Sex, War, and "Sin"

Sex, War, and "Sin"

Humanity's Path Toward the City of a Holy God

JAMES H. GAILEY

WIPF & STOCK · Eugene, Oregon

SEX, WAR, AND "SIN"
Humanity's Path Toward the City of a Holy God

Copyright © 2012 James H. Gailey. All rights reserved. Except for brief quotations in critical publications or reviews, no part of this book may be reproduced in any manner without prior written permission from the publisher. Write: Permissions, Wipf and Stock Publishers, 199 W. 8th Ave., Suite 3, Eugene, OR 97401.

Wipf & Stock
An Imprint of Wipf and Stock Publishers
199 W. 8th Ave., Suite 3
Eugene, OR 97401

www.wipfandstock.com

ISBN 13: 978-1-61097-834-7

Manufactured in the U.S.A.

To Edna Bryan Gailey, my mother, who gave me to God for the Christian Ministry; To Virginia Templin Gailey who agreed to share life and ministry with me; and to Landen Gailey, my daughter, who faithfully transcribed the final stages of preparing this book for print.

Thank God for the gift each one brought into my life and to this book.

James H. Gailey

Contents

Part 1: Biological, Cultural, and Religious Systems of Life
    1 Frames for the Experiment of Human Life 3
    2 The Biological Family and its Ancient Variations 15
    3 Understanding Sexual and Social Systems 26
    4 Discovering Sexuality 34
    5 Covenants and Sin 44
    6 Learning to Drive, and . . . 57

Part 2: Sex and Power Relationships in Some Israelite Stories
    7 Sin Lurking at Ancient Doors 73
    8 A Family Misstep Involving Sex 85
    9 A Childless Widow and a Lusty Patriarch 96
    10 Samson's Amorous Adventures 104
    11 Hannah and the Sons of Eli 112
    12 David's Wives and His Wars 117
    13 The Rhythms of Life and David's Adultery 133

    Michal's Lament 143

Part 3: A Natural History of Biblical "Sin"
    14 Sin's Reality 147
    15 How Innocent Anxiety Morphs into Guilt 172
    16 From Family Stories to the Adultery Commandment 182
    17 From "Unclean Lips" to Confessions of Sin 204
    18 Afterthoughts: Sin and Forgiveness in Retrospect 217

Part 4: Using the Hebrew Scriptures Today
    19 The Civilized Jigsaw Puzzle 235
    20 The Sustaining of Healthy Families 251
    21 Creating and Sustaining Cultural Entities 262
    22 Caregivers *Not* Anonymous 275

PART 5: In the Perspective of Hero Tales
- 23 Moses and the Name of God: Israel's Hero Tale 299
- 24 More Hero Tales 308
- 25 Creatio ex Nihilo, Imago Dei, and Talk with God 320

Bibliography 341

PART 1

Biological, Cultural, and Religious Systems of Life

1

Frames for the Experiment of Human Life

According to the scriptures—the Hebrew writings and the Greek New Testament—the most significant problem confronting the human race is the problem of "sin." Every other problem, medical, economic, inter-tribal or international can be seen as deriving from the failure of humans "to honor God as God, or give thanks to him, but they became futile in their thinking and their senseless minds were darkened" (Rom 1:21). In his letter to the Romans the apostle Paul announced the happy solution in Christ's redemptive work.

Church fathers and an established Roman priesthood claimed the power to dispense forgiveness for individual sins until Martin Luther called for a Reformation that would allow believers direct access to God. In the spirit of Luther, the French lawyer John Calvin wrote a major systematic statement, "The Institutes of the Christian Religion," for the purpose of freeing believers from the enforcing of belief in the Roman Catholic system by the arms of the state.

Following Calvin, spokesmen in several European countries wrote "reformed" creeds for the instruction and defense of their followers. The threefold statement produced in 1649 at Westminster Abbey was intended to give maturing believers three levels of theological insight and has remained as one of the creeds in the *Book of Confessions of the Presbyterian Church (USA)*. Having served as documents for advanced study for three centuries, in 1951 the Westminster "Confession of Faith," and the "Larger Catechism" were published in parallel columns with the "Shorter Catechism" as a "Harmony."[1] The heart of this system is in two covenants that propose to frame the relationship between God and the human race.

Covenants of Works and of Grace

As a child in a Presbyterian church and later as a theological student in the first third of the twentieth century I learned that my church focused on a particular form of evil known as "sin." The Shorter Catechism defines "sin" as "any want of conformity unto or transgression of the law of God," and the Westminster catechisms and Confession

---

1. Green, *A Harmony of the Westminster Presbyterian Standards*.

PART 1: Biological, Cultural, and Religious Systems of Life

of Faith explain that "sin" is endemic in human societies, as a sort of infection passed on from "first parents" to "posterity by natural generation."[2]

The human race, descended from Adam as a "public person, . . . sinned in him, and fell with him" in the first transgression, which occurred when he and his wife ate the forbidden fruit in the garden of Eden. Question 12 of the Shorter Catechism explains: "When God had created man, he entered into a covenant of life with him, upon condition of perfect obedience, forbidding him to eat of the tree of the knowledge of good and evil, upon pain of death." As a result of Adam's imperfect obedience to a command of God, the whole human race is now in a condition of "sin and misery," which could be remedied by God's gracious administration of a covenant of grace through "the preaching of the word" and the sacraments of baptism and the Lord's supper.[3]

It thus appeared that God had laid upon Adam a "covenant of works" as an experimental test of obedience, and failing that, the human race must live in sin and misery until a covenant of grace would offer salvation to all who believe in the redemptive work of Jesus Christ. The second covenant could be seen as a gracious offer by the Triune God, since the acquisition of "salvation" was no longer contingent on perfect obedience, but on the individual acceptance of the offer by each member of the race, all of whom suffered the consequences of disobedience to the moral law—a body of law including the Ten Commandments and laid out largely in books of the Pentateuch, but also detailed throughout the Holy Scriptures as laws to be obeyed.

Not all Protestants adopted this Calvinist frame but in a scientific age it haunts popular thinking about human life with large numbers of the world's people expecting a final judgment. In an age dominated by science both covenants can be interpreted as experiments conducted by God. Without focusing attention on a single man and his wife, the modern Calvinist can see all human beings confronted either with the test of obedience to the law of God or with the test of personal acceptance of the gospel.

New Uses for "Law"

A different confrontation developed after the term "law" was borrowed by the sciences from Roman and Church judicial practice. It involved two kinds of law—natural law and "the moral law"—and grew in intensity in the mid-eighteenth century and continues into the present "post-modern" twenty-first century when thoughtful clerics, journalists, political leaders and philosophers seek ways to relieve the tensions of the conceptual universe we all inhabit. There is perhaps a third conceptual regime that includes the term "law." It is Hebrew Torah, commonly translated "law," but it may be understood as one of many cultural forms of morality laid down by religious authorities on behalf of still Higher Authority.

In the 60's, during the days of the flower children, we experienced one of many collisions between nature and culture. More recently some Native Americans have

---

2. Answer to question 26 of the Shorter Catechism, J. B. Green, Harmony, 43–45.
3. Larger Catechism, Question 35, 51.

been calling attention to the disastrous cultural clash between "natural law" and "man's law." Assured by Steve Wall and Harvey Arden that they only wanted to hear whatever he wanted to tell them, the Onondaga Elder Oren Lyons said,

> that's good, because there are no secrets. There's no mystery. There's only common sense.... What law are you under? United States law and you pay a fine or go to jail—maybe. That's the way it is with Man's law. You can break it and get around it. Maybe you won't get punished at all. It happens all the time. People figure they can get away with anything and half the time they do. But they forget there's another law, the creator's law. We call it Natural Law . . . Natural law prevails everywhere. It supersedes Man's law. If you violate it, you get hit. There's no judge and jury, there's no lawyers or courts, you can't buy or dodge or beg your way out of it. If you violate this natural law you're going to get hit and get hit hard.[4]

The Native American confronted a people whose established laws were published in books for the guidance of courts. The Native American thought of the moral law as an aspect of the natural law, not radically distinct from every other law, except when law courts may or may not decide what they will do.

People's law: God's Law

The arena, "Man's law," originates with community agreement as to what is good and what is bad behavior. Thoughtful elders have always offered guidance through pronouncements that are frequently phrased as direction for the behavior of individuals. Such directions are often articulated as terse commands, "Just say no!" "Leave no child behind!" "Maintain family values!" or even shorter, "Stop!" "Danger!" "Slow!"

The traditional biblical saying, "An eye for an eye, a tooth for a tooth," expressed a common sense guide for insuring fairness in settling disputes over injuries. Public law grew out of these intuitive bits of advice when communities agreed to present them as formal rules for everyone's conduct.

The law codes of western civilization define crimes and assign penalties for those judged to have committed them. All legal structure testifies to a deep community need to describe the criteria for a workable society. In addition, much of the human race believes that the established rules of families, villages, states and nations are not simply systems of ad hoc social agreements, but are also reflections of a fundamental "law of God."

The biblical story of Moses receiving two tablets containing ten "words" from God on Mount Sinai has obscured the social origins of most moral laws. When Moses told his followers, "I was standing between the Lord and you to declare the words of the Lord" or a later prophet announced, "thus saith the Lord," Israelites believed that what they heard was divine revelation. But people seldom pay attention to the fact that the commandments were composed in language which identified and attempted to manage social problems common among the people. Likewise, when Hammurabi credited

---

4. Lyons, *Wisdom Keeper*, 64.

PART 1: Biological, Cultural, and Religious Systems of Life

the sun god with giving him a code of two hundred eighty two laws, many people accepted them as a divine gift for the ordering of the state of ancient Babylon. When the stone that bore that writing was set up, Hammurabi may have called the people together to praise and thank the god Shamash for intervening to establish order in the region. The old Babylonians might have said to each other, "We needed Someone to tell us how to settle our disputes without killing too many valuable people." No doubt customs already existed. With Hammurabi's code posted in the ancient "courthouse," divinely-given "law" certified that those customs belonged to the orderliness of the world which the gods had created and their human deputies ruled.

Whatever procedures were followed among an ancient people for the settling of disputes probably developed out of incidents in which elders intervened to cool the tempers of hotheaded youth. These events were formed into stories; which could be recalled as precedents when they were needed. Customary procedures developed long before the communities identified judges and wrote laws. The first to function as judges were no doubt the recognized heads of families, clans and tribes. Proto-law existed in the common consent of people to judgments made by the eldest respected members of the community. When it became time to write laws, the particular names and places of incidents were set aside and the law took one of two abstracted forms, "if a person does . . . , then he/she will be . . . ." or more simply "you shall (not) . . . ."

Parallel to social customs and political legislation in many cultures are the rules for relating to the gods. Here also we find stories—myths—and prescribed rituals; activities which guide the individual in relating to the invisible Powers that move the world.

Much that is called "revelation" can be seen as "discovery." What comes as direction revealed to an inspired spokesman for God is received as fresh insight and wisdom by the waiting people. It helps to be told by an authoritative voice that what we learn from experience is really right and good.

Socio-religious rules not only point to what is right and good in the eyes of our elders and our gods; they also provide the means for the survival of the people of our various tribes. Writing about self-deception in Paul and Matthew, Dan O. Via noted the wisdom of Proverbs 6:32–34, which says, "he who commits adultery . . . destroys himself . . . for jealousy arouses a husband's fury, and he shows no restraint when he takes revenge."[5] The book of Proverbs is full of the observations of ancient thinkers, who take note of the good and bad consequences of many human activities. And, to close the circle of wisdom, the law bringer of Deuteronomy 30:19 calls heaven and earth to witness "that I have set before you life and death, blessings and curses. Choose life so that you and your descendants may live." Evidences of this thrust toward survival can be seen in the stories we will be considering. In general the Bible presents the law of God framed in stories of *discovery* which are interpreted as *revelation* through prophetic voices and then followed by ambivalent popular *acceptance or rejection* of its wisdom. In this way the judgments passed down by elders were understood to be

---

5. Via, *Self-Deception and Wholeness in Paul and Matthew*, 75.

God's law, whether they were obeyed or not. Also in the people's acceptance of law we can see the roots of "social contract" thinking.

Nature's Law: Human Discovery

A different set of laws also has to do with survival, but in these the contemplated survival has to do with plant and animal species. It is unfortunate that we have used the word "law" to characterize the scientific discoveries of the modern world, since the word implies the same kind of authoritative—if impersonal—source of the formulation. Instead of a personal Deity, the secular mind has looked to an abstract "Nature" or "Science" for guidance. Researchers in various departments of the scientific community become the prophets who speak for Nature, telling us how things work, and by implication, how we can relate successfully to various aspects of the natural world.

The "laws of nature" are derived in a circular three step process of human investigation, beginning with *observations*, which are consolidated into *theories*, and which in turn are tested by *experiments* and further observations. This simplified model can be illustrated by dozens of familiar examples. Galileo challenged the theory that the earth was the center of the universe with his observations through a primitive telescope with which he witnessed the movements of moons around the giant planet Jupiter. Thought experimenting led him to examine the relationships between sun, moon and earth, and he concluded that the system of "spheres" devised by Ptolemy was not an adequate description of relationships between the heavenly bodies. Instead, he asked how the system would work if it treated the sun as a central point and visualized the planets orbiting around it. Isaac Newton supplied the mathematics for such a system, and the theory could be tested over and over as astronomers worked out the orbits of planets, comets, meteorites, and the more recent landings on the moon and Mars.[6]

Obviously *observing* is not simply looking at things. The primitive observer saw and remembered many repetitions of events in nature. Day after day he awoke to lengthening (or shortening) periods of light; month after month, she recognized a familiar flow of blood except at the times that heralded the experience of childbirth. Although the sun seemed to appear with great regularity, its dawning and setting were not always at the same places on the horizon. People noticed that its observed path was associated with changes in the seasons that marked a yearly cycle. The world operated in an orderly but complex way that appeared to belong to its "nature." This first step used memory as a tool to identify natural regularities and then to name them.

Theorizing emerged through that process of association, first of repeated events, and then of other events that could be observed at the same time or under similar circumstances. The woman noted that her flow of blood seemed to come at the same time each month. As she observed the moon, her mind raised questions: Was there a connection? Did some (divine) power control what she had no power to manage? Women used clay to shape the figure of goddesses to whom they could address their

---

6. The chapter on "Science" in *Genes, Genesis and God: Values and their Origins in Natural and Human History* by Holmes Roylston, III has a section on generating and selecting theories.

Part 1: Biological, Cultural, and Religious Systems of Life

concerns. Later, people came to understand and describe these natural cycles in the form we call "theories." Theories are the abbreviated form of stories of what happens, and are always descriptive.[7]

Concluding his study of *Coercion and its Fallout*,[8] Murray Sidman notes that "science always oversimplifies first. It then gradually adds the complexities that bring controlled experiments into contact with the uncontrolled conditions of the everyday world." So theories of human behavior begin with simple observations and are developed as thoughtful people formulate patterns they observe. A junior high school girl notices that a particular member of her class keeps looking her way between his moments of attention to the subject matter prescribed by teachers and administrators. She wonders if there is any significance in his glances.

Experimenting began when people started to help nature provide food. Having developed a rudimentary "theory" about the planting of seed, early humans began to test it. Whether they accidentally dropped seeds in particularly fertile spots, or decided to do so, they were experimenting. Experiment is the application of descriptive theory derived from past experience to future possibilities that people anticipate. A test is a consciously prescribed application of theory. Once people were aware that they could scatter seed with the expectation that in the cycle of weather it would produce a "crop," the agricultural revolution was under way, and people selected the places and times for the scattering of seed. New observations confirmed the theory, and we could describe the completed process as "discovery." Similarly, and probably earlier, people discovered that the planting of a man's "seed" in a woman's vagina produced a new life. However, the natural order does not always assert itself. An apparent pregnancy may result in a stillbirth. What alien "power" produced the unexpected event?

This method of taking the three steps—*observation*, *theorizing*, and *testing*—has confirmed thousands of specific discoveries, which are often stated in mathematical formulas. In common thinking, however, they are also described in diagrams or maps, which represent the patterns of relationships between the parts of particular entities in the cosmos. We also see "the complexity and unpredictability of historical systems, despite their ultimate determinacy" which Jared Diamond ascribes to "long chains of causation [separating] final effects from ultimate causes."[9] To the extent that we can speak of "laws," they are discovered by human minds and stated in verbal forms that people have developed since the earliest humans came to speech and self-awareness.

Every individual, not just every scientist, is capable of taking the three steps of scientific investigation, and in everyday life is accustomed to observe and experiment, while doing the peculiarly human theorizing. For Homo sapiens as distinct from other forms of animate life the power of speech has provided an otherwise unknown vehicle for theorizing and exchanging theories with other humans. For instance, in

---

7. Williams, *Doing without Adam and Eve*, 151 points out that natural laws are typically statistical and apply to groups rather than individuals. So, the natural sciences give us averages of a great many observations, but do not predict behavior for a single individual.

8. Sidman, *Coercion and its Fallout*, 242.

9. Diamond, *Guns, Germs, and Steel*, 423.

Guns, Germs, and Steel: The Fates of Human Societies, Jared Diamond tells how New Guineans acquired knowledge—rudimentary theories—of hundreds of local plant and animal species, and each species' edibility, medical value, and other uses, and also about dozens of rock types and each type's hardness, color, behavior when struck or flaked "by observation and trial and error."[10]

Laws of Nature, Culture and Religion

In his concluding chapter, "The Future of Human History as a Science," Diamond sketches the essential methodology of science in detail, and recognizes that history will never be subjected to controlled experiments. However, he sees observable "natural experiments" from which historians as well as biologists can formulate predictions using statistical methods.

The human development of self awareness has always been matched by the elaboration and clarification of a worldview, itself a kind of theory, which can be stated in a range of forms, including stories, laws, and the more sophisticated languages of philosophy and theology. No single system covers all kinds of observation and the human experiences that occupy our attention, though philosophers and linguists attempt to write theories of everything.[11] Along with theories regarding the material world we are now discussing a number of non-material, psychological and cultural observations, which include those of ethics and religion.

The two kinds of law that form the frame for our discussion of sex, conflict, and sin may be characterized by their stance in regard to time. The laws we discover by looking back to observations—in history or nature—are essentially *descriptive*; they describe observed and remembered behavior, of things or people that exist as part of the world around us, often including ourselves. However the laws we hear from our scientists and sociopolitical prophets also look forward to possible new behaviors, and are *predictive*; they tell us what we may or can do and often advise or command us to behave or not to behave in specific ways. They predict the possible consequences of our actions, so that our theories can be verified or falsified through our experimenting.

Descriptive law states the theories that have emerged from millennia of human experience and observation, and define the regularities of existence. Law as predictor contemplates these regularities and some surprising irregularities, and suggests what may be seen as possible experiments. When a scientist, a priest or some other authority recommends the repetition of some activity and the avoidance of others, laws become *prescriptive* as well as predictive. Laws both descriptive and prescriptive belong to the realm of human culture(s). As far as we know the natural world has never verbalized them.

It is evident, however, that many animals learn from experience. Gazelles in the Serengeti sniff the wind for the scent of lions and when a young gazelle senses a threat,

---

10. Ibid., 246.
11. Ken Wilber's *Theory of Everything* is the latest of which I am aware.

the herd flees together, moved by a wordless understanding that someone will be eaten. The jungle has its law, which operates without being formulated in words.

An Unfinished Jigsaw Puzzle

Although nature's time seems endless and we conceive a Creator God as somehow outside of or beyond time, we intuit and have confirmed, to the satisfaction of many moderns at least, that everything begins, endures, and ultimately ends. In our world of space and time a *dichotomy* appears—an intelligible division—between two realms. One apparently exists without words; it is observable in tangible substances. The other is expressed in human thinking and language. We call the one "material" or "natural," and the other "conceptual" or "spiritual." We confidently believe that our self is not mere matter, and that a soul or a mind is not just one more part of the body. Yet we intuit that world and self are not divided. Books continue to be written about this dichotomy, which has perplexed human minds for millennia. One of the most interesting is E. O. Wilson's *Consilience: The Unity of Knowledge*, which introduces the idea of a co-evolution of two realms, nature and culture, and tries to avoid the mental chasm between them. In what follows we will be concerned with both, exemplified in particular as biological and social. Physical sex and our social laws about sexuality seem to exist as a continental divide between nature and culture, which nevertheless recognizes a fundamental unity of the world. Unaware of the molecular materiality of air the ancients thought of breath as spirit or soul, and recognized it as different from the solidity of mountains, plants, and animals. Choose your metaphor: chasms and divides are both useful metaphors as we distinguish aspects of the world that our language attempts to describe.

Intuitively we believe, or "know," that the world we inhabit does not consist of two unrelated realms. Whether we think God created it all or that its forms came into existence through natural processes, we believe that the realms of matter and spirit are aspects of *one world*. Present and future theory, experiments and discoveries may help us understand the complex interrelationships between mind and body, nature and culture, science and religion, but most of us wake up each morning confident that we should be able to do what we want to do in the day that is before us.

The continuum of our history lies behind us as we awake and begin a day's activities, while the future is a *tabula rasa*, an unwritten and unknown void into which we will take our next steps, and about which we may only speak in guesses, plans, and hopes. Except for a hypothetical original creation we humans created many of the systems we leave behind, and we may model and structure new systems *like* but also *unlike* the systems of the past.

The question of creation by God is not trivial, for it introduces another possible dichotomy. Having recognized and agreed that the realm of matter and the world of thought are truly one intertwined world, we must consider whether there is yet a third and different realm in which God exists apart from the cosmos of space and time. Naming the Lord God as the Creator—*YHWH* in Israelite Hebrew—we tend to separate God from the creation, the result of God's work. The early chapters of Genesis can hardly be read in any other way. God appears to exist outside of everything mentioned, light, firmament, dry land, sun, moon, plants, animals, human beings. Even the heavens are God's creation. But should we think of a Heaven in which God exists, apart from the cosmos?

I think not. While we can test the laws of nature and the laws of culture, we have only the most limited capacity to test what belongs to an imagined God's realm, especially if such a realm were to exist apart from the universe. I believe that God, or the Being we take to be God, exists in the same world of matter and mind and spirit in which I live. Or possibly that *the world of matter and minds exists in God*. In either case, the realm of matter may be described appropriately as "the body of God" as Sallie McFague has suggested, and consequently the realm of spirit could be described as the mind of God.[12] Two realms are enough for this worldview, and both can operate under an interwoven set of laws, which philosophers, scientists, and theologians are seeking to define. Thanks to Einstein and his successors, it is possible to conceive of the extension of space-time beyond the range of possible observation, but our minds boggle at conceptualizing it all.

In *Doing without Adam and Eve: Sociobiology and Original Sin* Patricia A. Williams sketches a theory accounting for the common origin of the two realms. She suggests that at the Big Bang, "the basic matter-plus-law of the universe comes into being." She uses the word "stuff" as a term for the first almost unimaginable flux of energy the physicists consider to have preceded the appearance of radiation and the familiar particles of our world.[13] Her "stuff" is not an amateur physicist's term for God, and she does not pursue the existence of a Creator before the Big Bang.

With the idea that the four dimensional cosmos—three "solid" dimensions and the elusive dimension of time—began with the Big Bang we confront the question of the eternal existence of God, and also the question of a "beginning" of time. Following the leading of the socio-biologists, I believe that everything—social, cultural, theological, and philosophical—emerges from the realm of nature and *may also be considered the ongoing creative work of God*.

Everything, comprising nature and culture, exists *in God*, or that *God exists in everything*, not simply in the material part of the cosmos, but as the underlying Force binding matter and spirits together in continuing but time bound existence. Whatever we identify with a name appears to have begun at some point in the vast time frame of existence. Even the names and titles we apply to gods can be traced to their linguistic origins. Is that also true for the Entity behind the word "God?" Perhaps. But the most we can do is to apply metaphors to that ineffable Being. In a final chapter I will sketch my metaphor.

As we view ourselves in this world we recognize that we are like the surfer who rides gigantic waves when the sea is up, risking a "wipe out" while enjoying the

---

12. In Chapter 21 we will consider *The Mind of Man and the Mind of God* by James B. Ashbrook.
13. Williams, *Doing without Adam and Eve*, 160.

momentary exhilaration of the ride and then recalling it with fellow surfers at rest on the beach. For my purpose a better metaphor is our individual participation in a four-dimensional jigsaw puzzle. Like Lewis Carroll's chess game in *Through the Looking Glass,* we are the pieces; we must find pieces to mate with or eliminate as we find our places in the "big picture."

Apparently the Creative God has given creatures a power of adaptation through which "pieces" can change shapes as they experiment with groupings and separations in the puzzle. Non-human animate life has already "discovered" that species can develop new forms and adaptations so that life goes on in spite of catastrophic interruptions. The human species has been given the capability to develop tools and skills without involving radical changes in the basic human form. In *Genes, Genesis and God: Values and their Origins in Natural and Human History* the biologist and philosopher of science, Holmes Roylston III, has developed this thesis in detail. Roylston observes values at every level of increasing complexity in the cosmos from the emergence of energy and matter to the complex social orders of humanity, and concludes that everything is "a response to the brooding winds of the spirit moving over the face of these Earthen waters."

Meanwhile, in our human awareness God moves with us into the unknown future, recording the working of our experiments in the time bound patterns of the particles of the cosmos.

Experimental Behavior

Nature's laws are primarily descriptive but can be used prescriptively by human beings to propose experiments. The laws of culture and religion are also developed out of observations, but take on strong prescriptive forms as political and religious leaders "pass laws" to control people's behavior. While we may write ethical and religious law, an Ultimate Authorizer is needed for our various systems of law. The auxiliary verbs "can," "ought," "may," and "should" help to simplify the situation: Nature tells us what we *can* do; culture tells us what we *may* do; ethical religion tells us what we *should* or *ought to* do. A fourth auxiliary verb, "shall" and "will," expresses an individual or group decision to initiate action that moves from a present moment into the future. Thus individuals and/or groups create experiments which fit three dimensional shapes, which we imagine contain our selves, into the niches of our homes and families for the living of each moment and day.

Human laws, political and moral, serve to regularize our experiments by categorizing causes and their effects in the form of what James M. Robinson has called "the language world in which we swim." Robinson argues for

> a recognition, in terms of the historicness of man, that verbalization, linguistic formulation, is not to be understood ultimately as a secondary objectification (which in many cases may not ever occur) of a primary experience that itself is pre-linguistic . . . But once the cleft between deed and word has been transcended by the recognition that they are interlocked as eloquent action and effective word, as gesture and symbol, then language can be recognized in gesticulation

as well as in verbalization. Language is not merely the secondary expression of a more primary experience formed by the language world in which we swim, as conditioned reflexes. We live in style.[14]

Two systems are needed for our thinking, the system of law derived from observation of events in the realm of nature, and the ethical system established by socially accepted authority, human or divine. In what follows we will be examining the way an ancient people joined their pieces to form a picture within this double framework of law.

"Sin" arises, as we have been taught, when we either do not "conform to" a juridical law of God or actively "transgress" it. According to this definition sin is breaking a rule or stated law, normally an aspect of a culture. The Westminster Catechisms define sin in terms of the socio-religious laws of a biblically based church, not in terms of natural law. No one seriously argues that natural sexual activity is inherently sinful. Biblical laws define behavior in cultural terms, but include an underlying or overriding reference to God that lifts social crimes to offences against God.

In the world of nature a complex orderliness appears to be the rule. The world of human culture has found its way to massive disorderliness in spite of our best efforts to create order. Shall we ascribe that disorder to alien gods, powers or abstract forces? Or is the human species itself responsible for disorder in what appeared to be a good creation?

Should we continue to define "sin" as disobedience to God's law? Or can we devise a better definition for the concept? As we take a look at some incidents reported in the Hebrew scriptures, we can see how cultural rules emerged from a deep rooted sense of right and wrong, and how these rules came to be understood as divinely authorized. In the process we may be able to develop a functional definition of sin to replace the juridical one.[15]

A Way Beyond Law?

At times in its movement through history the human race has experienced an uneasiness or discomfort not only with the way things were but also with what we could see ahead. Not satisfied with our preliminary understanding of the operating laws of the material realm, we have continued a process of defining the rules for the happy working of the social order, using the judgments of the wisest of our kind. In the Hebrew Scriptures the "wisest" individual was King Solomon who is credited with collecting and "writing" the Proverbs, but we should also recognize that the editors of the three

---

14. Robinson, "The Enternal Word in History," 293-5. In Chapter 15 we will consider briefly Steven Pinker's distinction between crisp and fuzzy thinking and his term "mentalese," which I consider an alternate expression for Robinson's "primary experience."

15. In addition to Wilson's *Consilience* and Roylston's *Genes, Genesis and God*, my reading of the Hebrew scriptures is in the light of Victor Nuovo's translation and notes on Tillich's 1919 essay "On the Idea of a Theology of Culture," Peter Hodgson's *God in History*, and others to which specific reference will be made.

divisions of scripture brought together the accumulated wisdom of storytellers, lawgivers, prophets, Psalmists, and poets.

These efforts produced public systems of laws to regulate the behavior of individuals and groups, initially in the form of oral guidance by the more experienced, and later in written form as codes of formalized law.

However our uneasiness (*Angst*) has not been dispelled, and philosophers and theologians have continued to search for better, simpler statements, while lawmakers have produced book after book of new laws. The wordiness of our efforts is in itself a source of mental discomfort, and provokes new thinkers to add to the literature. Holmes Roylston asks how we got "from *is* to *ought*" and traces the emergence of a mental space for ethics and religion. Jacob Neusner in *Systemic Analysis* (1987) and other writings set his students to studying the elements of human systems in religious documents. Following these suggestions, I have sketched a less than complete "integral" worldview in this chapter.[16] It must be composed of natural and cultural elements.

As we proceed we will analyze the way ancient Israel expressed its worldview in the concrete affairs of its everyday life, limiting ourselves to those with components of sexuality and conflict. At the same time we will be aware of the way we successors of ancient culture are seeking to embody our worldview in caring social entities for our time. What guidance should we expect from the ancients, especially those who spoke for God? Can we escape the bindings of their oral and written systems without falling into chaos? Is there a better way than slavish acceptance of dated laws?

---

16. Wilber set out to provide a "psychological correlate of the Human Genome Project." in *A Theory of Everything: an Integral Vision for Business, Politics, Science, and Spirituality*.

2

The Biological Family and its Ancient Variations

WHILE NEITHER OF THE creation stories in Genesis are concerned primarily with sex and sexuality, both show a sensitive awareness of this aspect of human life. In Genesis 1:1–2:4a exilic priests wrote the more sophisticated, abstract narrative. Cultural overtones are heard at last on the sixth day of God's creative activity: "man" is made in the "image" of God; he is given "dominion" over other creatures, and is observed to be identifiably "male" or "female." God judges his "work" including its sexual aspect as "good" and "very good," and rests on the seventh day, which becomes holy, thus giving a religious tone to the story. In the Bible human life is thus framed as a specific form of emerging biological creation.

The Yahwist historian's work, in Genesis 2:4b–3:24, makes *family* largely biological and physical. Notice the references to "herb of the field," rain, water, rivers; a garden in Eden.

The woman is "bone of my bones and flesh of my flesh," according to the man's statement. Fruit of the trees is to be eaten; woven fig leaves become loincloths until God provides animal skins. Clothes seem to be a cultural afterthought. In the continuation of the story "the man knew his wife Eve, and she conceived and bore Cain." Thus the creation proceeds into the activity of procreation. At this point the first human family is a reality:

"Therefore a man leaves his father and his mother and clings to his wife, and they become one flesh. And the man and his wife were both naked, and were not ashamed." (Gen 2:24 NRSV)[1]

The Human Family

The basic unit of human existence is a family, not a single "Adam," which at its barest minimum is a couple. Alice Laffey[2] points out that in the Yahwists' Genesis 2 generic man, *'adam*, becomes *'ish* and *'ishah*, man and woman, just as the two sexes are de-

---

1. Unless otherwise indicated quotations of scripture will be from *New Revised Standard Version* (NRSV).

2. Laffey, *An Introduction to the Old Testament: a Feminist Perspective*, 22.

scribed in the priestly account of creation in Genesis 1 as "male and female." The sexual distinction is fundamental to the human species, like other species. Laffey rejects the patriarchal, hierarchical bias of the traditional translation "helpmeet" in 2:18, which imagines the woman as a subordinate "helper." Instead the words of the phrase, "meet for him," should be read as an indication of partnership as is done in the NRSV: "I will make him a helper as his partner." The woman with her different biological character will share in the creating of children, which the individual man cannot do alone. The Yahwist's account of the operation to release the first woman from the body of the first man is faulty biology, perhaps the writer's reflection on the proverbial "one flesh." It does not belong in a serious account of early history.

The Genesis accounts and the rest of the Bible are blissfully ignorant of much that recent biologists have learned including the significant place of proteins and the way a marvelous pairing of genes passes physical traits from one generation to the next.

Instead, Adam and Eve are prototypical human beings and equal partners in the drama of human life. The distinctive emphases of the two stories merge to become a model for human families that will exist in the world of interwoven culture and nature. The model is simplicity itself, basically biological, with an overlay of culture. Obeying the biological law, "be fruitful and multiply," a man and a woman can unite in repeatable events of sexual intercourse. From time to time sperm and egg unite and fertilization takes place inside the woman's womb, and a complete family is created. Earlier humans evidently discovered times in the monthly cycle when the woman was more likely to be fertile, and knew that "lying with" a woman meant having sexual intercourse.

The model is not purely natural, however, for "family" is a modern social expression that recognizes the personal relationships between husband, wife and child. Parents are needed not simply for the process of procreation, but also for the nurture of the infant during the relatively helpless first months of life. The mother provides first nourishment, and the father may or may not provide food for the nursing mother. We could elaborate with comments about the infant's need for TLC, "tender loving care," and the necessity for the social interactions of touch, play, song, and speech. The biblical books seldom refer to these aspects of the standard family, but do recognize that sons and daughters ideally "grow both in stature and in favor with the Lord and with the people" as Samuel is reported to have done. (1 Sam 2:26)

Intimate loving relationships between husbands and wives including various forms of physical contact are also important to the welfare of families. Perhaps consciously more important for wives, but in reality equally important for husbands, a commitment to provide both material and spiritual support to each other is essential for the happiness of couples as well as for the health, physical and mental, of children. We find more emphasis on this aspect in fiction than in biblical narratives, but we could mention occasional biblical allusions to love. We will follow illustrations of a covenantal paradigm in several biblical accounts and return to a look at family health in chapter 20.

The Biological Family and its Ancient Variations

Ita Sheres[3] has called attention to the way the redactors of the Genesis narrative have left moral judgments to their readers, who are sure to recognize the ideal character of the basic model. In fact, the realities of pain in childbirth, sweat and weariness in the labor of men, and the servile movement of serpents needed mention only in the "curse" pronounced by YHWH God. The curse prepares the reader for the transition from the ideal garden to the realities of common human experience, which can be described as both "good and evil." In fact, pain, weariness and hunger serve usefully to alert sentient beings to the needs of the body, and are good for the survival of individuals. That they also bring discomfort—"evil"—in families, goes without saying.

But while a baby's cry probably develops from an expression of discomfort to an early demand for attention, today no one thinks it is evidence of original sin. Correction! It is not actually true that "no one" thinks a baby's cry indicates original sinfulness. Patricia A. Williams[4] includes a critical treatment of the concept of original sin that was adopted from Augustine's Manichean dualism. The Manicheans gave equal emphasis to good and evil forces in the world, and Augustine, Calvin and the Westminster creeds kept the idea of a fall into sin from which a special work of God's grace would be needed. Though believers of some faiths ascribe an inborn sinfulness to very young children, only questions 25 and 26 of the Larger Catechism and section VI:6 of the Confession of Faith, speak of a transmission of an "original" or "first" sin. It is preferable to treat all forms of sin as cultural "memes" learned through human experience rather than as part of biological inheritance.[5]

It is probably significant that the mythologies of the ancient world imagined gods and goddesses, the creators and managers of the visible world, as members of families. Guerber began his *Myths of Greece and Rome* with Ovid's creation myth which describes a series of divine couples who share power until they are weary and are dethroned by their sons: "Chaos" and "Night" are replaced by son Erebus (Darkness), who then marries his mother. Their two beautiful children Aether (Light) and Hemera (Day), "acting in concert, dethroned them, and seized the supreme power.[6] On and on: their son Eros (Amor or Love) helped to create Pontus (the Sea) and Gaea (Terra, Earth). Ovid's Latin stories and the Greeks' can now be matched with the family tales of Canaanite, Mesopotamian and Egyptian deities. These pantheons project the experience of human procreative and sustaining parents into the obscurity of forces beyond the control of people. Early thinkers imagined gods and used them to certify the patterns of our life in a chicken-and-egg cycle of conceptualizing our world. The revelation of YHWH as masterful Creative Voice attempted to break that cycle, but few Israelites could give up their need for the male-female-child model either in their popular theology or religious practice.

---

3. Sheres, *Dinah's Rebellion: a Biblical Parable for our Time*, 18.
4. Williams, *Doing without Adam and Eve: Sociobiology and Original Sin*.
5. See chapter 18.
6. Guerber, *Myths of Greece and Rome*, 13.

PART 1: Biological, Cultural, and Religious Systems of Life

Childless Women

What is normal is sometimes described in contrast with the abnormal, and a group of biblical couples exhibit the problem of women who seemed unable to become pregnant. Abram/Abraham's wife Sarai/Sarah lived to old age before having her one son, Isaac. Jacob's favorite wife, Rachel, was long delayed in fulfilling her destiny, and Hannah offered soul-wrenching prayers and promised to return her son Samuel to YHWH if only God would allow her to be pregnant.

Having passed through menopause, Sarah laughed derisively at the idea that she might have "pleasure" when Abraham's guest announced that she would have a son "in due season." Climactic sexual pleasure was associated in ancient times with the presumed moment of planting the human seed in the woman's womb (fertilization) instead of being seen as one of the body's inducements to procreate. Perhaps she laughed again when Abraham slept in her tent, but the last laugh came when she could give Isaac his name: "God has brought laughter to me; everyone who hears will laugh with me." (Gen 21:6)

Rachel knew that Jacob preferred her to her sister Leah, but she complained that he wasn't "giving" her children. At that "Jacob became very angry ... and said, 'Am I in the place of God, who has withheld from you the fruit of the womb?'" (Gen 30:1–2) Each blamed the other for her infertility. Believing that increasing Jacob's family was more important than her personal satisfaction, Rachel offered her handmaid Bilhah to Jacob as a surrogate mother for Dan and Naphtali. Only later would she bear Joseph and Benjamin. Leah had no trouble getting pregnant, but perhaps to pacify her sister, she directed her handmaid Zilpah to bear sons for her. Sons were so important in the patriarchal story as told in the time of Davod and Solomon that additional women could be joined to the basic family. Each child could be welcomed and celebrated when initially childless women were normalized.

Hannah's story is told in some detail in the first chapter of 1 Samuel. Elkanah had two wives: Penninah had children, but Hannah did not. At the annual festival at Shiloh, Elkanah gave Penninah portions of the sacrificed meat for herself and for her children, but "to Hannah he gave a double portion because he loved her." When she returned to Shiloh year after year with a closed womb, she wept and would not eat. But Elkanah asked "Why is your heart sad? Am I not more to you than ten sons?" When the resident priest Eli found her praying bitterly, she vowed to give her son to YHWH as a Nazirite, after he assured her that she would bear the son she craved. The son was Samuel, who succeeded Eli to the priesthood at Shiloh.

These stories show how powerful is the woman's urge to bear a child, and how important is the emotional support of her mate and of the community. The Bible sees the biological and the social aspects of the relationships from the point of view of the woman, with emphasis on satisfying both biological and emotional needs. Nonetheless, Abram's prayer in Genesis 15:3, "You have given me no offspring, and so a slave born in my house is to be my heir," expresses the socio-economic interest of men. YHWH's pledge in verses 5–6, "look toward heaven and count the stars, if you are able to count them ... So shall your descendants be," answers his concern, just as Eli's response assured Hannah that she would become pregnant. Both matriarchal and patriarchal interests focus on offspring, with emphases nuanced according to the respective concerns.

Offspring have been considered the evidence of divine blessing on the normal family. Without a child not only the wife but the husband would feel cursed—or at least unblessed. This appraisal is neither purely biological nor purely social. Every birth assures the completion of the family and the continuation of the tribe and species. The achievement of a live human birth and the subsequent presentation of a son to his father may satisfy human expectations, but for believers it also represents a symbolic approval from God. Without such approval the believer can have a vague sense of being sinful.

Cultural Reflections

It is evident from any reading of the world's literature that the simple man-woman-child has never been the only family that existed. In fact a nuclear family of three has been the exception rather than the rule. Jacob's polygamous family of four sexual partners and at least thirteen children was more an idealized norm for Israel than the smaller family, especially for the affluent. The basic pattern of male-female-child was simply multiplied within the extended families of the patriarchs and in the other cultures of the ancient world, as well as in most so-called primitive societies in the world today. We may need to underscore this. Societies have generally accepted and approved the basic biological pattern even when they modified it. Cultures have often attempted to limit the number of men who might impregnate a woman, and have dictated which women a man might approach. In the patriarchal family, as Sheres points out, "Sexual desire became [the woman's] trap because while engaging in sexual intercourse, which is perceived by the text to be only procreational, she pointed to her social position, namely, her subjugation to the man."[7] Female family members were not counted in biblical reports of tribal population. Instead, military strength could be counted as a number of men, such as Abram's cohort of 318 men "born in his house" in the conflict with the five foreign kings of Genesis 14.

Thus the natural equivalence of the sexes became dichotomized in the development of human culture. Under patriarchy an ancient woman was bound to one man, and was confined to his household, while the ancient Israelite man was free to enlarge his family with more than one sexual partner. Some women were "handmaids," but prostitutes also contributed to the building of families and tribes.

We might assume that any deviation from the standard family pattern would be wrong and abhorred by an ancient community, and to a degree that was the case. The idealized pattern we have sketched as "normal" allowed little room for major deviation. What was important in the ancient world, as in the world of nature, was the survival of families, like the survival of species. Within social limits tribes, communities, and

7. Sheres, *Dinah's Rebellion*, 40.

PART 1: Biological, Cultural, and Religious Systems of Life

their leaders permitted productive couplings and accepted new members to extended families as they came.

The prosperity of a family or tribe was measured not only in cattle but also in the number of "servants," including women and girls as well as men and boys, who belonged to it. The more children his wives and servants had, the greater the prosperity of the patriarch and his tribe. In order for the tribe to survive and increase in wealth it was socially acceptable for men to take more than one woman.

Daughters, for whom the social contract of marriage was negotiated by adult males of the two families, became recognized wives of new families. Fathers exercised tight control, demanding bride prices within the customary limits, and permitting liaisons only with accepted families. Jacob was acceptable to Laban because he was related through his mother, who was Laban's sister, but he had nothing to offer as a bride price except his willingness to work. Laban's daughters were acceptable to Jacob's mother, Rebekah, because they were kindred.

Women could be married to only one man. Only if her husband died could a wife remarry. Otherwise a woman whom a man had "known" was considered to be too unclean or debased for any marriage except to the man who had deflowered her. The ancient custom became part of Torah/law in Deuteronomy 22:13–30.

Men, young and old, were not quite so limited if they had the means to offer an acceptable bride price, but their mothers might complain about their choice of mates. We are told that at the age of forty, Esau "married Judith daughter of Beeri the Hittite, and Basemath daughter of Elon the Hittite; and they made life bitter for Isaac and Rebekah." (Genesis 26:34–5) Were these Hittite wives hard to get along with because of cultural differences or because of some religious practice that was distasteful to the Hebrews? Sheres might argue that they were not acceptable to Rebekah because as matriarch she (or Isaac) was not involved in their selection. Other females with whom a man could produce children were slaves, concubines or prostitutes, and as long as he had the economic means to support them and their offspring, there appears to have been no limit to their number.

Mind you, the limits we are talking about were not biological. Put "two warm bodies" together and they could produce children. Hebrew men and women attempted to control the character and quality of the family and the tribal leadership that would succeed them. The older generations were concerned to designate legitimate sons and daughters. Though the term "legitimate" was unknown in Israel, I use it to distinguish recognizable levels of power and position within an Israelite family. So Jacob could designate the sons of the two handmaids as "legitimate," but only with the concurrence of "wives" Rachel and Leah. Likewise the son of Boaz and the Moabitess Ruth was a legitimate successor to leadership in the tribe of Judah. Their grandson David could have claimed a right to lead all Israel, as is suggested in the book of Ruth.

By requiring "all the men of his house, slaves born in the house and those bought with money from a foreigner" to be circumcised,[8] Abraham established an order of

---

8. Genesis 17:26.

membership in his clan, second only to his legitimate children. Circumcision significantly increased the number of his tribe's members and its economic and military potential without compromising its purity.

Israelite tribal identity was thus expressed through the circumcision of males. Wives and other females, including slaves, concubines and even prostitutes were identified through their relationships with the men in their lives, fathers, brothers, husbands, or masters.

These social devices succeeded in extending families, sects and tribes, producing the social building blocks of ancient Israel.

Within the family unit everyone was expected to contribute to its welfare. Women's activities were within or close to house or tent, while men's activities tended to be farther afield. All needed to be productive, not especially in a sexual sense, but throughout every aspect of common life. The "extended" family rather than the biological family became the norm for Israel.

Grandparents, uncles, aunts, and cousins had places in the Israelite extended family. The life span of three score years and ten provided occupation for women who were nominally superfluous to the procreative process but useful for the nurture of the young.

Creating New Families

The patriarchal system relied on two closely connected ritualistic arrangements for transferring young males and females from their families to a new family. It worked through the traditional structures of the covenantal paradigm. In Canaan and Israel transfers were essentially economic. Each new family became a living stone in the erecting of the clan and tribal structure, or, a "piece" as in my metaphorical jigsaw puzzle.

Young women became members of new families, and possibly of different tribes, when they were "given" in marriage to young men, or occasionally taken captive in war. Samson's unnamed Philistine wife should have become an Israelite of the tribe of Dan. And Dinah's brothers were afraid that she and her children would become Hivites instead of Israelites. We will look at the stories of Dinah and Samson in chapters 8 and 10.

Both families valued the economic benefits associated with the patriarchs to whom they "belonged." An increase for one family could have appeared as a loss for the other.

Possession of plots of land owned by the family always complicated the question of tribal identity, so the increases and losses involved tangible assets—the control of pasture land or fields—as well as the woman's change of identity. It is not at all clear, however, that Samson intended to move his Philistine wife to an Israelite plot of ground to set up a family, but it is evident that Shechem would have expected Dinah to move onto land he would control. The Israelites faced possible loss in both cases. With

PART 1: Biological, Cultural, and Religious Systems of Life

the identifying mark of circumcision on newborn sons the tribe would have to fight for Hivite or Philistine land.

In chapters 12–15 of the book of Judges, the Samson story precedes the migration of the tribe of Dan to its northern settlement, and apparently represented an early failure of a tribe to "drive out" both native Canaanites and the Philistines who appear to have been aggressive newcomers like the Israelites. The Philistines came into the Shephelah from the seacoast and took control of lands as far as Timnath. Samson's parents may not have been able to give him enough land to sustain a family.

Young women could expect to be looked after most of the time. Even the Moabitess Ruth could hope to find security as a member of an Israelite family and tribe. Independent women like Rahab who offered hospitality to travelers, possibly including sexual relationship, lived apart from male custody and protection. They were exceptions to the normal family pattern. Nevertheless they were accepted as useful members of Israelite society.

Young single men needed a plot of land or the beginning of a herd of goats to establish a home and family. Some fathers may have divided property for their sons, ideally giving each a share, but such a practice was probably rare. The granting of a birthright to only one of Isaac's two sons suggests that other sons were always subject to the first, and that customarily in patriarchal times a family's land was not divided. Without a share a second son faced a form of slavery to the eldest son or an uncertain future. Fathers could sell them into a seven year period of indentured service during which they could risk not earning enough wealth to establish themselves. But an early custom allowed a slave who married within the extended family of his owner to choose to remain with the owner as a permanent slave, who then might not be sold to foreign slave traders or released to be an independent youth in a community made up of families. The laws of Exodus 21:1–11 concern Hebrew slaves sold within the tribal limits of the covenant community of early Israel, and were intended to avoid the loss of young men to "foreign" tribes, but did not guarantee them economic self-sufficiency.

Jacob agreed to the customary seven years service for each of his brides. But some young men met their need for a mate by finding unusual ways to provide the bride price: when Saul's daughter expressed an interest in marrying the young man who had felled the giant Goliath, Saul saw an opportunity to let the Philistines take care of a potential rival to his son Jonathon, and since David confessed that he was too poor to offer the usual bride price, Saul challenged him to present a hundred Philistine foreskins. So, at the time of their marriages David outdid Samson in killing Philistines.

The gang rape of the Levite's concubine, at the end of the book of Judges, led to a small war to punish the tribe of Benjamin, and that involved the massacre of "every male and every woman that has lain with a male" in Jabesh Gilead. There followed the capture of four hundred virgins of this town, which had not joined in the war against Benjamin. When it was discovered that not enough virgins were left to marry the remaining men of Benjamin, the men were authorized to carry off wives for themselves from the yearly festival at Shiloh when "the young women came out to dance in the dances." The twenty-first chapter of Judges is devoted to this part of the episode, and it gives us a look at the way ad hoc decision making by assembled tribal representatives laid the ground work for the development of laws. Fortunately, the punishment and restoration of the tribe of Benjamin never became permanent law in Israel. However, patriarchy was enshrined in Pentateuch law, and thus provided structure for the management of family relations within the tribal confederation of ancient Israel.

"Certain Base Fellows"

One unintended consequence of the Israelite economic system was the presence of numbers of unattached young men like those of two communities pictured in the books of Genesis and Judges. The stories tell of two unplanned experiments, and at the same time suggest why they failed. The failed experiments helped establish norms (and memes) for the Israelite social fabric, but did not change the fabric.

The first incident occurred in Sodom, one of the "cities of the plain," a town which never belonged to Israel. Before Israel even existed, the two angels who had visited Abraham "came to Sodom in the evening, and Lot was sitting in the gate" of the town. When Lot offered them a courteous invitation to "turn aside to your servant's house and spend the night, and wash your feet," they said "No; we will spend the night in the square." That two travelers should expect to spend a night in a public square is puzzling. Clearly they did not have acquaintances in Sodom, but one wonders if travelers were regularly prepared to sleep on the ground wrapped in their cloaks. Jacob's solitary night at Bethel suggests that this was the common experience of lone travelers. The alternative in some communities was the "house of a prostitute" like Rahab.

But Lot prevailed and spread a hurried feast, baking unleavened bread. Before Lot and his guests lay down, "the men of the city, both young and old, all the people to the last man, surrounded the house; they called to Lot, "Where are the men who came to you tonight? Bring them out to us, so that we may know them." Lot "went out of the door to the men, shut the door after him, and pleaded that they not act so wickedly." He even offered his two virgin daughters in place of his guests, but the guests rescued Lot and struck the people of Sodom with blindness, "so that they were unable to find the door." (Genesis 19:1–10)

A similar incident is recorded in Judges 19 at Gibeah in the tribal land of Benjamin. A Levite had traveled to Bethlehem to bring his concubine back to the hills of Ephraim. As the evening approached he and his concubine bypassed Jebus (later Jerusalem) because it was a city of "foreigners," and made their way in the deepening dark to Gibeah where he was about to spend the night in the open square. But an old man returning from his field, stopped to inquire "Where are you going and where do you come from?" Learning of the journey ahead for the party, he insisted that the travelers pass the night at his house. While they were enjoying themselves, the men of the city, "a perverse lot"[9] surrounded the house, and started pounding on the door, just as the men of Sodom had done, demanding to "have intercourse" with the guests. Here

---

9. Hebrew literally "sons of Belial" or "good for nothings," RSV "base fellows." Belial may be taken as an abstraction and not as a deity.

PART 1: Biological, Cultural, and Religious Systems of Life

also the host offered his virgin daughters, but the Levite offered his concubine, and it was the concubine who was sacrificed to the mob.

Why were the men of these two towns, one Israelite and the other Canaanite, so perverse? What led to the bizarre attempt at the homosexual rape of strangers passing the night in a town? Of course the historians intended to contrast the bad social, not the biological, behavior with the ideal that they were holding before the Israel of their own day. You could expect no better from the corrupt "cities of the plain," but for the little town of Gibeah, the author of the Judges story wants the reader to see how low Israelites could fall in the days before a righteous king would bring order to the land. Benjamites behaved as badly as Canaanites. More exactly, *some* Benjamites behaved as badly as *all* Canaanites. The farmer host, however, was a model of hospitality just as Lot had been.

Was there something about foreignness in the antipathy toward passing travelers? Evidently any foreigner was looked upon with suspicion and fear in days when few people left their home communities. It is likely that Levites, Kenite blacksmiths, and Midianite or Ishmaelite traders, easily identified by clothes or tribal markings, moved freely from tribe to tribe, but the first impulsive reaction to any foreigner was evidently suspicion. Was the lone traveler a murderer like Cain, an outcast from his family? Were small groups of men spies seeking easily taken stores of grain and wine for a migrating body? But a few settlers were willing to extend the comfort of their homes to the occasional traveler, offering them food just as people of the Middle East do to this day when curious travelers appear in the streets of a town. Each such contact tests the covenantal paradigm.

How widespread in the ancient world was the malicious proclivity to sexual attack on defenseless travelers? Or why were there four hundred men who flocked to David at the cave of Adullam, "everyone who was in distress or debt, and everyone who was discontented?" (1 Sam 22:2) They were evidently *self-recruited* from among the "base fellows" who had not succeeded in establishing a normal family structure. What David offered was the security of a group large enough to demand or take what it needed from isolated homesteads, but at the same time he could enforce enough discipline on the members of his band to keep potential outlaws in responsible orderly behavior. His band became a faux family until its members settled individually in the midst of established communities.

The overriding concern of the stories in the biblical histories from Genesis through 2 Kings is the survival of all Israel, not the morality of individual Israelite men or women. The word "sin" is seldom attached to any behavior, except that of the sons of Eli, who "treated the offerings of the Lord with contempt" by insisting on the best pieces of the offered meat, and by lying with the women "who served at the entrance of the tent of meeting." (1 Sam 2:12–17,22–24)

The depravity described in these early stories resulted from the social and economic separation of young single men from women in the period of family life between childhood and full responsible adulthood. Forbidden to marry until they were self-supporting, youths gathered into gangs and devised ways of relieving accumulated tension. Eli's sons were no exception. Nevertheless, the reporting historians imply that the violence was displeasing both to responsible adults and to God.

What was normal in other mammal species, living in bands of males for a relatively short period of adolescence, was also the practice of the human species, notably in early Israel before the time of King David. Adolescent males normally test their increasing strength and skills in contests, which in modern times have taken the form of football, basketball, baseball and other sports. Many young adults in ancient Israel, like King David, developed useful skills for herding sheep and goats, or were indentured into seven years of slavery to more prosperous families, where they might settle permanently with a wife and service useful to the extended family. But some of those who lived in the populous towns of the growing Israelite community joined together either in lawless gangs or as the more disciplined followers of David. How else could adolescent males have become civilized? God evidently intended all humans not only to procreate, but also to build civilized families and tribal groups. Israelites would lead the way.

3

Understanding Sexual and Social Systems

BEFORE WE TRY TO place our feet on both sides of the divide between nature and culture, we need a quick look at sex. At the risk of being corrected by proper biologists I will sketch what I understand. It appears that only in the realms of plant and animal life can we be certain that sex occurs without the possibility of "sin." That is to say that Biology 101 will include a discussion of sexual reproduction, but will not normally require any comment about sin. Sex for mammals, however, must be seen in the broad context of kinds of "groupiness," as Holmes Rolston III characterizes the social aspects of the higher orders of animal life.[1]

Sex without Sin?

I remember my disappointment with a semester of introductory biology in high school which included diagrams of the reproductive process of some lower creature, perhaps a frog, but postponed the more dangerous topic of human reproduction for a more advanced course. I was too shy or embarrassed to raise my hand in class and inquire if human beings were reproduced by a similar process, believing that such a question would provoke derision from either teacher or classmates. At the time it seemed that everyone but I already knew "the facts of life" and the "birds and bees" scenarios. Atlanta's Boys' High School did not require any laboratory course in biology, but I doubt that my unspoken questions would have been answered in that setting.

My birth and the possibility of future births were topics we did not discuss at home, and all I knew about my sex organ was that my father discouraged any extended touching of it. One day when I was about eight years old, I was playing on our front porch with a little girl slightly younger than I, and without any preliminaries she asked if she could see my "peter." Without any hesitation I pulled up the leg of the short pants I was wearing and exposed my penis, and quickly satisfied her curiosity as to what it looked like. The same afternoon we had moved to a tent in the back yard, and without warning I kissed her awkwardly, probably on the cheek. After her family left I found

---

1. Rolston, *Genes, Genesis and God*, 86. Rolston considers that genes have a kind of "groupy selfishness."

my father inside the house and announced that I was going to marry Marjorie. He simply said, "Son, you'll have time enough for that later."

These events can hardly be described as sex without sin, but they approach the innocence of animal sexuality. What was it that Marjorie and I were so curious about? How did I recognize her term for my penis? Why did I not tell my father the whole story that led to the announcement of my prospective marriage? And why do I now connect these events with the dynamic of sexuality?

"Sex" is a convenient summary term for all aspects of the process of sexual reproduction. As human beings came to self-awareness, members of our species recognized—or discovered—that we, like practically all "higher" forms of life, reproduce through the mating of male and female elements produced by mature members of our species. Our ancestors devised specialized terms like "seed" and "pollen," or "egg" and "sperm," to identify these elements. Likewise they specifically identified the organs that produce them. Individuals of various species are identified as "buck" and "doe," "bull" and "cow," or "man" and "woman."

Our childish curiosity asks for a simple clinical understanding of the process of reproduction. Like the processes of digestion and waste elimination, this understanding is hidden from the young mind, which comes out of darkness into a hide and seek world of many mysterious events. In an ideal family, understanding of natural processes would increase gradually from the beginning of conscious life to maturity, and would no doubt continue into old age and to eventual death. There should be no place for "sin" in the thinking of young people who spent their lives learning the natural processes of digestion, waste elimination and reproduction. Likewise the discovery of laws of motion, electrical and atomic activity and a host of other features of the world would provide endless entertainment for the inquiring minds of human beings. Discovering how things work is a normal part of life for the embodied spirits of our species, and can satisfy the human hunger for meaning.

What We Later Discovered

It is not necessary to labor these comments, but it may be helpful to recapitulate several features of the reproductive process. First and foremost, it takes only one of the thousands of male sperm to fertilize the female egg. Thus, the survival of higher species is accomplished through the uniting of two distinct and different individual subtypes that appear within the species. Even the lowest species, the single cells from which all life originated, appear to have developed their complex forms through the union of dissimilar units of protoplasm. Strangely, the process of a sperm cell's fertilizing an egg cell in a womb looks like the process of consuming nourishment. Cells "eat" by absorbing what are essentially foreign bodies in the medium that surrounds them. The egg absorbs the invading sperm or "eats" it. The body is built, however, not entirely through a process of eating, but through a cooperative working together of individual cells. Dissimilar proteins are the active building blocks for the building of the specialized organs of a body, just as genes and cell walls cooperate in the replication of cells.

Part 1: Biological, Cultural, and Religious Systems of Life

Second, the thousands or millions of sperm produced in males are matched by a succession of eggs which females produce. At every level the forms of life are incredibly prolific, multiplying the possibilities for combinations that can survive. This means that there is ample opportunity for reproduction within most species. But the sperm and eggs that do not mate are not completely wasted. The body has its ways of passing unused eggs and sperm into channels for elimination, and what we eliminate becomes nourishment for the microbes that inhabit our public and private septic systems.

Third, the mating of sperm and eggs and the actual production of the new individual occur out of sight, deep inside our bodies, where many other processes are also hidden. This means that the outcome of a mating is not precisely predictable. Neither male nor female can know whether the product will be a male or a female, whether it will be one of the survivors or a waste product, or what features of one or the other will appear. Every union produces a *tertium quid*, a "third what?" something new and different from either of its parents. Rolston has written of the paradox of novelty in the midst of continuing identity:

> A paramount force that keeps enlarging the family is sexuality, combined with pressure toward out breeding. In sexually reproducing species, when the genes go through just that phase of the life cycle where the fully selfish genetic set might be expected to construct a faithful copy of itself, a cloned organism with identical genes, there are chopping up and reshuffling, as though to bar genetic fidelity as the only rule in the game. The system insists on variation. It is hard to be selfish, if one is a genome and must be slit in half at every reproduction.[2]

The beauty of sexual reproduction is this unpredictable creative novelty of result. It is safe to say that in nature no two matings, even between the same pair, produce clones. This makes for the tremendous variety of individual living beings, and provides a species with the resources to adapt successfully to new situations. Identical twins are only produced by one mating, but "identical" remains a relative term. Rolston uses the term "sexuality" in its proper biological sense of anything having to do with sexual function. In this book I use the term sexuality to distinguish the social aspects from the biological.

H. Allen Orr defines fitness as used in evolutionary biology as "the probability of surviving or reproducing in a given environment." He points out: "Adaptive evolution is therefore a two-step process, with a strict division of labor between mutation and selection. In each generation, mutation brings new genetic variants into populations. Natural selection then screens them; the rigors of the environment reduce the frequency of 'good' (relatively fit) ones."[3]

Fourth, we dare not use the term "process" casually, for nourishment, reproduction and elimination are all time-bound, proceeding moment by moment through the lifetimes of all the particles that make up whole beings. It is the coincidence of all of these features that results in the hide-and-seek quality of the natural world and all

---

2. Ibid., 96.
3. Orr, "Testing Natural Selection," 46.

its creatures. Recent discussions of physical reality have turned from seeking "initial conditions" to recognizing what some have called "determinative chaos," and others "intelligent design." The movement of sperm in the vagina is at once opportunistic and determined, that is, driven by a *vital* force that seems to "know" its destiny, as Bruce H. Lipton concluded when he first saw paramecia on a low power microscope in grammar school. He continues to believe in cell "knowledge" after years of observations with high power electron microscopes.[4] More exactly, Lipton sees the cell wall as the "brain" of a cell, and considers that its membrane functions selectively to absorb nutrients and to discharge wastes into its surrounding fluids.

Fifth, we may also note the cyclic character of natural processes. Repeated cycles of beginning, maturing, and completing occur at every level from cells to the most complex species. But the stages of living forms are not marked by cleanly distinct edges; instead new identities evolve seamlessly from pre-existing materials in the processes of life. John D. Palmer has recently written *The Biological Clocks: the Orchestration of Biological Rhythms*, but for humans clocks belong to the realm of planning and achieving goals.

Sexual reproduction has come to prominence in the natural world and has the special advantage of a continual juggling of the genes of species, mixing and matching to produce the infinite variety among individuals and the resulting flexibility to meet challenges that affect the survival of species. The biological world may be seen as a vast laboratory of unplanned experiments, some of which give rise to genuine novelties while others are doomed to the waste bins, or more accurately, to being recycled as nourishment for the more successful of other species.

These experiments have created not only unique individuals, but also new species and orders of being which bring with them their own operating rules in addition to those imposed on "lower" orders. The biological orders of animals and plants include but also utilize chemical bonding in new forms. Likewise the experiment of human thought utilizes the electrochemical activity of brain cells, which enables people to observe processes and theorize about them. In society, news reporters, scientists, philosophers and theologians carry on the experimental process, which becomes a highly sophisticated scientific method.

Applying the scientific method to culture, Richard Dawkins created the word "meme" as the social equivalent of "gene." Dawkins intended it as the unit of cultural transmission of melodies, fashions and learned skills that are passed on by social imitation. The term could be valuable in studies of the psychology of religious behavior.

Those who advocate the teaching of "intelligent design" (previously known as "creationism") apparently insist that every naturally occurring variant results from the determinative decision of a divine Creator. On the other hand advocates of "determinative chaos" see four essential forces producing actual order as well as apparent chaos beginning in the sub-atomic realm. The production of variety at every level can hardly be denied, but the riddles of Platonic forms, Aristotelian final causes and biblical

---

4. See Lipton's introductory chapter, "The Magic of Cells," in *Biology and Belief*.

PART 1: Biological, Cultural, and Religious Systems of Life

theistic creation remain unsolved. One may have to think along parallel tracks toward an infinitely remote vanishing point. The limited similarities between the processes of sexual reproduction and nourishment of the physical body should help to justify my thesis that "sexual sin" has no place in the natural world.

Competition, Dominance and Balance

A recent PBS Nature program focused on a young foal, "Cloud," and his growth to maturity.[5] The camera and commentary followed his early shaky steps and his movements imitative of his elders, both male and female, and followed his adolescence. As one of the "bachelors," separated from the mares by the band stallion, Cloud began unsuccessfully to challenge a particular stallion for the leadership of the band of mares, but finally, as a five year old, found a mare from a different band to mate with. The video showed the horses grazing in seasonal landscapes during five years of filming while the narrator verbally highlighted the stages of their interrelationships. Parallel hungers, which precede the hunger for meaning in humans, appeared to drive the processes of grazing and reproduction.

In the realm of nature neither of those hungers are satisfied by individuals living alone, at least through the full cycle of life. Ginger Kathrens, the human observer of Cloud's development, characterized the group of horses as a "band," a term which verbalizes the bonding between a stallion, his mares and the colts and fillies. Except when colts mature and act to assert their roles as developing stallions, banding functions to control grazing territory as well as sexual activity in its season.

In the animal world, particularly that of mammals, a third process which is not so easy to name must be taken into account. Natural selection has been associated with the theory of the evolution of species, but a degree of selection also takes place among individual animals. In the video viewers could see how self-selected males were able to keep young bachelors from the mares who followed them. Only when Cloud had found a filly that would accept his leadership could he become the "alpha male" of his own band. Both stallions and mares appeared to choose their mates once the basic necessity of nursing young colts and fillies ended. This social selectivity is even more fascinating to contemplate among our bird relatives, where it is often linked with a sort of "commitment" between one male and one female—like human marriage. However, sex is only one of the activities involved in the "groupiness" of mammalian species. Rolston invented that term to express the sense of community that appears among animals as well as human societies. His chapter on "Genetic Identity" in *Genes, Genesis, and God* is worth a careful reading.

Theory must also recognize the nurturing capability of both sexes. The genes that express themselves in mammal females provide the newborn with essential nourishment. The social links that form bands of horses, packs of wolves, prides of lions, and human families, provide for the continuing nourishment of the group. A sort of

---

5. The video essay presented footage made by Ginger Kathrens, and the interviewer offered an inside look at her procedure.

proto-culture can be observed in the bands of mammalian species. Somewhere I read of the procedure of a band of chimpanzees in choosing which way they would forage after their night of rest. As the members of the group awoke, stretched themselves and resumed grooming each other lazily, a younger individual would start out to forage, but would pause a short distance away and look back to see if anyone was following. If none followed, he returned to the group. Only when some senior followed would the whole band move toward the chosen direction for that day's foraging. The human observer characterized the procedure as "voting," which sounds like proto-government in the animal world.

According to evolutionary theory a species benefits from the virility of its strongest males, and any "weaker," recessive genes could ultimately be lost. The PBS Nova video included the violent killing of a defective colt by the alpha stallion, when the colt was unable to follow as the adults moved to a new area to continue grazing. Rolston has explored the behavioral relationships between "contexts, constraints, and consequences" of organisms in *Genes, Genesis, and God*. His study recognizes and celebrates the values that have emerged from the evolutionary processes associated with the genes inherent in all forms of life.

Studies of genetics have opened the microscopic hidden processes of reproduction, and brought to light the appearance of random variations in the gene pool of a species, some of which may be beneficial in times of stress, while others may be harmful but are seldom completely eliminated through normal wear and tear. As Rolston points out, genes are essentially neutral.[6] Species thus survive the transition from one generation to the next. Both males and females must do their parts in the ongoing story of life.

What I have briefly sketched may be summed up in a systems approach that observes repeated cycles of the behavior patterning of living forms. The cycle is initiated with the self-assembly of sperm and egg to produce what will be a fetus and later an adult. At every level the process of self-assembly continues to occur as disparate chemical elements, compounds, cells, and organs, nerves, muscles, and other tissues work together to create the individual. Finally, when two individuals, a male and a female, self-assemble into a couple, the cycle is completed and begins again with the creation of new individuals. The two who formed the couple may continue to live after completing the sexual cycle of life, probably producing more new individuals. Human custom names the resulting group "family." The covenantal paradigm has already taken shape in the activities of animal bands, herds and the beehive.

As we trace the cycle through its stages, each member of the family appears to make specialized contributions to the process. At any moment one or the other of an animal pair may appear dominant. The stallion actively manages the membership of the band, driving out some maturing young males. The filly, having matured as a mare, however, accepts or rejects the advances of an approaching stallion, and carries and nurses the foal until it can become independent of her care. Instead of observing a

---

6. Lipton, "The Magic of Cells," 65–66, notes that cells without nuclei can do everything but reproduce.

dominating male and a subservient female, we see a complex of balanced interactions. As the band grazes each member is nourished and energized to play its role in a process which anticipates the human stages of care giving and maintaining family health we will see in chapters 19 and 20. The role of the alpha male is analogous to what can be seen as a god-figure, but we must not overlook the way the mare also functions as a god-figure as she supervises the young foal.

Horse intelligence, or chimpanzee intelligence for that matter, is far from human intelligence, but each represents a step on the way toward what we think of as fully human. What does this mean? At a minimum it means a mind's capability to integrate sensations, to build a mental image of surroundings complete with indications of threat and possible benefit to ongoing personal life. A god-figure senses threats and possible benefits for the group's survival, and in acting makes "decisions."

Since we are discussing process, we must recognize that the fourth dimension, time, is required for the existence of all material substance. Mountains, seas, animals, trees and humans, even planets and stars exist in time, and may be observed at various stages. Unlike mountains and seas, for living creatures the all-important moment for survival is when two opposite forms unite sexually. "Sex" means more than a biological differentiation within a species. It often stands for the moment of agreed upon mating that marks the beginning of the cycle for many of the life forms in our world. For the materials that make land, sea and air we are told that the all important moment is in super-nova explosions when the more complex elements are created from hydrogen and helium, as protons and neutrons unite to form new elements, the "more from less," which is a theme of Rolston's book.

Form, Function and Fate

Our discussion has skirted two questions raised by philosophers and theologians. How did the remarkable sexual forms we observe come into being, and how, actually, do they work? In this chapter we have touched lightly on physical sex, but we have not yet clarified how the manifold variety of organisms came into being. Historically there are two essentially different answers.

Ancient people tended to see forms *as having antecedence over individuals*. Genesis 1:21 declares: "God created the great sea monsters and every living creature that moves of every kind." History followed as creatures diversified and multiplied. Where Genesis writes of "kinds," Plato wrote of permanent *ideal forms* which existed apart from the shadowy figures in the cave. For the ancient mind the source of species was outside the systems of the cosmos (creation *ex nihilo*): "So God created humankind in his image, in the image of God he created them; male and female he created them" (Gen 1:27).

On the other hand, since the age of Linnaeus, Darwin and Mendel *moderns have traced the shaping of forms to the requirements of function*. The architect Walter Gropius expressed the concept in his simple formula "form follows function." Forms grew from pre-existing materials just as seed grew in the fruits of trees. And, adapting to new uses, newer forms, new breeds of domesticated sheep, horses, dogs and cats, for instance, become part of the array of living creatures.

The ancients could conceive only of designing Mind or named Deities in a realm apart from the created forms, and some religious teachers have clung to the idea of the "intelligent design" of distinct forms by a transcendent God. Students in the school of evolution study the functioning of the physical parts of the animate as well as the inanimate features of the cosmos, and only rarely refer to God. When they do, it is mostly as an aspect of their personal religious faith and their commitment to a fellowship of believers, while they prefer separately to explore the operation of a wide range of forces and powers in their laboratories. In *A Theory of Everything: An Integral Vision for Business, Politics, Science, and Spirituality*[7] Ken Wilber discusses several approaches to the dualism of science and religion, but insists that "the integral Map helps make sure that you are 'touching all the bases.'" In *The Integral Vision* he identifies five "essential aspects of [personal] awareness" which correlate with stages of human and social development.

Natural Cycles without Sin

To conclude, we do not observe any "sin" in the systems of nature. Certain patterns of behavior are favored in the circumstances and setting—the "niche" a species occupies—and many aberrations from normal behavior are tolerated though not favored. Nothing we think of as "sin" appears in the lives of plants and animals, or of any microscopic creatures.

Instead we look at the niches, the time they are occupied, and the moments of transition that mark the boundaries within and around particular lives. The death of individuals and the demise of species do not appear as punishment for sins committed, but as the closing of shorter and longer cycles of natural existence. Lifeless material offers nourishment for the life cycles of plants and through them of animate creatures. In Darwinian evolution variations appear and develop successors, some of which may survive while others fail. In nature neither success nor failure is related to sin.

Animate species follow cycles from beginnings through maturity to death, which are generally recognized as "natural." The sexual cycle and the cycle of dominance and subservience are completed normally with the emergence of new individuals. An animal species fails to survive when an insufficient number of individuals complete the sexual cycle, and/or when new individuals become prey to other, stronger species. Except in our closest kindred species cycles and behavior may be studied without consideration of sin.

Only in the human species do moral questions rise, whether behavior should be considered right or wrong, just or unjust, good or evil, creative or destructive. The biblical stories we will consider illustrate the working of some of the intermediate cycles in the dual world of nature and culture. Only in a community of personal beings may we begin to look for sin.

7. Wilber, *A Theory of Everything*, 60–63.

4

Discovering Sexuality

THE ADVENTURE OF CONSCIOUSNESS expresses itself in curiosity about the processes of digestion and reproduction. Human curiosity, going beyond animal seeking, looks below the surface activities of feeding and mating, and perceives or creates a different world, one of social and religious relationships. We humans are not satisfied with the bare experience of "raw sex," or raw food for that matter. We have to think and talk and fit sex into the wholeness of our lives with the theories and experiments that are the substance of community, business, science, philosophy, and religion. The acquired habits that develop from the interaction of cultural training of an individual's body may be characterized as "second nature."

James B. Nelson has pointed the way to a responsible contemporary discussion of male aspects of sex in his book *The Intimate Connection: Male Sexuality, Masculine Spirituality*. Nelson's chosen term "sexuality" may stand appropriately for our look at sex in the whole experience of human life. Persons with a religious orientation are well equipped to explore the tensions between the physical attractions of sex and the spiritual aspects of sexuality. Some biblical stories focus on women, the "other" from the male point of view.

The *Sexual* System

Nelson's title and our common experience suggest that the peculiarly human experience of sex can best be described in terms of relationship. "Relational" characterizes the coherence of one element to another in any whole. At the physical level the male relates to, joins with, the female. In the cultural world a similar meeting and joining occur as social barriers are breached and penetrated. This is to say, human beings distinguish and can speak about a cultural system that overlaps and transcends the natural system of male/female mating.

Notice how many of the words end with the suffix *-al*. Language, the verb*al*izing of relationships, uses adjectiv*al* forms to call attention to the difference between natur*al* and cultur*al* realms. We speak of the development of soci*al* control, of ethic*al* concepts, or leg*al* restrictions, and in our exploration of the religious interest in sex, of covenant*al* relationships. It is all ment*al* with spiritu*al* overtones in a song parallel to the physic*al*. One additional adjective distinguishes the system of sexuality from raw sex. It can be described as emotion*al*. The cultur*al* is deeper and broader than the ration*al*. "Animal" is one more -*al* word, suggesting spirit-like or breathing, i.e., more like a human than a plant. It would be diverting to observe the metaphors contained in these words, for such figures of speech are a fundamental aspect of human thought processes.

Primitive thinking appears to have distinguished the sexual roles of man and wife by an analogy or metaphor of seed and soil. The man's semen provided the seed, which was believed to be a sort of homunculus, an extremely small human being, while the woman was the "soil" into which the seed was sown. More recent thinking keeps the idea of seed, but recognizes the sexual mating of sperm and egg as well as the mating of man and woman. Neither need be dominant in the cooperative process, which is essentially relational. We may be tempted to hear a word-play on two senses of the English word "soil" when we read of defilement in the biblical holiness laws, but in these it is the woman who is soiled, "defiled," not by her husband, but by any other male.

While animals sense pain or comfort in the functions of their bodies, only the most advanced species can be characterized as experiencing self-conscious pleasure. Experiments with dolphins, chimpanzees, crows, and ravens have demonstrated that many animals and birds have limited capabilities to recognize and respond to signals, to name objects, to plan actions, and to enjoy comfort. Perhaps more interesting than the conceptual skill of laboratory animals which these experiments have demonstrated, is the interrelationship between the experimenters and the creatures. Although we cannot speak with authority of what the animals are thinking and feeling, it is evident that both experimenter and creature are enjoying the games they play, as well as experiencing a bonding between them.

Our pleasure with sex shows itself all the way from the sensations of the physical act to the reading and writing of novels, operas, and letters and e-mails to those we love. We have endless curiosity about the sexual experience of other people, and few people can resist the temptation to indulge that curiosity. Television, which combines images with stories, is currently the medium for many of the stories people enjoy, and is rightly considered "entertainment." Stories in the Hebrew Scriptures anticipated this entertainment.

Female Sexuality

Anita Diamant's novel *The Red Tent* illustrates the experience of female sexuality as she imagines the family of Laban's daughters and their handmaids as they prepared themselves to bear Jacob's twelve sons and one daughter. Diamant has evidently read Susan Ackerman's careful study *Under Every Green Tree: Popular Religion in Sixth Century Judah*, which explores the religious meanings of women's practices in ancient Israel. Another student of the biblical text, Ita Sheres, has analyzed the setting of *Dinah's*

Rebellion: A Biblical Parable for Our Time. Diamant sketches life in the tents of the women in the patriarch Laban's extended family.

Laban's daughters, Leah and Rachel, children of his marriage to Adah, together with his daughters by other women, Zilpah and Bilhah, spent their days preparing food, planting and harvesting grain, spinning and weaving, and tending the goats' kids. They also attended to a common menstrual cycle with rituals intended to prepare for eventual marriage and parenthood, which they hoped would be goddess-blessed with male and female children for their husbands. They shared the awareness that their father Laban no longer had sexual intercourse with Adah, but was still "lustful" and from time to time made sexual approaches to his goats, just as the young boys of their acquaintance did.

Diamant pictures Jacob's entrance into Laban's family as a significant sexual approach welcomed by each young woman with an individual response. Rachel, having not yet experienced her "first blood," decided at the moment he kissed her at the well that she would marry Jacob. Leah, Zilpah and Bilhah all had mixed feelings in Jacob's presence, strongly attracted by his male sexuality, but required by custom to accept the family's decisions as to who would be permitted to bear Jacob's children and when this would take place. For his part Jacob was ready to negotiate for the bride he had come from Canaan to find.

Managing Sex

The distinctively human aspect of sexuality is this conscious and intentional management or domestication of sex. Its earliest form was apparently matriarchal, as a number of women writers have pointed out. In *The Chalice and the Blade* Riane Eisler develops a picture of the early management of human life by women and shows how men supplanted this with the patriarchy familiar to readers of the Hebrew Scriptures. In *Hagar the Egyptian: The Lost Tradition of the Matriarchs*, Savina J. Teubal suggests that each of the women in Abraham's family exercised a powerful priestly role, which included her sexual relationships. In *Sarah the Priestess* Teubal collected what can be surmised about the Mesopotamian life of the women of Genesis prior to migration to Canaan. Thomas Cahill begins his *Gifts of the Jews* with an imaginary Babylonian ritualized sexual intercourse initiated by a priestess with a chosen adolescent male. These fictions offer a glimpse at realities now lost to us.

Since the biblical record has illuminated the dominating male management of sexuality, it is appropriate that we imagine what probably took place in the tents and rooms where ancient women spent their lives. Anita Diamant pictures the "red tent" as the locus of the women's management of physical sex from births to the completion of the sexual cycle. The exception was when one of the women welcomed Jacob to *her* tent for dinner. The novel builds on a clue found in Genesis where Jacob's wives decide which of them will sleep with him on a particular night. Having bargained with her sister and prepared his evening meal, "When Jacob came in from the field in the evening, Leah went out to meet him, and said, 'You must come in to me, for I have hired you with my son's mandrakes'" (Gen 30:16).

Preparing for their childbearing, women performed experiments, testing what would work to produce a child: they collected their blood and offered it in libations; baked three cornered cakes and burned them as offerings to the queen of heaven or to a lesser goddess who might be more favorable than the distant mother of the gods. Their experiments also included the use of a variety of plants, such as Leah's mandrakes, some intended to assure a successful pregnancy, while others were known to bring about the termination of an unwanted pregnancy.

Susan Ackerman notes Jeremiah's prophetic denunciation of the time-honored rituals still practiced by women in the cities of Judah prior to the exile: "The children gather wood, the fathers kindle fire, and the women knead dough to make cakes for the queen of heaven, and they pour out drink offerings to other gods to provoke me to anger" (Jer 7:18). And the book of Jeremiah tells how the people responded to Jeremiah's sermon:

> And all the men who were aware that their wives had been making offerings to other gods and all the women who stood by, a great assembly, all the people who lived in Pathros in the land of Egypt, answered Jeremiah: As to the word that you have spoken to us in the name of the Lord, we are not going to listen to you. Instead, we will do everything that we have vowed: make offerings to the queen of heaven and pour out libations to her, just as we and our ancestors did, our kings and our officials, used to do in the towns of Judah and in the streets of Jerusalem. We used to have plenty of food, and prospered, and we saw no misfortune. But from the time we stopped making offerings to the queen of heaven and to pour out libations to her, we have lacked everything, and have perished by the sword and by famine" (Jer 44:15–18).

The sexual relationships we observe in Genesis fit the pattern of the covenantal paradigm and rest on the coherence of elements found in the natural world with an overlay of customs practiced by people. In the harmonious interweaving of physical and social activities note the conscious pleasure of Sarah when she named Isaac: "God has brought laughter for me; everyone who hears will laugh with me." Earlier when one of three visitors had told Abraham that Sarah would have a son, she had laughed to herself, saying, "After I have grown old, and my husband is old, shall I have pleasure?" (Gen 18:13). The unusual word "pleasure" may reflect an ancient belief that a woman's orgasm anticipated a pregnancy.[1]

From our perspective extended families and tribes appear to have been learning/teaching organizations, with elder women, variously described as midwives, priestesses, or witches, preserving the memory of successful and unsuccessful experiments. As with early agriculture the ways of sex were apparently the discovery of women, though distinguishing science from superstition was still in the future. As Susan Ackerman has noted, Israelite women continued to practice rituals dedicated to several goddesses

---

1. Genesis 21:6 and 18:12.

Part 1: Biological, Cultural, and Religious Systems of Life

into the sixth century BCE, well beyond the orthodox insistence that only one God, YHWH, could answer an Israelite's prayers.[2]

Rituals

In the ancient family setting religious, physical and social aspects of every human experience were interwoven. The actions of gods and goddesses mirrored those of human families and could be invoked to assist human living. Both men and women could serve as intermediaries between ordinary people and the gods, and many of the rituals were thank offerings that returned a "first fruit" portion of a god's gifts in the expectation that the god would be induced to continue the blessing. The rituals, however, were not always joyous. Aware of the uncertainties of planting and breeding cycles, worshippers offered their prayers and sacrifices with an anxious note of pleading. The prayers of women in ancient Israel took the form of tangible gifts, libations, potions drunk by the petitioner, visits to holy places, or the holding of statuettes. Their private rituals centered on the birth and health of the children they expected to bear.

Circumcised men in Israel sought the pleasure of releasing their sexual tensions as men have always done, seeking partners with wombs wherever these could be found. We could note examples from the scriptures, but at this point suggest how men's sexuality differs from women's. In general, women appear to wait, more or less passively, for sexual fulfillment; men actively and publicly seek objects for sexual relationship. James Nelson uses the verb "embracing" as he discusses sexual mystery, friendship, mortality, and masculinity. The social aspects of sexuality parallel the physical: as sperm appear to seek an egg to fertilize, the male human "embraces" the female, ideally in the complete range of the four Greek words translated by the English word "love," which Nelson interprets: "Without eros, agape is cold and devoid of energizing passion. Without philia, epithymia becomes a sexual contract. Without epithymia, other ways of loving become bloodless. Without agape, the other dimensions of loving lose their self-giving, transformative power."[3]

As chromosomes connect and the double helices of DNA carry information to shape the living forms of the new generation, culturally parallel "ideas" or "memes"[4]—thoughts and feelings—prepare men and women for the intimate physical contact of marriage, and then sustain the relationships needed to preserve families, clans, tribes and nations. Rituals are the active embodiment of thoughts and feelings, and, as Victor Turner suggests, they enable social change.

Putting Feelings into Words

Modern humans think thoughts in their minds or "heads," while feelings come "from the heart." The ancient Israelite referred to both with the word "heart." When we ver-

2. Ackerman, *Under Every Green Tree*, 5, 7.

3. Nelson, *The Intimate Connection*, 62.

4. Richard Dawkins, coined the term as the cultural equivalent of biological "genes" in *The Selfish Gene*; Rolston, *Genes, Genesis, and God*, 1435 prefers "ideas."

balize our sexual feelings, our minds name them "love," or we write poems like the Song of Solomon, celebrating the dialogue of relationship—the interacting longings of *epithymia*.

> "Tell me, you whom my soul loves,
> where you pasture your flock,
> where you make it lie down at noon;
> For why should I be like one who is veiled
> beside the flocks of your companions?"
>
> "If you do not know,
> O fairest among women,
> follow the tracks of the flock,
> and pasture your kids
> beside the shepherds' tents."
> (Song 1:7–8)

The shepherdess must wait for the return of her lover with impatient but almost nameless longing.

Women and men also express their feelings of longing for each other through subtle changes of facial expression (smiles) or movements of the body (extended hands and arms) as well as through the cultivation of physical beauty or handsome figure. The rituals for preparing for a "date" are a major preoccupation of people's minds in the modern world. Advertisers advise people about products to enhance attractiveness, pointing to the values of marketable products. However, verbal communication is essential for human beings, for it is through talk that men and women specify how they feel. Hugs, kisses, hand holding and other forms of touching body to body also express feelings between the sexes, some of them not necessarily sexual.

Relationship and its Various Paths

Nelson's four meanings of the word "love" are only the beginning of the complex of ideational relationships in human societies. While genes are interwoven in a fifty-fifty pairing in the biological realm, and remain constant through a person's life, ideas can be shared in an infinite number of ways, not only at the moment when two bodies meet for conceiving a child, but throughout the lives of the man and woman who create a social context for their children. Rolston insists that while biological information is transferred genetically, ideas are practically free from the "long leash" of genes. Ideas and memes are not bound by time or kin connection.[5] One wonders how much of this Abram/Abraham understood as he left Mesopotamia.

The four Greek words suggest the path traced by an individual "in love." Relationships begin with a subtle *erotic* attraction that may be verbalized as "Can we have supper on Saturday evening?" Friendship (*philia*) develops as individuals continue to spend time talking with each other. If there is no longing (*epithymia*) for the time together, such as the dialogue in the Song of Solomon voices, relationship is

5. Rolston, *Genes, Genesis, and God*, 248.

PART 1: Biological, Cultural, and Religious Systems of Life

"bloodless" or casual, subject to the accidents of ordinary living, like meeting the same clerk in the post office regularly. With *agape* a meeting to satisfy a need for food or shelter becomes a mutually satisfying pleasure that can lead to a permanent commitment.

Biblical incidents in which water was drawn from wells illustrate *agape* or its near equivalent, Hebrew *hesed*. Rebekah offered to draw water for the camels of Abram's servant. Jacob assumed the role of owner of a well and rolled its large stone cover aside for Rachel. Moses came to the defense of the daughters of a Midianite priest when other shepherds were harassing them. (Exod 2:15–22) It should be obvious that head and heart cannot be separated, though our minds delight in distinguishing and defining our feelings.

For women an interdependent relationship with a husband, or with the limited group of men and boys in the extended family, is important. Men on the other hand tend to be more independent, particularly as regards the economy of the household, compared with the family's relationships with the larger world. Within the family both men and women are anxious for the survival of the family lineage or "name." With patriarchy the name was that of father or patriarch. Links to a king's female ancestors, however, are found in the mention of the queen mother in Israel, as Susan Ackerman has pointed out in *Warrior, Dancer, Seductress, Queen: Women in Judges and Biblical Israel*. The linking of two Israelite families was remembered as the linking of the two individuals who discovered each other through the communally approved bargaining process.

A few more comments on the anxieties of both sexes should complete our observations on Israelite thinking about sexuality. First is the question of the identity and name of the deity to whom offerings would be made. Every woman would no doubt have had a favorite, but if, like Rachel or Hannah, she had a problem getting pregnant, she may have inquired of a less familiar goddess, just in case. It was Rachel who carried away the family's household gods on the journey from Harran to Canaan where El was the generic god worshipped by the patriarchs. On the other hand, Hannah's anxiety and suffering could not be relieved until the priest Eli told her that the male god YHWH had heard her prayers. Both Abram/Abraham and Sarai/Sarah spoke with visiting YHWH of an heir whose coming had been greatly delayed.

Another concern might have been finding the right sacrificial offering or the proper ritual to manage an immediate problem. As Anita Diamant pictures it, midwives were essentially priestesses who used a wide variety of herbs and prayers some of which were passed from one midwife to another or were self discovered or developed. In Genesis 15 YHWH specifies the offerings Abram is to present when the patriarch expresses his concern that a foreigner, Eliezer of Damascus, would be his heir. Abram performed as priest for the patriarchal family, while YHWH offered priestly guidance as to details of the ceremony.

The presumed transition from matriarchal to patriarchal management of sexual relations must have taken place as families developed into clans and tribes, and as these claimed territorial control of specific lands. Patriarchs effectually "owned" their sons and daughters, and decided who might unite with whom. In particular, daughters were "given" to the sons of selected other families, while chosen sons were endowed with sufficient land or flocks to enable them to support their families. The giving of a daughter was essentially a barter transaction with the husband's family returning a *mohar* or "bride price" for the bride. Remnants of these exchanges continue to color marriage ceremonies to this day.

Thus, at least from earliest historic times sexuality has been managed through socio-religious conventions, largely economic, with which people have clothed the natural functions of sex. These covenantal conventions have had a profound influence in shaping the whole human experience. In post-exilic Judaism many sexual practices became taboo when devotees of YHWH sought to satisfy what they believed to be God's rigorous expectations and requirements.

By the time YHWH was understood to be "the living God" and the Creator of the world and all within it, the wise priests of an Israel in transition toward Judaism saw much behavior as the author of Deuteronomy 30:19–20 expressed it, as a choice for death instead of life. This falling short of God's expectations for his human creatures has been defined by Barbara Brown Taylor in *Speaking of Sin* as: "Sin is the turning away from life, whatever form that destructiveness may take."[6]

Melodies with Sexual Overtones

Societies' priests are the persons most acutely aware of the tension between sex and sexuality. Representing or presenting God in the midst of human community, the priest has frequently been required to abstain from physical sexual relationship. But his or her ministry must be to persons of both sexes in the whole range of human activities. It is not surprising that the priests are addressed in terms of reverence, sometimes as "Father." Their proper role is to channel the blessings of God to men and women, boys and girls, but they dare not ignore the sexual component of their relationships. Candidates for ordination, who visit churches, meet with youth groups or visit in homes as part of their preparation for ministry, quickly recognize possible temptations.

Before lunch prepared by a mother and her thirteen year old, the visiting Seminary student found himself pleasantly entertained by, and for some weeks corresponding with, the daughter, who seemed to need to relate to him as father/friend. During World War II after leading a church service two Seminarians were invited to dinner by two young wives whose husbands were in France with Patton's army, and after dinner the students were persuaded to postpone their return to the campus until they enjoyed a swim. On a weekday in an empty church the unmarried "preacher" was confronted by an obviously nubile adolescent who made him think of himself as the disgraced Rev. Dr. Shannon in *The Night of the Iguana*.

Small town protestant churches in the South have frequently been served by single students just out of Seminary who have been advised by their professors to "Marry as soon as possible, and as often as necessary!" But they were also advised not to "make

---

6. Taylor, *Speaking of Sin: the Lost Language of Salvation*, 85.

shipwreck" of their ministry. One such young minister never dated a member of his congregation or anyone in his community; another cautiously sought the advice of his landlord's wife before asking attractive bank tellers or social workers for dates. When an Elder in his church kidded him about losing a girl friend to a young lawyer who had just come to town, he thought, but did not say, "Just wait until I date *your* daughter."

Sixth grade school children insisted that he join the PTA in the name of his anonymous "girl friend."

The songs of sexuality must remain harmonious with the deeper melodies of hymns to God and the work songs of daily tasks. It is impossible to avoid some physical contact with other people of both sexes. Ministers are not the only professionals who must ensure that no unintended promise or overture is expressed in day-to-day relationships. Doctors, lawyers, business owners and their employees engage in human relationships where physical sex is socially excluded, but sexuality, communicated without words, can add an undeniable quality of pleasure even to transactions with the postal clerk. Casual flirting adds spice to life.

The harmonies that sound through many of our stories represent our feeling of delight at the tangible and personal expressions of Darwinian "fitness" for survival or of the Hegelian "synthesis" of sexual opposites. Sexuality is at least as complex as sex. Thought has intruded into a world whose highest expression of complexity was heretofore biological. Thought has produced culture, where stories could be told, songs could be sung, satisfactions and disappointments shared, customs developed, laws written, and sins forgiven. Thank Sigmund Freud for beginning the scientific exploration of this aspect of the world of culture.

In our cultural settings we tend to think in dichotomies. At first is an inchoate awareness of the otherness of a world beyond the intuited "self" which the infant can act upon. Next is awareness of an "opposite" gender. Beyond this fundamental biological division of life forms are all kinds of social dichotomies, which organize complexity into kin and non-kin, friend and foe, husband and wife, master and slave, priest and people, etc.

Probing the mystery of sexuality suggests that a necessary symbiosis appears at every level of life. Symbiosis is "the living together of two dissimilar organisms, as in mutualism, commensalism, or parasitism."[7] In the stories we will examine we will see one individual confronting "the other," often as potentially "alien" or "foreign." The story's plot concerns the learning—or failing to learn—of a pattern of living together, sometimes biological but always cultural. The biblical word "covenant" (Hebrew *berith*) expresses the social uniting which is the cultural equivalent of symbiosis, and reduces the action of natural law to a conceptual abstraction, the covenantal paradigm of chapter 5. In the life of an individual, however, the conceptual abstraction must be embodied in flesh and blood. Such embodiment can be called maturity.

Although biblical stories which present sexual relationships from Hebrew history have been considered normative by some religious groups, the writers and editors of

---

7. *Random House Webster's College Dictionary.*

the Hebrew scriptures presented most of them without comment, as events which YHWH God used to shape the history of their ancestors. Walter Wink writes, "the Bible has no sexual ethic. Instead . . . a variety of sexual mores."[8] The stories vary in the details of the scenes they present, sometimes offering two distinct perspectives or different sequences of events, but these complement each other when we look at the human family through their eyes. We should not be vexed when we do not know exactly what happened in past settings. Instead we can learn from the reported successes and failures of our ancestors.

---

8. Walter Wink, *Engaging the Powers*, 44.

5

Covenants and Sin

LAWS, MORAL AND POLITICAL were formulated by people to avoid social conflict or chaos, but before we look at biblical laws, we may profitably look at the lives of people in general. The biblical concept of family (Hebrew *beth ab*, "father's house") comes to us from writer/editors who looked back from the sixth-century BCE exile of Jews from their homeland to the earliest beginning of the human race. As they reflected on the experiences of generations of their ancestors, the Judean writer we identify with the initial letter "J" began his history with a solitary male who needed a companion with whom he could share conversations, a sexual relationship, and life in a garden. Waking after an especially deep sleep, he found a partner for his social, sexual and life extending needs (Gen 2:4b). The letter "J" comes from the German spelling of the Israelite name for God, and identifies the writer/editor who preferred it above all other names for God in his narratives. We will reproduce its four consonants YHWH, more or less as it was first written, without vowels. Early Hebrew manuscripts contained only consonants and no vowels (aeiou). Later commentators added the vowels to Hebrew manuscripts in the second or third century BCE.

After losing their childlike innocence in the garden, our biblical "first parents" began to extend themselves into a future beyond individual lifetimes through the procreation of children with all the attendant problems of sibling getting along peaceably with sibling in the ever-expanding human family. The priest (P source) who added the first chapter of Genesis during the Babylonian captivity articulated the combination of privilege and obligation in the relationship of the human race to the God of Creation, adding the positive command, "be fruitful and multiply," to the prohibited eating of the fruit of the mysterious tree of J's story.

Though theologians have interpreted God's conversation with Noah as the initiation of a second covenant between the human race and God, it is more reasonable to recognize that all relationships are "covenantal," that is, as having the qualities of formal covenants without the formality. The English noun "covenant" comes from a Latin verb meaning to "come together" and in the thirteenth century of the current era (CE) it represented the agreement of two persons to do or not to do something. Even the chemical elements, molecules and DNA helices could be described as "coming together" in our test tubes and in our bodies, though we reserve the term covenant for consciously intended agreement.

The history recorded in the Hebrew Scriptures can be described as a process of putting together a jigsaw puzzle in four dimensions. The men and women of the stories appear as live pieces of the abstract puzzle trying to fit themselves together, sometimes in sexual relationships, always in power relationships, as they met on the map of the ancient middle east. First a man and a woman agreed to live together, though in Genesis it appeared they had no other choice. At times covenants took the form of treaties between political groups. Often people glimpsed only parts of the big picture while joining with each other to become families, tribes and nations. The thousand pieces of popular picture puzzles have an odd resemblance to male and female sexual parts while plumbers regularly borrow the terms "male" and "female" for the threaded ends of pipes and fittings.

A significant pre-Israelite use of the word and concept of "covenant" is found in the legend of King Keret's quest for a bride from the kingdom of his neighbor King Pabel. Pabel's daughter, the lady Hurriya, was a "chess piece" on the board of the treaty between two city states in western Syria during the second millennium before the common era (BCE). Like biblical Job, Keret had lost his "house," i.e., his sons—one of whom would succeed his kingship. In a dream the god El, "Father of Man," advised him to stop weeping, go to the top of a tower and sacrifice to El, then go down, bake bread "for a city" and muster his people for battle. The troops march, threatening villages, awaking King Pabel, who sends messengers offering "silver and yellow glittering gold, friendship by covenant and vassalage forever." Keret refuses, and demands:

> Give me Lady Hurriya, the fair, thy first begotten,
> Whose fairness is like Anath's fairness,
> Whose beauty like Ashtoreth's beauty . . .

In addition to the dream conversation with the god El, the legend reports the successful establishing of a treaty, including the gift of Pabel's daughter, chariot steeds, silver and gold. After seven years the lady Hurriya had delivered "the sons of Keret . . . even as was stipulated in the vows."[1]

Meeting Human Needs

In this study we begin with two elemental human needs which always involve what can be called covenantal transactions: the securing of food, shelter and comforts, and the bringing of new lives into the picture. Many secondary activities are obviously involved in these primary activities, but we must not be diverted by considering how a hunter's muscles coordinate to kill his game or how a gatherer remembers where the tasty fruits are to be found. Since we are human, however, we must consider the power of an individual's thinking and speaking in the family and tribal group. The invention

---

1. Ginsburg, *Ancient Near Eastern Texts Relating to the Old Testament*, 142.

of coherent speech has given humans the capability of managing all the other available powers. My thesis is that this management is accomplished through asking and receiving, giving and expecting a gift in return, or the more violent taking and paying a punitive price. These transactions are inherent in social settings, and are analogous to the physical, chemical and biological activities studied in the sciences.

Jared Diamond has traced in detail the way groups of living beings—plants, animals, and humans—have used their inherited powers to exploit the resources of our planet by developing such essentially human activities as food production, plant and animal domestication, writing, governance, and technology.[2] To a reader whose attention has been focused on the covenantal relationships of the Bible, Diamond's discussions provide illustration after illustration of an essential paradigm that has operated in both natural and cultural systems. In the chapters that follow I propose to sketch the working of the biblical system in terms that should be meaningful to the minds of people of the secular twenty-first century.

Covenantal Bonding

Writer/editors identified by letters "J" or "E" and "P" provided the framework of the history found in the Hebrew scriptures, building on Martin Noth's base narrative "G," which was probably a congeries of oral traditions (not even a conscious collection). As noted above, "J" came from the German *Jahweh*, Anglicized as Yahweh, and associated with writing produced in Judea; "E" identified Elohist or Ephraimite writing, identified by the use of "Elohim," one of the generic words for God; "P" abbreviated the word "priestly" for the priests of the exile.

Like a writer who reads and edits his or her own work, successive storytellers added afterthoughts or remnants of other traditions to the narrative, particularly in the legal sections. They traced the way a basic family model reproduced itself to build the extended families, clans and tribes of the people of Israel, and also of the human race.

In contrast to most science, history is cultural, concerned with social relationships between people. These are established through conversations in which people agree (or disagree) about their adult obligations to each other. After agreeing on the terms of a relationship, both parties in this system are obligated to be faithful to their commitments to each other. The Hebrew word *hesed*[3] expresses that faithfulness and means more than a vague "loving-kindness." It represents the fulfillment of obligations and is important to the working of good relationships. Since there is no exact English equivalent for it, I will use it in italics to represent the social equivalent to biological synergy. In biology we speak of "genes" which serve in the reproduction of living bodies; in social and religious systems we may speak of an equivalent set of "memes," which function to establish the working parts of personal/social entities.

2. Diamond, *Guns Germs, and Steel*.

3. Some authors transliterate the word as *chesed*, but I prefer to represent the first letter as an English "h." Scholars distinguish the letter *heth* from the softer Hebrew *he* (pronounced "hay") by placing a dot under it. Hebrew *heth* should be pronounced like the "ch" after the vowel in the Scottish "lo*ch*" but not as in "*ch*air."

In the Hebrew scriptures, relationships ideally took shape as covenants were formalized between individuals in marriages, food bartering and land transfers, and also between tribes to form a united Israel, all under YHWH/God, who sat as supreme Judge and Enforcer of the terms of these agreements. While the scriptures focus on the broader covenantal relationships of tribal and national history, they are aware of the special bonding between parents and children, husbands and wives and between other people living in communities together.

An overriding covenant between Israelites and God has dominated the biblical record. If God's people are faithful in offering their worship only to YHWH/God and are not seduced to serve other gods, they may confidently expect their fields, flocks, and families to be fertile and to enable them to fulfill the essential law of survival. Failure to fulfill commitments to other people or to God may be identified as "sin," but in the Bible sin is never so specifically defined. Often, however, sin is the subject of talk between people, and occasionally between God and a person.

Jacob's Survival

Within covenantal relationships, men and women should have been free to enjoy innocent sexual relations and the resulting offspring just as they enjoyed the fruit of the trees in the primitive paradise. How and when did the natural feelings of ancient people about family matters become transmogrified into feelings of sinful guilt? What were the feelings and thoughts of the men and women in the stories that are before us? Why do the storytellers introduce ideas of right and wrong, good and evil, sin and salvation into their pictures of ancient Israel? The answers are found in biblical clues that can be interpreted in modern sociological and psychological terms, or in analysis of the term covenant (Hebrew *berith*), which has taken on a religious connotation. What appears at first to be an established status quo in a society, can be seen as the momentary position of dynamic forces reaching for equilibrium through covenanting.

Perhaps the earliest feelings of which men and women were aware—after fear and anger—were longings, a man for a particular mate, or a woman for a particular man, or for the health of the newborn son or daughter.

Feelings were ultimately verbalized abstractly as "love," "grief," "sadness," "joy." At the same time families were forged through the expressive language of covenantal relationships: "*I want you* (or "*her*" addressed to her father in ancient Israel) as wife" and answered by affirmative gesture or word. Jacob's relationship with the family of his uncle Laban, retold in Genesis 29–31, is typical of the way covenantal relationships worked. When Jacob presented himself to Laban after meeting Rachel at the well, he asked for the "gift" of Laban's daughter as his bride. The wily Laban agreed, but bargained for seven years service in his household, since Jacob could not offer anything as bride price. Seeing no alternative to what was already a customary social arrangement for young males, Jacob accepted the bargain and a wedding took place.

Laban, however, deceived Jacob by presenting him with the veiled Leah instead of Rachel, and insisted on seven additional years of service for Jacob's first choice. Both daughters accepted the bargains that were made between the men. In these transactions we can see the operation of informal covenanting, but the historian does not use the word covenant until Jacob left Laban's establishment. We can also see how anger could seethe in the heart of a weaker, cheated, bargaining partner.

Jacob's story continues with another seven years of bargaining for the accumulation of wealth as a share of the goats belonging to the establishment. At the end of twenty years Jacob was ready to declare his independence from Laban's household and return to Canaan, but in the final confrontation between the two clans Laban continued to claim ownership of all the herds and his daughters and grandchildren. Evidently believing that his eleven-son clan was stronger than Laban's, Jacob stood firm on the rights to which they had both agreed in their twenty years of bargaining. And finally, Laban, to avoid harming his children and grandchildren, agreed to a formalized covenant with the setting up of a cairn to mark the permanent separation between the two clans.

This story of the survival of Jacob and the creation of his family is a good illustration of the way human level covenants were established with words and enforced with the possibility of violence between stronger and weaker parties. Sworn in the names of the gods of their fathers, the covenant of separation between Jacob and Laban left final enforcement to an ambiguously named God/Power, who would not be called upon to act as long as Laban and Jacob went different ways. It was possible to reach an agreement because the two clans were nearly equal in strength. Sexual relationships were only a small part of the total covenantal picture, which covered all forms of wealth—animal, human, and territorial. The writers of Genesis sketch the material arrangements, but also mention God's overriding management of critical aspects of the story. Jacob's survival depended on his assertive domestic activities, in which the historians saw God's guidance and blessing. But the bonding that lasted twenty years could not go further into exchanges of goods and services between the two clans. We do not hear of a Jacob clan and a Laban clan sharing in a larger community. Jacob had to start over back in Canaan, while Laban and his sons could continue to increase their wealth in Syria. They disappear from the biblical tradition.

Relationships in Society

How do covenants work? In any society relationships between people can be visualized as covenantal, and the theoretical structure can be diagrammed as two human persons under a superior human power or a personal God.

Every relationship may be understood as a two-way street on which intelligent beings meet and exchange their wares, with God looking on from time to time. Recent reports by researchers at the Yerkes National Primate Center in Atlanta have demonstrated "How Animals do Business."[4] Frans B. M. deWaal illustrates the key features of a reciprocity mechanism between laboratory capuchin monkeys, which appears to be similar to human exchanges.

4. DeWaal, "How Animals Do Business," 72–79.

```
              GOD
            FIGURE
              blesses
         //           \\
        //             \\
       //               \\
      //                 \\
     //                   \\
        ------ asks ------→
  WEAK  <= /\/\/\/\/\ GIFT /\/\/\/\  STRONG
        ------ pays ------→
```

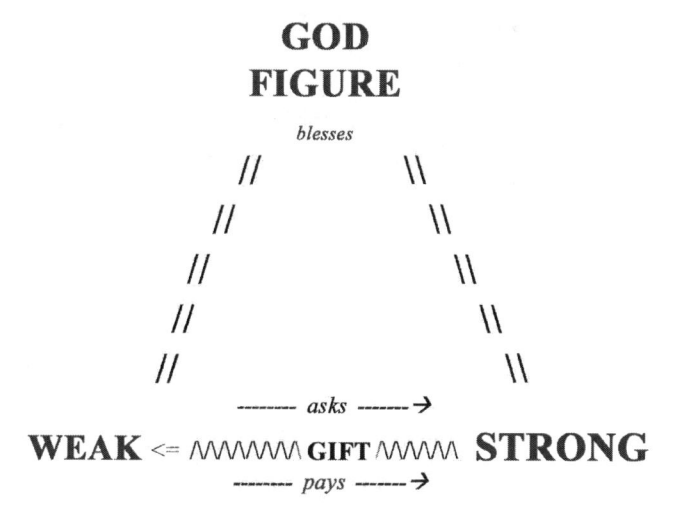

In any exchange each *"gives"* to the other and *"receives"* from the other something of value, whether it is the product of labor or the commitment of devotion and moral support. Above the human interaction is the ultimate Source of the good things being exchanged, and also the Arbiter of the fulfillment of pledges made by parties to an agreement.

In the diagram each party is designated in different size type to indicate relative strength or power in the relationship. Historically, relative inequality became institutionalized as slavery or marriage. However, the use of capital letters indicates that each person is theoretically self-directing or autonomous, and has a relative capability to accept or reject the conditions of any relationship.

Society is the network of such basic units or nodes of giving and receiving among persons who come within the orbit of others. The covenantal relationships of the Bible could be diagrammed with God at the center of radiating concentric circles or above fields of clustering people. But the Hebrew Scriptures prefer to tell family stories.

Jacob and Esau

The stories of Jacob and Esau illustrate power relationships within families and also an early diversification of economic roles in society. When Rebekah's birthing process began, the Lord (YHWH) said to her:

> Two nations are in your womb
> and two peoples born of you shall be divided;
> the one shall be stronger than the other,
> the elder shall serve the younger.

At the birth "the first came out red, all his body like a hairy mantle, so they named him Esau. Afterward his brother came out, with his hand gripping Esau's heel, so he was named Jacob" (Gen 25:23–26, NRSV: "He takes by the heel" or "He supplants").

As the two boys developed Esau was a hunter like his father and Jacob preferred to stay close to his mother and turned to her for his training. One day Esau came in, typical teen-aged hungry from the hunt, and found Jacob tending the fire under a pot of lentil stew. The conversation can be written as a bit of drama:

> Esau: Let me eat some of that red stuff, for I am famished!
> Jacob: First sell me your birthright.
> Esau: I am about to die; of what use is a birthright to me?
> Jacob: Swear to me first.

Or it can be diagrammed with a wavy line representing dialogue between Jacob as the stronger in larger type and Esau as the weaker in smaller type.

ESAU /\ JACOB

The actual transaction can be represented with straight lines with arrow heads as Jacob "gives" Esau the bread and lentil stew and Esau *promises* the birthright (inheritance) to Jacob:

JACOB -------------------- bread & lentil stew ------------------> ESAU
ESAU /\/\/\/\/\/\/\/\/\/\/\/\ *birthright (inheritance)* /\/\/\/\/\/\/\/\/\/\> JACOB

The brothers are represented as nearly equal in the final line where the birthright is promised, but in the delivery of the birthright, Rebekah intruded to help Jacob deceive his father.

Her scheme: While Esau hunts for game to prepare a savory meal for the formal investing of the birthright to Esau, Rebekah directs Jacob to bring a couple of domesticated kids from the household for her to prepare with seasoning like wild game.

Also she dresses Jacob in Esau's clothes and puts goatskins on the backs of his hands, so that when he presents the meal to his father, he will be disguised as Esau.

The scheme works, and the actual transaction may be diagrammed:

JACOB (as ESAU)--------- gives savory stew --------------------> ISAAC
ISAAC ---------------------- gives birthright --------------------> JACOB

Genesis 27 reports the preparatory conversations and the actual transaction.

The Role of God-inspired People

It is evident from the traditions, that the common people in early communities turned to certain individuals who seemed to *know*, not just know about, the unseen powers that ruled the world, including its living forms. Perhaps the diagram should include such a mediator within a circle representing God or as a separate figure under an invisible God, but still indicated in the largest type allowed to humans.

In the later altercation between Jacob and Laban both men reported that they had received words directly from God in dreams, telling of God's interest in keeping their families alive.[5] Individuals who received such messages came to be recognized and identified with titles such as seer, prophet, priest, Levite or witch. Abraham, Isaac and

---

5. Alan Jenks, *The Elohist and North Israelite Traditions*, has noted that the reception of prophetic insight through dreams is a particular characteristic of Ephraimite (E) traditions found in Genesis, Exodus and Numbers.

Jacob received word directly from God much of the time, and should be considered as predecessors of priests and prophets. Any such person may be thought of as having inner eyes and ears that open to sights and sounds not perceived by most people.

Other members of a tribal community looked to them for guidance at those special times when the survival of the community or of an individual was at risk, or at the celebrations of critical times of the yearly calendar. Anita Diamant portrayed midwives in her story of Jacob's daughter Dinah as just such significant mediators between the unseen powers and the day-to-day life of women. Called to assist in the critical process of childbirth, the midwife is pictured in her book, *The Red Tent*, as offering guidance and providing herbal aids as needed.[6] Although the story is fiction, it suggests the important role these specialists in relationship with unseen powers played in the life of every ancient community. Practitioners of medicine, psychology, sociology, anthropology, politics and religion are modern heirs to this tradition.

The mediator/manager from an unseen Power may have been a recognized prophet or priest or simply a stranger who delivered a message, and who would be described in retrospect as a messenger or "angel." Entertaining three travelers at the oaks of Mamre, Abraham was asked by one of them "Where is your wife Sarah?" And he said "There, in the tent." The Guest went on to declare, "I will surely return to you in due season, and your wife Sarah shall have a son" (Gen 18:9–10).

The mother of Samson was absolutely certain that the person who promised her a son was "the angel of YHWH" or "a man of God, whose appearance was like an angel of God" (Judg 13:8), but her husband Manoah was not at all convinced that the messenger was bringing a word from YHWH.

Later, for Hannah, the word from YHWH came through the priest Eli. And next it was the boy Samuel who brought words from YHWH. Susan Ackermann has devoted a chapter to barren women in the Bible, commenting that in the second act of the stories of such women who bore a son, "Yahweh exercises God's rightful claim upon the life of that child."[7] Human promises to God must be fulfilled.

While the ordinary role of these mediators was to assist members of the community in relating properly to the layered systems of life created by God, and thereby to God, at times they found it necessary to correct their neighbors. Thus, occasionally they suggested that in some way an individual somewhere in the community had offended God and that the famine, foreign invader, or barrenness was the result of a human fault or "sin." Such an announcement no doubt increased whatever anxiety the individual, family or clan felt about their lives. Skimpy crops must have occurred often enough to prompt the careful observance of the community's rituals of assembly and sacrifice.

Although biblical stories seldom spell out the feelings and fears of their characters, especially in sexual matters, we can imagine the nagging anxiety as women wondered if an infant's death or their childlessness was the result of some fault they

---

6. Anita Diamant, *The Red Tent*, 279–424.
7. Ackermann, *Warrior, Dancer, Seductress, Queen*, 192.

had committed. When Rachel demanded a child from Jacob, he angrily referred her to God: "Am I in the place of God, who has withheld from you the fruit of the womb?" (Gen 30:2). Thus the anxiety the community felt when enemies approached or crops failed was felt by a childless woman. Her people's survival depended on women's fertility, and if God withheld the blessing of children, she must be under some curse. She would want to know what sin had brought God's condemnation. The word "sin," however, is seldom applied, and never used for barren Sarah, Rachel, or Hannah.

Men also could feel anxiety. After God told Jacob in a dream to return to the land of his father, Jacob sent and called Rachel and Leah into the field where his flock was, and said to them, "I see that your father does not regard me as favorably as he did before. But the God of my father has been with me. You know that I have served your father with all of my strength, yet your father has cheated me and changed my wages ten times, but God did not permit him to harm me" (Gen 31:5–7).

With his anxiety confirmed by the insight gained in his dream, Jacob began his separation from Laban by calling his family together "in the field where his flock was," that is, out of the doors of his wives' home. There he could tell them what he could see clearly: the oppressive working of his father-in-law's patriarchal management of their lives. Later, priests, seers, and prophets similarly supplied guidance for anxious people, and gradually came to spell out the laws of sexual purity and national justice, which took their final shape after the exile under the leadership of high priests of the restored temple in Jerusalem.

The Biblical Covenant

The materialistic secular thinkers of the eighteenth, nineteenth, and twentieth centuries were content to study the workings of social, economic, physical, biological, and chemical (both organic and inorganic) interactions, effectively ignoring the source of the energies being studied. Nuclear physics and electron microscopes opened the sub-atomic world to view, with its previously unknown energy. Biologists could investigate what happened inside the individual cells that compose the working parts of animate living entities.

Bruce H. Lipton used wavy lines with accompanying directional arrows to indicate bidirectional communication of energy that could be used constructively or destructively like the waves on the surface of a lake. His medical example was the way in which doctors use sound waves to break kidney stones into small bits that can be passed easily out of the body.[8] What he and others found is a whole new microscopic set of relationships that act in giving and receiving energies similar to what I am calling "covenantal" transactions or exchanges.

Can the biblical traditions tell us anything (or everything) we need to understand about the relationship with a divine Creator to supplement or undergird what we are learning about the processes of the natural and cultural regimes? The Shorter

---

8. Lipton's theme is the recent development of a "new biology" which studies intra-cellular forces and activities. Lipton, *The Biology of Belief*, 114–21.

Catechism tells Calvinist believers, "The Scriptures principally teach what man is to believe concerning God, and what duty God requires of man." The Hebrew Scriptures give accounts of the failure of early humans to satisfy God's expectation. Although made "in the likeness of God" and capable of begetting a succession of long lived sons and daughters, humankind's "wickedness . . . was great, and every inclination of the thoughts of their hearts was only evil continually." (Gen 6:5) So, in spite of the human race's domestication of livestock and developing of crafts, YHWH ("the Lord God") was sufficiently grieved to declare: "I will blot out from the earth the human beings I have created—people together with animals and creeping things and birds of the air, for I am sorry that I have made them" (Gen 6:7).

But one man, Noah, "found favor" in YHWH's sight, and was directed to build an "Ark," stock it with two of every creature, and set out with his family on the perilous journey above the flood. When the waters subsided, God said to Noah and his sons,

> I am establishing my covenant with you and your descendants after you, and with every living creature that is with you, the birds, the domestic animals and every animal of the earth, as many as came out of the ark. I establish my covenant with you, that never again shall all flesh be cut off by the waters of a flood . . . This is the sign of the covenant that I make between me and you and every living creature that is with you, for all future generations. I have set my bow in the clouds, I will see it and remember the everlasting covenant between God and every living creature of all flesh (Gen 9:9–16).

In that ancient tradition humans *may* have discovered and engaged in covenantal relationships, but these evidently became corrupt and went awry. After destroying most of Noah's generation, YHWH established a permanent covenant with Noah, his family and the creatures they had saved in the Ark. The scriptures tell of further bad human behavior and the consequent deaths of many individuals and groups, but also report new beginnings with selected individuals and their descendants upon whom would fall the duty of living in ways pleasing to God. This story is also told by native Americans and other cultures in a variety of forms, testifying to the universal human sense of responsibility to please a Supreme Being as well as to relate adequately to persons and forces within sight and reach.

The stories of Israel's patriarchs exhibit the covenantal structure as their historians told the national story. Early family-sized covenants prepared the way for, and fitted into, the broader structure of a covenant initiated by God with the family of Abram, whom the Deity brought from Mesopotamia and rescued from slavery in Egypt. In the biblical narrative the authoritative Covenant was finally bestowed on Israel at a mountain in the Sinai desert to fulfill the promise God made to Abram in Mesopotamia.

Although individuals in each generation were selected to share in God's covenant with humankind, the historians and modern readers can all see a duty to behave in a way that pleases God. As we read the biblical text, we may recognize a process of human covenanting, which has led to social and ethical laws that can describe and guide, the ritualized behavior of people in corporations, states, and churches. This pattern of covenantal relationships continues to provide for the beneficial functioning of society.

PART 1: Biological, Cultural, and Religious Systems of Life

When Abram arrived in the region between the Jordan River and the Mediterranean Sea, he and his son Isaac found that in order to survive they had to work out covenantal arrangements with the natives, but they also needed to maintain good relationships within the family. The relationship between Isaac's sons, Jacob and Esau failed, and Jacob might not have survived Esau's wrath. When Jacob traveled to his uncle's home in Haran, he had to establish good relationships with the members of Laban's family, and for twenty years he succeeded in living in an uneasy peace with Laban and his sons. He evidently learned how to survive through covenantal relationship, and could meet his brother Esau peacefully at the Jabbok without claiming the southeastern land that Esau chose. Jacob's sons would go on to settle in Canaan, and thus Jacob would survive as a tribal entity with the name "Israel" granted to him by the wrestler at the Jabbok: "You shall no longer be called Jacob, but Israel, for you have striven with God and with humans, and have prevailed." (Gen 32:28) Jacob would no longer be a simple man with twelve sons, but Israel. whose sons would be the ancestors or eponymous heads of twelve tribes. Israelites told the stories and believed them as history.

Human Talk Often Precedes Action

The triangle of relationships omits something of great importance to an understanding of human covenants. At the human level actions of giving and receiving are often preceded by arguments/conversations between the persons who do the acting. Also, in many biblical stories we find words from God. How should we represent this verbalizing? My first thought was simply to treat the language component as substantive information to be given and received, bought and sold like the bride for whom Jacob bargained. Then I remembered the way Richard Feynman devised to show reactions between subatomic particles in cyclotrons. Because he conceived of particles as waves in these almost instantaneous reactions, Feynman represented them as oscillating lines. Likewise, human speech is modulated in audible waves of sound that carry them between people, just as the energy of a tsunami is carried thousands of miles across oceans, which continue their less energetic tides and waves relatively unaffected.

The analogy is not perfect, but it should serve to distinguish what works in a cultural medium from what works in a material world. It is cultural and social to ask for bread, while eating the bread is biological and can be a social event. Securing the bread may be agricultural, economic, political, or religious depending on which system in the immediate context is being considered.

Neither scheme conveys the ongoing movement in time of participants in covenants, though every material transaction takes place in time, and no conversation, however brief, is without its time component. We, and all existence, live at the cusp of creation, taking steps into an unseen dimension or being blocked in the fulfillment of plans.

In what follows we will be retelling some biblical stories that feature inherently human and personal transactions. However, the personal aspects are always constrained as more or less impersonal aspects—structures—appear to operate within the vital and personal activities portrayed.

From time to time we will be noting powers that emerge from natural and cultural situations to be exercised by the characters of the stories. Is one dominating individual or group forcing another into submission? Situations present choices that *can, may* or perhaps *should* be made in the complexity of life. Choices appear in *now* moments in which humans can look both forward and backward in time. Forward for decision-making and backward to recall experiences that provide the information on which decisions may or must depend. Human minds are capable of what might be called a calculus of change from present situations to the realization of hopes, fears, or loves. Human vision is not limited to the immediate and tangible, but can range throughout what we can now believe to be a four-dimensional cosmos. In the cosmos the cusp of time is in an infinite series of *now* moments.

In Plato's Republic, his quintessential philosopher, Socrates, chose the concept of the Greek "State" as the social context for the development of society. In contrast, the biblical pattern features family, tribe and "people". Socrates (Plato) conceives the origin of the State "out of the needs of mankind . . . And they exchange with one another, and one gives and another receives, under the idea that the exchange will be for their good."[9] In Plato's state, reproduction was taken for granted; in Israel's stories it preceded the acquisition of shelter and the arts of civilization. The writers of both texts considered praise to the gods an essential recompense in divine-human transactions. Praise or worship is the highest form of giving thanks.

Many moderns see that faithfulness to a covenantal commitment is more important in the ongoing life of society than the purity of sexual relationships. Faithlessness or failure to fulfill an obligation breaks one thread in the fabric of family and society. It can be called "sin," and may lead to a more extensive tearing of the fabric.

Evolving into Culture

In the 1920s children in residential neighborhoods were occasionally delighted to hear the sound of an "organ grinder," an exotic man with a small monkey on a long leash and who pushed a little cart and turned the crank that produced a happy tune. When children came out to the street, the monkey would jump from its perch on the cart or on the man's shoulder and with outstretched hand would beg hopefully. Parents would dig into pocket books or pockets and find pennies to give to the monkey, which quickly returned to the man and handed the penny to him, in return for a bit of food. The process was repeated as long as neighborhood children were supplied with pennies and the music continued. Of course when money ran out the little cart moved into the next block to find more children, and it would be months or years before the children would see it again.

The monkey was not quite a pet of the organ grinder, nor was it a wild animal fresh from a jungle. Parents who would have been quite angry at the outcome of the Scopes trial in Tennessee had no trouble letting their children relate in this way with one of their closest semi-civilized biological kin. The irony of the scene is delicious

---

9. Plato, *Republic*, 2.369.

Part 1: Biological, Cultural, and Religious Systems of Life

three quarters of a century later: "master" and "slave," owner and owned, working together wordlessly to support the family to which they both belonged.

Not quite wordlessly! The exotic man did use a few words which the monkey and the children could understand, just as trained family pets understand the commands their owners issue: "Sit!" "Stay!" and "Lie down." The monkey, however, could not respond with appropriate human language, but could only obey commands that called for physical behavior. A fine line remains to separate the human from the animal.

Most infants quickly cross that line when they not only understand what mothers say to them, but also begin to make sounds like words they have heard. "Baby talk" is a transitional language between "infancy"—the Latin word means "not talking"—and human speech. Adults who watch their young children are amazed at how quickly the process of learning the family language is accomplished. In the car going home after a Christmas party a remark that our daughter has said "tars" instead of "stars" is all it took to establish the correct English pronunciation forever.

While the human learning of words seems almost instantaneous, learning to use arms and hands takes time for both monkey and human baby, as muscles and nerves develop apparently effortless coordination that evolved over many millennia. No diagram is needed to represent this activity. A mental picture of a young child giving a penny to the organ grinder's monkey will have to suffice. We will be more interested in the social and moral development of the people of Israel, not only as individual descendants of Abraham, but as tribes which must relate to their chieftains and to their neighbors. We will also be interested in the way "churches" can offer "salvation" to people.

Personal and cultural patterns, "memes," are often ignored or treated sketchily in the telling of national stories, but in the story of Jacob's survival to become the father of all Israelites, Genesis calls special attention to the love he had for Rachel and the more business-like relationships he had with Leah and the two slave girls who were the mothers of his sons. Even if fictive, the personal-social component is never completely absent from any human relationship whether it is the master requiring work from the slave, the husband demanding sexual relationship from his wife, or the king ordering his soldiers to attack an enemy. The physical and the social are two interwoven aspects of every human relationship.

But beware! In every human relationship "sin" is possible. The biological or physical can be corrupted by humans. In what began as bargaining transactions such as Laban made with Jacob, either party—the stronger or the weaker—could see the possibility of gaining control over the other. What begins as a willingness to serve for pay can be subtly transformed into an intention to own the ranch or the household. We will consider whether such a transformation should be called "sin."

6

Learning to Drive, and . . .

OLD TESTAMENT STORIES HAVE us assuming that the bodies of young males know all they need to know about the experience of sex. There is no need for learning. In a patriarchal setting the young man has only to "know" the particular mate chosen for him. Whatever learning is required is foreshortened into the moment of meeting in the bridal tent during the public celebration of the marriage. The tent flap parts and closes, robes are dropped to the floor, and the intimacies begin. Onan was the only Israelite who refused the experience of sexual "knowledge" when he was assigned to "raise up seed" for his deceased brother.[1] Otherwise young males probably approached marriage as we approach a new computer, eager to know how it works.

It is not insignificant that the Hebrew Scriptures omit mention of the bride's "knowing" her new husband. The expression "he knew his wife" describes sexual intercourse as a male experiences it and seems to assume an active male and a passive female. The bride may come to "know" her husband, but the Hebrew Scriptures do not talk about it. The other expressions, "he *slept* with her," and an Egyptian woman's invitation to Joseph, "Lie with me" suggest but say nothing specific about sexual activity. It is possible that this reticence of scripture represents a suppression of the earthier expression "he went in to her," which could be understood as "he went into her tent" but means sexual intercourse. If so, it may be an early literary device to clothe—and conceal—the sex act in poetic language, in effect maintaining the hiddenness of sexual activity.

Nevertheless for the sons of patriarchs, kings, and every head of a substantial household, it was important that the family lineage be sustained. How would a lineage begin?

Self-Discovery

It is worth noting that the Old Testament has almost no need for self-discovery. The first man and woman learned that they were naked only when YHWH came to visit. Neither men nor women in Israel were given manuals about their body's parts and

---

1. Genesis 38:8–10; see more fully in chapter 9.

PART 1: Biological, Cultural, and Religious Systems of Life

functions. Teenagers in ancient and modern societies have always had to learn the mechanics of sex as they approached adulthood. Learning how to manage the sex "drive" is similar in a few important ways to learning to drive a car, that western rite of passage, which is sometimes accompanied by the acquisition of an automobile. My education took place in the twentieth century and some details may seem quaint, but the realities of sexuality, conflict, and sin were essential parts of it.

The sex drive comes into full conscious power in the bodies of young men and women with a suddenness like the arrival of an automobile from the factory or the used car dealership, ready to roll. Each vehicle has a finely tuned set of essential parts. The sex "motor" is in male and female glands and their surrounding tissues and nerves. It can be turned on and off as occasion demands. A couple can switch on the act of sexual intercourse with almost no instruction at all, each learning from the other. But many young people enjoy a little private experimenting to learn how the parts work.

The biological aspect is extremely user friendly. Unlike most other animals, for people sex is always available. It is not only available but it intrudes on the consciousness of young teens both female and male without much warning. Human societies have, therefore, found it necessary to provide some restrictive instructions in the operation of the marvelous reproductive equipment in the form of rules, laws and habits to be learned, which are the software comparable to driver training.

When I was first permitted to switch on the motor of the family car in the early 1930s, I worried about where I was steering the car. Sitting left of the centerline of the vehicle I sighted across the hood to avoid a ditch on the right of the road, but that tended to take the car across the center of the road. Centerlines were not marked in those days, at least on the road we chose. Fortunately we were practically alone on the road. My father did not say very much, but I quickly realized that I needed to steer between the boundaries of an imaginary centerline and the ditch on the right side of the road. Smoothing gear changes with the clutch was another problem, as those who have driven a stick shift will testify. The sense of knowing and not having to know where your body is and what it is doing is called kinesthesiology. It is a sixth sense that, like the other five, develops through experience and observation. One can be aware of the presence of one's body especially in contemplating or reflecting on its actual movements, as when the new driver mentally rehearses the steps needed to start the car. Later, awareness of the process of driving sinks into habit.

What boy has not imagined sitting in the driver's seat, racing effortlessly faster than he had ever been able to move on bicycle, skates or homemade soapbox car? Children's play may have rehearsed for the performance, but the event brought problems that I did not anticipate. One day in making a turn into a narrow street I found myself steering straight toward a street sign. Before I could get my feet on clutch and brake, the car had knocked the street sign down, and I was ashamed. Years later when I was the father guiding a son into the ritual of driving the family car, we began by experimenting with the brakes on a quiet sloped street as we coasted before turning on the motor.

Learning to Drive, and . . .

The biologist Bruce Lipton tells how he discovered his subconscious mind in a chiropractor's office when he was asked to resist downward pressure on his outstretched hand while saying "My name is Mary." He had been able to resist when he said "My name is Bruce," but now a second mind, sensing the falseness of the "Mary" statement, weakened his muscles, and his conscious mind lost control. Lipton clarifies much of what I had begun to think before reading his book.[2] In chapter 19 we will discuss our two minds again, but here we will consider another indication of the hidden mind.

For a boy the end of childhood may be marked with a strange dream, not about cars, but about a very childish thing. He wets his nightclothes. Embarrassed and unable to share the experience with anyone, he realizes that in his dream he had been astride a pulsating fire hose near a burning building. He made the connection with sexual experience later. After hearing a few lectures on controlling sexuality and recalling that dream, he worries about losing control over this new power. Before turning on the full power of the sex motor, some adolescents welcome guidance as to how to keep the vehicle from running away with them, while others experiment.

Imagine a group of young people on a snow-covered hillside in the days before cars were common among teens. Eight or ten friends in the church's youth fellowship have found a sled that is just big enough to hold two for the ride down the hill. With a little push the sled gains speed until it reaches the level ground at the bottom of the hill, where it glides to a stop. The reader, who may recall such an experience, will recognize that the pleasure in the dynamics of movement was matched with a few moments of physical contact, body to body, boy embracing girl for the fifteen second ride—a delicious feeling not otherwise socially available to teens in those days. Matching of couples by chance or choice permitted a range of feelings that were shared briefly but safely between the sexes. Reflecting on those moments of pleasure, one sees the operation of the covenantal paradigm on several levels: dragging the sled up the hill asked the natural world to store the energy that would be released on the downhill slope; the slope ended safely at a turn around where no cars would come. Agreeing on which girl would ride with which boy was not a random choice, since a stated preference vaguely anticipated a future permanent partnership.

Parents and community elders have recognized that young people need brakes that will at least slow the headlong rush into sexual relations. The patriarchal families of Israel kept the brakes on maturing girls and boys in two distinct ways. Families kept daughters at home until fathers or elder brothers could steer them to an eligible husband. A son was denied marriage until his father was ready to set him up with enough land or cattle to support a wife and the expected children. Esau was allowed to acquire wives, but Jacob was not. Their father apparently intended to deny Jacob an inheritance, and leave him to live as a junior partner, with his brother in charge of the family estate.

---

2. Lipton, *Biology and Belief*, 159–60. Lipton clarifies much of what I had begun to think before reading his book.

Instead of isolating young men and women from each other as the Israelites did, *our* culture has encouraged a mutual acquaintanceship between numbers of boys and girls, with the implicit promise that each young person will be free to find a suitable mate. The common sense of the community recommends that both boys and girls get an education—at minimum a high school diploma—to prepare for jobs that should pay enough to support a young couple with food, shelter, clothing, and entertainment. Western nations generally have a minimum legal age for marriage, which is more or less at the completion of basic education. But we seldom enforce the rule or restrict the associations of our teens.

As a result talented and capable young couples experiment with unprotected sex and sometimes discover that they and their families have to deal with an unintended pregnancy or a sexually transmitted disease. At times alcohol dulls the usual inhibitions and sex becomes a group affair with the increased possibility of sharing disease. When these things happen, career plans are set aside or postponed, all for the few moments of exhilaration gained from the fast ride.

Many young couples find the support of a child a burden that requires financial help from parents or government programs. Some European nations provide childcare so that both parents can work, thus helping to carry the load when the vehicle is driven into a lifetime career. Brakes and steering mechanisms have not proved enough. Instead of the family car the metaphor of a train of linked cars more appropriately describes traditional societies where the rails of carefully laid track guided the forward movement from one generation to the next.

Owning the Car

We need go no further with the analogy of learning to drive, except to note that it is not an accident that in the twentieth century the automobile became the vehicle of choice for courtship between the sexes. How else could young persons escape the enclosing walls of homes and the watchful eyes and ears of parents and guardians? In twentieth-century United States the first breakthrough for many was the use of the family car, more recently many families can afford to give their teen a car to expedite going to and from high school and the part time job, plus the privilege of socializing.

"Owning" a car, even if it was the temporary use of the family's, made possible the phenomenon of dating. In the still patriarchal family settings of early twentieth century it was usually the fathers who owned this new vehicle for moving about in cities or from farm to neighboring farm. Young males, first drivers of cars, as their fathers had been drivers of buggies, could plan for those brief hours alone with a selected member of the opposite sex. Of course, a young woman who owned a car could initiate a date with a carless male for a swim and a picnic at a secluded creek, and as the century progressed it became common for both sexes to initiate these plans.

Note the feeling of ownership that comes to boy *and* girl sitting side by side in the movie theatre or driving *his* or her car.

There was a moment when little boys and girls who never dreamed of anything but tussling with the neighborhood kids, suddenly noticed a newcomer and wondered how to get his or her attention. The magnetic polarity between the sexes asserted itself, replacing the asexual competition of childhood. A powerful force began to draw the two together, while at the same time driving former playmates apart. I overheard one girl say to her girlfriend, "He's mine, leave us alone." When dating became "steady," friends began to speak of "his girl" or "her boyfriend." More recently one simply moves into the other's apartment.

The "family car" can be understood as metaphor for the homes from which the two young people have come and for the family to which they both aspire. It is the entity larger than either of them toward which both are driving. Their brief association for a date can be seen as an experimental fitting together of the jigsaw pieces that could result in a family.

"Falling in Love"

The enjoyment of contact between bodies may be characterized as a law of nature, essentially descriptive. For human beings a parallel social "law" is falling in love. However, falling in love is only a moment in the warm sunlight of human relationships, a foreshortened minute in the progress from an infant's earliest awareness of parents to commitment to spouse, children, community, and God. Culture transcends nature with constraints consisting of advice, rules, or laws designed to regulate the establishing of families.

Between the earliest awareness of parents and the decision to commit to a shared life with another, youths of both sexes begin with a search for friends. Mentally emerging from the shelter of home, youths survey the people around them looking for a reciprocal response from another likeminded person. Among neighbors, schoolmates or siblings the child has spent hours and days in play; activity which often simulated the activities of parents as the child observed them. "Playing house" is a child's activity, with miniature cups and saucers, kitchen equipment and dolls made to look like adults. The goal is to gain familiarity with household furnishings.

Adolescent friends are chosen not so much for the physical contact as for the sharing of thoughts and ideas. There is not necessarily anything sexual in these thoughts. More often than not career preparations are the context and recreation the content of the relationships that are formed during the teen years. At Atlanta's Boys' High School we studied our Latin, Physics, and Math or memorized poems with our male classmates, even challenged each other in experimental writing of articles for school papers. The important thing was that we did not do these things alone, even if monitors punished us for talking during study hall. The girls in our church youth groups did their studying at Girls' High. Today's boys and girls study together and develop "steadies."

It is surprising that the word "love" does not appear in the early chapters of Genesis. The writers of early history neglected to mention love between the sexes until

"Jacob loved Rachel." After that it was bargaining: Jacob said to Laban, "I will serve you seven years for your younger daughter." In the patriarchal world love was usually ignored or assumed to be an insignificant byproduct of mating and marriage contracts.

Instead of romance Biblical stories focus on the possessions of men. Adam awoke from a sleep of childhood to discover a willing partner in his exploration of the garden, "bone of *my* bone and flesh of *my* flesh." The patriarchs journeyed to Canaan to possess land, women, sons, daughters, slaves, and cattle. Wives were needed to bear the heirs who would carry on the family name and own the land. YHWH promised to bless Abram, making of him "a great nation" and making his name great. To accomplish YHWH's program, political, economic, and sexual relationships, good and bad, would enliven the history. David came from following his family's herd into the world of men at war, and met two of King Saul's children with whom he entered into serious relationships. Jonathon became his beloved companion in the Philistine war, and Michal became his wife. Rolston's "ideas," Dawkins' "memes," were the intangible linkages that cemented these friendships.

Translate that moment between Jacob and Rachel at a well in the desert into modern terms: What meeting of eyes and minds led this young man and that young woman to decide that each wanted to know the other better? Was it a sudden awareness of a familiar figure across a street that impelled the two to arrange for further meetings? Or was it a mutual "sizing up" in a work place? Our modern Jacob sees Rachel, *and perceives* a person with whom he wants to share new experiences. Falling in love can lead to an ongoing process of seeing, perceiving, agreeing, *and disagreeing*, always in the present tense from day to day. Two lives intertwine as two minds see their differing paths leading to common goals. When the process of courtship is successful, a family is created.

Success depends on agreements that in modern times involve fitting times of togetherness into times of separation. Sometimes one or the other must arrange to travel to meet and share a weekend or a few hours together. The commitment necessary for a lasting partnership may be tested repeatedly in the fulfilling of these small agreements to meet for a date. Breaking a date can signal the end of a romance. Like a seed attaching itself to soil and beginning its growth into a plant, love between two people develops in successive agreements to share time for activities both enjoy.

Looking back on those adolescent years a husband and wife may revive the feelings of guilt they remember when certain kinds of touching between the sexes were forbidden. They remember the powerful urge to be close in the seat of the old Chevrolet and the trained inhibition not to "go too far." Whether they thought that "touch" was inherently sinful is not to be decided here. It was clearly exploratory with intent to "know" the previously unknown. What were the limits? At least since the beginning of the twentieth century western societies did not consider brief hugging or extended cuddling in roller coasters or cars to be "going too far."

But the first kiss! Not a casual good night kiss at the door after a pleasant evening, one step beyond a hug, that signaled only a willingness to begin or continue a friendship. The meaningful kiss engaged one of the most sensitive surfaces of the body, and posed a quandary for two people. Without words the two separately and simultaneously faced the question "do we want this relationship to continue toward possible permanence?" Jacob's was a cousin's kiss for Rachel, but as he reflected on it, he decided that his relationship with her would be more than that of mere kinfolk.

"Getting Hitched" as a Team

Metaphors have limited usefulness, and new ones are needed to explore some aspects of our relationships. The metaphor of learning to drive a car has run its course, since it is obviously too mechanical for the personal relationships between the sexes. The early twentieth-century metaphor of partnership between horse and rider lost its usefulness when male dominance was seriously challenged. We do admire, however, the skill of jockeys who ride racehorses, and know that their partnerships harness the energies of the animal with the guiding hands of the rider as the pair seeks to win a race. Horses, riders, and trainers in Kentucky work as members of a team, but should not be considered a model for a dominating male and a subservient wife.

A better analogy for marriage is the team of horses hitched to an elegant carriage, or the team of mules pulling harvesting equipment. Today most city people can only vaguely imagine the complicated process of matching two horses, but our elders knew that not every pair of horses could be hitched as a team. When properly trained each mare knew her place in an equal partnership, right or left. With teams, however, the animals do not decide where they are to go or what they are to do. It is Santa Claus who directs the reindeer to deliver Christmas toys and the farmer who guides the plough.

The analogy does not flatter a youth's dreams of moonlight and roses and of sharing a cottage or a flat with the most charming girl he has ever met, but it is important to see where the team is going, and how it will get there. At least some sense of direction is required. The letters to Annie's Mailbox syndicated column regularly reveal conflicts between husbands and wives, parents and children, brothers and sisters, and families with their closest neighbors. A great many of these conflicts are about control: Who decides where the family will live? Who controls the family's money? Who manages the children's social life? What school will the son or daughter attend? Should Juliette have been locked in a tower like Rapunzel?

These are not problems for animals in the wild. Two stallions may contend for a mare or for several of them, but when horses have been broken to harness, they learn that they will be rewarded with their oats when they work as a team. Human beings long ago found that the path to survival leads through becoming families. So the senior members of a family encourage and sometimes require their children to form families similar to their own. It should not be surprising that the Hebrew scriptures trace the families of one patriarch after another, Abraham, Isaac, Jacob, twelve tribal chiefs, Saul, David, Solomon, and on and on. In an earlier time women had held extended families together by establishing dens or "nests" for their children and a welcome for the selected adult male, but as families grew it was men who directed the affairs of "their" tribes.

Part 1: Biological, Cultural, and Religious Systems of Life

Parental examples and directions lead children into mental patterns and social activity that we call customs. Customs are the social expression of personal habits. Habits and customs develop as people repeat behavior that satisfied their needs and their wants. People need supportive relationships with other people both male and female, but there is a widespread preference for companionship with members of the opposite sex. It dominates the lives of most adolescents.

The descriptive memes of social science abbreviate the stories of human behavior and set them into more or less abstract formulas. Community custom goes beyond tradition to become prescriptive law, which requires the formal initiation to the sexual relationship we call marriage. Social conventions have shaped the exercise of physical processes. The archaic expression "getting hitched" for the marriage ceremony recalls the nearly forgotten context of matching working mules or horses in a farming community. How else should an earlier generation of human beings have described the creation of families?

Who Drives the Family Car?

When two young people are ready to create a family, important questions arise in the minds of all those involved. These questions must be answered through agreements arrived at through conversations which involve the surrounding community. This can be represented schematically in the covenantal paradigm by letting the stronger human be identified as head of the family, or chief of the village, the tribe or the nation. Simple conversations morph into laws and a chief sits as a father figure.

Although there is such a thing as a "bicycle built for two," two people cannot be allowed to drive the family car *at the same time.* When Henry Ford produced the model T at a price low enough for many families to afford, it was usually the husband who first learned to drive, though our next-door neighbors' car was always driven by the wife in the 1930s. Ancient Israelites agreed on a *hierarchy* with fathers deciding who managed the family wealth. Jacob thought he had succeeded in subverting Isaac's intention to give the family's birthright to Esau, but had to flee when his brother discovered that he and his mother Rebekah had deceived the aging patriarch. However, in Harran he met and married his cousins, earned considerable wealth, and returned to make a final peace with Esau—a peace achieved with each going separate ways again. Do modern American families solve such disputes over family wealth any better?

When his father-in-law caught up with Jacob after he had gathered his wives, children, and possessions and started the journey back to face his brother, Laban accused him of stealing the image of the family's household god. Jacob was angry and said, "What is my offense? What is my sin, that you have hotly pursued me? Although you have felt about through all *my* goods, what have you found of all *your* household goods?" Only later did Jacob discover that his beloved Rachel had hidden the image, but at the time Laban reluctantly agreed to let Jacob's family continue peaceably on their journey.

This incident in the life of Jacob epitomizes the perennial problem of creating a new family. Parents accept the responsibility for managing the new lives that come into their care, but sometimes attempt to hold on to the children when they are ready to start their own families. Having laid down rules for the behavior of their little ones, they try to prevent activities that break those rules—having sex before marriage, for example. To enforce the family (or community) rules, people appeal to God as the supreme Rule Maker, and declare that anyone who breaks a rule has committed a "sin."

Most of Jacob's sexual and economic relationships had followed the customary practices of the time, and no specific "punishment" from either family or God was actually applied. Twice in Jacob's life, however, he had to leave a situation he (or Rachel, for whom he was responsible) had created. Perhaps living in the consequent exile was punishment enough. The storytellers report the consequences of Jacob and Rachel's actions without telling us that either actions, consequences, or the individuals were "good" or "bad." If Jacob had chosen not to leave his parents, Esau might have killed him. If Rachel had not taken her family's idol, her father would have had no reason to accuse Jacob of theft. Two breaches of trust practically destroyed the sense of solidarity for the extended family.

The only mention of sin was in Jacob's question to Laban, and it asked how *he* had committed a sin within the family. A modern monotheistic reader might think that the idol Rachel took was insignificant and therefore its theft was petty and not a real sin. But in Jacob's day the theft was wrong, as Jacob would have agreed, and Rachel was guilty. An idol was not a family heirloom; it was viewed as a tangible connection with a spiritual deity. Rachel had a guilty attachment to a god she should not have been worshipping. But the God of Jacob, the "fear of Isaac," Abram's "Friend," did not intervene to destroy Jacob and his family. Instead, the pious writer of the story saw the unseen God guiding the family of Jacob toward its destiny of nationhood in spite of the theft. Apparently God treated the deceptions of Jacob and Rachel as social sins rather than as more religious sins against God's Self. Were they also "learning moments" for Jacob in his maturing process?

Traveling Together

By now our metaphor is nearly worn out, but there remain more relationships to explore in family life. In an address to Presbyterians at the 2001 Covenant Conference, Peter J. Gomez urged his listeners "not to yield to the temptation of defining the identity of one of God's creatures simply in terms of sexuality."[3] The caution reminds us that there is much more to family and community life than sex. In our tapestries we weave sex along with the burdens of work and the pleasures of entertainment. Creating a functioning family clearly involves sexual relationship, but it includes many other relationships, happy and unhappy.

Jacob's polygamy is usually passed over as ancient custom that has no meaning for modern society. Western cultures have outlawed the practice, but very rarely

---

3. Gomez, *Covenant Connection*, December 2001 (Volume 4, Number 4) p. 4.

attempt to punish it. Which person should be selected for punishment, a modern polygamous Mormon or any one or all of his submissive wives? The harm done by any judicial punishment for breaking the law against polygamy would clearly exceed the damage to society's sense of right and wrong. American courts face this dilemma in dealing with occasional cases of polygamy, while Christian missionaries created problems of support for the second wives of their converts when they insisted they be given up. Nehemiah (13:23–27) reported that he "cursed and beat and pulled out the hair" of some of the Jews who had married foreign wives. Much harm has been done by those who zealously sought to enforce what they believed were God's laws for families. Family arrangements for food and shelter are often disrupted in cases of divorce. Jacob's two wives and their two handmaids lived in semi-independent quarters, and bargained with each other for the right to sleep with him, probably telling him when he returned from work, "You will have dinner in my tent today." (Gen 30:16, author's paraphrase) The conflict between Rachel and Leah was settled through the bartering process. Meanwhile every member of the family had other responsibilities for the welfare of the developing clan. The ancient Israelite family was a functioning organism with every member contributing in specialized ways to its continuing life. Sex between the chief male and his selected partner was incidental, occasionally managed by women. Genesis tells us that Jacob fathered twelve sons and one daughter, but the book of Genesis is more interested in the ongoing progress toward the family's anticipated greatness than in the more mundane lives of wives and children. Only when Simeon, Levi, Judah, and Joseph became adults and made their own decisions do we read about their sexual relationships and raise questions about sin. The obscure, thoughtless acts of the fathers occasionally involved sex, but were largely questions of how those in control related to the lesser people around them.

In today's world we dare not judge sexual relations to be sinful without looking at the broader relationships between the people involved. Our Sunday comics offer terse comment on many of the problems that arise between individual members of families, as husbands, wives, parents, and children test their strengths against each other. Although the cartoons distinguish genders in these relationships they do so with only the barest allusions to sex, but the social context involved is often visible in the cartoon's background.

Refueling and Traffic Management

As we mature we realize that we cannot operate the family vehicle very long without refueling, and for this we are dependent on arrangements our parents and their peers have provided for us. Our highways are dotted with "service" stations that provide fuel for our cars, food to nourish our bodies, lodging for more extended travel. We discover that civilized social systems offer more than enough to meet our basic needs, tempting us to indulge our more frivolous wants. We seldom remember that all of this refueling of our bodies, minds, and spirits is the gift of God's ongoing creative work channeled through human intermediaries.

When a great many people who own cars are ready to leave their homes at the same time, we need arrangements to manage the traffic. Our political structures tell us who has the right of way at intersections, how fast is safe speed on our roads, and where to stop. We also license cars and drivers, intending to keep the immature and irresponsible from endangering others. And we preach courtesy for all drivers. Signaling our intentions is more courtesy than warning, though laws may require it.

The book of Genesis does not trace a development from animal-like behavior to social systems, but it does recognize that human behavior needs to be guided by moral considerations. God approves sexual relations between a man and a woman. The physical comes first: "The man knew his wife Eve, and she conceived and bore Cain . . . Cain knew his wife, and she conceived and bore Enoch . . . To Enoch was born Irad . . ." *just as YHWH God intended.* (Gen 4:18) But then: "When people began to multiply on the face of the ground, and daughters were born to them, the sons of God saw that they were fair; and they took wives for themselves of all that they chose"— probably without the parents' approval. The reported result was the birth of legendary giants, and *God was not happy with the "wickedness of humankind."* A pattern of evil had replaced the ideal paradigm. What should God do? So YHWH said, "I will blot out from the earth the human beings I have created." (Gen 6:1–7)

"Sins of the Fathers"

Shortly after the great flood, "Ham, the father of Canaan, saw the nakedness of his father, and told his two brothers." Perhaps the text is hiding more than a casual look, but as a consequence of reporting that look of his father's sex organ, Ham's son Canaan was cursed and made the slave of Shem. So, with only a curse uttered by Noah, the custom of slavery between peoples began. No law was required, but as the Israelites told it, the relationship of slave to master was established. Desert Semites could own expensive cars and drive the freeways while the Hamite inhabitants of Canaan must drive old used cars to the back doors of their "betters." As this is written, Palestinians are literally being barred from roads built to join clusters of Israelis from their settlements in the West Bank to the centers of Israeli power. Learning to drive involves more than the controlling of mechanical equipment. The driver must learn about good relationships and his/her moral and religious obligations.

God's involvement in some legendary incidents introduced the moral considerations that led to hierarchies. The specific considerations are obscure to us. Why was it wrong for women to mate with "sons of God," as reported in Genesis 6? Why was it wrong for a son to see his father's penis? (Gen 9:22) Israelites were taught through these stories that both *were* wrong and deserved punishment, even though in a patriarchal world the "daughters of men" could hardly have resisted being raped, and an accidental discovery of a parent's sexual parts does not appear to deserve perpetual enslavement. What these two stories reveal is, nevertheless, that storytellers shaped the development of guidelines for Israel before formal laws were issued from Mount Sinai. As in every family, parents, and other storytellers establish and communicate

Part 1: Biological, Cultural, and Religious Systems of Life

the "rules" for life. A sort of natural "hierarchy" exists without formal appointment, since a mother and a father are given the care of every newborn, and their talk with children structures the social and religious world of privileges and responsibilities for family and community life.

The enslavement of grandson Canaan introduces the idealized social hierarchy that Joshua attempted to impose on the tribes that inhabited Canaan prior to the completion of the conquest by Israel. Figuratively, Israel's SUVs crowded everybody's smaller cars off the road. Traveling from Mesopotamia to Canaan, Abram and Isaac had met little interfering Canaanite traffic until their herdsmen met Abimelech's in the vicinity of the wells at Beer Sheba, where the herdsmen found a covenantal way to share the well water (Gen 26). In contrast, Joshua's campaign was not satisfied with multiplying Israel's children in the land. It aimed to clear the land of everyone but Israelites, and to enforce Mosaic laws on the whole population. It may have been what YHWH wanted, but was it what God intended?

The laws which are associated with Moses' name, however, are embedded in a narrative that shows indications of gradual development in the promised land over some five or six hundred years after his time. Community approved custom was gradually shaped into bodies of law in Exodus through Deuteronomy. In a burst of lawmaking, ascribed to Moses, the priests who returned from the exile sought to lead their fellow Jews to become a holy people, pure enough to live in the vicinity of a Holy Temple where a holy God would reside (Exod 19:5-6). Sin—the breaking of divinely given law—would not be allowed in the Holy City. God would only be pleased with a people who followed God's rules. The long journey to the promised parking place should be over, and the rules for an expanding population would serve for many generations—with some further modifications—to guide the Holy City's traffic. The ancient dicta "you shall not murder, . . . commit adultery, . . . steal, . . . bear false witness, . . . etc." became an abbreviated monument, a "one way" sign symbolizing all the laws of God.

In the biblical stories we see very few labeled sins. Younger Israelites were simply trying to live their lives in a setting that gave them freedom for sexual expression within the customary patriarchal limitations. Older Israelites acted to hold young adolescents in virtual slavery, insisting that they work for their own support and often withholding the economic basis for independence. Some modern youth find themselves in similar straits, the exception being the proportion of affluent modern youth who have been able to marry in spite of the hardships that young couples face.

It may surprise some readers for us to point to the fathers in Israel as the chief culprits in the stories we will examine. Thinking that they were doing service to God, they established customary rules and laws to keep youth from indulging in promiscuous sex. The result was (and still is) an almost obsessive interest in sex and sexuality. Israelite women sought sexual relationships in order to bear the children that would enlarge their communities. Young men sought to emulate the fathers whose sexual and physical prowess they admired and feared. Patricia Williams characterizes behavior that breaks family or community rules, laws or other constraints as structural sin:

> Sociobiology suggests that personal sin is inherent in our good and necessary nature. . . . We are sexual beings, and sexual desire produces good, constructive results in our lives. Sex provides pleasure, knits powerful bonds between slightly related kin, enhances love, and produces children. Sexual desire can also turn destructive, becoming lustfulness willing to rape and jealously capable of murder. . . . Structural sin seems even more destructive than personal sin because it can manipulate and corrupt the best in us against our better judgment. Moreover, good individuals caught in structural sin can do horrid deeds.[4]

Recent reports on the state of sexuality in the United States, particularly in women's prisons, show that severe sexual and physical abuse of women and children is far more excessive than anything found in the Hebrew Scriptures.[5]

Another vicious legal arena of structural abuse involves same sex partners who are deprived of the full economic benefits automatically available to legally married couples. When two men or two women choose to live together and want to support children, they find themselves caught in a web of political and economic structures that penalize them. Higher individual Income Tax and medical insurance rates pose serious financial obstacles for the creation of these families.

The thorny problem of medical insurance for every member of our population remains as one of the structural "sins of the fathers." In a time when cars with two or more passengers have the privilege of special freeway lanes, one would think that two or more people living in happy, healthy companionship should also be rewarded when they share the cost of necessities. Why not recognize such groupings as "families" and pay them and tax them so as to enable them to meet all the basic needs of their families?

The operation of the complex and powerful machinery of the twenty-first century is more involved than was the operation of early social and economic structures, but it is not less intriguing to try to design gentle controls to guide today's committed couples when they drive through the traffic surrounding their lives.

---

4. Williams, *Doing Without Adam and Eve*, 173, 174.

5. See for example Herman, *Trauma and Recovery: The Aftermath of Violence from Domestic Abuse to Political Terror.*

Part 2

Sex and Power Relationships in Some Israelite Stories

7

Sin Lurking at Ancient Doors

PATRICIA WILLIAMS HAS EFFECTIVELY destroyed the concept that one act of eating a forbidden fruit in Eden produced a taint of sin which would be passed on through sexual reproduction in the lives of all of the descendants of the first man and woman pictured in the early chapters of the book of Genesis. She surveys theological treatments of sin and salvation and concludes that the idea of original sin evolved out of an effort by the Christian church to understand a primeval catastrophe that led to the crucifixion and death of Jesus. She concludes, "Augustine's misreadings of Paul lead him to misinterpret Genesis 2 and 3."[1]

In fact, the careful reader of Genesis 3 finds that the story of human survival is not about sexual reproduction at all, but about eating a food that might extend human life indefinitely. The fruit of one tree is forbidden by the Owner of the garden but is eaten anyway. The know-it-all serpent questions the limitation that has been placed on his two intelligent companions, "Did God say, 'You shall not eat of *any* tree in the garden?'" Innocently, the woman repeats God's instruction, interpreting "you shall not eat" to include "you shall not touch it." As we know, in the patriarchal narrative the woman was the first to satisfy her curiosity and the man quickly followed. Together they discovered good and evil: "The eyes of both were opened, and they sewed fig leaves together and made loincloths for themselves." This is all the Bible has to say about the evolutionary transition from animal to human life. Today the idea of evolution remains controversial because of the lingering belief that biological genes determine moral developments in life forms.

We now know that Neolithic humans wore carefully designed clothes, and lived in houses as well as caves, neither of which are mentioned in the story of the Garden of Eden. When a high school student once asked "which came first the cave man or Adam and Eve?" I suggested that the cave man was our biological ancestor and Adam, our theological ancestor. In *The Chalice and the Blade*, Riane Eisler pictures an early time of peace and plenty when Adams and Eves lived as equal partners venerating a female goddess as the source of life.

---

1. Williams, *Doing Without Adam and Eve*, 43.

PART 2: Sex and Power Relationships in Some Israelite Stories

When the first human "gave names" to the creatures in the garden in Genesis 2:20, we note a definite advance beyond wordless animal existence. That advance of humans, which Genesis almost ignores, was the development of culture. Sexuality was an incidental discovery in the garden, and it would not be very significant even in the cities built by many generations of Cain's descendants. However the metaphor for cultural self-awareness required the covering of the sexual organs. Against who's seeing? Have the man and woman suddenly discovered the need for personal modesty after eating a bit of fruit? The serpent and the other animals of the creation have not been disturbed by their lack of clothing. Why did these two think their nudity was not good? No other creature in the garden wore clothes. The answer is obvious when the pair of humans hide themselves from God, adding one more layer in an attempt to cover themselves from God's seeing. It was not their sexual nature they were hiding but their effort to live forever, like God.

In fact, to live forever we need not only to eat from any and every tree in the garden, but also to extend our lives through reproducing. Individual men and women, like the animals, will "surely die" but their seed, like cubs and kittens, will survive. The socio-biologists and Holmes Rolston recognize that evolution is concerned with the survival of species rather than individuals. It is not good exegesis of Genesis to suggest that its authors anticipated the "survival of species," as an alternative to the deaths of individuals, but preachers take such liberties all the time. In doing so we are speaking what we believe to be an insight from God. All this emerging awareness has been telescoped into the briefest of sentences by the author of the third chapter of Genesis.

Dare we ask why the Creator reserved the knowledge of good and evil for God's Self? The traditional answer of Calvinist Augustinian theologians points to a first "law" which people must not disobey. We have been told that the prohibited fruit was a test of human obedience, anticipating a string of laws that must be obeyed forever. However, the editors of the Pentateuch reserved God's announcement of those laws for the book of Exodus.

In the meantime mankind is pictured as discovering that actions have consequences both good and bad. Perhaps we should understand the garden of Genesis as a hedged nursery in which God planted various trees to see whether their fruit would be edible or not, and also settled animal creations in it to see how they would behave and which of them—the "fittest"—would survive.

Finally, it appears, God created a truly amazing animal that could enjoy conversation with God and create names for the various plants and animals (Gen 2:20), managing and discussing the fantastic qualities of everything in creation! Wow! Whatever scenario led to the moment of confrontation with a disappointed God, Adam and Eve had disobeyed, and were ushered out of paradise. If only they had asked for explanations!

Believers see themselves in the story, and remember the rest of it.

Sin Lurking at the Door

What parents sending their seventeen year old son or daughter off to college for an education have not wished and prayed that their child could be saved from experiences of evil that are lurking outside the sheltering doors of home? Should we not think of God as such a parental figure, already foreseeing the terrifying possibilities of the education ahead for the human race?

The biblical record recounts the race's experiences of those possibilities in definable arenas, which will be settings for this study. Interwoven with our experience of sexuality is always the primary effort to secure sufficient nourishment from the plants and animals in the garden/wilderness in which we find ourselves, together with efforts to create shelters of various shapes against the vagaries of the world's weather. Human beings are aware of another sphere not bound to space, time and materiality that we may tentatively identify as *life's meaning*. Thoughtful humans have sought to understand the meaning of our existence, intuiting that an adequate answer is not limited to the way material things work and how social creatures survive in a largely material world.

Genesis 4 takes the reader into our world, the world around the garden, and past enough years of begetting, birthing and naming, childhood and adolescence, farming and shepherding, until the biblical telescope focuses on two brothers who present their annual thank offerings to the proprietary Lord. The new setting is not pictured in the text before us, but it draws on the customs and conventions of the patriarchal period when the earliest ancestor of Abram paused in his labors to "call upon the name of YHWH" (Gen 4:26).

We may imagine a visiting God/Person before whom the brothers spread a table with the products of their labor. Instead of the traditional picture of gifts on an altar, Abel offers a savory pot of lamb stew, and Cain, the fruits of his toil with the ground. At this primitive feast neither beer nor wine have been discovered, but animals and grains have been domesticated. As the three share this feast Cain observes that their Guest seems to prefer the stew that Abel has cooked rather than the bread he has baked, and he becomes angry. Noticing the expression on Cain's face, the Guest comments, "If you do well, will you not be accepted? And if you do not do well, sin is lurking at the door; its desire is for you, but you must master it." I hazard an update to God's remark: "You did okay, why not leave well enough alone."

As we explore this imagined picture we have all kinds of questions. Feminists might ask whether the two men actually cooked and baked their contributions to the meal. Were there no wives or servants who prepared the meal for their men? Anthropologists could ask if the brothers met in an open space between two tribal encampments or in a precursor of Cain's city. We could wonder why the two men did not blend their contributions into a typical nomad's single pot, Abel's meat made tasty with the addition of herbs from Cain's garden and eaten by dipping Cain's bread in the stew? How should "doing well" have been played in the scene? Theologians have wondered needlessly whether God was actually seen by early human eyes, a visible Guest, or only heard as an inner voice.

However we imagine the setting, out of doors, sheltered by the opened flaps of a tent, or inside the doors of a house, the climax of the story is apparently a fight in a field, and Abel is killed. The field is mentioned only in the Greek translation of Genesis, but needs to be there to receive Abel's blood. The fatal outcome seems to require some sort of fight. Good-natured tussling between pre-adolescent brothers does not fit. The story pictures men who have honed their skills in their respective fields of labor. Abel is the herder who followed the small cattle as they foraged in the open country, Cain, the settler who has learned to seed the ground and wait in a permanent dwelling for a crop.

The fight occurs at the border between the open country and the first farm. The brothers have domesticated a bit of the wilderness, completed the yearly cycle, and meet to celebrate with the products of their labors. The happy thanksgiving ceremony seems already to have been marred by contention: have Abel's goats found the pit where Cain's grain is stored? Apparently their disagreement was about the products of their toil that were offered as thanks to God. It was not about a woman. Women are notably absent from the incident.

After the feast the brothers argue; their covenantal relationship falls apart. Before they separate to return to their chores, their conversation is heated, and Abel is killed. God hears the cry of blood from the ground, and returns to ask Cain, "Where is your brother Abel?" Cain answers, "How should I know which way that herdsman has gone?" Cain is settled on the land he has chosen to till; his brother has no permanent address. God's question is ridiculous. Still angry, Cain does not tell God what happened. He is not Abel's "keeper." Worse, he has lost the feeling of brotherhood he could have enjoyed in a shared preparation of the feast.

Sin *had been lurking at the door*, but in his innocence Cain had not realized that he should have controlled his feelings. Isabel Carter Heyward asks if "human innocence and human irresponsibility in the world are indistinguishable" for the God of the early chapters of Genesis.[2] In telling the story the Yahwist sees innocence that has not yet matured to responsibility.

This, like the eating of the restricted fruit of the garden, was a new development in the life of the first humans. Thus the Genesis narrative introduces the term "sin." Not the actual killing of Cain's brother, but the uncontrolled anger that led to a fight is what the word from God refers to. In God's enigmatic sentence the key word is "desire," which stands for an inclination of a personal spirit toward something not yet attained. Cain wanted God's approval, and felt that he had not received it. Yielding to his anger, he overpowered his brother, but in the end he could not feel that he had done "the right thing" (Today's English Version). He went out a fugitive and wanderer, unable fully to trust himself or anyone else.

---

2. Heyward, *The Redemption of God*, 151.

The "Door"

Like the clothes of Genesis 2 and the guardian angel at the border of the garden the door is symbolic and meaningful. Each stands for protection from an outside world that is often seen as hostile. Doors are not natural objects but are products of culture and civilization. Inside the shelter of tents, houses and clothes it may be either cooler or warmer than the weather outside. Inside the shelters people erect there is a degree of protection from other people who *may* actually threaten to steal the crops that have been reaped, the lambs that have been born, or the virtue of the innocent. Inside the shelter of the door, the women owned by a patriarch are relatively safe from rape. Inside the door "a man's home is his castle." Shepherds build sheepfolds; cultivators of the soil arrange hedges or fences. Doors may also shelter many forms of evil from public view. Sin can and may occur both inside and outside of the doors we erect.

People may choose, however, to open their doors or remove their clothing. Such opening reveals what is otherwise hidden. It invites intimacy. Although an opening anticipates good relationship with an outsider, it risks bad relationship. Several biblical stories feature the opening and closing of doors. In the story of the attack on Lot's residence in Sodom harm—a rape—was intended, but it was thwarted by a closed door. (Gen 19:5–11) In the story of the Levite's concubine harm was done in the street. (Judg 19:22–30)

Ita Sheres underscores the "going out" of every one involved in the rape of Dinah. Dinah "went out to visit the women of the region;" "Hamor the father of Shechem went out to Jacob to speak with him" (Gen 34:1,6,20). David's son Amnon was permitted to enter the bedroom of his half-sister Tamar (2 Sam 13). Bath Sheba was invited from the shelter of her husband's home to the palatial residence of King David (2 Sam 11:1–6). A door is always a limited protection from evil. Sin lurks outside the door, as a poisonous serpent threatens the unsuspecting householder who ventures outside for work or community relationships.

It is not sin to open the door to relationship. Sin has to do with the quality of relationships within the house or with people beyond its protecting walls and doors. In the case of Cain and Abel "sin" arose within the family, as serpent-like *"sin"* poisoned the relationship between the brothers. We may imagine the two men emerging from the fabric of their respective tents to come separately to the place where the sacrificial meal was to be celebrated, each eyeing the other and the other's sacrifice: "Will God favor *my* offering?" Perhaps only one of the brothers had been bitten by sin, while the other may have thought only of giving thanks to God. Genesis does not attempt to probe the thoughts behind the murderous act, but we sense that sin is deeper than action. It roots in what one intends when one opens doors and eyes. Both brothers were "doing well" as long as they thought to please their Guest, but when Cain thought God favored Abel's meat, he did not put the thought out of his mind. He did not master the "sin lurking at the door."

PART 2: Sex and Power Relationships in Some Israelite Stories

The "Law" of Vengeance

When the Lord speaks in the Yahwist's account, God identifies the consequences of the action without describing it as "sin." God questions Cain twice, requiring him to look at his anger, locate his brother, and consider what he has done (Gen 4:9). Having killed his brother, Cain will discover that the ground he has tilled has now become an antagonist with which he must wrestle alone. He will be a fugitive and a wanderer apart from other people: "anyone who meets me may kill me." Finally, the Lord confirms the *descriptive* law of vengeance: "Whoever kills Cain [or any person descended from Cain] will suffer a sevenfold vengeance." This "law" does not *prescribe* executions; it *describes* anticipated actions. Once the human race has discovered the power to kill, the act will be repeated. The next victim may be the first killer.

We no longer believe that the death of Cain should have been avenged by seven other deaths. The saying simply states the significant social consequence of killing a human being. Relatives of a murdered man may want and often will seek a vengeful death penalty, or "justice," as we prefer to say. People tend to overdo in the effort to retaliate, just as Cain did when he attacked Abel after the latter may have tried to assure him that both were actually receiving God's favor. We have no business using this proverbial word to justify executing murderers or adulterers.

Investigative Reporters and Tainted Cousins

All of the stories in the early chapters of the Bible are the imaginative work of storytellers who presented their ancestors as literary characters representing the legendary first man, woman, and family. Their tales, however, are not "just stories." The writer whom scholars call the Yahwist was inspired by his concept of a God who, like many early people, preferred meat to barley, was curious about his creatures' behavior, and did not hesitate to allow the soil to harden itself against those who would harm each other. We are blessed with the sense to see a better way. Our God grieves when he finds his children killing each other.

Believing that the whole human race is descended from Adam and Eve, the writers of Genesis traced the multiplying descendants in heroic terms with lifetimes of hundreds of years until the time of Noah, when the Lord set a one hundred twenty year limit because of his displeasure with the way "sons of God went in to the daughters of humans, who bore children to them" (Gen 6:4). We are not told if this opening by the daughters of humans annoyed God, but in the next verse we read, "The Lord saw that the wickedness of human kind was great in the earth, and that every human inclination of the thoughts of their hearts was only evil continually." Though the behavior was displeasing, God was distressed to observe that thoughts—those internal dialogues that precede decisions—could lead to bad activities. Wickedness is a synonym for sin, but its motivating source is obscure. Did the Yahwist believe that humans were corrupted by the example of the "sons of God?" And if so, how is it that actions spring from thought?

When the flood was over and a fresh covenant bound Noah, his sons and every living creature to the Lord, all seemed to go well until his third son looked at him lying drunk, while his brothers, "walking backward," closed the door on their father's nakedness with a blanket. (Gen 9:10–23) The nakedness was not sinful, but for Ham's sin of disrespect his descendants, the Canaanite tribes, received Noah's curse, assigning them to be slaves to the descendants of Shem. The Bible's human authors believed that words of a curse could affect those upon whom a curse was laid.

Again when the people spread over the earth, speaking one language, some settled in the plain of Shinar [Sumer] and agreed to build a city with a tower, intending to "make a name" for themselves, that is, to create the first identified state or empire. Building a city was apparently not sinful, but the Lord was displeased with the arrogance of a people who thought they could do anything they chose to do without consulting him. Since their cohesion as a people depended on their ability to make plans together, the Lord confused their speech by letting "corrupt" dialects and languages develop. Or perhaps they just argued about how to proceed (Gen 11:1–8).

Genesis does not say that Shem's descendants were immune to corruption, but the story resumes with Shem's unbroken line to the family of Terah, "the father of Abram, Nahor, and Haran," and singles out Abram with his wife Sarai for attention. (Gen 11:10–32).

Abram and his nephew Lot pastured their flocks together until their herds were numerous enough to be the occasion for strife between their herdsmen. Lot decided to move south toward Sodom, was captured by a coalition of foreign kings, and rescued by Abram. Lot needed to be rescued again when a mob came to his door just before the destruction of Sodom, but his wife "looked back [as they escaped] and she became a pillar of salt" (Gen 13–14).

Lot settled in a cave in the hills with his two daughters, and the two women despaired of finding a man to give them children. So they made their father drunk and on successive nights each had intercourse with him to produce Moab and Ben-Ammi, the ancestors of the Moabites and the Ammonites, who became near neighbors—and were kin—of Israel (Gen 19:30–38). Later on, Leviticus 18:6–30 would see the behavior of Lot's daughters in the secrecy of the cave as impurity and depravity.

These incidents may seem irrelevant to the main thrust of Genesis and to our treatment of sex, war, and sin. Sex appears to have a very small but important part in the stories of Noah, Ham, Lot, and his daughters, and since the word sin is absent from the stories one may legitimately ask why they should be considered significant. Sex is always incidental to the principal movement in the scriptures toward populating the world with the "right" kind of people. And law would not be announced until long after the lives of the first patriarchs. But according to Levitical rules both Ham and Lot became impure and produced lines of descendants who would be excluded from the post-exilic congregation of Israel. When God called Israel to be a "holy nation," and a "kingdom of priests," the children of Canaan and Lot, Canaanites, Moabites, and Ammonites would not qualify. These "others" would be destined for slavery or destruction. But because of their close ties with the selected line of descent from Noah,

PART 2: Sex and Power Relationships in Some Israelite Stories

these cousins were allowed inferior positions in God's plans. As the history developed, we see them as Israel's tainted cousins.

Cain did not master the lurking sin, but he succeeded in building a city with many doors. The people of Sodom and Gomorrah had deadly instead of constructive thoughts. When a great outcry over the "grave sin" of those cities of the plain arose, the Lord went with his friend Abraham to find out what was happening. According to Genesis, when the two investigators could not find ten righteous people, the two cities were destroyed. Was Lot's wife destroyed because she looked back with regret at leaving the life she had enjoyed? (Gen 19:12–29)

Today's investigative reporters have assumed the role of the curious God and of his friend Abram/Abraham, focusing attention on the actions of people, both men and women. Many members of our species appear to be tainted, often characterized as "evil" but it is a mistake to assume that "kill the evil one!" is God's final word.

Wives at Risk

In several events of the early history the connection between sex and sin is left undefined except to suggest how the significant people found shelter in their migrations. The book of beginnings has three versions of a story about a patriarch who passed off his wife as his sister, and had to reclaim her from the harem of a local chieftain or king. Two of the stories concern Abram/Abraham, and the third is about Isaac.[3] Local details and identities differ, but the stories are similarly structured: A patriarch, variously identified as Abram, Abraham, or Isaac, still on the move in the new land, finds a measured hospitality with a local "king," who is attracted to the patriarch's wife, Sarai/Sarah/Rebekah. In the two stories concerning Abram/Abraham, Sarai/Sarah is taken within the doors of the king's harem. In consequence members of the king's household are threatened with plagues or death. The king confronts the patriarch with the question "What have you done to me?" The patriarch replies, "I was afraid for my life." But at the reconciliation the foreign king rewards the patriarch with expensive gifts or the privilege of settling on lands he controls.

All three stories center around the possibility of adultery between the foreign king and the wife of the patriarch, who has risked his wife's purity in order to preserve his own life. However, the action of the foreign king in each case was innocent of intent to harm the patriarch's wife. The most detailed of the stories includes a dream in which God converses with Abimelech:

> God came to Abimelech by night, and said to him, "You are about to die because of the woman whom you have taken; for she is a married woman." Now Abimelech had not approached her; so he said, "Lord, will you destroy an innocent people? Did he not say to me, 'She is my sister'? . . . I did this in the integrity of my heart and the innocence of my hands." "Yes," [God replies] "I know that you did this in the integrity of your heart, furthermore it was I who kept you from sinning against me. Therefore I did not let you touch her. Now then, return the man's wife; for he is a prophet, and he will pray for you and you shall live.

3. See Genesis 12:10–20; 20:1–18; and 26:1–5.

But if you do not return her, know that you shall surely die, you and all that are yours" (Gen 20:4–7).

As the Israelite storytellers told it, adultery was *almost* committed in each of the three cases, but God blocked it each time. If God had not blocked the adultery, an even more serious consequence than the closing of the wombs of his household could have befallen the foreign king. But God declared in Abimelech's dream, "it was I who kept you from sinning against me." Likewise in the other stories the reader senses that God was involved in protecting the patriarch, his wife *and* the foreign chieftain.

We remind ourselves that in Genesis there was no revealed law to guide either the patriarch or the foreign king, and that custom may have dictated an exchange of gifts between a visiting chieftain and a local king. Having little else to offer, the patriarch permitted his wife to be attached to the king's harem, perhaps trusting that she would not be harmed. She may have been a hostage to insure the visitor's good behavior. As usual, we can only speculate. It is clear, however, that neither adultery nor deceit was acceptable in either community. Abimelech accused Abraham: "What have you done to us? How have I sinned against you, that you have brought such great guilt on me and my kingdom? You have done things to me that ought not to be done" (Gen 20:9).

In place of laws both men had a sense of right and wrong: no one should do the kind of thing that Abraham had done. Abimelech tentatively assumed responsibility asking, "have I sinned?" but expecting a negative answer. Alternatively, he suggested that Abraham may have been at fault for making him feel guilty. The story does not explore every aspect of the situation, but leaves the impression that it was Abraham who had sinned, although *Abimelech might have sinned against God.*

The only way these seemingly contradictory judgments make sense is that a personal God was Abraham's friend and patron, as the biblical historian believed. Abimelech recognized that his guest was under the protection of such a God, and a sin against this visitor was a sin against God. But then, a sin against *any* visitor should also have been seen as malicious, a breach of pre-covenantal relationship with a traveler. Repeatedly in the biblical story the treatment of a traveler tested the quality of hospitality between people who were not seen as kin. Yet in God's eyes all people are kindred. The Hebrew word for good relationship is *hesed*. It means the fulfillment of obligations between people whether between close kin or between strangers who agree to covenants.

Physical sex is not even peripherally involved in the three stories, and neither sexual nor social abuse actually occurred against God's friends. Social experimenting, testing whether settled communities should open doors to the homeless, took place at every turn as the patriarchs faced new challenges on the way to becoming a nation.

God's Oversight over a Brother in Jeopardy

The book of Genesis includes an incident that strangely contrasts with these stories. Joseph, sold into slavery by his brothers, finds himself managing the household of a wealthy Egyptian named Potiphar. He has free run of the household and catches the eye of Potiphar's wife (indoors!). When she asks him to satisfy her lust, he refuses with the words: "Look, with me here, my master has no concern about anything in the house, and he has put everything that he has in my hand. He is not greater in this house than I am, nor has he kept back anything from me except yourself, because you are his wife. How then could I do this great wickedness, and sin against God?" (Gen 39:8–9).

This is possibly more than a man in Joseph's position would actually have been saying, but it does spell out heroically the sort of understanding masters and servants shared in the ancient world, which I consider not as a formal covenant but as covenantal. Potiphar had probably detailed the things that he was placing in Joseph's hands, and no doubt identified the various women and girls who belonged to the household, making sure that Joseph knew which had lesser functions and who was his wife.

Without doubt Joseph referred to his relationship with his master and to a secondary commitment to his owner's wife, but what is interesting is the way Joseph transfers those commitments from the moral or social to the religious/theological level. No clearly defined covenant between Jacob's sons and God had yet been expressed, but Joseph acted in the spirit of covenant rules. He refused to commit adultery with the foreign woman who was nominally his mistress, but practically his equal in the household. Contrast the wives of Abram/Abraham and Isaac, potential victims of rape in a foreign household with this young son of shepherds in a sophisticated Egyptian home, seriously pressured into a sinful relationship. Trusting God for protection and that his mistress would understand, Joseph behaved in a way he believed a just God approved. His unseen Sponsor would protect him and through him guide a small tribe toward its destiny.

So, the book of Genesis closes with no specifically adulterous liaisons, no wildly sinful sexual escapades. Instead, abuses were committed in several relationships between members of God's chosen family and foreigners. Seldom called "sins," these wrong acts broke the trust a superior had invested in inferiors, and consequently the damaged egos would assert their rightness, just as the blood of Abel had cried to heaven. The incidents in Genesis presage the wars of history.

Viewing the story of Israel's earliest beginnings from the point of view of God, the biblical historians saw a series of gifted men facing the double challenge of finding food and shelter to sustain their bodies and of keeping mates who could join in completing the cycles of life from one generation to the next. God, the authors and editors of our texts, and we readers observe unscientifically, empathize with, and judge what we see the figures of the stories doing. *We all watch*, just as Katherens hoped that the wild stallion Cloud would take his first steps, find his mother's nipples, follow her to pastures, and grow into a successful band stallion himself.

All the divine Observer was willing to do for the chosen men of Genesis was to invest each actor with the twin forces of life, the hunger for nourishment and the need for sexual reproduction. Standing apart like God from the actual struggles, we judge their actions as right or wrong, and then, as events determined outcomes, we re-examine our judgments. Was it a sin for Abraham to seek grain in Egypt when there was little of it Canaan? Did he sin by offering his wife's virtue for his own safety? We have hardly any doubt that Joseph's brothers sinned against him when they traded his freedom for their anticipated dominance in the family. They admitted as much before they could face him in Egypt: They said to one another, "Alas, we are paying the penalty for what we did to our brother; we saw his anguish when he pleaded with us, but we would not listen. That is why anguish is come upon us." (Gen 42:21)

This inadvertent confession was among the brothers, and because their Hebrew words to the Egyptian official were not being translated, they believed Joseph did not know what they were saying to each other.

None of Jacob's sons committed the sin of adultery, at least as Genesis tells the stories. The apparent exception was Judah's affair with Tamar, but both of her husbands had died before that took place, so technically Judah was not committing adultery. Genesis is concerned about keeping the sexual relations of the ancestor patriarchs within one Mesopotamian family, evidently to assure the start of a pure lineage in Canaan, untainted with foreign influences. Abraham and Isaac succeeded in pruning undesired branches (Ishmael and Esau), but Jacob began a process of assimilation in which servants were included as the mothers of some of his sons. Adultery would have occurred if a patriarch took the wife of another man It was a crime involving property, not personal relationship. Joseph did not allow himself to be seduced by Potiphar's wife, but later married Asenath, "daughter Potiphera, priest of On," mother of his two sons, Manasseh and Ephraim, in Egypt.[4] Marriages with non-Israelites were not prohibited until the Deuteronomic reporting of the conquest of Canaan, and were not thought to be sinful until Nehemiah's time.

Cain's "War" Culture

The two significant concerns of the Israelites were wives and land. The first involved the sex drive and the procreation of at least one heir, but the drive to possess and build on the land God promised was at least equally important. The conflict between Cain and Abel heralded future power struggles over land that male heirs in the family would control.

Robert Coote has called attention to this dimension in the stories of the patriarchs and their families. In his study of the Elohist History, *In Defense of Revolution*, Coote writes, "In agrarian Israel, the household was more than a family and its resources. It was the primary center of power." Demonstrating how E materials in Genesis and Exodus mirror the experiences of Jeroboam I, Coote calls attention to the vulnerability of the sons of the patriarchs as well as of the families of their Canaanite hosts and antagonists. The sons of Jacob believed they had removed Joseph as a rival heir to the blessing promised to Abram, but the tables were turned, and Joseph turned out to be the God-ordained savior of the whole family. Kept, or keeping, from sinning, Joseph confronted his brothers and they confessed their guilt to each other. The survival of the family depended on the faithfulness (*hesed*) of its savior and his willingness to

---

4. In later Jewish and Muslim tradition she is given a Persian name, "Zulaikha."

forgive. The brothers' confession of sin was not made to Joseph, but to each other in a language they did not expect the Pharaoh's officer to understand. Joseph did understand, however, and reconciliation could be accomplished.

Even if the stories are fictitious, they have been preserved to illustrate a fundamental paradigm of relationship which enabled the families and tribes to grow and be successful Failure to fulfill covenantal conditions, Israelites and their successors believed, would have brought harmful consequences to Israel.

Behavior that we might call sinful does not show any evidence of being a consequence of actions by Adam and Eve. Instead, most of the activity in Genesis appears to be self-motivated or a response to actions of others who possess their own powers. Power struggles between people lead to murder and war, whether the prize is a woman or a plot of ground. Within Hebrew families word of a patriarch or his favorite wife often served to prevent violence in disputes in all arenas of life. Later, judges and priests assumed responsibility for restraining violence in Israelite communities until anointed kings became the designated human judges. These believed that they were acting for God, and when laws were spoken or written they were believed to have come from the God YHWH who spoke or wrote them for Moses in the wilderness of the Sinai peninsula.

Like art, sin is in the eye of the human beholder, and also, according to scripture, in the sight of God. This ambiguity continues in declarations of faith today. We care for the memory of our spiritual ancestors because without them we would be something other than what we are. When they tell of surviving their mistakes and building cities, we rejoice, knowing that we also may survive our sins and the forces that could undo us. The biblical record is the primary source for the stories of our spiritual ancestors. Secular sources can give us physical detail about our biological ancestors and the cities they built. Sin lurks at doors, material and spiritual, and a trusting alertness might not save us from harm, but it did save Joseph from sinning. Today we can rely on the Spiritual Presence that surrounds and infuses all living creatures, offering protection more secure than many of us believe possible.

8

A Family Misstep Involving Sex

GENESIS 34 RECORDS A serious misstep by the sons of Jacob on the way to becoming the people of Israel. Although the bargaining conversation that could have led to a covenant of marriage is present in the chapter, neither the words covenant (Hebrew *berith*) and "good faith" (*hesed*) nor the social realities they represent appear in the telescopic view of the author/editor (JE). Also, there is no reference to God in the story. YHWH is not invoked as God to bless the proposed relationship. Elohim (or El) does not intervene with verbal blessing or curse. All the action is on the human level, between members of the recently settled but still tenting tribe of Jacob and the settled Hivite (or Perizzite) town whose chief was Hamor. Genesis 33:19–20 reports that Jacob had purchased the land on which his tent was pitched for one hundred pieces of silver, and erected an altar dedicated to "El, the God of Israel" on it.

The story introduces Leah's daughter Dinah, the only daughter of Jacob mentioned in Genesis, a younger sister of Simeon and Levi. The Hivites had evidently accepted the family of Jacob as migrants—temporary neighbors with whom they might trade—but had not yet agreed with Jacob for the most delicate relationship, intermarriage between families. However, Dinah visited "the women of the country, and Shechem, son of Hamor, . . . saw her; he took her, lay with her and dishonoured her" (vs.2, New English Bible). What the sons of Jacob and the sixth-century writer considered a rape may well have been a case of two young people making love before marriage, what we would call statutory rape. Feminist writers insist that Shechem raped Dinah, and Ita Sheres correctly translates the verb and its object "he *laid* her" instead of he "lay with" her, a difference in vocalizing the Hebrew consonants. Immediately, the young Shechem "comforted" Dinah, and asked his father to arrange for a proper marriage. Anita Diamant has given us an imaginary account of Dinah's life in *The Red Tent*. I was delighted to find that she pictured a romantic relationship between the young Shechemite and Jacob's daughter.

Without delay father Hamor approached Jacob—before the sons of Jacob had come in from tending their flocks in the open country. Discussions continued with Jacob's sons present, and when they asked that Hamor's men should be circumcised,

PART 2: Sex and Power Relationships in Some Israelite Stories

the Hivites agreed, probably because Shechem was the popular son of a chieftain and other young women of Jacob's extended family were attractive. An agreement for one marriage between the two families would also open the way for members of the tribe of Jacob to marry the local girls. Hamor and his sons came to the city gate and addressed their fellow citizens with these words:

> These people are friendly with us; let them live in the land and trade in it, for the land is large enough for them; let us take their daughters in marriage, and let us give them our daughters. Only on this condition will they agree to live among us, to become one people: that every male among us be circumcised as they are circumcised. Will not their livestock, their property, and all their animals be ours? Only let us agree with them, and they will live with us. (Gen 34:21–23)

In effect covenant relations between two tribes would be established, or to put it in terms of the covenantal paradigm, the not yet settled and thus "weaker" Israelite tribe became politically strong enough to dictate terms of an agreement. Everybody could see that it was the right thing to do.

Socio-Political Aspects

The young men in Hamor's tribe faithfully fulfilled their part of the bargain, "doing *hesed*." Though the word *hesed* is not used in this chapter, it expresses the mutual fulfilling of agreements between people, and later between God and people. Hamor had used a synonym in declaring his eagerness to win Jacob's "favor" (vs. 12). As the historians retold the story, we can only speculate as to the relative strength of the parties in the incident. It seems that the increasing numbers of Jacob's family were becoming a threat to the Hivites, and to maintain peaceful association they agreed to the condition his family imposed. Thus, instead of being dominated by Jacob's family, the people of the town believed that they would be able to assimilate the future Israelites into their community, "Will not their herds, their livestock and all their chattels then be ours?" (vs. 23).

But assimilation was not what Dinah's brothers wanted. "Two days later, while [every able bodied Hivite male] was still in great pain, Jacob's two sons, Simeon and Levi . . . armed themselves with swords, boldly entered the city and killed every male" (vs. 25). With the Hivite community weakened, the rest of Jacob's sons used the opportunity to plunder the city and its surrounding territory. Dinah was snatched away from Shechem's house, and disappears from the record, while Jacob and his sons had to face the displeasure of the wider Canaanite world.

No Israelite leadership is visible in the story until word of the massacre reached Jacob. Even then, no word from God would be heard, nor appeal to organized government. When the patriarch spoke, he pointed out with parental authority how the surrounding people would see the situation: "Jacob said to Simeon and Levi, 'You have brought trouble on me, you have made my name stink among the people of the country'" (vs. 30).[1] Commentators have noted that Jacob was not involved in his sons'

---

1. Quotations are from the New English Bible.

A Family Misstep Involving Sex

scheme or in the family's negotiations with Hamor. When he had heard that "Shechem had defiled his daughter, . . . [Jacob] held his peace until [his sons] came" in from the field. He evidently did not assert the patriarch's right to deal with another patriarch, and left the negotiating to his two sons. Maybe his sons overruled him. But in the end he may have remembered sadly that he had settled his differences with Laban without violence, arriving at a covenant to go separate ways. The sons of Jacob moved away from the area, probably forsaking the land their father had purchased from Hamor. The historian's interest was in the acquisition of the land, not in the personal fate of a daughter of Jacob.

In the larger frame of Genesis we have one more lesson in the learning of good and evil. Simeon and Levi forgot an earlier lesson of necessary good faith between Abraham and Abimelech. Jacob, however, after all his experiences of good and bad relationships with Esau and Laban knew that his sons had not "done *hesed*" with their neighbors, and as a result would be in danger from other neighbors. The social consequences of their action, "the sin of the father," could last into the third and fourth generation.

When tribes were competing for the two most vital "properties" in the ancient world—wives and land—the alternatives were either some form of covenant or violent conflict. Throughout Genesis the patriarchal families were concerned with the problem of finding and keeping suitable mates for their male offspring. Abraham and Isaac both risked parking their wives in the establishment of a local chief named Abimelech in order to be secure as migrant shepherds in the vicinity of his settled land. Jacob's quest had led him far from his own family and he secured four mates but no land in a far country. In the case of Dinah, the family wanted an acceptable marriage for her, while Shechem disregarded the custom of Jacob's tribe, if not of his own kinsmen. Both families appeared ready to make the best of the situation and accept the new more friendly relationship between wandering tribe and established village. The Hivites were ready to welcome sons and daughters of Shechem and Dinah, for the increase of families was a mark of the favor of God, whether known as YHWH, El, or by some other name. But the younger male members of both families had their eyes on the livestock the region could support and, of course, the land itself.

The incident was a small-scale intertribal crisis, like the larger scale conflicts in today's world between people who see their neighbors as alien to their core values. Evidently the two tribes had already engaged in friendly trade. Children played together until daughters were old enough to be considered for marriages, while older boys and men were busy with their herds in the open ranges. Two tribes with different backgrounds had not reached the point of accepting marriages across the invisible line between them. That line also marked the distinct ownership of material goods and persons by two groups identified by tribal names and particular customs. At the time the only land that could be claimed was where both groups actually lived. The range was not owned by either tribe, but was shared when shepherds kept flocks at some distance from other herds. Wells, dug by tribal groups, could be held by the tribe with the stronger or more numerous men. Other tribal properties were the herds of Jacob's sons

PART 2: Sex and Power Relationships in Some Israelite Stories

and the herds and garden patches of Hamor's sons. Since property was held by males, and daughters were treated as property, two distinct people could exist side by side in semi-covenantal freedom. No larger government existed, and the border incident over Dinah delayed the ultimate assimilation of the two groups.

The sexual incident was only a tiny part of the situation, a pretext for the conflict that was waiting to occur. If there had been no tribal custom or family "rule" against marrying outside of the kinship group, Dinah and Shechem might have produced the first members of a new clan or tribe or nation that could have joined Hivites to Hebrews. We note that Jacob is not called Israel in this story, and the word "Israelite" had not made its way into the vocabulary of the period. The unnecessarily violent episode did lead to identifying "sons of Israel" rather than "sons of Shechem," but that would probably have occurred anyway. If there had been no patriarchal zeal for a pure line of male succession for the holding of property, the natural course of events could have led to a mixed population in Canaan long before Moses, instead of the separate settlements of distinctively identified tribes. If Dinah's brothers had not planned to use force to avenge what they saw as an insult to the dignity of their family, the assimilation of the native population into a future "Israel" could probably have been accomplished peacefully through the natural attraction between adolescents. Would the resulting mix have been "Israel" or one of the identifiable local tribes?

Throughout the first seven books of the Old Testament there are occasional references to groups of six or seven Canaanite tribes that inhabited the land before the twelve or thirteen Israelite tribes arrived to possess it. Also the line between tribes and smaller clan groups is not consistent, with several of the latter rising to prominence from time to time.[2] Feminist writers have pointed out that Isaac and Jacob followed the custom of seeking a cousin as bride, while Jacob's sons (and daughter!) broke with that tradition.

The only kingdoms mentioned in the patriarchal period are two consortiums whose conflict involved Lot. The record reports an ad hoc association of the kings of Sodom and Gomorrah against eastern kings who took Lot captive before Abraham called on his friends to rescue his nephew (Gen 14).

Paying the Bride Price

The Greek story of "Pyramus and Thisbe" and Shakespeare's "Romeo and Juliet" have kept the tradition of patriarchal decision-making concerning marriage alive. In mid-twentieth century my wife Virginia gently insisted that I formally ask her father for her after she had agreed to marry me. Cultural "memes" maintain social realities and values.

Up to a point the Dinah incident appears to fit the standard (biological and social) family model as we have understood it: Boy likes girl; girl is physically responsive whether she initially likes the boy or not, and the first step toward the creation of a

---

2. Norman K. Gottwald explores Israel's terminology for tribal groupings in *The Tribes of Yahweh: A Sociology of the Religion of Liberated Israel 1250–1050 BCE.*

family is taken. It is strange that several biblical stories involving rape seem to suggest "one night stands," although normal human experience requires a number of copulations to achieve a pregnancy.

Since Shechem and Hamor so readily agreed to the proposal of Simeon and Levi, we may assume that the payment of a bride-price for a seduced virgin was a long-standing, socially approved precedent for both groups, It would later be incorporated in the laws of the Covenant Code ascribed by Moses to YHWH: When a man seduces a virgin who is not engaged to be married, and lies with her, he shall give the bride-price for her and make her his wife. But if her father refuses to give her to him, he shall pay an amount equal to the bride price for virgins (Exodus 22:16).

Genesis does not mention this law since the incident occurred before the giving of laws at Sinai, but we note that the transaction fully illustrates the covenantal paradigm of human taking and giving diagrammed in chapter 2.

The law in Exodus does not suggest that seduction or a willing response by a virgin should be considered a sin before God. Such an incident customarily was dealt with by mutual agreement between the two fathers of the "defiled" daughter. In both the law and the story of Dinah the problem is one of "goods" which are considered to be too devalued to be worth anything for a possible future transaction. A young woman no longer an intact virgin was immediately assumed to be contaminated by her sexual contact with a male. Whether she became pregnant or not or whether she was a willing partner made no difference to the judgment. All that mattered was whether her hymen had been pierced.

In the story the young "prince" Shechem acted responsibly by offering a customary bride price for Dinah; undoubtedly he expected to be asked for one or more animals from the herds of his family. His father approached Jacob with the offer: "The heart of my son Shechem longs for your daughter; please give her to him in marriage. Make marriages with us; give your daughters to us, and take our daughters for yourselves. You shall live with us; and the land shall be open to you; live and trade in it, and get property in it." Shechem added his word: "Let me find favor with you, and whatever you say to me I will give. Set the marriage present and gift as high as you like, and I will give whatever you ask me; only give me the girl to be my wife."

The sons of Jacob made their counter proposal, answering "deceitfully" as the narrator says: We cannot do this thing, to give our sister to one who is uncircumcised, for that would be a disgrace to us. Only on this condition will we consent to you: that you will become as we are and every male among you be circumcised. Then we will take your daughters for ourselves, and we will live among you and become one people. But if you will not listen to us and be circumcised, then we will take our daughter and be gone."

In rejecting the hospitable offer of Hamor and Shechem Jacob's sons seemed to give higher priority to God's command to circumcise than to the overall project undertaken by Abram/Abraham to share in the making of a great nation in a land that YHWH would show them. What led them to insist on the circumcision of potential

PART 2: Sex and Power Relationships in Some Israelite Stories

members of a united people as a prior condition to sharing in the development of a nation? Why was being circumcised so important?

The Meaning of Circumcision

The circumcision ritual was more than an incidental pretext for conflict over ownership of land and tribal wealth. Abraham had marked himself, his son Ishmael and "all the slaves born in his house or bought with his money, every male among the men of [his] house . . . that very day as God had said to him. Abraham was ninety nine years old when he was circumcised." (Gen 17:23–24) Circumcision was to be *the* covenantal mark for every one of his male descendants, but also for all purchased slaves or who would bargain to be a part of Abraham's super-tribe.

In the Shechem incident the Hivites had no similar bargaining chip, and by accepting circumcision they were perhaps unaware that they were binding themselves to be fictive descendants of Abraham, Isaac and Jacob. Their persons, flocks, and land might still belong to a Hivite clan, but also would be part of the Israelite confederation still in the process of formation. As a settled community the Hivites had evidently neglected the practice of physically marking members of their "tribe." Tribal facial marking was still recognizable in settled communities in parts of Africa in the late twentieth century of the Common Era, but evidently such marking was neglected in some Canaanite towns during the patriarchal period.

There are no references to God in Genesis 34. The only vestige of religious ritual is the concern of the sons of Jacob that the men of Shechem be circumcised before Shechem and Dinah could be married. The reader may remember that God, identified as "Almighty" (*El Shaddai*) in Genesis 17:1–14, had required the Hebrew Abram/Abraham to observe this ritual as a sign of the covenant which promised many nations to the patriarch. Thus the reader should understand the religious motivation to adhere to the one condition of the covenant, which would mark the sexual organ of every male Israelite (Genesis 17:12). Jacob's sons may have thought they were obeying YHWH when they insisted on the circumcision of the Hivites, but the story does not credit them with religious motives. We could also mention that Moses' wife Zipporah insisted on circumcising his son on the way from Midian to Egypt (Exod 4:24–26), making the unnamed son a proper Israelite before the Exodus.

The Hivites on the other hand were apparently unaware of the religious motivation, or ignored it, and accepted the condition as a tribal marking peculiar to the tribe of Jacob. In the biblical account they simply wanted to "do the right thing" and make everyone happy. The result of the painful ordeal would be increased prosperity for all. At the time they were not concerned with satisfying an Israelite god.

We can, however, look at circumcision through the lenses provided by Victor Turner's studies of ritual. Bobby C. Alexander has broadened Victor Turner's definition of ritual as "a symbolic, self-reflective, performance that makes a transition to a time and space out of the ordinary in order to reflect on an ideal or community and to create, sometimes through routine and sometimes through experimentation, the experience of community . . . Turner recognizes ritual's capacity to suspend social norms, criticize social structure for its inability to meet the need for direct and egalitarian relationships, present alternatives, and to transform the existing social structure."[3]

The ritual was intended to function at two social levels; circumcision was primarily a symbol of the crossing of the boundary between two tribes so as to create a *new community* out of the two. Social change was about to occur, with Turner's "antistructure" replacing "structure," i.e., full friendly trading relations replacing preferred intra-tribal relations. The payment of "bride price" together with circumcision would have completed the establishment of a *new family unit* in the community. The "anti-structure" would have been Dinah's unplanned—experimental—assumption of adulthood.

The reader will recognize that this hypothetical analysis does not qualify as genuine anthropology, since we "observers" receive the "data" through the historian's lens instead of through observations in the field. Nevertheless, the data of the story appear to fit the theory. Missing, however, is recognition that the new relationship would belong to the covenant with God.

Dinah's Rebellion?

In a world of male dominance it is virtually impossible for a male to tell a woman's story adequately. The text of J (the Yahwist) and redactor JE, possibly influenced by Deuteronomic thinking, managed a factual report of events as they were remembered, but their view precluded telling what Dinah thought. Women writers, however, have been attracted to the story of Dinah. Anita Diamant created a fictional picture of *The Red Tent* where women managed their private sexual lives, preparing to bring the next generation into being. In her fictionalized setting Dinah was allowed to enter into a loving sexual relationship with young prince Shechem, and after that relationship was destroyed, to become a priestess, expert at guiding another generation in the art of living.

Ita Sheres titles *her* study *Dinah's Rebellion: A Biblical Parable for our Time*. She concludes with comments on the ironic parallel provided by Hebron and Shechem, "two clear geographical centers that serve also as symbolic centers in the present day confrontation between the Israelis and the Palestinians in the occupied territories. Both Palestinians and Jews attempt to show their strong links with these sites in order to carve for themselves a place in the heritage and a firm hold on the territories."[4] The parallel efforts to control the land are obvious.

However, the story offers more than a geo-political parallel when one explores Dinah's actions and motivation, as Sheres does. First she notes a double powerlessness suffered by women: sometimes they could not have children for natural reasons but often because of the protective shield created by the patriarchal society that surrounded them. Then, comparing Dinah with Eve, Sheres comments that the biblical

---

3. Alexander, *Victor Turner Revisited*, 14–15.
4. Sheres, *Dinah's Rebellion*, 116.

PART 2: Sex and Power Relationships in Some Israelite Stories

narrators treated the two women "as transgressors who made an effort to widen the realm of their experiences and in the process offended patriarchal values... Eve's story finally echoed the story of the Hebrew people, who abandoned the commands of their God and lost their Canaanite Eden. Dinah's tale evolved into a nationalistic parable of exclusion with the Hivites functioning as the Canaanite 'strangers' and enemies whom the redactor abhorred."[5]

Attempting to widen her experience as Jacob's only identified daughter, Dinah made the fatal mistake of "going out" to meet members of a neighboring family who were not recognized as kin. "Accordingly, Dinah's misfortune was transformed into a warning to women about the dangers, personal and familial, that lurk outside of the house."[6] Sheres stresses the view of the narrators that "the woman is excluded from participating in social functions outside of the home without the permission of her protective man because people outside of the home are described as dangerous and prone to vicious attacks. The woman is believed to be too weak—perhaps too unreliable—to handle peril."[7] Sheres argues that the narrators deliberately connected the story of Dinah with the story of Absalom's vengeance for the rape of his sister Tamar in 2 Samuel 13, and did so to remind their readers that women are vulnerable.

Was Dinah's behavior rebellion? "Dinah goes out to associate with the Hivites; like the woman in Eden, she is playing the game of inclusion, while the brothers' response is exclusion. In many ways, the woman's rebellion is a declaration against ignorance and manipulation by the powers that be, as well as an assertion against those who hold different opinions."[8]

The transgression was against the customs of patriarchal society; there is no reference to laws of God or to the command forbidding covenants between Israelites and Canaanites, though editors of the scriptures may have seen an anticipation of Torah/law in the story.

A declaration against ignorance may be seen in a positive light as legitimate curiosity about the "other." The explorers who arrived in the Americas with Christopher Columbus were amazed to discover that the inhabitants were people like themselves, not the weird beings imagined in legends. Very quickly the conquistadors "took wives for themselves of all that they chose" just as the sons of God were reported to have done in Genesis 6:2. In much of Latin America as a result of these unions a Mixtec population and religion developed, until recently without racial disharmony. More recently a small number of Israeli women have been meeting with Palestinians to learn of each other's customs and religious beliefs,[9] but almost no intermarriage has been reported.

---

5. Ibid., 16.
6. Ibid., 17.
7. Ibid., 46.
8. Ibid., 48.
9. See the website of the Interfaith Encounter Association chaired by Yehuda Stolov: http://interfaithencounter.wordpress.com/

The legendary story from fourteenth-century BCE Ugarit told of the marriage of King Keret to the lady Hurriya, daughter of King Pabel, which was accomplished through a formal covenantal bargaining between Keret's invading forces and Pabel's fortified city.

Like many narratives in the Hebrew Scriptures, the storyteller gives a detailed account of the plan in the words of El, and then repeats the details in the execution of the plan, writing in the typical parallelism of Hebrew and Canaanite verse. The story focuses on the feelings of Keret and on the dialogue between gods and humans in a way that is barely suggested in the bargaining between Shechem and Hamor on one side and Levi, Simeon and Jacob on the other. In the Ugaritic story no ritual of circumcision blocks the friendly relationship accomplished through the more benign rituals of festive meals. Since the "sons of Keret are even *as was stipulated in the vows*,"[10] it is evident that the peaceful outcome was a result of bargaining like the covenantal paradigm.

Sin?

So far in our retelling of the story we have not identified sinful *acts*. Dinah's going out was more unfortunate curiosity than rebellion. Shechem's sexual act was socially premature but not a sin. The specific bride price was unexpected and unusual but not treated as an abuse of Hivite good will. Only when the sons of Jacob used the opportunity to massacre male Hivites and pillage their stores do *we* think of sin, but neither Jacob nor the narrator of the story used the term.

Jacob's mild rebuke could be understood as a prophetic judgment on the deceitful and violent actions of his sons. Jacob and God were "not angry, but disappointed" as Ruth Bader Ginsburg described her feeling about some of the majority decisions of the Supreme Court against which she had dissented.[11] Am I right in thinking that God was silent, did not put a label on the killing, and let the sons of Jacob face whatever consequences followed their actions? We are not told of immediate specific consequences, so there may have been no deaths as a result of the fevers occasioned by the minor surgery on the Hivites or within Jacob's family as "wages" of a "sin."

Jacob and God, however, may have had a final word. In her study of the book of Numbers Mary Douglas reminds us that long after "Jacob's first three sons sinned . . . the leaders of the tribes descended from them have sinned again. Reuben seduced his father's concubine, was disinherited (Gen 49:4), and in Numbers his descendants joined Korah's revolt against Moses' leadership . . . and Jacob denounced Simeon and Levi together as brothers in cruelty, fierce in anger and treacherous conspiracy (Gen 49:5–7)."[12] As Jacob's prophetic poem in Genesis 49 foresaw, Judah would displace

---

10. Three forms of the legend, which may be based on a historical incident, were discovered in 1930 and 1931, and are translated by Ginsburg in Pritchard, *Ancient Near Eastern Texts Relating to the Old Testament*, 142–49.

11. Ginsburg expressed herself with these words when asked by Public Television's Nina Totenberg how she felt in writing her dissents to the Supreme Court's 5–4 decisions.

12. Douglas, *In the Wilderness* (1977), 204–7.

Part 2: Sex and Power Relationships in Some Israelite Stories

the three as political leader of the tribes, "your father's sons will bow down before you" (Gen. 49:8). Reuben sinned by defiling his father's bed, an act as much political as sexual. Simeon and Levi sinned by killing men *in anger*, also for political and economic motives, but as Douglas points out, "Vengeance for the honour of Israel was meritorious" and even commanded against the Midianites (Num 31:2). Having no other word to use, I have characterized the action of Dinah's brothers as a misstep, since the brothers could not carry forward the settlement of Israelite tribes in Canaan. Some may call it "sin," but in the patriarchal narratives the word sin occurs only in other contexts.

The term "sin" may have originated as an expression for failure to satisfy the expectation of another person, initially in a social relationship with another human before it was related to the will or expectation of God. If this tentative designation stands, then what the sons of Jacob did could be described as sin—against Shechem's people, against Jacob, and against the whole disrupted community. One could add "against God," and recognize that although God had not yet published rules for the behavior of the descendants of Abraham, except for the requirement of male circumcision, those descendants were aware that both God and the surrounding communities expected them to behave morally after performing a ritual atonement/"covering." However, God was even more silent than Jacob, sending no prophet to rebuke the sons. Better to see the evil in the actions of the sons as a vicious and stupid misstep, which set back Abraham's God-assigned project of settling his descendants between the Mediterranean coast and the Jordan river.

Jacob's rebuke was the word of a thoughtful elder who foresaw disastrous consequences. Perhaps reflecting on his youth with Esau and his business dealings with Laban, Jacob voiced his awareness of natural human retaliation for a perceived "wrong."

We can visualize the three stages of the episode as a social experiment in human relations: Dinah innocently visited a neighboring household. Shechem initiated a closer relationship by thoughtlessly stepping across the invisible boundary between two tribes. Dinah's brothers proposed the next step, offering to strengthen the tie between the two families. Why did that experiment blow up in the laboratory instead of ending with a firm bonding of the two groups? The narrator's word is "deceit," already applicable to Abram/Abraham and Isaac in their relations with the natives. But the Judeo-Christian tradition has preferred the more general term "sin" for such behavior.

The sin was in the way Jacob's sons made the building of the nation of Israel into a competition with the indigenous people for Hebrew domination instead of a friendly and peaceful assimilation through intermarriage and trading. Tribal acquisitiveness characterized the attitudes of both peoples, expressed in immediate group action by the sons of Jacob, but also in a restrained expectation of future wealth by the Hivites. No law required the sons of Jacob to commit themselves to close relations with the Hivites, but once they did so they erred in breaking faith with them.

The sexual aspects of the episode were neither inherently good nor evil, and could or should have been means to the creation of new people instead of means to conquest. Israel did grow and prosper, but it was at the cost of the good will and help of some native population groups, and her growth in prosperity and power was delayed until after 430 years spent in Egypt. Exodus 12:40 gives us the exilic priests' calculation of the period from the move of Jacob and his family to Egypt. Several of the sons of Jacob were involved in selling Joseph to slavery in Egypt. They wronged a brother within Jacob's family, while Levi and Simeon wronged their sister as well as hurting the Hivites.

Thinking only of the family's purity, Dinah's brothers broke faith with her, and we are not told of any child of hers. Naturally, not every mating produces a child, nor every seed becomes a tree, but because the seeds of life are many, populations grow and prosper in spite of setbacks.

9

A Childless Widow and a Lusty Patriarch

GENESIS 38 TELLS THE story of another Israelite woman caught between natural law and social pressures. Tamar became a significant part of biblical history as a result of the way she handled her plight. After Jacob had brought his extended family into the land promised to his grandfather Abraham, his son Judah became a patriarch in his own right. He had a son named Er, one of three sons of Bathshua, the daughter of a Canaanite. Er married Tamar, but for some unnamed wickedness "in the sight of the Lord" YHWH "took his life." Judah decreed that the second son Onan should take Tamar in accordance with the custom that a widow's brother-in-law should "raise up seed" in her husband's place. But "whenever he slept with his brother's wife, he spilled his seed on the ground so as not to raise up issue for his brother." Whatever land belonged to Er's inheritance should have passed to Tamar's son and could not be joined to Onan's property. What he did was "wicked in the Lord's sight, and the Lord took *his* life" (Gen 38:9–10).

Since a third son Shelah was too young for marriage and the responsibility to provide an heir to Er's property, Judah sent Tamar back to her father's house, where she waited patiently for a few years, long enough for Shelah to grow to manhood. Judah forgot about Tamar. We may note that when missionaries first came in contact with the tribal culture of Cameroon "a barren woman was regularly disposed of by divorce or abandoned to a life of prostitution."[1]

Tamar could live with her kindred but she did not forget, and was grieved at her inability to fulfill her role as a mother in Israel. After all, she had accepted the decision that bound her to Judah's family, and had done her duty as wife to two of the sons of her new family. God had not blessed her with a child for Er, and Onan had denied her the possibility of a child. Then Judah had treated her the way automobile buyers would treat a car that turned out to be a lemon. She was sent home, and must have thought that Judah's family considered her cursed or diseased or a hopeless failure. In fact she had become an economic liability to Judah and his sons, one of whom would have to provide her food and shelter for the rest of her life. It looked as if her parents or her

---

1. Anderson, *Incidents and Recollections of Missionary Service 1926–1965*, 74.

brothers would have to support her as she became an "old maid" aunt, the childless woman in a society that expected children and grandchildren from every woman.

A Bold Deception

One day somebody told Tamar that Judah had gone to Timnath for sheep-shearing, and she "veiled her face, perfumed herself" as a prostitute and sat where Judah was to pass. Prostitutes had a place in Israelite society just as they have a place in western society today. Veiled because they needed to be anonymous, perfumed because a woman would not otherwise attract attention. Independent of normal family connections, women could support themselves principally by meeting the demands of men who were not sexually satisfied for one reason or another.

Lori Rowlett, in a paper entitled "Inclusion, Exclusion and Marginality in the Book of Joshua," has called attention to the existence of independent women in Israel. She comments, "Although Rahab is a woman, she is described as a head of household in patriarchal language, almost as though she were a man." Tamar may have set up a temporary tent-brothel complete with the fragrance of perfume to lure Judah into fathering a child. Without an unattached woman's need for a "profession," the existence of harlots in a community of families is difficult to explain.[2]

Tamar took advantage of the recent death of Judah's wife, knowing that widowers might be expected to visit a prostitute after their days of mourning were over (Gen 38:12). She decided to entice him to an "affair" on his way home from the business of collecting the season's wool. As we recall from the story of Samson, Timnath was on the Philistine border of Judean or Danite lands, so perhaps Judah "needed" an overnight stop in a "motel" on the way home.

The NRSV has Judah asking his friend to find the "temple prostitute" (literally the feminine for "holy person") when he sent the kid as payment whereas by the roadside he had noticed her as a common prostitute. Evidently an unattached woman could become a part of a local shrine's "family," sharing her fees with the priest's family and thus finding shelter. Before Israel had a temple, some landless men and women evidently attached themselves to local shrines and provided sexual intercourse as sympathetic magic to promote other forms of fertility. The physical pleasure of the ritual could be justified as needed to ensure the next year's products of field or flock. Today a visit to a prostitute is rarely seen as therapy for a failed sexual relationship.

Susan Ackerman has discussed the widow, the prostitute and the divorced women of the Bible, including Rahab and Delilah. She comments: "As the story goes . . . Tamar does not linger to receive her fee; instead, once pregnant, she trades her prostitute's veil for her widow's garb and, simultaneously, from the story's perspective discards a prostitute's autonomy to reassume the encumbrances placed upon her as a levirate widow."[3] Judah pledged future payment for her services with his seal and cord, in effect giving her his credit card for the customary fee, which was probably

---

2. Chalcraft, *Social-Scientific Old Testament Criticism*, 379.
3. Ackerman, *Warrior, Dancer, Seductress, Queen: Women in Judges and Biblical Israel*, 229.

the calf that Samson would bring to his Philistine wife or to any of the prostitutes he visited. These transactions were more business than sex, just as they are today. There were evidently no tender feelings between the couples or concern for the welfare of the possible offspring. The prostitute might become a single mother, and her child a man without proper family connections like Jephthah, who is described in Judges 11:1–2 as "the son of a prostitute, a mighty warrior" and whose half brothers drove him away, saying, "You shall not inherit anything in our father's house, for you are the son of another woman."

Men who visited prostitutes had the minutes or hours of pleasure that men crave without incurring the long-term responsibility for the care of wives and children. Masculine honor, however, required an exchange of something of value in every transaction even if the actual values were highly disproportionate. Earlier, in taking Tamar as wife for his sons, Judah had implicitly promised that the family would provide her support, food, and housing for which she would bear his grandchildren. But at the time of the first son's wedding he or his family had only provided a bride price, customarily live cattle, but not a documentable pledge. In giving Tamar the equivalent of a blank check for her service as prostitute Judah paid more than he expected for his moment of relaxation and pleasure.

When word came that she was pregnant and she was brought before the community elders for judgment, Tamar announced that the father of her child was the owner of the seal and cord. Judah accepted responsibility saying "She is more in the right than I am, because I did not give her to my son Shelah" (Gen 38:26). The storyteller lets us imagine Judah's embarrassment, not that he had visited a prostitute, but that he had failed to do the right thing with his third son and his daughter-in-law. Genesis does not say that what either of them did was sinful.

Situation Ethics!

This story in the Yahwist's history may be treated as a case study in situation ethics, where no clear right or wrong is evident to the participants in a conflict situation.

Popularized in the United States by Joseph F. Fletcher,[4] the term appears to have originated with *The Christian New Morality: a Biblical Study of Situation Ethics* by O. Sydney Barr. Fletcher begins his book by rejecting the two extreme approaches to the making of moral judgments or decisions, the legalistic and the antinomian. His "situationist enters into every decision-making situation fully armed with the ethical maxims of his community and its heritage, and he treats them with respect as illuminators of his problems. Just the same he is prepared in any situation to compromise them or set them aside *in the situation* if love seems better served by doing so."[5] Thus a mature adult views situations thoughtfully and is prepared to act responsibly.

In the end the wrong was identified not with Tamar's deception or Judah's visit to a prostitute but with his failure to follow the established custom of the levirate marriage,

---

4. *Situation Ethics: the New Morality* (Westminster, 1966 and 1997).
5. Fletcher, *Situation Ethics*, 26.

which provided a widow with the support of a husband and the future support of a son or daughter. The action of Tamar was, according to the Yahwist's treatment, more pleasing to the community—and to YHWH—than Judah's behavior, because it re-established justice. In this story the narrator ascribes the deaths of the two older sons to YHWH's action, but he does not explain God's action in the death of Er. On the other hand an ancient Israelite would have believed that Onan did wrong in withholding his seed from Tamar. Since YHWH had commanded people to multiply and gave them the socio-biological incentive to procreate, Onan's act could have been considered sinful. It was Tamar's right *and* duty to bear sons into the family of her husband.

In retrospect we might describe what Tamar did as an acted prayer. By her daring act she succeeded in forcing Judah to right the wrong done to her and thus she fulfilled the cultural expectation that she should bear children. Patriarch Judah had failed to use his authority for justice, but YHWH intervened as judge on behalf of Judah's wronged daughter-in-law. The twins born to Tamar were a double blessing from YHWH.

This story focuses on the covenantal relationships that exist within a family, in this case between a patriarch and his daughter-in-law. Judah was clearly derelict when he failed to send for Tamar after Shelah reached adulthood. In a day when every male child counted, either as a worker or as the heir to a part of the family's land, every woman should have had the privilege of bearing children. Tamar had a "right" to bear children to the third son of Judah. Her father or brothers could have forced the issue with Judah. Instead, Tamar took a dramatic action that made her appear to have violated the moral code of the community, the unwritten personal morality of subjection to the man who headed her family. When her pregnancy was evident, and it appeared that she had played the whore, Judah had to admit that it was he who had violated the family's code of right and wrong. The family felt that someone should be punished: God had removed Er and Onan. What should the patriarchal community do about Tamar? Execute her or shame Judah? When Judah accepted responsibility for Tamar's pregnancy, the community was satisfied, and Judah bore his public shame.

The birth of Perez and Zerah provided divine approval, "blessing," to complement the community's approval of Tamar's action. Perez was an ancestor of David, and through this son Tamar has a place in the genealogy of Jesus in Luke's gospel. Almost immediately it was evident that YHWH approved.

The stories of Dinah and Tamar have more significance than first appears. Because Tamar's twins would belong in David's lineage, they would have more value in Israel than any child of Dinah and Shechem. At the time the community recognized a tribal value in the seed of Judah, which should have been planted in Tamar's womb by Shelah after his two brothers had failed to impregnate her. The connection of Tamar with King David, significant for the Judean kingdom, is not the only value of the story for us. Whatever the actual realities in the lives of the legendary patriarchs, we see a breach of human covenantal relationships and its repair in Tamar's story.

The story of Dinah on the other hand concerned a situation *between* tribal families not yet in covenantal relationship, while the story of Tamar was an affair *within* a family that recognized covenantal values. Each case called for the fulfillment of a commitment, spoken or unspoken, a commitment often characterized by the Hebrew word *hesed*. The breach of covenantal relationship brought adverse social rather than legal consequences, and in these stories was not explicitly related to the covenant with YHWH. The sons of Jacob could not escape hostile suspicion from their neighbors after the massacre at Shechem, and Judah must surely have suffered public disgrace, which persists to the present day in the minds of readers. One additional sexual breach of relationship (and later law) within the family of Jacob is mentioned in Genesis 35:22: "While Israel was living in that district [Migdal-eder] Reuben went and lay with his father's concubine Bilhah, and Israel came to hear of it."

These incidents are set in a time before the giving of the law on Sinai/Horeb, so the only "laws" that were broken were the bonds of faithfulness and good relationship between people. In the absence of legislation given from Sinai/Horeb the actions are not called "sins" by the writers of Genesis. But that cannot mean that "laws of God," similar to laws of nature, did not operate in the patriarchal age.

My thesis is that while the men and women obeyed the "natural" law of sexual reproduction, they were often guilty of violating the social customs and values of the communities of which they were a part. How can we think of customs as divine law? To what extent should we consider these socio-religious customs to be permanent aspects of the created world? In Judah's day the men of the community gathered at the "gate," in a public space, to decide what to do about Tamar's pregnancy, and left the question of divine approval to the evidence that would come from Tamar's womb. No "law of God" was established, but God and we agree that the community treated the unexpected twins with ethical responsibility. In chapter 19 I will suggest that the mind of God is distributed in the dialogues of people who deal responsibly with human social problems.

A Judgment from God

The biblical perspective on law begins with Moses shortly after the exodus and extends to the end of Moses' life in the last chapter of Deuteronomy. Although all the laws of the Pentateuch are ascribed to YHWH's communication with Moses in the region of Horeb/Sinai, we can see a progression from the simpler family customs that the Israelites shared with their Canaanite neighbors in the Covenant Code (Exod 22:13–30) to the reminders in the Deuteronomic Code to be YHWH's "holy people"[6] and finally to the strict punishment of being "cut off from their people" of the Holiness Code in Leviticus 18:29. Pragmatically, laws were formulated to restore justice in problem situations. However, there appears to have been an underlying feeling among people that certain situations were not "right," among them pregnancy of a widow nominally reattached to her father's household.

The biblical laws against incest in Leviticus 18 were not written until the sixth or fifth century BCE. They include a specific prohibition of Judah's unwitting act in a

---

6. Deuteronomy 22:13–30.

long list of kin whose nakedness should not be uncovered: "You shall not uncover the nakedness of your daughter-in-law: she is your son's wife; you shall not uncover her nakedness." (vs. 15) The Covenant Code did not call for the execution of adulterers, but lists a series of three death penalties in Exodus 22, only one of which (vs.19) is concerned with sexual relations with an animal.

In the spirit of Joshua's mission to drive out iniquitous Canaanites, Deuteronomy 22:22 includes a broad puritanical rule: "If a man is caught lying with the wife of another man, both of them shall die, the man who lay with the woman as well as the woman. "The stated reason for the law is simply, "So you shall purge the evil from your midst."

Although the human writer is ostensibly Moses, the commands come from God: "The Lord spoke to Moses, saying: 'Speak to the people of Israel and say to them: I am the Lord your God. You shall not do as they do in the land of Egypt, where you lived, and you shall not do as they do in the land of Canaan, to which I am bringing you. You shall not follow their statutes. My ordinances you shall observe and my statutes you shall keep . . . by doing so one shall live'" (Lev 18:1–4).

This tacit recognition that customs belong to a common store of human values expressed in the laws of nations, however inadequately expressed, may help us understand the intent of the editors of the biblical books. None of the laws of Leviticus appear to have been in written form among the patriarchal families of Genesis or among YHWH's tribes during the period of the Judges.

Genesis 19:30–38 reports that after the destruction of Sodom, Lot settled "in the hills" and lived in a cave with his two daughters, who became restless since "no man on earth" would "come in to us after the manner of all the world" (vs. 31). They therefore gave their father wine to make him drunk and slept with him with the result that each bore a son who became the ancestors of the Moabites and the Ammonites. Although Israelites looked down on these other peoples, the narrator recognizes the situation and does not characterize their acts as sinful.

A man could kill his wife and her paramour with impunity, just as he would have avenged the murder of a relative. But the family in which Tamar lived brought her to confront the community, perhaps suspecting that the father of her child was one of the elders who were accustomed to deciding disputes. Were Judah and Tamar threatened with stoning? Judah had suggested that she should be burned. It did not turn out either way.

The rituals in Numbers 5 include an ancient procedure for a woman whose husband believes but cannot prove that she has been unfaithful.[7] In the case of Tamar, however, there was no need to discover who was guilty of impregnating her; she had the goods. The question for the elders was what judgment they should make. Seeing that Tamar was pregnant, and hearing Judah's admission of guilt, the community evidently accepted the pregnancy as God's will to maintain the family's place on the land, accomplished through faulty, irregular means. A social rule had been broken; a custom

---

7. Numbers 5:5–31.

had been ignored; but good could come out of the biological situation. The concept of "sin" did not enter the discussion. Acting on behalf of justice and community well being the people favored letting the pregnancy continue. Thus the community exercised its judicial authority, not to take several lives—Judah's, Tamar's, and the expected child's—but to preserve them all.

Intercourse as Covenant Love in Action

In Tamar's day Jacob's descendants had not yet clearly identified themselves as Israel or defined laws of God, but in the concept of *covenant* they may have seen a social pattern established by God in the creation of human beings. The English word "intercourse" can be used in the two senses that express the biological and the social aspects of Tamar's situation. An act of sexual intercourse between father and daughter-in-law had led to a problem pregnancy and an anticipated birth. Now in its sense of "communication between people" the community representatives came together to discuss what should be done with the two adults.

Accepting the situation as the operation of biological reality, the community agreed to extend parental care for the unexpected child, in effect declaring that Tamar's child would be welcomed as legitimate. Neither she nor Judah would be treated as adulterers, since execution by stoning would have meant killing the unborn child. Why was there apparently no concern for the unborn child in other cases of presumed adultery? In any case, for Christians the motivation for decision-making in every situation should be loving care for every member of the widest circle of people involved.

As it turned out Tamar had twins, whom she named Perez and Zerah. In the delivery Perez was marked as the elder by a crimson thread when his hand appeared before his brother was born, and his seniority was remembered in the genealogy of David found at the end of the book of Ruth.

The family value of covenant love parallels and trumps the biological law of procreation. A man and woman agree—"intercourse" either silent or verbal—to a sexual act the woman carries in her body the physical consequence of that intercourse while the man *ideally* supports her with food, shelter, and the comfort of his presence not simply during her pregnancy but at least until the child reaches maturity. Whether the term "covenant" is used or not, the loving nurture of the child is anticipated as a part of the transaction.

Since the oversight of God was often invoked in the making of covenants, Judah's fault could have been considered a sin in the sight of God, but the storyteller was not ready to describe it that way. The relationships between a patriarch and the members of his extended family may not yet have been thought of in terms of formal covenant making, so the necessary commitment and the expectation of God's blessing or fear of being cursed were *not defined* in the situation. However, in telling the story the historian saw that Judah had wronged his daughter-in-law, and that the community acted—for God—to right that wrong.

We can analyze the nature of that wrong by looking at the socio-economic context of the story. Wealth and the gaining and distributing of it was in the hands of heads of families. Having accepted Tamar as a member of his extended family, Judah was responsible for providing for her, in exchange for her mothering of his grandchildren. She had not produced a child, but his family's responsibility had not ended. When Judah sent her back to her family and turned to his sheep shearing and other affairs, he compounded the "sin" initiated by his son Onan. That sin was the breach of the loosely defined commitment between Judah's family and the young woman. The sin could be "forgiven" when the commitment to support Tamar and her children was re-established.

The story of Tamar's pregnancy comes as close as any biblical story to testing the question of the common human ban on incest. Modern ethicists recognize that although closely related individuals can produce offspring, it is not a good idea for the relationship to be too close because of the possibility of multiplying defective genes. In addition there appears to be a built-in sibling inhibition that inclines an adolescent to look outside the family for a sexual partner. The social experience of life in a family can be seen as establishing a "rule" or meme which can be understood as either natural, cultural, or divinely decreed. E. O Wilson would treat it as a custom that emerged from the co-evolutionary development of natural and cultural processes.

To modern minds it may seem strange that a patriarch's visit to a prostitute was mentioned so casually while a protected family member's unexpected pregnancy was cause for community judgment. But the incident warns us to attend to every aspect of any questionable situation and do our evaluations in terms of social contexts that are not uniformly the same in different settings. It seems that words from God are not the same everywhere.

The priestly legislation of Leviticus 18 quotes God directly, detailing a list of family members a man may not approach sexually, including "your daughter-in-law; she is your son's wife." In verse 3 these ordinances are distinguished from the "statutes" of Egypt and Canaan, which the exilic priests evidently believed permitted incestuous relationships. For the reconstituted post-exilic Israel the rules were strict, a top-down set of dicta from YHWH, spoken to Moses. Though Genesis 38 does not mention the word "sin," Judeans returning after the exile believed that the Mosaic dicta defined sinful relationships. In Leviticus the sin appears to be a composite of a defined "uncleanness" and an unstated moral abuse of persons who live in the covenantal relationships of family. In Genesis only the latter are evident. When the community considered Tamar's situation, the people decided that she had been "more right" than Judah, and he assumed responsibility. God appeared to confirm that judgment when good consequences followed. The historians and most readers of the story have agreed.

10

Samson's Amorous Adventures

AFTER JUDAH'S AFFAIR WITH Tamar two other Israelite leaders indulged in amorous adventures with consequences that affected the development of God's people. Although each contributed publicly to the progress from tribal life to the kingdom that history remembers, we cannot praise either man for his relationships with women. Samson began life as a more or less conventional Israelite, a member of the tribe of Dan, and in spite of his personal life he was listed as one of the judges who provided leadership between Israel's entry into Canaan and the establishment of the monarchy under Saul. David was a Judean, the youngest of seven brothers, who rose finally to kingship over the twelve Israelite tribes. He linked his life with a series of wives whom he attracted to himself during a forty-year public life. Since the Mosaic watershed between custom and law had presumably been crossed as migrating Hebrews became settled Israelites, we may properly ask how well our two heroes obeyed the newly revealed laws. What sins, if any, did they commit? Or better, how well did they perform their covenantal obligations? First, Samson's adventures.

I

Samson was born to a pious woman and a slightly skeptical father in the low hills that had been apportioned to Dan (Josh 19:40–48), and were later disputed by the Philistines. Manoah's wife had been visited by a man "who was like an angel of God." He told her that she would have a son with a special destiny, who was forbidden to drink wine or to cut his hair. These were the marks of individuals being prepared to serve as Nazirites. The young Samuel would be similarly trained from infancy for special service to God, though the nature of that calling would become apparent only as the youth approached maturity. Samuel would discover his ministry as "priest;" Samson as "judge." The ambiguity of Samson's life is evident from his name, which honored and identified him with the powerful sun god Shamash, not otherwise recognized in Israelite records.

As the young Samson matured he eyed the young women of the region instead of choosing one from his tribe or a nearby Israelite tribe. He told his father that he wanted to marry a certain Philistine girl. "Is there not a woman among your kin, or [at least] among all our people, that you must go to take a wife from the uncircumcised Philistines?" his parents asked (Judg 14:3). Clearly the anticipated calling would not be to the priesthood.

No, he liked her looks, so his parents went down the hilly road to Timnath and made arrangements with the girl's parents for the marriage. According to the custom of both families, the groom made a feast, and thirty young men of Timnath came out to celebrate. It was also customary for the young men to engage in a contest of wits, and Samson proposed a poetic riddle that could be answered only by a matching couplet during the seven days of feasting and lovemaking. Samson bet his Philistine friends an outer garment each that they could not answer correctly, and each agreed to give him a "new suit" if they failed. This was his riddle:

Out of the eater came
something to eat.
Out of the strong came
something sweet.

On the fourth day of the celebration the bride's friends despaired and asked her to coax the answer out of Samson. By the seventh day she had worn Samson down with her tears, and he gave her the answer:

What is sweeter than honey?
What is stronger than a lion?
(Judg 14:14, 18)

The reader already knows that on his way between Zorah and Timnath Samson had stopped to see and refresh himself with a honeycomb that bees had built in the carcass of a dead lion. Presumably the whole community knew of it, but only Samson saw it as an appropriate riddle for the wedding feast. Both couplets have been understood as referring to sexual love with its linking of virility and tenderness. One could speculate on the allusive features of male sexuality and virility that could have occurred to Philistine and Danite minds when the riddle was solved.

When the merrymaking was over, Samson went down to Ashkelon, killed thirty men, took their clothes to pay his debt, and returned to the home of his parents, leaving his bride to be given by her father to the [Philistine] "best man." When he returned with a kid for his wife some time later, her father said "I was sure you had rejected her; so I gave her to your companion. Is not her young sister prettier than she? Why not take her instead?

But the offer only increased Samson's anger and he caught foxes, tied lighted torches to pairs of them, tail to tail, and loosed them into the Philistine fields of grain. Of course that terrorist act ended Samson's marriage and any friendly relations between the two communities.

PART 2: Sex and Power Relationships in Some Israelite Stories

II

Samson's virility could not be satisfied with freeing himself from the ropes his countrymen used to bind him at the request of the Philistines, so he visited a prostitute in Gaza. This was another Philistine city, and the people of Gaza lay in wait at its gates thinking they had him trapped. But Samson rose at midnight, strode to the doors that protected the city and walked off with everything movable, doors, posts and bar before the Philistines could touch him. The prostitute in this story was an ordinary one, not a temple prostitute. Her business was simply to satisfy the sexual demands of men, and Samson obviously cared even less for her than for his wife or her sister. We note the casual way our storyteller introduces a prostitute into the personal life of a biblical hero.

At this point in the narrative the reader begins to see that more than a casual contest for personal superiority between individuals is going on. Philistines saw Samson as the potential leader of a small war against their extended settlements. Samson's countrymen were not yet involved in his contests, but the next generation of Israelites would retell his feats of strength and, with some exaggeration, make him into a legendary hero in the contest between an Israelite tribe and the Philistine cities.

III

The most famous of Samson's women and the only one named in the Bible was Delilah. She lived across the border from his home somewhere in the valley of Sorek near Timnath. Not a common prostitute, she was evidently an independent woman who could entertain a male friend without asking permission from parents or brothers. Samson apparently fell in love with her, and she seemed to reciprocate. Her initial motives are not clear, but it is likely that she welcomed his attentions the way some women students admire college football heroes. Naturally, the Philistine political leaders seized the opportunity, and schemed to capture Samson. "Coax him," they told her, "and find out what makes his strength so great, and how we may overpower him, so that we may bind him in order to subdue him, and we will each give you eleven hundred pieces of silver" (Judges 16:5).

Delilah may not have cared where Samson's strength came from, but the possibility of eleven hundred pieces of silver from each of the five lords of the Philistines appealed to her business sense, so she wheedled him and he gave her false leads until he told her that his uncut hair was his secret. He was not only a strong man, but he was also a Nazirite, a man dedicated by vow to serve his God, not as a priest, but in some special way. Samson thus had not only physical strength but also the power supplied by a god to support his terrorist attacks against the Philistines.

A Contest on Several Levels

The outcome of the story is familiar and does not need to delay us here. Pulling down the pillars of the dining hall associated with the temple of Dagon in Gaza and killing a large number of Philistines appears to have been a success in the opening stages of conflict over the border territory between Philistines and Israelites. Like the other harassments Samson inflicted on the Philistine countryside, it could be scored as preparation for a war that would reach a stalemate during the reign of David.

It appears that Samson started the war. Or, from the narrator's point of view, YHWH was behind Samson's harassments. The story's editor included an ambiguous comment when Samson asked his parents to arrange his marriage that "*he* was seeking a pretext to act against the Philistines." Who was the "he"? Did Samson actually intend to harass the Philistines and provoke them with violence when he married his wife? Or was it YHWH who needed a pretext to provoke conflict and end the expansion of Philistine territory? Either way the Deuteronomic editor who preserved the story believed that YHWH intended Israel to destroy the Philistines or at least slow their expansion. The story does not indicate that Samson shared the desire to cripple the Philistine government or its cities. His vendetta was a personal affair, but the reader can now see how it became a contest between rival villages and also at a third level the power struggle between Philistines and Israelites.

At first it was personal, the male "taking" the female, but it had quickly become a contest of wits between the friends of the bride and the lone groom, and extended into several Philistine cities as Samson secured the garments to pay his debt.

Interesting questions come to mind: what if Samson had stayed with the wife he had chosen and established a normal family instead of disappearing to kill people for their garments? Suppose he had not given his wife the solution to the riddle. Suppose his Philistine buddies had accepted their defeat and each had given Samson a garment as a wedding present, good-naturedly joining in the fun and accepting Samson [with fifteen minutes of fame] as a hero in a novel mixed community, Philistines and Israelites together, like the aborted Hivite-Hebrew community at Shechem. Or suppose he had not risked everything on the outrageous gamble that he would have to find thirty garments to pay his debt?

What If?

The contest between Philistine and Israelite, between YHWH and Dagon, might well have been settled without the violence that actually developed. Would Dagon's uncircumcised followers have dominated the region? Or would the circumcision of a son of a popular Samson have led other Timnites to become followers of YHWH? It would have been Samson's prerogative to insist on circumcision for a son, but this story is not concerned with that religious ritual. Which faith would have shaped the community after that day? How many men in a mixed community would have chosen to worship YHWH over Dagon? Or could the people have thought of Dagon and YHWH as one God with two names? Not likely. Dagon was represented by an image, and YHWH forbade his followers to make images. But what about Israelites who made images and worshipped Baals through them? What features of the two religions would have determined the final solution to the dilemma? What qualities of YHWH might have appealed to Philistine men, or would Israelites have been seduced to follow another less exacting god? How can we be sure that Samson was doing what the Creator in-

PART 2: Sex and Power Relationships in Some Israelite Stories

tended? Would the religion of YHWH have survived unchanged? In sum, what if, through Samson's marriage some Philistines and Israelites had continued the potentially friendly relationship?

Three interwoven factors determined the story's development. Each can be characterized by adjectives, some with *-al* words. The first is *economic*. Samson's marriage was more economic than sexual, although initially the sexu*al* was uppermost in everyone's thinking. He or his family was obligated to provide a "gift" in exchange for the gift of the Philistine bride. Samson wagered a considerable bet on the solution of his riddle. As one Israelite matching wits with thirty Philistines, however, he was in a politic*al* minority, and was driven to resort to physic*al* violence to pay his debt. The riddle was a game in small-scale power politics with the overtones of sexu*al* virility providing entertainment.

The fact that Samson did not take his bride to a home in Israel suggests that he did not own a residence. Does this mean that his father had not given him a share of the family's wealth? Or did his dedication to the Nazirite vow preclude owning land, just as Levites received no land among the tribes of Israel?

A second factor had to do with the rite of circumcision as the practical expression of *tribal* and religious identity. Today a man's circumcision is a private matter, but in early Israel where men urinated against any convenient wall, an Israelite's circumcision was a public testimony to his faith in YHWH and to his identity as a descendant of Abraham, Isaac, and Jacob. Philistines were clearly different. Wives and daughters were not marked, but were considered the property of their fathers or husbands and of no political consequence. Samson's unnamed wife was passed from her uncircumcised father to circumcised Samson, and then back again to another Philistine. In the exchanges her identity probably changed twice, from Philistine to Israelite and back again.

We can say almost nothing about the theologic*al* factor in this story beyond the identification of two deities, YHWH, God of Israel, and Dagon, God of the Philistines. What these names meant to the participants is obscured by the emphasis on the power struggle between them. The contest for Israelite dominance over Philistines begins with little more than the concept of YHWH's superior power to kill Israel's enemies. It would be tested in the loss of the captured ark and its return to Israel at the end of Eli's priesthood, also in David's securing Philistine foreskins as his bride price for Saul's daughter, which is anticipated in Samson's securing outer garments for his Philistine friends.

The concept of YHWH as God for a settled agricultur*al* community was exceedingly thin and undeveloped in this period. Dagon was a grain deity, probably a Baal (Lord) of the fields tilled by the Canaanite natives recently subjected to Philistine seagoing invaders from the Indo-European north. Indo-European Hittites had invaded the Semitic world by land, and among them the Philistines had come by boat or along the coast. Ethnic Philistine invaders were apparently relatively few in numbers, and although they came to political power they did not succeed in imposing an Indo-European language on the native Semites in the coastal territory. YHWH was a desert deity, a god whose followers tended sheep and goats. It is evident that both deities were considered to be leaders of their people in the contest for possession of rich agricultural land, but the herders needed what the farmers produced and the farmers wanted the meat of the flocks.

Finally, we observe the relative political strengths of the two populations. Philistines and Israelites were both governed by chieftains supported by councils of elders during the period. Israelite tribes were loosely confederate, led by "judges." Some of the tribes came to the aid of threatened brothers when they were called, but in Samson's time the other Israelite tribes failed to support him. The five Philistine cities appear to have been a little more advanced politically than the Israelite tribes, and were ruled by "lords." The word for "lord," (Hebrew *seren*), is a loan word related to Greek "tyrant," and along with the name Philistine is our clue to the Indo-European origin of the chiefs of the five cities which controlled the coastal area west of Dan and Judea.

When the Philistines "came up and encamped in Judah, and made a raid on Lehi, the men of Judah said 'Why have you come up against us?'" When the Philistines asked the Judeans to bind Samson and surrender him, they did so meekly, and Samson saved himself by tearing the ropes apart "like flax" and used the jawbone of an ass to "kill a thousand men." (Judg 15:9–17) The historian explains the secret of Samson's great strength with the expression "the spirit of YHWH rushed upon Samson." The augmenting of Samson's strength occurred three times before he told Delilah of his Nazirite vow.

Neither side was ready for war, but the Philistines had five fortified cities with gates closed at night, while the Danites and Judeans in the area lived in villages without walls. Political power could not protect Philistine grain fields from Samson's terrorist tactic of tying foxes' tails together with firebrands. In the end the Philistines found his weakness in the secret of his strength. When he told Delilah that he was a Nazirite, committed to special service for YHWH and pledged never to cut his hair, no Israelite could or would save this hero from capture, humiliation and death.

Where were the traditions of the Exodus and the giving of the law? What religious rituals other than circumcision and the Nazirite vow did Samson and his parents observe?

What had happened to the idea of human covenanting watched over by the Creator? Had Manoah and his wife allowed their sacrifices to become dull routines with little meaning, except when the "man/angel of God" visited with word about the expected son? Was Samson ready to bring his Philistine women to Israelite altars for sacrifices three times a year? The only significant religious ritual in the region was a community feast dedicated to a god, but at the end of the story the feast was held in a building dedicated to Dagon, and Samson's role in it was to amuse his captors.

PART 2: Sex and Power Relationships in Some Israelite Stories

Samson's Failure

In retrospect one can imagine a story different from the biblical account. Either of two scenarios could have built a mixed culture—the kind forbidden to the Israelites by Moses and Joshua. In one scenario (very oversimplified), ordinary people would have made personal choices to follow either YHWH or Dagon, families journeying a few miles to the separate altars of competing "churches." This was apparently the situation when neighboring Philistines traveled to Gaza to worship Dagon while Israelites journeyed a longer distance to Shiloh. Neither "god" would have won the worship of all the people, but the mixed culture might have prospered with exchanges of grain for meat.

In the other scenario, one altar and one priest might have served a mixed community with people worshipping a "Baal" known either as Dagon or YHWH. But YHWH's angel/messenger who visited Samson's parents—probably more prophet or seer than priest—provoked conflict between the two peoples. When both Dagon and YHWH claimed the title Baal, "Lord," irreconcilable religious denominations would develop. The circumcised would belong to YHWH's "church"; the uncircumcised, to Dagon. Samson was outnumbered, and he was no missionary. He relied on his wits and his strength to win the contest with the Philistines, but there was no love in his behavior. It may have been YHWH's way, but was it God's? Did Samson sin by harassing his in-laws and their neighbors? Without a will to live peaceably together, Philistines and Israelites would attempt to eliminate each other from the fertile coastal plain.

Traditionally believers have not condemned Samson or his Philistine adversaries, since neither had any clear guidance toward a better way to manage Israel's settlement at the edge of Philistine territory. But Samson *was* guilty of forsaking his wife after he found the thirty changes of clothing for his friends. His wife's father can also be considered guilty of impatience since he did not trust Samson to return. Whether Samson's wife was pregnant and needed a man to support her is not part of the biblical account. Neither Samson's or his father-in-law's actions were considered "sins" by the other participants or by the editor. However, we can see that there could have been a more excellent way if all participants had fulfilled their covenantal obligations and done *hesed*.

In fact, the ancient Hebrews, particularly Jacob, and their neighbors had discovered the healing power of covenant making when tensions leading to violence erupted between communities, and between emerging families like Jacob's, while tribal confederations experimented with enlarging their territories. What I think of as the standard family model is a good example of solving problems by covenanting, which probably anticipated the integrating of the Israelite confederation of tribes, as well as the Philistine confederation of cities.

One reads in Genesis 14 that a Mesopotamian coalition of kingdoms made war with a coalition of Canaanite kingdoms, each probably bound together through covenanting. Since Abram's nephew Lot had been captured in that instance, the biblical patriarch called on his covenanted allies to join him in rescuing Lot. The covenantal concept was not an Israelite invention.

The sons of Jacob failed to follow through with their covenant with the Hivites in the Dinah affair. Samson's parents and his Philistine father-in-law negotiated a marriage agreement, but Samson did not follow through with what might have led to an integrated community on the border between Philistines and Danites.

It was not until the post-exilic period that a mixed marriage such as Samson's was formally and legally condemned, though Rebekah was not happy with Esau's Hittite wives. Only in the story of Ruth is a cross-cultural marriage treated as an opportunity for absorbing the foreign woman into Israel. Neither Samson, his women, nor the historian saw the possibilities his attraction to Philistine women presented. Likewise American culture, particularly in the southern United States, was slow to see the possibilities offered by sexual attraction between members of our racial and religiously mixed society.

Israelis and Palestinians living in close proximity today have also been blind to the possibilities of peaceful covenanting with regard to pieces of land, and appear to be repeating the failure of Samson. In the United States, however, stars of the entertainment world and heroes of the sports world have led the way in successful mixed marriages as Samson did not. And in spite of marriages of service personnel with Japanese and Vietnamese women we do not value that possible enrichment of our culture. Instead, by social rejection of the marriages that do occur, we have delayed the creation of a multicolored united world with greatly enriched culture.

The saddest note is the current bitter conflict between Israel and Palestinians, who are possibly as close genetically as any two peoples in the world. Political and religious differences, which I believe are memes created by leaders and not by God, enforce a physical separation that prevents the operation of natural attraction between neighbors. There are, however, a few hopeful signs in the region. An Israeli film crew has produced a film, *The Olive Harvest*, with a cast of Palestinians. National Public Radio reported that cast and film crewmembers fell "in and out of love" with each other. The film written by Hanna Elias was submitted for an Academy Award in 2005.

Is there something sinful in human cultures? Is it time to evaluate the concept of structural sin? Capitalizing on the attraction between the sexes, but under no social compulsion for association across social and religious dividing lines, society's web of good relationships *could* be tightly woven into a beautiful fabric—one world truly united "under God with liberty and justice for all."

11

Hannah and the Sons of Eli

Two incidents surrounding the call of Samuel epitomize the contrast between sexual innocence and behavior a secular society could only condemn. They also contrast good and bad covenantal behavior. 1 Samuel opens with a picture of a barren woman who lived in the hill country of Ephraim with her husband and his second wife and the latter's children. Although her husband loved Hannah, she was vexed at Penninah's obvious superiority. "Her rival used to provoke her severely, to irritate her because the Lord had closed her womb," but her husband Elkanah said to her, "Why do you weep? Why do you not eat? Am I not more to you than ten sons?" This bit of dialogue occurred every year when they "went up to the house of the Lord."

At the annual festival, she prayed with such intensity that the aging priest, Eli, noticed her agony. Thinking her to be drunk with the new wine of the festival, "Eli said to her, 'How long will you make a drunken spectacle of yourself? Put away your new wine.'" When Eli understood that she was speaking "out of great anxiety and vexation," he assured her with a priest's benediction: "Go in peace; the God of Israel grant the petition you have made to him."

Hannah returned home with her husband, I imagine, with face glowing with assurance. She had promised to give a son to God, and God would provide. No strange or miraculous procedure would be involved; it was a bargain with YHWH. God kept his part of the bargain: Hannah had prayed and "in due time" she bore Samuel. Eli's word to Hannah was the simple word of a reassuring pastor, and at the same time a prophetic word, mysteriously fitted into the larger movement of Israel's history. Hannah believed Eli and God, and her faith was rewarded. What is interesting about this episode is the way a simple woman's asking and receiving could illustrate the covenantal paradigm.

As soon as Hannah had weaned Samuel, probably at five years of age, she and Elkanah took him to Shiloh and with appropriate sacrifices, "a three year old bull, an ephah of flour and a skin of wine," delivering her son to serve as a Nazirite, a person achieving holiness through the performance of his own or his mother's vow.

Eli directed Samuel's service in the house of God, and evidently they lived in rooms adjacent to the sanctuary. Hannah would bring new robes for her growing son each year, and Eli would bless Elkanah and his wife, saying "May the Lord repay you with children by this woman for the gift that she made to the Lord." The prayers of Hannah and Eli were answered: "the Lord took note of Hannah; she conceived and bore three sons and two daughters," not quite the seven sons and three daughters of Job's second family, but a typical example of the pious Israelite's model family.

Eli's Failings

Eli's prophetic insight had spent itself along with his failing eyesight, and he began to hear reports of the way his sons were treating their priestly ministry with contempt. They were greedily taking the tasty parts of the sacrifices, which belonged to YHWH, and sleeping with the women who served at the entrance to the tent of meeting. An unnamed man of God came to Eli announcing that because of the sons' behavior no member of the family would live to old age. But it was not until the boy Samuel learned from God that Eli's family would be replaced by a faithful priest that things changed.

All seemed to be going well until one night the young Nazirite heard a voice calling "Samuel! Samuel!" Thinking Eli had called him, Samuel got up and went to the aging priest only to be sent back to bed. When the call came a third time, Eli directed Samuel to reply to the Voice: "Speak, Lord, for your servant is listening." When he did so, YHWH said to Samuel,

> See, I am about to do something in Israel that will make both ears of anyone who hears of it tingle. On that day I will fulfill against Eli all that I have spoken concerning his house, from beginning to end . . . I am about to punish his house forever, for the iniquity that he knew, because his sons were blaspheming God, and he did not restrain them. Therefore I swear to the house of Eli that the iniquity of Eli's house shall not be expiated by sacrifice or offering forever" (1 Sam 3:11–14).

Although the word "sin" appears only in the historian's telling of the story, the parallel word "iniquity" is prominent in the message Samuel was to deliver to Eli. Eli had known of the iniquity of his sons, and had not "restrained them." As a consequence the iniquity of the three of them could not be propitiated by the ritual of sacrifice and offering *forever*! The sexual aspects of the indictment were secondary to the sins of blasphemy and greed, but had been mentioned in the public's complaint along with the charge that the young priests who had enjoyed the "choicest parts of every offering" brought to Shiloh. Offerings that had been bought to atone for the sins of the people were being used to fatten and indulge the priests responsible for presenting them to YHWH. Eli had done nothing about it. The old priest had failed in another way. As man of God, ironically he had not recognized a word from God when it came from another prophetic voice.

Sex at the Door of the Tent

The abuse of the women "who served at the entrance of the tent of meeting" is almost lost in the telling of the story, but it is nonetheless significant in highlighting the con-

PART 2: Sex and Power Relationships in Some Israelite Stories

trast between the two families. Hannah and Elkanah faithfully followed the Lord's means to increase their family by asking YHWH and trusting God's response. Eli's sons either seduced or raped the women who had come to serve at the sanctuary, and in the end went to their deaths on the battleground between Aphek and Ebenezer when the ark of YHWH's presence was captured by the Philistines. At the altar, Hannah had innocently asked for a child. Eli's sons were guilty of contempt for the altar and may have impregnated some of the serving women.

First Samuel does not delineate the thinking of the women who tended the altar. Were Eli's sons the only men with whom they could engage in sexual relations? Were they barren wives who blamed themselves, like Hannah, for not presenting sons to their families and sought relief with the young priests? Were they widows or spinsters? Were they innocent or guilty in the whole affair? Did they bother to rationalize their behavior? Is the line between being seduced and being raped as clear as we would like to believe? We cannot answer these questions, but we can imagine how young priests tempted wives unable to become pregnant: "Let me give you a son!" Even those who tended the altar could be guilty of corrupting their charges.

A Lawless Time

In the account of the establishing of Samuel's priesthood there is no question of YHWH's law, and Eli's leadership of the tribal confederation was ineffective. Instead it was the unordained people who expressed their outrage at Eli's sons. The young Samuel had felt that same sympathetic anger and disappointment as he saw Eli's sons taking the best pieces of the sacrificed meat and sleeping with the women. He may have heard the "man of God" rebuking Eli for not correcting his sons. However, Eli *had* spoken to his sons using the word "sin" both for human relationships and for relationship with God: "I hear of your evil dealings from all these people. No, my sons; it is not a good report that I hear the people of the Lord spreading abroad. If one person sins against another, someone can intercede for the sinner with the Lord, but if someone sins against the Lord, who can make intercession?" (1 Sam 2:23–25).

Neither the man of God nor the young Samuel used the word "sin" when it was time to tell the old priest that YHWH would end support for his family,[1] but they both recognized that God was not pleased with the people under Eli's care.

Finally, YHWH brought the episode to its end. In the larger story of Israel's gaining possession of the Promised Land Eli and Samuel are characterized as judges, and both filled the role of political leader before Saul was anointed to be the first king. One wonders why it was necessary for the Lord to reveal himself to Samuel at Shiloh "by the word of the Lord"[2] instead of through the laws delivered to Moses. It appears that at the time "Mosaic" laws were not fully developed or that the sexual sins of young priests had not come to the attention of the human lawgivers. Perhaps the voice and power of a priest turned prophet were what was needed to guide the transition from

---

1. See 1 Samuel 2:27–36 and 3:10–14.
2. 1 Samuel 3:21.

Hannah and the Sons of Eli

the period of the judges to the time of the kingdoms. The setting was an early form of "church" instead of "state."

Contrary to the impression given in the book of Exodus that a complete Decalogue, judgments, and statutes became law for Israel when the two tablets were delivered to Moses in the Sinai desert at "the third new moon after [they] had gone out of the land of Egypt" (Exod 19:1), it is probable that a "Ritual Decalogue" was the first set of rules to gain acceptance by the settled tribes in the Promised Land. In an alternate account of the delivery of the "tablets of the covenant" Exodus 31:18—32:35 tells how Moses discovered the people worshipping the golden calf when he returned from the mountain and threw the two tablets down and broke them. After Moses pleaded with God, YHWH agreed to accompany him on the remainder of the journey and directed him to cut two tablets like the first. To seal that agreement YHWH dictated rules scholars call the "Ritual Decalogue" (Exod 34:11–26).

These rules are quite different from the Ten Commandments, being largely taken up with directions for times and forms of worship. The law of Exodus 34:23 requires "all your males" to appear before the Lord three times a year, and it is possible that wives and children came only once a year, or not at all if they chose to remain in their homes.

When the Israelites arrive in Canaan the Ritual Decalogue requires them to appear before YHWH three times a year, bringing the first fruits of the ground for priests to sacrifice. They are *not* to worship any other god or make a covenant with the inhabitants of the land, lest they be invited to eat another god's sacrifices and thus "prostitute themselves" to the gods of the land (Exod 34:15–16).

In the time of Eli and Samuel these rules for worship do not appear to have been known or fully effective. Elkanah and Hannah apparently sacrificed only once a year, at the time of the fall festival, instead of the three times mentioned in all three of the pre-exilic law codes. Neither Hannah's family nor Eli's appear concerned to avoid the worship of other gods, since they were evidently not competing with YHWH in the immediate vicinity of Shiloh at the time. Hannah's family lived by whatever customs prevailed, but Hannah was clearly faithful to YHWH. The public felt that Eli's sons were guilty of abusing the people's offerings and of sexual license, neither of which would ever be specifically mentioned in the written laws of Israel. However, Eli was the only authority for the enforcement of customary ritual and political practices, and he had failed. The historian's judgment, "there was no king in Israel," extends from the final chapters of the book of Judges into the early chapters of 1 Samuel. It was truly a lawless time.

When the outraged tribes were called together to avenge the rape of the Levite's concubine in Gibeah (Judg 19), the tribe of Benjamin was saved from extinction not through any use of commonly accepted law, but through the decision of all the tribes, *except Benjamin,* to attack Gibeah and "cut down" their fighting men and set fire to the towns belonging to the tribe. The graphic account of the three-day battle in Judges 20 shows how Israel, lacking laws, resorted to violence to "teach" YHWH's way to the erring. Many "courageous men" died to avenge the crime of Gibeah's "worthless fellows."

PART 2: Sex and Power Relationships in Some Israelite Stories

The book of Judges concludes with the agreement that the remaining Benjamites could each "carry off a wife" for themselves when the "young women of Shiloh come out to dance in the dances" (Judg 21:21).

The Judgment of God

Eli was notable as the priest who presided over a major transition from a loose confederation of tribes led by God-selected leaders to a period of confidence not only in a specific leader but also in a stronger system. A crisis was precipitated when Israelites were defeated at Aphek near the Philistine border. When the survivors came back into the camp, they asked that the Ark of the Covenant be allowed to accompany them when they met the Philistines in the next battle, and Eli allowed it to go, perhaps insisting that his two sons accompany it.

In the second battle Israel was defeated, the two sons of Eli were killed, and the Philistines captured the Ark. The deaths of Hophni and Phineas and the subsequent death of Eli opened the way for Samuel to take charge of Israel. The loss of the Ark led the people away from trusting in their fighting skills and from less superstitious trust in what was a recognized holy object. The Ark had been treated as a magical totem, and even the Philistines were afraid of its power, but in the battle they had rallied, and left the Israelites briefly without leadership or the Ark.

The first step toward establishing the rule of law in Israel was the bargaining that went on between the people, Samuel and God over their demand that the priest find a king for YHWH's tribes. Hannah's son struggled to understand YHWH's ambiguous messages regarding political power, moral authority, and ritual practice in the Israel of his time. How would Israel fulfill the destiny laid out in God's word to Abram and in the later word that announced the end of Eli's family? What was in store for the defeated tribes? How would YHWH and his Israelite companions accomplish God's purpose?

12

David's Wives and His Wars

David did not set out from Bethlehem to marry the king's daughter or to spend his life fighting for land. Although the priest-prophet Samuel had come to his home looking for YHWH's choice to succeed King Saul, no one knew what to make of the anointing that had taken place, and Jesse's household had gone on as before. Before long, however, the three older sons joined Saul's army in the war against the Philistines that the Danite Samson had started, and David was back in hills that belonged to neither Philistines nor Judeans. He followed or guided the family's sheep and goats to feed on the wild grasses until the day when father Jesse asked him to take provisions to supply his brothers and their relatives as they defended Israelite lands against their aggressive neighbors.

Interwoven in the story of the development of the Israelite kingdom are a number of intimate details about the experiences of one of the central figures of biblical history. David's interactions at the personal level had much to do with the creation of a social group (government) that brought loosely confederated tribes into what has been called a "transitional early state," under a dominant chieftainship.

Chrita Schaefer-Lichtenberger[1] characterizes two earlier development stages of states as "inchoative" and "typical." In *The Origins of the Ancient Israelite State*, Schaefer-Lichtenberger maintains that in the transitional state kinship becomes marginal, private ownership of the means of production develops, a market economy leads to social class antagonisms, and law is codified and overseen by full time judges. In the preceding stage kinship was balanced by local relations, taxes were levied, and the state became landlord. In the Pentateuch we can see the transition from kinship dominance in the earliest inchoative state to the typical early state. In Joshua 13–22, however, the Ultimate Landlord is YHWH with Joshua acting as distributing agent.

Was David aware that his decisions were taking him toward being the king over all Israel? First Samuel 17:12–14 describes David as the youngest of Jesse's eight sons, so it is likely that he would not inherit family land. Instead he was assigned to herd the sheep and run errands while the three eldest sons could support Saul's army.

---

1. See Claessen, *The Early State*.

PART 2: Sex and Power Relationships in Some Israelite Stories

A Battle between Two Citizen Armies

Picture a confrontation between two small armies.[2] A wedge of Philistine control had penetrated deep into the territory the Israelite tribal confederation believed God had given them. Citizen armies of the two confederations met for a battle between Socoh on the east, "which belongs to Judah," and Azekah toward the west, which at the time was recognized as Philistine territory. In the valley of Elah the Philistine champion Goliath challenged any Israelite to come forward for a personal duel. The Israelites stood on their side of the creek abashed until the kid brother, David, stepped forward, accepting the challenge, and broke the hold of Israel's enemy with a single smooth stone from the brook.

From the viewpoint of a historian a battle, or a war, is something like any business transaction. Two sides meet in a bartering situation. Each wants something tangible that neither holds securely, and they begin by mentally estimating costs and relative strengths before field-testing their powers. Battles are also like football games or chess matches where opponents seek to own the playing field and seize a goal, which in war is a center suitable for human habitation. Two villages were evidently the goals of the opposing armies. The Judeans were holding Socoh, which the Philistines evidently wanted for their expanding population. YHWH had promised the Mediterranean as Israel's western boundary, Gaza's outpost village Azekah stood in the way.

Ambiguity is always present in war, since neither side knows what the actual strength of the other side is. Also ambivalence. Ambivalence is in the feelings of the contestants. There would always be some uncertainty, whether the Israelites would win this battle and move the unfinished conquest forward or have to fall back and regroup for the next battle.

But successful regrouping calls for a common understanding of and commitment to the policies that lead to a war. David D. Kirkpatrick in the Hendersonville, NC TIMES-NEWS, June 15, 2008, reported John McCain's thesis that the military should teach recruits not only how to fight but also the foreign policy reasons for the particular war, which at the time was the war in Vietnam. What David brought to the valley of Elah illustrates McCain's thesis that soldiers need to understand what they fight for. Modern Israel and the Palestinians have been fighting to possess the territory involved in David's first battle.

Philistine power was centered in "five lords" who ruled five city-states. Israelite power centered in King Saul, a Benjamite anointed by the priest-prophet Samuel at the request of a people's delegation. Saul had structured a citizen's army from several Israelite tribes to take the offensive against encroaching Philistines. Though the adjacent tribes of Benjamin and Judah were represented in Saul's army, we are not told how the Benjamite Saul brought them together nor which other tribes were represented when David came with supplies from Bethlehem.

---

2. The biblical account underlying this chapter begins with 1 Samuel 17:1 and continues through the remainder of the book.

When the two armies met in the valley, there was no ambiguity about the immediate situation. Evidently it involved an implicit, crudely shouted, agreement to settle the question of who would own both sides of the creek and the two villages. The matter could be settled on the spot by a duel between two champions. Probably no one on either side really wanted a battle, but possession of land could and would be changed by the outcome of the battle. In joining battle both sides agreed to that. The victors would take possession; the defeated would retreat. The power we can see at the outset would be raw and physical, man against man.

But first there would be two champions, man to man. Michelangelo's statue of David in Florence is not an accurate representation of the Judean shepherd boy, who probably looked like a teenager dwarfed by the size of a seven-foot tall giant. The sculptor has given David three times the proportions of Goliath.

Fighting between the two armies broke out when David cut off the head of the giant he had felled, and the Israelites drove the Philistines from the field. Once the battle was under way it was a more united and confident Israel against a less united Philistine army. Before the battle, the Israelites had not been so united, and perhaps the Philistines were not united either. The situation appears to have been a stalemate with neither side eager for the fight.

Why, after the anxious moments and stalemate, were the Israelites able to drive the Philistines off the field? What was the secret of David's power to turn the tide of the Philistine advance onto Judean land? Why did it take a youth from the fields of Judah to tip the power balance from frustrating equality to a victory?

Are rational and religious explanations incompatible? The account in 1 Samuel 17 gives us an ambiguous mix of the two. David introduced a spiritual factor, the element of an optimistic confidence—religious faith—into the situation. But he also remembered his own skill, honed against the country's lions and bears, and then he declared that his skill had been given him by God for just such a moment: "The Lord, who saved me from the paw of the lion and from the paw of the bear, will save me from the hand of this Philistine" (2 Sam 17:37).

David, by word and action, introduced a new dimension to the situation, the recollection of a skill he had developed when his family had sent him out to tend the sheep that were their livelihood. They had trusted David to be resourceful and God to send only occasional predators. Having done thousands of practice shots, he knew what he could do with his sling and staff. A few minutes earlier David had asked the soldiers: "Who is this uncircumcised Philistine that he should defy the armies of the Living God?" (vs. 26).

His question evoked a memory of the legendary war by which Israel had taken the Promised Land under Caleb and Joshua. The new situation called for *continuity* with the old tradition of lightly armed desert tribes marching around the city of Jericho to fulfill the plan that brought Abram/Abraham from Ur of the Chaldees. David recognized that God operates through the powers of people willing to take step-by-step actions to *change* things. The secret of this kind of power is in the combination of physical strength with a thoughtful confidence in developed skill. America celebrated the coordinated action of the two or three men who interrupted the hijacking of Flight 93 on 9/11/2001, and many of us saw their action as God's intervention to save the nation's capital.

In this first action between Israelite and Philistine armies, focused on David and Goliath, we can see the operation of two powers, the one physical, sometimes organized as military and expressed in brute force; the other spiritual, ordered by means of words and ideas, and relying on the presence of an unseen God.

Rewarding the Popular Hero

The next scene focuses on three people who operate largely in the social, spiritual arena where each has an underlying physical presence and power. In that arena relationships between David and Saul and between Saul and his daughter Michal could change. Saul had promised a daughter in marriage to anyone who faced Goliath successfully. He no doubt expected a seasoned veteran to claim the reward, but here was a young shepherd boy from the hills of Judah claiming the prize. The power situation was suddenly ambiguous: a nobody with no wealth to marry the king's daughter? But David was a popular hero, and the women were singing like in a Greek chorus: "Saul has killed his thousands, and David his ten thousands" (1 Sam 18:9).

Pause a moment and listen, not to the numbers in the song, but to the meaning of it. The chant was an endlessly repeated news item measuring the perceived strength of two military leaders. When compared with King Saul, David appeared the stronger. Body counts on the battlefield were one measure then as now of an intangible military capability. Saul, of course, was remembered for his earlier victories; but this time he had not rallied his troops, and David *had* inspired them. Neither Saul nor his son Jonathan were in evidence when David had heard Goliath issuing his challenge, but after the battle they had lost some of their luster, and a comparative weakness would be an issue with public opinion giving David the stature of Michelangelo's sculpture.

After the battle Saul temporized about his offer of a daughter, taking David into his household as the musician who would play the lyre to quiet his spirit and as an armor bearer and companion for Jonathan in the continuing war with the Philistines. What he didn't do was to reward David immediately with one of his daughters. Instead he went into a traditional bargaining mode as Laban had bargained with Jacob. Since neither Jacob nor David had the wealth to buy a bride, they would have to serve the family chieftain. After David admitted that he did not have the wherewithal for the elder daughter, he agreed to bring Saul a hundred Philistine foreskins as the price of his marriage to Michal, Saul's younger daughter. His exploits in warfare would be the measure of his value to the family of Saul and to the kingdom, and would further devalue Saul.

At first from Saul's point of view it was a good bargain. He was buying a fifty-fifty chance that some Philistine would knock off David, and his son Jonathan would be around to take over the throne when the time came. And the wobbly kingdom would not be threatened by as many Philistines. The hundred count was probably a more accurate measure of the size of the battles than the ten thousands in the chant. But the thousands *were* a measure of that intangible strength that sustained the people's hope for victory over the Philistines. The measure of final victory would be in territory controlled either by Israelites or Philistines. You would know victory when the mapmakers issued new maps. In trying to show the location of this episode I turned to Mapquest for current maps of the area. Guess what! Maps of today's Israel did not show an international border with Palestinian territory, but included a numbered national highway through "Gazzah" all the way to the Egyptian border. For the mapmakers at this writing the Gaza strip belongs to modern Israel along with the valley of Elah.

Ambiguous Transfers of Power

We will return to the ambiguities in David's marriage, but we need to take a short look at an early "sin" of Jonathan. Although Jonathan seems to have been somewhere else when the battle near Socoh took place, he had distinguished himself in a daring raid against a Philistine camp at Michmash. He and his armor bearer companion, just two of them, approached the edge of the Philistine camp, and instead of hiding when the Philistines noticed them, they boldly attacked, and killed about twenty Philistines, who were evidently scattered and unprepared for fighting. The rest of the Philistines panicked, and Saul and his troops joined in the confusion. To assure a fight to the finish Saul announced a curse on anyone who paused during the day to eat anything, but Jonathan did not hear his father's curse, and tasted some honey "on the tip of his staff" as he was pursuing the fleeing Philistines. The curse had reinforced the order to keep fighting all day, and when the priest who was with the Israelites refused to authorize further pursuit of the Philistines later that day, the fighting stopped and they consulted the sacred lot, asking who had sinned. Saul, his priest and the people were evidently prepared to enforce the curse with the execution of the guilty soldier, such was the superstitious belief of in the power of curses.

This part of the story is found in 1 Samuel 14:36–46 where it is embedded in an account of the hasty slaughtering of captured sheep and oxen without draining their blood. The unnamed priest judged that everyone had sinned, but apparently manipulated the sacred stones to fix the charge of sin on Jonathan. The incident indicates the waning power of the priesthood in the early days of the Israelite kingdom. As always God's guidance was channeled through human voices, first through "angel"/messengers later through priests, seers and prophets. The announcement of Saul's fate would be channeled through the witch of En–Dor who called Samuel back from the grave to speak to the king.

When pebble after pebble was drawn from the priest's ephod, it came down to a choice between the people on one side and Saul and Jonathan on the other, and then it was between father and son, and the black rock fell to Jonathan. "Saul said to Jonathan, 'Tell me what you have done.' Jonathan told him, 'I tasted a little honey with the tip of my staff . . . here I am, I will die.'" But the people absolutely would not let Jonathan

Part 2: Sex and Power Relationships in Some Israelite Stories

die, and Saul weakened and let the matter drop, while the Philistines continued their retreat to territory they controlled.

The incident is a perfect example of ambiguity in kinds of power. In ancient Israel everyone believed that the human enterprise of battle was under the control of a people's god, often represented through a patriarch's authority, but also subject to a priest's veto. Power was initially thought of as physical, but in society it became authority, i.e., socio-political and religious. We note that in the incident Jonathan had invoked neither a priest's religious authority nor his father's parental-political authority when he and his companion made their decision. Instead the two men decided to attack when the men of the Philistine garrison "hailed Jonathan and his armor bearer, saying 'Come up to us, and we will show you something'" (1 Sam 14:12).

Jonathan's action can be characterized as autonomous or self-generated. He had looked for a sign in the situation and found it in the overconfidence of the Philistines, so the two men could kill twenty men, one at a time, until the rest of the Philistines panicked. For us the question is whether the victory was the result of Philistine overconfidence, Jonathan's trust in God, or both. Likewise for David's meeting with Goliath. For the Israelites the ambiguity was whether Saul's son was properly respectful of his father and the priest's god-inspired guidance. Jonathan had transferred decision-making power from the "authorities" to himself as any healthy young person must do at some time.

Now perhaps we can see why Jonathan and David decided that they were soulmates. Jonathan appears to have been a little older than David, but when David moved into the household and Saul told him to go out and kill Philistines, the two of them made a pact to go together. David arrived as the political and social inferior, serving as Jonathan's armor bearer, but it was Jonathan who asked David for a covenant at the family confab, in effect recognizing that he would be David's inferior.

The dictionary defines "ambiguous" as "having more than one meaning," so the symbolic transfer of power in that moment indicates the ambiguity or ambivalence in David's relationship to Jonathan and Saul. The historian tells us, "Jonathan stripped himself of the robe that he was wearing, and gave it to David, and his armor, and even his sword and his bow and his belt." (1 Sam 18:4)[3]

The historian points out that what Jonathan did was because his soul was bound to the soul of David, but we get the subtle suggestion that Jonathan was handing over his right to the kingdom, though not quite the way Esau allowed Jacob to buy his birthright for a mess of pottage. At this point in the story nobody but God, or the historian, knows that both Saul and Jonathan would die in a battle with the Philistines on Mount Gilboa, while David was in the south getting out of a temporary friendly relationship with other Philistines. Saul had noticed the women's chant praising David, and he said, "they have ascribed to David ten thousands, and to me they have ascribed thousands, what more can he have but the kingdom?" (18:8) Ambiguous relationships appear throughout this history.

---

3. The exchange of gear for authority might be delineated in the covenantal diagram of chapter 2.

Triangles of Love and Fear

Things get complicated when more than two people are involved. Thus far the attractions and repulsions of power have been between more or less equally matched pairs: David and Goliath, Saul and David, David and Jonathan. In ancient Israel, however relationships between fathers and daughters were never equally matched. Daughter Michal, no doubt, had looked forward to the day when father Saul would "give" her to a man who would own her as property and when her prospective husband would "give" some items of his property in return as "bride price." The custom of such exchanges persists today in many parts of the world. My wife was startled when a young man in a class she was teaching in Nigeria suddenly asked if she had a daughter! When Virginia said, "Yes, why do you ask?" he explained that he was looking for a wife, and he went on to explain the customs of his village, which are like what we see in the Hebrew Scriptures.

Michal's marriage to David was not an entirely unequal bargain for her. Like the Israelite women who chanted David's praises, Michal had fallen in love with him. And when her older sister was given to another man, word was passed to Saul that his younger daughter loved David. He could fulfill his promise to reward the man who had killed Goliath, and Michal would get the prize other women coveted. She was still subject to her father's decision, but possibly Saul gave her a chance to refuse. We can imagine her breathless "Yes" when he asked her if she wanted to marry David.

With two of Saul's children affected with the love bug for David you might think that a triangle would develop, and to some extent it did. David was pulled in at least three directions in that household, but a wave of fear and hatred engulfed Saul, while a tension between loyalty to the king and their developing independence involved Jonathan, Michal, and David. Saul sent David out to kill Philistines; Jonathan was his companion in the defense of Israel; the new bride, Michal, was left behind. Michal's potential to produce a new member of the family was evidently wasted because David was out fighting Saul's war. David may have been away too much to father a child who would have combined the threads of Judean and Benjamite tribal leadership into a truly Israelite kingdom.

But a triangle of fear developed. Things got ugly when David was home with Michal, since his father-in-law was insanely paranoid about David's popularity. When no Philistine could rid him of his son-in-law, Saul resorted to force, lunging at him with a spear in the house, and pursuing him over the countryside. One morning Michal learned that Saul was sending his bodyguards to kill David in his bed. Quickly, she sent David outside by a back window and prepared an effigy in the bed to delay the soldiers. On another occasion when Saul had ordered a family feast, Jonathan made excuses for David's absence, and sent his servant to bring back the arrows he had intentionally shot past the target as a warning to David to stay away.[4]

There was nothing ambiguous about Saul's intention to destroy David. Like the family of Jacob and Esau where two heirs to the family fortune were one too many,

---

4. 1 Samuel 19–20 reports several attacks by Saul against David, and Jonathan's loyalty to David.

this time a kingdom was at stake. Isaac had believed that one or the other of his two sons would replace him as a God-blessed patriarch. Saul saw David as an unwelcome intruder not only in the family, but also in the kingdom dominated by the tribe of Benjamin. However, the historian and the reader know that the last word and act would not be Saul's. God could and would override Saul's insane struggle to keep political power in his family. The significant triangle in this part of the story was not a woman's ambivalence about choosing between two men. Michal and Jonathan both favored David over their father, but the strands within Saul's family were unraveling.

Saul's fears led him to seek guidance from a medium at En–Dor, and the ghost of Samuel confirmed his fears, telling him that YHWH had "turned the kingdom" out of his hand. Both Saul and Jonathan would die in battle, leaving the way open for David to claim the power Saul had coveted for his son. In the scene in 1 Samuel 28, Saul learned from the ghost of Samuel that the transfer of God's approval to David was final. The wording of this private conversation, as of most of the incidents in the history, is not to be taken as verbatim, but rather gives the substance of the interchange between Saul and the medium. Samuel's presence was in Saul's mind.

Opportunism: Might makes Right

David was forced into going his way rather than choosing it. For a while he and his band of followers associated themselves with Achish, the Philistine king of Gath. This may seem strange, but earlier a number of Israelites had joined or were conscripted into the Philistine army when it was extending control over Israelite territory. When the Israelites began to win battles, the conscripted soldiers forsook the Philistine leaders and returned to their kindred.[5] Now it was David's turn, and he found a temporary ally in a Philistine chief.

Here is an ambiguity of power we'd rather do without, but we would do well to understand. Power is fluid, like water under pressure, capable of penetrating dividing walls whether they seem solid like the Berlin Wall or are only in the identifying slogans of political parties. A militaristic use of the name YHWH had a place in the stories we're looking at, earlier when Jonathan launched his two man blitz against Philistines at Michmash, and then when David struck down Goliath. Both heroes recalled that YHWH, the named God of Israel, had shown himself capable of blitzing the Canaanites out of their land. Jonathan and David believed YHWH could do it again, and some six hundred men eventually attached themselves to David to help.

We may wonder how so many would be free to follow a leader who was in disgrace with the king. It seems that many landless young men, independent of fathers, were abroad throughout Canaan during this period of Israelite history. We glimpse them in Lot's experience in Sodom and in the rape of the Levite's concubine in Gibeah. Also, Nabal's refusal to share food with David mentioned "many" runaway slaves. They

---

5. 1 Samuel 14:21 reports that "the Hebrews who previously had been with the Philistines turned and joined the Israelites who were with Saul and Jonathan" during the battle which followed Jonathan's daring raid. There is no mention of their circumcision. We may assume that they were not marked as Israelites or that the Philistines did not care as long as they shared in battles.

were probably sons of Israelite families or their non-Israelite neighbors who could not inherit property when they most needed it or perhaps were indentured for seven years service to more prosperous neighbors. Probably these youth could neither marry nor support wives.

Now David was reduced to opportunism. He went to territory more or less controlled by the Philistines, and for a while based his operations with them. Among his adventures he found a second wife. That came about when his band of six hundred freebooters needed to resupply with food. Part of his troop showed up at the gates of a prosperous ranch owned by a man aptly named (or nicknamed) "Fool." David sent ten men who politely asked Nabal "Let my young men find favor in your sight; for we have come on a feast day. Please give whatever you have at hand to your servants and to your son David."

The men reported back to David that Nabal had said, "Who is David? Who is the son of Jesse? There are many servants today who are breaking away from their masters. Shall I take my bread and my water and the meat that I have butchered for my shearers, and give it to men who come from I do not know where?" (1 Sam 25:10). Meanwhile "one of the young men told Abigail, Nabal's wife, 'David sent messengers out of the wilderness to salute our master, and he shouted insults at them. Yet the men were very good to us, and we suffered no harm, and we never missed anything when we were in the field . . . they were a wall to us both by night and by day . . . Now . . . consider what you should do; for evil has been decided against our master and against all his house; he is so ill-natured that no one can speak to him'" (25:1, 5–17).

Abigail took matters in her own hands and "hurried and took two hundred loaves, two skins of wine, five sheep ready dressed, five measures of parched grain, one hundred clusters of raisins, and two hundred cakes of figs" (25:18). That was not all. Abigail went with all those supplies and presented them to David with an apology for her ill-natured husband: "Do not take seriously this ill-natured fellow, Nabal; for as his name is, so is he; Fool is his name, and folly is with him . . . Now, as the Lord lives, and as you yourself live, since the Lord has restrained you from bloodguilt and from taking vengeance, now let this present be given to the young men who follow my lord. Please forgive the trespass of your servant, for the Lord will certainly make my lord a sure house."

In Nigeria a man who makes such an apology does so lying absolutely prone on the ground in the middle of the street if that is where he meets the person he has insulted, so 1 Samuel 15:24 says that Abigail alighted from the donkey, fell before David on her face, bowing to the ground." There is nothing ambiguous about her complete humiliation before David, but the ambiguity that remains is whether we should ascribe the happy outcome to God, to David, or to Abigail.

We will return to the rest of Abigail's rather formal address to David and his gracious acceptance speech, and at this point turn to the rest of the story. When Nabal found out what his wife had done, he had a stroke and died within a few days. David promptly invited her to become one of his wives. The historian reports, "Abigail got up hurriedly and rode away on a donkey, her five maids attended her. She went after the messengers of David and became his wife." (1 Sam 25:42) The historian continues without a break, "David also married Ahinoam of Jezreel; both of them became his wives. Saul had given his daughter Michal, David's wife to Palti son of Laish, who was from Gallim."

Building a "Sure House"

The history turns at this point from personal relationships to the tribal relationships through which the united kingdom of Israel was formed. In David's acquisition of his wives we have seen a "covenantal" pattern for handling the ambiguities of several persons working in and around an expanding society. David's marriage to Michal was accomplished through the traditional negotiation between patriarch and prospective bridegroom. As a newly independent woman, however, Abigail dealt directly with David, and one suspects that Ahinoam may also have been independent, free to make her marital arrangements (1 Sam 25:43–4).

Three interwoven activities were involved in building David's kingdom. The one that engages most history books, including the Bible, is *war*. But as every warrior learns, war is more destructive than constructive. Killing an enemy or destroying a house only makes a vacant place in a social order that must be filled by another person and a new house, if the society is to function efficiently. And the anger and bitterness of the defeated make rebuilding difficult.

It is not easy to characterize the second activity, for "peace" doesn't tell us much about the way it works. It is better to describe what is needed as *secular economic activity*, or simply *trade*. Visualize the situation in a small, relatively insignificant region named Carmel where Abigail and Nabal had their establishment. Before David's troop showed up, their ranch was thriving with its men as shepherds and sheep-shearers and its women in a household managed by Nabal's wife and run by competent servants. Some dozens of people were evidently involved, and Nabal was what we might call an entrepreneur with a recognizable incorporation. We are not told, but may presume, that the activities of Nabal's establishment included sacrifice or a priesthood similar to that of the independent "man of the hill country of Ephraim whose name was Micah" and whose idol was taken by the tribe of Dan and relocated to the northern town which was renamed for that tribe (Judg 17). It appears that Nabal owed political and religious *allegiance* to neither Philistine nor Israelite powers. We do not hear whether he sacrificed to Dagon or YHWH or to some other god. He thought himself politically and religiously neutral, economically independent and prosperous. When David's troop arrived Nabal had assets they both needed.

David and his troop represented the possibility of a hostile takeover by a start up corporation looking for a share of the market. Nabal voted against the merger, but Abigail overruled his vote, and turned over their assets to David. In those days a wife of childbearing age was also considered a human resource that could produce other human resources. Abigail and the other woman mentioned in 1 Samuel 25:43 both bore sons to David who would one day be possible contenders with Solomon for his throne. But that is another story.

Back to the way David handled the ambiguities of increasing power: David seems not to have had enough of war, and was ready to use the sword in the expansion of his economic and political base. He had not yet made the temporary alliance with Achish, the Philistine ruler of Gath, but was apparently already raiding neutral towns of Geshurites, Amalekites, and others in territory that would soon belong to the Judeans. When he did link up with the Philistine Achish, his policy was to approach a settlement as a friendly protector, ask for and accept supplies when they were given. His disciplined band of outlaws, like gangs in cities of America, were careful to give "protection" when their offer was accepted, but if they were refused, David saw to it that every man, woman and child was destroyed so that no one could return to tell king Achish what had happened. All David would tell king Achish was that he was raiding Judean towns and villages. In this way David expanded his control over the southern and western highlands, until he could establish Hebron as his capital, where he governed Judean territory for seven years.

This strategy gave David the elements of a kingdom, though his title was probably the ambiguous "chief" at first. Only when he had settled in Hebron was "king" appropriate. His relationship with women was also ambiguous. Instead of taking Abigail captive in an assault on her establishment, David sent her a proposal of *marriage*. When she accepted, she was obviously acting out of interest for herself and the servants of her household. She became in effect the same kind of servant as every wife in Israelite or Canaanite communities. Was she attracted to David, and if so in what way? Was he simply a strong man who could offer protection for Nabal's ranch, while she continued to manage it? Or did she actually take a liking to him, and if so, was the liking mutual?

Men built their power in ancient times by attaching wives to themselves; a woman's role in this mutual dance was to accept the offered protection and bear a son. But Abigail could verbalize her feelings in her negotiating statement, which is found in 1 Samuel 25:23–31. In spite of her vulnerable position when she approached David with the foodstuffs for his followers, Abigail declared, "the Lord has restrained you from bloodguilt and from taking vengeance with your own hand." And she continued with a series of prayer-petitions: "let your enemies . . . be [dead] like Nabal . . . let this present . . . be given to the young men who follow my lord. Please forgive the trespass of your servant." Such petitions would normally have been addressed only to a stronger person from whom a suppliant was asking a great favor; the mention of "trespass" makes her guilty of Nabal's rudeness. Finally, Abigail became prophetic, "the Lord shall certainly make my lord a sure house, because my lord is fighting the battles of the Lord [YHWH] and evil shall not be found in you so long as you live."

In this remarkable statement, not all of which was literally true at the moment or even her exact words, Abigail (or her editor) voiced YHWH's appraisal of David's life as she saw it. The central declaration has several possible meanings: David's battles were the Lord's way of building Israel into "a sure house" in contrast to the divided households of Saul and his son Ishbosheth. Abigail could become wife of the strongest chieftain on her horizon, as young women become second wives to wealthy men in third world countries because they and their own families know the economic and social security the large establishments offer. And Abigail sensed that YHWH was profoundly involved in guiding the building of a secure and prosperous nation. She could hope that David would fulfill her personal dream, but also that his leadership would unite Israel in a prosperous peace.

In David's youth war was the prime instrument for taking the land and ridding it of people Israel considered alien. Abigail may be credited with turning David to a less violent way to build a kingdom. As a strong woman, she shared her food with his troop and accepted life as one of his wives.

Uniting Israel for YHWH

We've been tracing the ambiguities of power through a series of episodes in two parallel stories. On the one hand we've seen the personal story of a shepherd boy on the way to becoming a king, and on the other we've seen the broader struggle of an identifiable Israel to possess and control the land in which they were living. The Hebrew Scriptures are devoted to this broader story, and it is a narrative of the adventures of ancient Israel as it had to contend with groups of hostile people. In David's time the "enemy" was not only Philistine foreigners, but a part of Israel itself.

Like the situations in twenty-first-century Israel/Palestine and Iraq two or more parties contended for the power to manage what should ideally have been a peaceful and prosperous country. At the dawn of the tenth century BCE the two principal contenders identified themselves as Israelites and Philistines. Not contending as strongly but clearly factors were small groups of Amalekites, Geshurites, and very small settlements known by geographical names such as Nabal's Carmel or clan names derived from eponymous ancestors. Today's mapmakers do well to omit sharper boundaries of controlled lands.

The final episodes in this chapter tell of David's achievement of a unified nation and incidentally mention Michal's revenge. For seven years after the deaths of Saul and Jonathan two kings controlled two regions of the country that needed to be united. David was firmly established as king over the remnants of two or three southern tribes, Judah and Simeon among them. In the north the rest of the Israelite tribes were loyal to a second son of Saul known to Judeans as Ishbosheth, "man of shame." Saul had given him the name Ishbaal, "Baal's man," but the historians could not bring themselves to use it.

When the tribal leaders gathered at the call of the commander of Saul's army to install Ishbosheth, a group of David's followers objected and launched a brief but violent war. When the two commanders agreed to a cease fire, three hundred sixty northerners were dead and nineteen southerners, and the two sides separated until Abner, the northern commander, and Joab, the southern commander, would negotiate for David to be king in Jerusalem.

According to the subtext of the biblical story *YHWH intended a united country to serve Him* with regular three times a year gatherings of all the people at the place He had designated to deposit His name. That place was Shiloh when the little boy Samuel had come to minister with the aging priest Eli. God's name was contained in an old wooden box, the "Ark of the Covenant," probably on the stone tablet that contained the opening words of the Ten Commandments. But that box and its stone tablets had been captured by the Philistines and later returned to an Israelite farmer during the period we are discussing. It served no unifying religious or political function until the two commanders began to negotiate for a way to unite the country some time after Saul's death.

Women as Links between Tribes

Sifting through all the ambiguities of a divided situation, Abner remained loyal to Saul's remaining son, until he took a fancy to a concubine of Saul's named Rizpah. That was too much for Ishbosheth and the king called his commander to account. Angrily Abner sent messengers to David offering to "bring all Israel over to you." David accepted the offer with one condition, spelled out in words preserved by the historian: "Good, I will make a covenant with you. But one thing I require of you, you shall never appear in my presence unless you bring Saul's daughter Michal when you come to see me."

It was done. "Ishbosheth sent and took her from her husband Paltiel . . . but her husband went with her, weeping as he walked behind her all the way to Bahurim. Then Abner said to him, 'Go back home!' So he went back" (2 Sam 3:6–12). Why did David insist on having Michal with him?

In her youth Michal may have felt that she could share with David in the uniting of the northern tribes with the tribe of Judah, but the wedges of war and her forced marriage to Paltiel left her angry and bitter when David required her to be a part of his court. The men around her gave her no opportunity to share in the building of the kingdom.

Abigail had seized her God-given opportunity to contribute to the building of the kingdom when David's path led him to her home. Her actions, even without the words reported by the historian, showed that she understood the need to replace anarchy with the only form of stable government known to the ancient world. As an active piece in the jigsaw puzzle, Abigail joined herself to the future king instead of being merely a bargaining chip in the men's political game.

A Marred Celebration

Loyal followers were also active in creating the emerging political structure, using a traditional symbol of the presence of a unifying god. David did not depend on the superficial unifying of the northern tribes brought by Abner with David's southern tribes, but decided that Hebron was too deep in southern territory to serve as the capital of his kingdom. So he planned to enter his new capital in Jerusalem with a huge celebration. First he had to capture the city from the tribe of Jebusites who still held it. He did that by entering that fortified city through the tunnel that supplied the city's water. Then he found the "ark of God" moldering away in a rural farmhouse, had it placed on a cart, and began the procession to Jerusalem.[6]

It looked as if David's power was absolute on that day, but two untoward incidents took place to remind him of the ambiguities of human power. Along the way, perhaps climbing a steep rise, the ark slipped on the cart, and a man named Uzzah, who reached out to steady it, was struck dead. It seemed that YHWH was saying, "I don't need people to take care of my ark, my stone tablets, or me."

The other incident may seem trivial, but it also points to the ambiguity of interwoven divine and human powers. After the procession in which David was a central figure along with the ark, Michal met him at the door of their house with a reproach. She had looked out of the window and had seen David "leaping and dancing before the Lord," evidently in sexually exhibitionist ways. So when she met him, she said, "How the king of Israel honored himself today, uncovering himself today before the eyes of his servants' maids, as any vulgar fellow might shamelessly uncover himself." The historian adds, "Michal, the daughter of Saul had no child to the day of her death." She evidently locked her bedroom door, and David could not or did not force her to have a child.

Weaving a Kingdom Fabric

Seen from the human standpoint, David's early career met ambiguities at every stage, and like other events from the Hebrew scriptures, the way these ambiguities worked brought David to serve either the mysterious movement of God's providence or as a power driven opportunist. The author-editors of the Deuteronomic Succession History saw God's guidance at every step of the way, but also give detailed reports of the human shaping of the pieces of the jigsaw puzzle.

Is the biblical view the only way to read the story? Without arguing for a dissenting view, I want to make a few points. First: although the Succession History affirms a mysterious guiding power from the God Israelites knew as YHWH of hosts, "mighty in battle," this God could and often did appear to tip the scales of battles to frustrate his chosen people or His chosen leader, as when Saul was rejected through Samuel's word.

The historians ascribed this frustration to a God who changed His mind, whereas we can see human powers locked into nearly balanced conflict with each other, some acting against God and others in harmony with God.

Second, the mystery of God's creative presence leaves individuals free to direct their own paths, make mistakes, and even abuse the people they were chosen to lead. Saul could succumb to jealousy, fear, and hate. He could break covenantal relationships between father-in-law and son-in-law, and he could repudiate the marriage of Michal to David and give her to another man. It is surprising that the historians did not tag any of this behavior as sinful.

---

6. This sequence is logical and may not appear from reading the Deuteronomic history.

David's Wives and His Wars

A third observation is more subtle, but it too probes the mysterious ways of God. Planted in or emerging from the hearts of many of the characters of this story was an almost irrational devotion to one heroic figure. Two of David's companions "loved" him and many others enabled him to take steps to his kingship. Michal's love can be understood as adolescent infatuation, but in spite of what must have seemed long absences, she continued to care for him until she was given to Paltiel. Jonathan's love can be described as a normal bonding between men who face danger together, but when he went to Mt. Gilboa with his father, he might have had a conflicting ambition to be king. It is not said that Abigail loved David, and she probably hoped for the stable establishment for herself and her servants that David represented. Each wife hoped that David would be a savior.

These complex personal relationships interwove themselves into the relentless political development that enabled David to build a united Israelite kingdom. Neither we nor the historian can say that David loved Saul's daughter or Abigail or any of his other wives, at least in any romantic sense. But in a broader sense David loved God and the people, and he became the patriarchal king for the nation that Saul was not. He expressed his love for the nation and YHWH at his first appearance before the duel with Goliath by claiming the tradition of the holy war. In spite of Saul's vicious treatment David managed to show respect for the king as the Lord's anointed, which can be seen as a sort of "love." It can also be seen as clever political strategy.

Though his tactic of allying himself with the Philistine chief led his followers to kill many men and women, David caught a glimpse of a better way when Abigail sensibly preferred to live as his wife instead of being slaughtered. Instead of labeling David a sinner, someone describes him as a man after God's heart, but with "unclean hands." After his meeting with Abigail, he seems to have modified the early strategy of brutal conquest that had subjected the tribes of Canaan to the *herem* or "ban"—the complete wiping out of populations as a religious duty to YHWH. Instead David adopted a secular strategy, destroying every person in the southern settlements who resisted, but letting his men colonize and assimilate with those who were willing to cooperate and meet the material needs of his followers. He appears to have anticipated the rule for war laid down in Deuteronomy 20:10–18 which directed Israelites to offer terms of peace to a targeted town and allowed those who accepted Israelite identity to serve the nation as a laboring class. Males in any town who refused to convert were to be put to the sword, while women and cattle were treated as spoil. It appears that after the Philistines would not allow David to go with them into the battle in which Saul and Jonathan were killed, David encouraged his followers to integrate the scattered settlements of the Negeb into his kingdom at Hebron by marrying their women.

The program was somewhere between a complete annihilation of Canaanite settlements, which forbade any intermarriage with the women of the land, and David's need to occupy the villages of the south. After the independent Abigail agreed to David's marriage proposal, his men evidently chose women from the scattered settlements of the territory previously unclaimed by either Israelites or Philistines. In this

PART 2: Sex and Power Relationships in Some Israelite Stories

way we may conclude that David used both war and sex as he built a united Israel. Perhaps Abigail should be given credit for his program of assimilation.

In the context of their time the historians were right in seeing an overruling God behind the story. But we may also be right in seeing the power of an idea held by a sufficiently large body of followers of a charismatic leader. David's concept of Israel as the chosen people of YHWH was grasped by citizen soldiers at the valley of Elah, by the women in their song, by Michal, Jonathan, Abigail, the six hundred men who followed David in the southern wilderness, Joab and Abner and many others who were swept into David's path.

Underlying the history told in 1 Samuel we can see the operation of a dynamic movement of people relating well (or badly) in covenantal structures, "Our" story was told from the point of view of those who won in David's day. No Philistine storyteller was given the opportunity to tell a different story.

13

The Rhythms of Life and David's Adultery

THE HISTORIAN-THEOLOGIAN'S ASSESSMENT THAT David was a man after God's own heart ignored David's darker side and presumed to speak for God in a way that some modern critics feel is not justified. David's life after he established his capital in Jerusalem was marked by a change from the discipline of holy war to the indulging of his libido.

David's adultery with Bath-Sheba is generally treated as more significant than Samson's amorous adventures, and since David became king over all twelve Israelite tribes while Samson "judged" only the tribes of Judah and Dan, the proportionality is probably correct. Both men, however, were important to Israel and their behavior led to adverse consequences. Samson's actions led to war with the Philistines; David committed the first publicly recognized sin in the united Israel.

Life can be seen as multiple cycles of activities in the rhythms of several systems that operate in time scales ranging from extremely short to the full length of a human life. The Decalogue's week of work and rest is not the only cycle that concerns people. Even the fields were supposed to be allowed to rest one year out of seven. But Job complains that he can no longer rest at night:

> Do not human beings have a hard service on earth,
> and are not their days like the days of a laborer?
> Like a slave who longs for the shadow,
> and like laborers who look for their wages,
> so I am allotted months of emptiness,
> and nights of misery are apportioned to me,
> When I lie down I say, 'When shall I rise?'
> But the night is long,
> and I am full of tossing until dawn. (Job 7:1–4)

What the author of Job does not mention is that the typical worker looked forward to an evening meal and sleeping with his wife after a day of work.

PART 2: Sex and Power Relationships in Some Israelite Stories

A Quiet Afternoon "Affair"

David could rest from warfare after he moved the seat of his power to Jerusalem, and no doubt could have called upon any one of several wives for sexual satisfaction. His story is so well known that it hardly needs retelling. Well into his forty-year reign, David could rely on his generals to conduct a small war against the Ammonites, who lived in what is now the Hashemite Kingdom of Jordan east of the Dead Sea. The Philistines, who lived to the west of Judea, had been held within a narrow strip of land along the Mediterranean coast, largely by David's guerilla attacks when he was younger. Now a middle aged king, David could rest and nap during the heat of the day while others suppressed an uprising against David's attempt to annex Rabbah to his kingdom. "Late one afternoon, when David rose from his couch and was walking about on the roof of the king's house, he saw from the roof a woman bathing; the woman was very beautiful."[1]

Evidently David did not recognize his neighbor, but learned that she was "Bath-Sheba, daughter of Eliam, the wife of Uriah the Hittite." In spite of the fact that Uriah was one of the soldiers who was at that time defending the border of his kingdom, David sent for the woman, and she came. Imagine the preliminary conversation: "You are married to Uriah the Hittite?" "Yes, we've been married some time." "He's a good man, one of the best of our soldiers. How long has he been away at the front?" "Well, it's been a few weeks; the spring campaign has just begun." "I'm afraid it's going to be a long siege. Rabbah is well fortified, and even at this season it is probably well stocked with provisions." "So I've heard."

Was Bath-Sheba wondering by this time why it took the king so long to get to the real reason for his invitation to visit the palace? Why had the king summoned her to his residence on a warm spring afternoon? She must have known, for his reputation was no secret. Whatever her thoughts and feelings, she did not "cry out," as respectable women were expected to do if they were sexually harassed in the towns of Israel.[2]

Bath-Sheba returned home, and a week or so later she sent word to David that she was pregnant. Until modern times people believed that semen contained the "seed"— a tiny human being—of the future son or daughter, and that the woman was only the seedbed in which the seed germinated and matured So Uriah's outrage at David's intrusion into his "field" would be understandable. Foreseeing that, David took steps that only a king could take, attempting to make it appear that Uriah had planted the seed in Bath-Sheba's womb, He ordered his general to see to it that Uriah be sent back to Jerusalem.

"So David sent word to Joab, 'Send me Uriah the Hittite.'" Uriah came and David asked questions about the campaign, how Joab was managing the siege, how the troops were getting along, and what the prospects were of taking Rabbah. Small talk: news

---

1. Quotations from 2 Samuel 11–12 are from the NRSV.

2. The earlier Covenant Code does not include this provision, which would have made her innocent of having agreed with her attacker. Deuteronomy 22:22–26, however, does specify that an innocent woman should escape being stoned with the man. However, it is highly unlikely that the Deuteronomic law had been formulated and adopted in the time of David.

from the front. Then he dismissed Uriah, suggesting that he go to his home and relax. In addition, "there followed him a gift from the king."

Instead of going home Uriah "slept at the entrance of the king's house with all the servants," and probably did not know that the servant who delivered the present would report that he had not gone to his wife. When David asked why he had not gone to his home, Uriah spoke as a good soldier, "The ark and Israel and Judah remain in booths, and my lord Joab and the servants of my lord are camping in the open field; Shall I then go to my house, to eat and to drink, and to lie with my wife? As you live, and as your soul lives, I will not do such a thing." An oath on the honor of the two men, not in the name of YHWH.

David kept Uriah in Jerusalem an additional day, and feasted him, making him drunk, but Uriah stayed with the servants again. In the meantime, David wrote (or probably dictated) a letter in which he asked Uriah to deliver to Joab. The letter directed Joab to put Uriah in the front line in the next assault, and then to leave him exposed "so that he may be struck down and die." It was done; Uriah was killed; and word was brought back to David: The attack had gotten very close to the wall of the city, and " . . . Your servant Uriah the Hittite is dead too."

Bath-Sheba publicly mourned the death of her husband for the conventional period, and David waited silently as a member of the community, having commented officially to Joab: "Do not let this matter trouble you, for the sword devours now one and now another; press your attack on the city, and overthrow it."

A Public Marriage and a Case for the "Supreme Court"

What was to that moment a personal matter between two men now became public property. When the mourning was over, David sent for Bath-Sheba "and brought her to his house, and she became his wife, and bore him a son." Bath-Sheba was not the only widow whom David had taken into his household. In the previous chapter we recalled how David came to marry the widow of a wealthy man named Nabal who had refused to help David's band of outlaws with food and drink in their flight from Saul. There may have been no week long celebration of either marriage, only the sending for and bringing the women into David's quarters. The king could give himself any woman he chose. One may wonder what sort of love David shared with Abigail and Bath-Sheba, and how two strong women related to each other in his household, but the historian does not tell us.

Bath-Sheba was neither an independent woman nor a prostitute when she first attracted David's attention. He might have considered the risk he was taking when he learned that she was the wife of one of his soldiers, but he was not one to weigh the possible consequences before acting impulsively. It is probable that publicly Israel had few written laws in the eleventh century BCE, possibly only oral versions of the Ten Words brought down from the mountain by Moses. "Thou shalt not commit adultery" would have been one of those laws, but the commandment offered no guidance to Israel's judging elders as to how to punish a violation of this Torah. Instead tribal

Part 2: Sex and Power Relationships in Some Israelite Stories

custom permitted men to avenge wrongs done to them even if doing so led to further reprisals, as we observed in the case of Dinah. So, it would not be until the writing of the Covenant Code a century or more after David's time, that Israel's local judges could look to a law book for guidance.[3] In the meantime Israel's tribal elders and priests were shaping oral rules that would implement the intuitive sense that certain behavior was wrong not only in the sight of people but also in the sight of YHWH. If David had been an ordinary Israelite, he might have considered the consequences detailed in this oral tradition, but how often are strong men deterred from trying to seduce an attractive woman? Every Israelite knew that Bath-Sheba's husband would have attempted to kill a man who slept with his wife. Uriah would incur no guilt for doing "what was right."[4] But David was king, and he had a reputation as a powerful fighter.

Since the king was one of the elders of Israel, and in fact the chief elder of the nation, David was the judge to whom difficult cases were brought when the lower "courts" failed to satisfy the community's demand for justice. So it seemed quite natural for the prophet Nathan to present a case for David to consider. In narrative form an outraged citizen turned prophet approached the king and said:

> There were two men in a certain city, the one rich and the other poor. The rich man had very many flocks and herds; but the poor man had nothing but one little ewe lamb, which he had bought. He brought it up, and it grew up with him and with his children; it used to eat of his meager fare, and drink from his cup, and lie in his bosom, and it was like a daughter to him. Now there came a traveler to the rich man, and he was loath to take one of his own flock or herd to prepare for the wayfarer who had come to him, but he took the poor man's lamb, and prepared that for the guest who had come to him. (2 Sam 12:1–4)

David's intuitive, instinctive reaction to the injustice pictured in the story was immediate and visceral, "As the Lord lives, the man who has done this deserves to die; he shall restore the lamb fourfold." But until Nathan said "You are the man!" David did not notice that the prophet did not identify the "certain city" of his story, as would have been customary with cases brought to the king for judgment.

Nathan's indictment of his king recalled all that YHWH had done for David, even voicing YHWH's word, "If that had been too little, I would have added as much more." Then returning to his own voice Nathan asked, "Why have you despised the word of the Lord?" and declared, "You have struck down Uriah the Hittite with the sword, and have taken his wife to be your wife, and have killed him with the sword of the Ammonites." Two indictments for murder, one for veiled adultery, and another for public contempt for the word of God. Nathan went on, detailing the punishment

---

3. The book detailing "the rights and duties of the kingship" which Samuel "laid up before the Lord" (1 Sam 10:25) could have included only a broad statement of covenantal relations between king and people, if it was more than a figment of the historian's mind. The Covenant Code apparently originated in the northern kingdom no earlier than fifty years after David's time, and Deuteronomy's laws followed a century later.

4. Pinker, *How the Mind Works*, 490: "All over the world, men also beat and kill cuckolds and suspected cuckolds . . . rivalry over women is the leading cause of violence, homicide, and warfare among foraging peoples."

to come, in YHWH's words: "I will raise up trouble against you from within your own house; and I will take your wives before your eyes, and give them to your neighbor, and he shall lie with your wives in the sight of this very sun."

The prophetic "I" stands outside the human affairs as only God can, whose eye attends to one situation now and then another, observing behavior and its consequences, and inviting bystanders to judge whether the actors have done well or badly. Finally the actors must see their little scenarios for themselves, and the guilty must judge himself.

"I Have Sinned"

All David could say was, "I have sinned against the Lord." At that moment a man who was practically above human law not only took responsibility for acts he had committed, but also recognized that his actions concerned a Power beyond the covenantal arrangements people make with each other. This simple admission of guilt is profoundly significant for our understanding of the moral universe in which we live.

Remember that one aspect of the social, cultural world of Israel was belief in a supreme personal God, who was not only the world's Creator but also its supreme Judge, a living, thinking being like humans. Since human communities included wiser, older men and women, the ordinary Israelite in the village had no trouble looking beyond the local elder or priest to a Being who approved or disapproved the choices people were making. Even if the villager in Nathan's story had not entered into formal contracts with his neighboring landholder, he believed in the power of the elders of his community or the tribal judges or priests, who could be appealed to for justice. In David's day no one questioned the reality of personal gods who ruled above the tribal leaders. David himself was particularly God-aware, or more exactly, YHWH-aware. Preeminent in David's thought world was Israel's God, YHWH.[5] At least in moments of crisis, David had turned to the living deity, calling for help in battle as he and Jonathan had helped each other. He frequently used the oath "As the Lord Lives," (in Hebrew simply "YHWH lives!") to give emphatic stress to a declaration or decision.

David had grown to manhood relying on a companion God to support his arms. For David and his kinsmen YHWH was not only the giver of young lambs, babies, and agricultural products; the God of Israel cared for the social as well as the physical welfare of people. He had led a generation of Abraham's descendants into and out of Egypt, and had given Torah/Law to guide them to behavior that pleased Him. Three of the ten words brought down from Sinai told Israelites to worship YHWH alone, to make no image of Him and not to use His Name lightly. Whether he knew the Decalogue in the form familiar to us or not, David took the first command very seriously, and apparently gave less thought to the others. Although he used the name YHWH freely, it was always to express deep commitment, usually to what he believed to be a just cause. YHWH was just as much companion to David as Jonathan had been.

---

5. It should not be necessary to remind readers that the Hebrew text reads four consonants YHWH which we suppose were pronounced Yahweh and have been rendered in English with the word "Lord."

When Nathan told his story of the wealthy man who took his poor neighbor's ewe lamb to provide a feast for a guest, David's response did not refer to the Decalogue's "thou shalt not steal." Instead he decreed, "the man who would do such a thing deserves to die . . . at least he ought to repay his neighbor four times." The King's sense of right and wrong was outraged, and he burst out with two possible punishments for the rich man. He did not refer to a legal rule, which had probably not been written in his day, but to one of many "judgments" held in the common memory of all the tribes. The wealthy man had done wrong to his poor neighbor—a personal injury—for which no punishment or repayment could atone. In the deepest meaning of the word, he had *sinned*. He might take a neighbor's lamb in haste and pay later, but neither one nor all of the four lambs he might offer could replace the pet his neighbor's children had played with. The harm was beyond the material; it was moral and spiritual.

Sin may involve personal injury, but also a failure to uphold or fulfill the communal relationships which people take for granted within families, tribes, towns, or nations. People do not think first of a law that has been broken; they *feel* that a wrong has been done and impulsively say so, as David did when Nathan finished his story. Today he might have said, "There ought to be a law . . ." but since *he* could give judgment, David uttered an oath, "YHWH lives," [in extended form "I swear by the God who lives,"] binding himself to right the wrong done by the wealthy man of the story. Seeing YHWH as Supreme Judge above all Israelite relationships, David identified the taking of the lamb as an insult to YHWH, who must feel as angry as David at the breach of the common good. So the human level injury cried out to YHWH God for a retaliation the poor man could not effect, a perfect example of the need for the God apex of our covenantal diagram of relationships.

Sin's Consequences

Nathan did not use the word "sin" or mention the Ten Commandments. He spoke only to David's sense of right and wrong, that deep feeling of sympathetic anger or disappointment that struggles from the depth of a person's being to find action, words, rules or laws, expressed in a few words. The young Samuel had felt that same disappointment as he saw Eli's sons taking the best pieces of the sacrificed meat and sleeping with the women who served at the entrance to the tent of meeting He may have heard the man of God rebuking Eli for not correcting his sons and he certainly heard the people's gossip. And Eli *had* spoken to his sons using the word "sin" both for their abusing people and for their failing relationship with God: "I hear of your evil dealings from all these people. No, my sons; it is not a good report that I hear the people of the Lord spreading abroad. If one person sins against another, someone can intercede for the sinner with the Lord; but if someone sins against the Lord, who can make intercession?" (1 Sam 2:23–25).

The true nature of sin comes into focus in the setting of the first substantial kingdom in ancient Israel. A sin is "evil dealing," literally a bad "word" or metaphorical "thing" between people *and* between an individual and God. The Hebrew uses the common term for "word" and metaphorically indicates that something valuable has been moved from one person to another as in a business transaction, but without the consent of the giver. As crime, what happens is bad; the second person is injured—physically, economically, socially, politically, or religiously. Eli's sons had abused the people they were supposed to be serving, and the report of their behavior "spread abroad" and offended YHWH himself. Perhaps more significantly, mutual relationships break down in all directions from the "sinner." My diagram could be modified to show the raw red wound of sin in the social fabric. As sin, David's actions had damaged his moral authority with his people, a responsibility committed to him by YHWH, and Nathan hesitated to intercede with God for him, just as Eli had explained to his sons.

We customarily think of sin as an offense against God even when there has been an abuse of a human relationship. When we are aware that we have injured another person, we can ask that person's forgiveness, and we have been taught to pray also for God's forgiveness, but we learn that God does not turn aside the consequences of our action. Prayer, with or without the mediation of priest or prophet, does not avail to avoid consequences. So David could neither require Bath-Sheba to abort the fetus nor turn aside the wrath of her husband Uriah. David, Nathan, and the people of Israel must live with the consequences of his action.

The immediate consequences were both good and bad. Bath-Sheba bore a son, but "it became very ill" and died. In the meantime the people learned that Uriah's death was no accident, but had been engineered by their king. Later, the problems within David's family to which Nathan's prophecy alluded would sour David's final years. Amnon would rape his half-sister Tamar, and would be murdered at Absalom's command.[6] However, Bath-Sheba would bear another son, and Solomon would succeed his father instead of one of David's other sons, Adonijah, Absalom, or Amnon. The historians' judgment was that this consequence was good.

Modern thought looks for direct and essential connection between cause and effect, but ancient wisdom believed in the personal intervention of human or divine beings to avenge wrongs. Biblical stories recount the process in personal terms: If David had Uriah killed, YHWH would see to it that someone close to David would die. The ancient proverbial formula: "an eye for an eye, a life for a life" recognized the natural rhythm of giving and receiving whose operation people expect. In our day underprivileged people say, "What goes around, comes around!"

Rape and Murder in the Family

Amnon actually raped his half-sister Tamar, and Absalom ordered his servants to murder Amnon, just as David had ordered Uriah to be killed in battle by the Ammonites. These incidents, told in some detail in 2 Samuel, like many others in the biblical history, seldom use the words "guilt" and "sin." They report events and let the reader provide the categories of right and wrong or good and evil for the actions. And since

---

6. Wilson, *Divine Symmetries*, 130, Victor M. Wilson comments, "As the linchpin of justice and order, David's conduct is appalling. He invites anarchy within his household."

PART 2: Sex and Power Relationships in Some Israelite Stories

the stories are about David's children, we can presume with the historians that what Amnon and Absalom did were delayed consequences of David's sin.

When David "sent to his daughter Tamar, saying, 'Go to your brother Amnon's house, and prepare food for him'" because he had pretended an illness that only his sister's cooking could cure, Tamar went obediently, "took dough, kneaded it, made cakes in his sight and baked the cakes. Then she took the pan and set them out before him." When he refused to eat, and ordered everybody to leave his room, "he took hold of her, and said to her, 'Come, lie with me, my sister.'" She answered, "No, my brother, do not force me, for such a thing is not done in Israel; do not do anything so vile! As for me, where could I carry my shame? And for you, you would be as one of the scoundrels in Israel. Now therefore, I beg you, speak to the king; for he will not withhold me from you" (2 Sam 13:12–13).

If only he had asked! Would that coupling have been wrong? Amnon was forcing Tamar to cross a socially forbidden line. Tamar's father was the master of his household and king of the nation; his word was final, and whether Tamar cared to be married to her brother was not the question. She would have accepted her father's decision to give her to Amnon just as she had accepted the order to care for her "sick" brother by preparing his meal. From childhood every young woman knew the customary social structure of intra-family care giving.

After the rape "Amnon was seized with a great loathing" for his sister and ordered her from his house telling "the young man who served him, 'Put this woman out of my presence, and bolt the door after her.'" So, "Tamar put ashes on her head, and tore the long robe that she was wearing; she put her hand on her head, and went away, crying aloud."

Brother Absalom asked, "Has Amnon your brother been with you? Be quiet for now, my sister; for he is your brother; do not take this to heart." So Tamar remained a desolate woman in her brother Absalom's house. When David heard the story, he was angry, but would not punish Amnon "because he loved him, for he was his firstborn. But Absalom spoke to Amnon neither good or bad,"—the "silent treatment" with nursed anger.

After two full years Absalom had sheepshearers at Baal-hazor, which is near Ephraim, and Absalom invited all the king's sons. Absalom came to the king, and said, "Your servant has sheepshearers; will the king and his servants please go with your servant?" But the king said to Absalom, "no, my son, let us not all go, or else we will be burdensome to you." He pressed him, but he would not go but gave him his blessing. Then Absalom said, "If not, please let my brother Amnon go with us. The king said to him, "Why should he go with you?" But Absalom pressed him until he let Amnon and all the king's sons go with him. Absalom made a feast like a king's feast. Then Absalom commanded his servants, "Watch when Amnon's heart is merry with wine, and when I say to you, 'Strike Amnon,' then kill him. Do not be afraid; have I not myself commanded you? Be courageous and valiant" (2 Sam 13:23–28).

So the servants of Absalom did to Amnon as Absalom had commanded. Then all the king's sons rose, and each mounted his mule and fled.

Was Absalom wrong to avenge the rape of Tamar by a planned murder? The historians declined to force a judgment, and did not always tell us how God felt, but we like to believe that our feeling is more or less the same as God's. Amnon should have *felt* guilty of rape, for he *was* guilty. Absalom yielded to *his* anger, but since he was following ancient custom he had no need to *feel* guilty.

"Life for Life"

Thus, the *lex talionis*, "eye for eye, tooth for tooth, life for life," served as the master formula both for assessing guilt and for removing it. Amnon had penetrated his sister's virgin hymen, presumably occasioning enough bleeding to mark the bedclothes. The text does not mention blood, but recall that the father and mother could certify their daughter's virginity by offering evidence of her recent menstrual flow when her new husband did not find evidence that he had broken the hymen. Both guilt and innocence could be marked with blood.

When he ordered Tamar out of his bedroom, Amnon knew that he was guilty. Because he had violated the family's implicit rule of care giving love, it was incumbent on a near kin person to shed "blood for blood" to restore a sense of order in the family, thus to remove "blood guilt."

Procrastination, if not ambivalence, seems to have characterized king David, Absalom and YHWH God. Absalom waited two years for the opportunity, and thought he had relieved the tension of guilt in the family. Unfortunately, his act created a new tension which could only be relieved by *his* death—if then. Absalom began to assume his father's responsibility and power to judge in disputes people brought to David, since David did not concern himself about them. Finally, he proclaimed himself king of Israel in full rebellion (2 Sam 15). Remarkably, almost absurdly, both nature and culture conspired to accomplish God's vengeance when Absalom's "head [his remarkably long hair] caught fast in the oak, and he was left hanging between heaven and earth," until "Joab's armor-bearers, surrounded and struck him, and killed him" (2 Sam 18:9–14).

Mary Douglas offers clues to Israelite thinking about a number of social matters. In her book, *In the Wilderness*, a study of Levitical legislation in the Pentateuch, she writes:

> The doctrine of Leviticus 17:11 is that God has allowed blood for making atonement. If we change the translation to, 'I have given it to you upon the altar to make atonement for your souls; for it is the blood that makes atonement for the soul', this brings *talion* as described in Exodus 21:23 and Leviticus 24:18 within the scope of the covenant. If a life for a life can be translated as 'living being for a living being', or as 'a person for a person', or 'a soul for a soul', the phrasing implies that the sacrificed blood (which is the soul or the life of the animal) is the intended ransom or substitute for the human soul. We are back to Professor Drai's argument that biblical *talion* has been taken out of context. It is artificial to suppose that the discussion of blood as forbidden food and blood for atonement on the altar has no evocation of blood of birth and blood of homicide. When

such contrived compartmentalization is corrected the book's teaching on blood becomes a vital part of the theology of covenant. [Leviticus] is a book about life and death and everything that blood stands for, violence, injustice, betrayal, killing, and atonement.[7]

For the ancient Israelite guilt was everywhere and the offering of blood was the only way to restore a semblance of innocence. Mary Douglas comments further: "The systematization of sin in Leviticus makes all human creatures unavoidably liable to defilement. Regardless of good intentions defilement in one form or another is going to happen to everyone and anyone at any time."

It may seem that I have anticipated the legal and ritual developments promised for a later chapter, or that I have retrojected the thought of a post-exilic writer to a pre-exilic situation, but the rules of Leviticus, whenever written, returned to the traditional desire for vengeance with its parallel feeling of abhorrence for blood. Both are merged in the early "eye for eye" formula. The Israelite believed that one who has shed blood offends the Living God as well as his injured neighbor. For the offense to God, the "sin," sacrificial blood must be shed; for the neighbor's life another life must be taken. The death of Bath-Sheba's first son had proved the point, and the murder of Amnon and Absalom's later death added further exemplifying proofs to the Israelite ethic of retributive justice and the practice of sacramental ritual. *Talion* became both legal dictum for justice and a ritual for cleansing. Cycles of guilt and punishment, uncleanness and cleansing were completed in David's later years.

---

7. Douglas "Sacred Contagion," 100–101. Also see Jackson, "Talion and Purity," 112.

Michal's Lament

Yahweh, you came to our house that day!
Celebrating the victory, applauding the hero,
Cheering the shepherd, the troops at our door;
David appeared with my father the King.
Kings promise daughters to heroes in battle.
Daughters are always the gifts of their fathers.
Suddenly I knew what I wanted—that man,
Ruddy and tanned, and glistening with sweat.
From a corner I saw him. My father inquired,
"Whose son are you. young man?"
I already knew the answer, "the son
Of your servant Jesse of Bethlehem."
But it was Jonathon my brother
Who captured the heart of the shepherd.
They went off to fight Philistines,
And my father forgot his promise.
Always the women were there
When the soldiers came home from a battle,
Singing and dancing, "Saul his thousands
Has killed, and David ten thousands."
He stayed in our home, and I waited.
My sister was married, but not to David.
Then father and he came to terms:
A bride price to be paid, Philistine foreskins.
He returned for his prize; my joy was unbounded.
"Avenge me of my enemies," my father said,
Thinking, *"he may fall by the hand of a Philistine."*
So my husband went back to the wars again.
Always the women were there

When the soldiers came home from a battle,
Singing and dancing, "Saul his thousands
Has killed, and David ten thousands."
My hero returned from the wars, and I hoped
We could plan for the future, peaceful with family,
A little one who'd be king after David.
But father had one of his rages one day.
My husband was playing his harp, but that day
The storm that was brewing exploded.
The spear just missed, and David escaped,
His battlefield strength no help in the house.
I lied to my father when his guards came searching
And found only an idol and a heap of bed clothes.
Our last night of love ended too quickly,
In ignominious flight before dawn.
A king's daughter has problems others don't have.
When David did not return, it was decided
I should be the wife of good Paltiel,
A favored friend of the family.
He was no hero, but he loved me, perhaps
For reasons of his own. He never knew my heart,
But when the King decreed I should return
To him, good Paltiel wept, and I was grim faced.
I knew it was not for love of me that I
Was called back. The king was busy cementing
Alliances between tribes, and needed me
A Benjamite, to link with Judah, and the others.
I do not complain, for what woman has not
Known such usage from the man she hoped
Would love her as an equal partner
In the building of his house?
We built a glorious house—in time—
A temple for Jehovah God, but it was
Another's son who finished what we began.
Bath-Sheba took my rightful place.

Part 3
A Natural History of Biblical "Sin"

14

Sin's Reality

As we explored a set of stories in the Hebrew Scriptures, we found no definitive picture of generic sin and almost no evidence to build a definition of it. The first man and woman may have sinned when they ate fruit from a particular tree, but we are not told why eating it was wrong. In the light of Deuteronomic commands to obey everything God directs, *the first couple* must have understood that their older Companion expected obedience to His commands.

Having received no instruction from God, Cain was told after he killed Abel that sin was "lurking at the door." At the egocentric stage of personal and social life, Cain had not yet learned rules or definitions of sin, but at that point he did hear that he must learn to control his [right brain?] impulses. His family probably treated the first manslaughter as a crime and excluded him from family gatherings.

The *people of Babel* may never have thought that building their tower was either criminal or sinful, especially if it was mostly their king's idea. And a vague feeling of corruption connected with sexual relations between "the sons of God" and the "daughters of men" is the only explanation for the worldwide flood.

In his dream it was no close kin of Abraham, but the Semite *Abimelech*, who learned that God—a good Spirit who talked with him—had prevented him from sinning by warning that Sarah was Abraham's wife. Like Cain he learned that some behavior, adultery, could not be allowed in a culture of human relationships, even in relationships with foreigners. The editors of Genesis included three versions of this incident, identifying the host as Pharaoh and the patriarch as Abram in 12:10–20, and the host as Abimelech and both Abraham and Isaac in 20:1–18 and 26:6–11 as the visiting patriarch. The stories are substantially the same but only in Abimelech's dream does God say "it was I who kept you from sinning against me" (20:16).

When *Rebekah and Jacob* deceived the aging Isaac into giving dominance to Jacob instead of Esau, neither the historian nor God seem concerned that a sin might have been committed in the deception. In the modern world most deceptions are called crimes.

PART 2: Sex and Power Relationships in Some Israelite Stories

When he invoked future mastery over slaves for Jacob, was Isaac (1) announcing a judgment on an abusive regional practice, (2) foreseeing Jacob's future, or (3) praying that each son would fulfill his destiny?

> Let peoples serve you,
> and nations bow down to you.
> Be lord over your brothers,
> and may your mother's sons bow down to you. (27:29)
> And slavery for Esau?
> By your sword you shall live,
> and you shall serve your brother;
> But when you break loose,
> you shall break his yoke from your neck. (27:40)

The historian simply reports the fury of Esau and Rebekah's arrangement to send Jacob to her family. When *Rebekah* decided that neither Jacob nor Esau should be allowed to murder his brother, did she commit a "sin?" Her unhappiness with Esau's wives was the ostensible reason for sending Jacob to Paddan-Aram and came close to being a deception, but the historian does not identify it as either deception or sin. Which designation should we choose? What were God's feelings and thoughts?

It is possible that *Simeon* and *Levi* may have reflected that their massacre of Shechem's clan was a sin, but all we can call it was a serious misstep, since God apparently let it pass without penalizing the family of Jacob.

Judah should have remembered his obligation to bring Tamar back to be the wife of his third son. Why didn't he? We can only guess that having lost two sons, he felt that somehow Tamar was demon possessed or that she would utter a curse if or when she returned to his family. However, when he was confronted with his responsibility for Tamar's unanticipated pregnancy, Judah said, "she is more in the right than I," not "I have sinned." God and the family were apparently more interested in the growth of the tribe than in the effects of an unformed curse.

Joseph's brothers belatedly realized that they might be paying the penalty for what they had done when they sold him to traders, implying that the sin they had committed might explain their predicament in Egypt. Discussing their situation, Reuben commented, "Did I not tell you not to wrong the boy? But you would not listen. So now there comes a reckoning for his blood." For NRSV "wrong," which is the sense of the comment, the authorized version and the RSV translate the Hebrew of Genesis 42:22 literally, "sin against the lad." None of the brothers mentioned God until one of them opened his sack to give his donkey fodder at the lodging place, and found his money. At that moment they asked, "What is this that God has done to us?" (Gen 42:28) The members of Jacob's family almost never mentioned the possibility that they had sinned, and Joseph did not accuse them. But they believed God knew what they had done.

When *Miriam and Aaron* "spoke against Moses," and asked if YHWH's speaking through them was not as significant as what Moses had done, Aaron begged God not to punish Miriam for "a sin we have so foolishly committed." This instance of forgiveness for a thoughtless sin was like the modern "time out" imposed on an obstinate child, through exclusion from the camp for a week (Num 12). Like the child today Miriam had time to think about how she and Aaron had stepped out of their places in line.

Shortly after the fall of Jericho, *Achan* and probably many others "took some of the devoted things" in the aborted attack on Ai, and YHWH told Joshua "Israel has sinned; they have transgressed my covenant . . . stolen, acted deceitfully, and have put them among their own belongings. Therefore the Israelites are unable to stand before their enemies; they turn their backs to their enemies [taking booty to their tents], because they have become a thing devoted for destruction themselves." In Joshua 7:10–12 the customary "eye for eye" practice has become God's judgment on Israelite soldiers. To teach Israel a lesson, Achan was stoned to death, his body was burned and a great heap of stones was raised over his ashes. Had those who were not caught sinned? And if so, why were they not punished?

David's clear and unambiguous confession, "I have sinned," focused attention on his personal sin, and linked two destructive actions to the concept. It is almost ironic that his adultery and the contrived murder that followed are among the core ethical prohibitions of the Decalogue, and that Nathan's story of the rich man's lamb brought a third of the principles, theft, to bear on David's conscience. David, however, did not "bear false witness" about himself. Which of the commandments defined his "sin?"

His declaration, "I have sinned," addressed God as well as the prophet, and accepted responsibility for the consequences of his behavior. In so doing David broadened his perspective to see his actions as God might see them. The context broadened from David's involvement with Bath-Sheba to his relationship with everyone whom YHWH could see. In David's mind, that might have involved a united Israel, and possibly all its neighbors. Looking back, David saw the significance of what he had done and he may have realized that before he sent for Bath-Sheba he might have asked, "Is my personal pleasure more valuable to Israel than the stability of the family relationships of the people of the kingdom?" Today's reader may think of the sexual misdeeds of popular political and sports figures and ask the same question.

This group of "sins" from early stories in the Hebrew scriptures illustrates some broad commonalities in notable sins as writer/editors reported history from God's viewpoint: (1) eight or nine incidents tell of deceitful failures in covenantal relationships when what was promised was not delivered either in whole or part to its prospective owner; (2) about half the cases involved *persons as property* that was to have been cared for in a family setting; (3) only in the case of Achan was *valuable material property* involved, but his case may have uniquely punished only one out of hundreds of guilty individuals. (4) The Achan incident involved *property that was recognized as God's*.

In addition to the commonalities of the "sins", a sort of progression appears: in place of damaging actions, the biblical storytellers give attention to underlying motivation and the conversations in which motivations are only partially exposed. David's adultery stands out as a physical act; afterward the motivations are exposed.

In contrast, the motivations of Miriam and Aaron to stand equal to Moses in reporting the words of YHWH are central to the story in Numbers. The only physical aspect was the ritual week of exclusion from the camp to cure Miriam's leprosy. Two kinds of relationship can be distinguished, one predominantly physical (biological) and the other more social and conceptual. Both are aspects of the world, but Miriam consciously crossed from the secular to a special form of the conceptual we know as "the sacred" in her "sin" while David violated a social convention, suppressing his awareness of it. A common thread in the sins is God's interest in the events.

When members of the human family see what they have done in a context broader than the physical and social, that is, with God's view of their activity, an act may be considered a sin if it intended adverse effects against one or more individuals whom God had created. Not all acts with adverse consequences need to be called sins, since motivation must always be considered. On the playground an injured child can be told, "He (or I) didn't mean to hurt you." The Hebrew histories tell a variety of stories in which people did harm to other people without intending it or acted in such a way that harm might follow, so our summary observation is that only God has sufficient insight to label "sins," while early humans had to learn through experience.

The true nature of sin comes into sharp focus in the dedication of Solomon's temple. The sins of the patriarchal period were largely failures of personal or tribal covenanting between people whom God brought into relationships. But when Deuteronomy's Moses reminded the Israelites of the forty years of wandering in the wilderness with its "poisonous snakes and scorpions," he urged the whole assembly to keep the commandments and walk in YHWH's ways and not to turn aside into a "bad way." (Deut 8:2,6,15) Shortly after receiving the law, however, Israel had refused to follow the path YHWH had laid before them.

A moment of "sin" was briefly acknowledged in the Israelites' confession in Deuteronomy 1:41, after the people refused to go forward to the Promised Land. "We have sinned against the Lord! We are [now] ready to go up and fight, just as the Lord our God commanded us." A parallel and more extended account of the return of the spies and the unfavorable report of ten of them is found in Numbers 14 which also reports the immediate death of the ten pessimists while promising that Caleb and Joshua would lead the next generation into the land. The word "sin" is not mentioned in the parallel Numbers account, but the incident does point to the power of leaders to influence rebellious behavior in their followers. Having been forgiven for their immediate refusal to move into Canaan, the people "presumed to go up to the heights of the hill country, even though the ark of the covenant of the Lord, and Moses, had not left the camp. Then the Amalekites and Canaanites who lived in that hill country came down and defeated them." (Num 14:44–45) After two disobedient actions, "sins," which we might call a sin of omission and a sin of commission, a whole generation would die in the wilderness for its waywardness.

At Shiloh *Eli's sons* abused the people they were supposed to be serving—even priests can be greedy—and the report of their behavior "spread abroad" and offended YHWH (1 Sam 2:22–25). Eli's fumbling behavior, a "sin of omission" and David's two sins of commission—adultery and arranged murder—damaged their moral authority with the people, a responsibility committed to them by YHWH, but neither Samuel or Nathan interceded with God for them. God would deal with them as God chose.

Samuel, Nathan, Elijah, Micaiah, and other priestly/prophetic figures sometimes spoke to YHWH *for* the people, but they often spoke for God *to* the people. Were their disapprovals genuine communication from the God we worship, or did they use rational processes to compose messages that they could ascribe to God? The question is as troubling as the question of the reality of sin.

Having discovered that events can be "caused," believers declare that disapprovals of human acts come from God who both created humans and notices their actions. Secularists prefer to ignore God's role and declare that at the heart of the cosmos is an uncaused randomness into which every activity is meshed. Between the general randomness and the idea of causation modern humans tend either to believe or deny that priests and prophets can actually speak for God. Secularists think that many acts should not be called sin, that is, referring to disobedience of a command of God, but should be labeled "crimes," violations of human laws or ethics. When a modern speaker uses the term "sin" loosely, it often carries no reference to God. Both believers and secularists, however, agree in being concerned with much human activity that occupies a vaguely defined region of human instigation.

"When . . ." or "If . . . then . . ."

Israel crossed a watershed in more than one way during the reign of David's son Solomon. Politically, Solomon completed the consolidation of the twelve tribes whose identities were remembered from patriarchal traditions.[1] What security David had accomplished through his wars, Solomon and the nation should have enjoyed in the cultivation of peaceful trade and growth, but after a time their bad behavior could be called sin.

Religiously, the completion of the temple established a visible center for the nation's worship of YHWH, whose spiritual presence was symbolized in the Ark of the Covenant that David had brought to Jerusalem. Solomon completed the nation's climb to the "holy place of the Most High" and the people could expect an era of security, protected from enemies by YHWH's sacramental presence. Solomon could stand wisely like Moses in Moab and proclaim the beginning of a time of peace for Israel under the Davidic dynasty. The language of 1 Kings 8:14 is a Deuteronomic version of what Solomon said on the occasion of the dedication of the Temple. The wording of his prayer in 1 Kings 8:22–53 / 2 Chronicles 6:12–39 was evidently prepared by theologians who, during the sixth century BCE, also wrote the present text of Moses' oration in Moab.

Our bibles give us what Solomon was supposed to have said. Biblical literalists may object that this emphasis on the literary activity of historian speechwriters detracts from divine inspiration, but it does not need to. We may understand the "mind

---

1. Norman K. Gottwald clarifies the socio–political history in detail in *The Tribes of Yahweh*.

of God" about "sin" without being concerned whether editors believed Solomon consciously referred to Moses' words or whether Moses and Solomon actually said specific words. What is important is that we get as deep insight as possible into the realities of our good and bad behavior.

Having assembled the elders of Israel and all the heads of the tribes for the installation of the Ark in the temple, Solomon first "blessed the people" with a brief look back to God's leading out of Egypt and his choice of Jerusalem as the place where the Name should dwell; (1 Kgs 8:14–21 / 2 Chr 6:1–11) The prayer recognized that no temple on earth could contain Israel's incomparable God YHWH, but it also asked that God confirm the promise to David that "there shall never fail you a [political] successor" and "that your [God's] eyes may be open night and day toward this house, the place of which you said, 'My name shall be there'" (1 Kgs 8:25, 29). Finally, Solomon looked prophetically into the future of Israel, using the language of Israel's Deuteronomic law code: "If someone sins against a neighbor and is given an oath to swear, and comes and swears before your altar in this house, then hear in heaven, and act, and judge your servants, condemning the guilty by bringing their conduct on their head, and vindicating the righteous by rewarding them according to their righteousness" (1 Kgs 8:31–2).

In the next verse Solomon changes from "if" to "when" in his references to the people's anticipated sinning: "When your people Israel, having sinned against you, are defeated before an enemy but turn again to you, confess your name, pray and plead with you in this house, then hear in heaven, forgive the sin of your people Israel, and bring them again to the land that you gave to their ancestors" (1 Kgs 8:33–4).

Without mentioning Moses' Deuteronomic farewell address, Solomon implies a cause and effect relationship between the people's sin and the afflictions they will be suffering, and sounds as if he is preparing God for the prayers they will bring to the Temple. He says, "If they sin against you—for there is no one who does not sin—and you are angry with them and give them to an enemy . . . yet if they come to their senses in the land to which they have been taken captive, and repent, and plead with you . . . then hear in heaven your dwelling place, their prayer and their plea, maintain their cause and forgive your people . . . and grant them compassion in the sight of their captors. (8:46–53).

With the "when" clause, Solomon anticipates that sins will actually have been committed. In Solomon's prayer sin is the reality of behavior to which people will ascribe afflictions, plagues, and wars, and from which they will turn to God to seek forgiveness.

Today we consider this loose ad hoc cause and effect thinking to be superstitious, particularly when drought, famine and plagues are treated as the effects of unnamed sin. Likewise national defeat and the Exile may have seemed to the ancient Judeans, coached by their priests and prophets, to be consequences of religious sinning, the worship of gods other than YHWH. The wise king Solomon and/or his editor had no better understanding of these afflictions. Solomon had no reason to mention specific sins since he could point out that "there is no one who does not sin." One hears these words as a precursor of verses 23–24 of the third chapter of Paul's letter to the Romans: "since all have sinned . . . they are now justified . . ."

This parenthetical observation in Solomon's prayer states as fact the principle of human fallibility. It is the principle underlying the Satan's charge against the character of Job when the Lord invited his heavenly servant to consider that "blameless and upright" human servant. The Satan charged: "Does Job fear God for nothing? . . . But stretch out your hand now, and touch all that he has, and he will curse you to your face" (Job 1:9, 11). Bring serious affliction on Job and he will sin just like everybody else.

According to the Deuteronomic language of Solomon's prayer, everyone is guilty of sin or *some sin*, and hence has a need for the healing rituals provided by the custodians of YHWH's temple. Real sin is so obvious in the life of people that it does not need to be catalogued. But prayers will go up with the smoke of offerings and be heard where YHWH dwells in heaven, and though the afflictions may remain, the sin factor—the way an abusive act appears in God's eyes—may be erased and disregarded.

What is essential is honest communication about the problem: the human "sinner" needs to own up to the thought and the act. In the Psalm 32 David, or an exilic poet writing as David, chose to "declare my transgressions to the Lord" and found that God was ready to be "a hiding place" who would "preserve me from trouble; and surround me with glad cries of deliverance" (vs.7).

Personal and Communal Sin

Because of its consequences sin appears to be real, and therefore it requires significant measures to remove it from the life of people chosen to serve YHWH God. Solomon's prayer asks God to condemn guilty individuals and reward the righteous when they come before the altar and swear about a controversy between two individuals. But the remainder of the prayer looks forward with if's and when's to broader afflictions that will come upon the whole people. As certainly as drought will come from time to time, Israel will need to come to the Temple, confess the Name and turn from their sin (1 Kgs 8:35–6). Or if the problem is famine, plague, blight, mildew, locust, caterpillar or whatever sickness, then Solomon asks God to "forgive, act, and tender to all whose hearts you know . . . so that they may fear you" (8:37–40). Even foreigners from distant lands or Israelites who go out to battle should be heard no matter how far from the Temple. Solomon implores YHWH to hear any prayer directed toward the Temple, even by those "carried away captive to the land of the enemy, far off or near" (8:46). When they say, "we have sinned," Solomon explains that they will have "come to their senses if they repent with all their heart and soul in the land of their enemies" (8:46). God should understand and forgive.

Afflictions and the sin linked to them will be real not only in the thought of Solomon, but in the experiences which God's favorite people would bring to the Temple in their prayers. As the people experience *real* afflictions and pray, God's *real* forgiveness can be granted: "Whatever sickness . . . whatever prayer, whatever plea there is from any individual or from all your people Israel, all knowing the afflictions of their own hearts so that they stretch out their hands toward this house, then hear in heaven . . . forgive, act, and render to all whose hearts you know . . . so that they may hear you all the days that they live in the land that you gave to our ancestors" (1 Kgs 8:37–40).

Confessions of individual Israelite sins can be brought to the temple and sorted out by God who knows the human heart, but Solomon declares that the same principle will apply to other peoples. Foreigners who believe may come to the temple to pray, or pray from afar. Those who confess sins, however vaguely, and "repent with all their hearts" will be forgiven. Solomon's prayer is remarkably unspecific and insubstantial regarding sins, but readers and hearers of the Deuteronomic literature could easily think of their own and their parents' sins to give the prayer a sense of reality. The very existence of the Temple would assure the reality of forgiveness for sin.

A king's sin could affect his people. 1 Kings 9 reports that YHWH appeared to Solomon a second time to confirm the promise of "a wise and discerning mind" which was the message of the first of three manifestations of God to him. In this revelation YHWH made a conditional promise that "there shall not fail to you a successor on the throne of Israel" (9:5), which was a specific answer to Solomon's prayer. But it both promised and threatened the whole of Israel, in effect making the people's future depend on the obedience of Solomon and his descendants. "If you [Solomon] turn aside from following me, you or your children, and do not keep my commandments and my statutes . . . I will cut Israel off from the land that I have given them; and the land that I have given them, and the house that I have consecrated for my name I will cast out of my sight, and Israel will become a proverb and a taunt among all peoples" (9:6–7). The possibility of Solomon's turning aside into sin is clearly real enough to have disastrous consequences not only for David's dynasty, but also for the nation.

Parenthetically: when the Chronicler reported the second epiphany to Solomon, YHWH offered opportunity for repentance for the people and a reward for obedience to Solomon, who is not mentioned as a probable sinner: "if my people who are called by my name humble themselves, pray, seek my face, and turn from their wicked ways, then I will hear from heaven, and will forgive their sin and heal their land . . . As for you, if you walk before me, as your father David walked, doing according to all that I commanded you and keeping my statutes and my ordinances, then I will establish your royal throne" (1 Chr 7:14,18).

The NRSV notes that in 2 Chronicles 7:19 the "you" for the conditional turning aside from YHWH's commands is plural. The Chronicler apparently left Solomon in free possession of his throne.

In a third appearance when Solomon was old, however, YHWH declared, "because *his* heart had turned away from the Lord . . . I will surely tear the kingdom from *you* and give it to your servant. Yet for the sake of your father David, I will not do it in your lifetime. I will tear it out of the hand of your son. *I will not, however, tear away the entire kingdom*, I will give one tribe to your son, for the sake of my servant David and for the sake of Jerusalem, which I have chosen" (1 Kgs 11:9–13, emphasis added). Thus YHWH, looking at Solomon from heaven, anticipated the fulfillment of Deuteronomic law, which Solomon, in his dedicatory prayer, had told God he understood. Without mentioning the word "sin" both Solomon and YHWH had agreed to the terms of the national Covenant, which had been established in the days of Moses. The king must now be told that the kingdom would be divided as a consequence of his forsaking God, following other gods and not keeping "the commandments and statutes" YHWH had given.

"In the later days of Solomon's reign the reality of sin was exemplified in Solomon's loving many women along with the daughter of Pharaoh . . . For when [he] was old, his wives turned away his heart after other gods, because his heart was not true to the Lord his God, as was the heart of his father David" (1 Kgs 11:1–4). The Deuteronomic principle of wayward sin could also be seen in other acts of Solomon. In chapters 9 and 10 of 1 Kings and in the parallel chapters of 2 Chronicles the historians report how he conscripted forced labor to build the Temple and other buildings of Jerusalem, including a house for Pharaoh's daughter. Solomon's expansive commercial empire included a seaport on the Red Sea and the sale of cities to Hiram of Tyre. The historian reports all of this without comment, leaving the reader to remember that Samuel had warned the people when they asked for a king that the king would act in these very ways to aggrandize himself and his kingdom (1 Sam 8:10–18). Though the sin factor of an act may be forgiven and the sinner restored to good relationship with God and community, the consequences would be relegated to remembered history, and might continue to plague both sinner and community.

A friendly observer, the Queen of Sheba, toward the end of Solomon's reign, was clearly impressed with the commercial success and glories of his kingdom, but she should have been able to see at least two questionable features of it. What term but "sin" should a religious observer or God have used to characterize the forced labor of Israelites by their king and the selling of Israelite towns? (1 Kgs 9:10–11). No Israelite should have been required to do what their ancestors had been required to do in Egypt. And the traded cities belonged to the tribe of Naphtali, not to the nation Israel. However, no one living in Solomon's time or when the scriptures were written gave attention to the forces that led to the division of the kingdom.

Israel had been delivered from forced labor in Egypt. Were its men and women not to be free from oppressive conditions in work camps or at the king's residence in Jerusalem? How could cities and their people who were part of a tribal confederation be separated from their nation for the enrichment of the king's treasury, or the payment of his debts? A serious breach of covenant relationship occurred in each of these situations. The historians report them, and we draw our conclusions.

Sin may be seen as the breaking of the Covenant bond between Israel and YHWH that required Israelites and their families to do justly, to love *hesed* faithfulness and to walk humbly with YHWH. Only a Yahwist Israelite or a Levitical priest— or YHWH—would have considered the introduction of alien gods in the worship a breaking of covenant relationship, so the historian reports that when Solomon made his alliances, he "loved many foreign women along with the daughter of Pharaoh" and "when he was old, his wives turned away his heart after other gods." (1 Kgs 11:1,3) As the exilic priests saw it, he not only broke covenant with YHWH, who was "angry with Solomon," but as we see it, he broke covenant with his own people. For us the ruptured relationships within the body of Israel appear more significant than the introduction of the images of foreign gods in shrines. The connection between them is clear enough when Solomon permitted his foreign wives to worship a god other than YHWH. For a superstitious people led by their priests to believe that YHWH reacted in anger whenever any Israelite looked toward another god for help, the thinking about sin remained fixed on unorthodox worship instead of the culture of sin.

A Culture of Sin

In a third epiphany YHWH told Solomon that most of the kingdom would be torn from him. Sin had its consequences, but the general concept remained undefined. From the early biblical stories we get the idea that sin was a personal breaking of covenant relationships, which could be formulated as social and moral "laws" directed to individuals by way of Moses' Deuteronomic sermon. The idea persists in Solomon's prayer and God's responses to him, but when he looked to the future of the kingdom, a wider horizon came into view.

Instead of the local and personal problems of families Solomon foresaw the problems of the nation, and anticipated the national misuse of the Temple he had just completed. In the background of his thought are the traditional defensive and aggressive uses of the Ark of the covenant. In Solomon's time the Temple became a fortress that God would defend against foreign attack, *if and when* enemies, famine, and/or plagues attempted to destroy Israel. Solomon recognizes in his prayer, however, that afflictions will certainly come as a result of the failure to obey all the "statutes and ordinances" of Torah/law which is Israel's precious heritage. God's part in the Covenant was to maintain his people's cause. Remember the vertical dimension in the covenantal diagram. As the law became public property and the Name YHWH became a memory of a treasured secret within the Ark and Temple, a subtle shift occurred. Sin became more national than personal. Instead of defining sin as the breach of private commitments, we must write about the culture of sin that developed in the kingdom under Solomon.

In the second of God's epiphanies to Solomon, God had said, "If you turn aside from following me, you or your children, and do not keep my commandments . . . but go and serve other gods and worship them, then I will cut Israel off from the land that I have given them; and the house that I have consecrated for my name I will cast out of my sight; and Israel will become a proverb and a taunt among all peoples. This house will become a heap of ruins" (1 Kgs 9:6–8).

Cultures do not suddenly rise or disappear without warning like an attack by terrorists on buildings in New York and Washington. Instead, cultures evolve from the give and take of social groupings, and, as Thomas Kuhn might have written, nobody announces, "Yesterday the Middle Ages ended, and now we are in the Renaissance." After his *Confessions* Saint Augustine wrote *The City of God*, which signaled the reversal of the church/state paradigm for the world when Rome lost control of more and more of its empire. In Western Europe, however, the church adopted the weapon of coercion, religious, political, and military.

Solomon's prayer, apparently written by a Judean Deuteronomist, signaled the anticipated agonies of the terminal illness of Israel-Judah as a nation, but barely glimpsed a paradigm in which loving relationships, arising through forgiveness and positive reinforcement, could supplant threatening and punishment. Murray Sidman writes: "we do not have to punish in order to prevent or stop people from acting badly. We can accomplish the same end with positive reinforcers, without producing the undesirable side effects of coercion."[2] A common policy of positive reinforcement works toward good behavior; forgiveness removes the psychologically painful results of bad behavior. In chapter 19 we will consider how positive reinforcement works, but we may remember it as the way God supports.

Israel's sin culture had roots in the conquest under Joshua, when some of the men took booty from the cities they didn't finish destroying, took non-Israelite wives, and shared in the worship of the "other" gods of the people of the land. Individuals like three of Jacob's sons also ignored the commitment they had made to other Israelites and to the foreign people who were their neighbors, using coercive force to win the land.

By the time of David and Solomon Israel's culture was in full bloom, and Solomon led the way to the excesses of his retinue. Every Israelite might aspire to be like the king and enjoy as much of the luxuries as were within reach; everybody but the displaced workers and the foreign slaves.

Three features of the dark side of the culture stand out as we read between the lines of the biblical record. Solomon began by employing non-Israelite workers from Tyre to build the Temple, then houses for himself and his wives and concubines, and finally he rebuilt many of the Canaanite cities "in all the land of his dominion." (1 Kgs 9:19) Some of the cities were designated as store cities; others were for chariots and cavalry, as Solomon developed a small empire that reached into Lebanon and to the friendly border of Egypt. We do not know at what point he required resident aliens (*gerim*) to work at these tasks, or whether the needed foreign workers from Tyre were gradually assimilated into Israel's new towns. But evidently many of the people living within the boundary of the united kingdom, some the descendants of unassimilated natives mentioned in the first chapter of Judges who lived in Israel-Ephraim, became second class Israelites subject to coerced labor in Solomon's forty years. Punishment was evidently the chief instrument in the management of Solomon's public works.

Workers must be housed and fed, and cities must be defended—just in case—so the building of Solomon's empire disrupted the ordinary home building that should have characterized a natural and peaceful development. It was Solomon's chief of staff, Jeroboam son of Nebat, who noticed the unrest among the workers. Apparently during Solomon's administration he raised questions before he resigned under pressure

---

2. Sidman, *Coercion and its Fallout*, 212.

PART 2: Sex and Power Relationships in Some Israelite Stories

and fled to Egypt. Returning after Solomon's death, he led the secession that divided the kingdom into "Israel" in the north and "Judah" in the south.

Solomon's wives were a special class of slaves, though no one at the time thought of them as such. Instead, most Israelites probably envied them for the luxuries Solomon showered on them. But many must have lived restricted and unproductive lives. That they demanded or were given shrines for their alien deities suggests that many were homesick and unfulfilled in their new lives. That Solomon "loved" many foreign women apparently meant that he got "trophy wives" who were the results of successes in diplomacy with their fathers. The process may have been like the quest of King Keret, which we sketched in chapter 2, the neighbor king arriving with military force to capture a bride. Of course the actual numbers of such women were probably less than the "seven hundred princesses and three hundred concubines" reported in 1 Kings.

It is probably impossible to build an empire without falling into what may be called *national* or *communal* sin. Or, as Lenin is reported to have said, "You can't make an omelet without breaking eggs." Solomon's mini-empire is a case in point. Though he was not called an emperor, Solomon extended the kingdom that David had begun. While David had used mostly military tactics to win territories around the core tribes and had enslaved many of his captives, Solomon used the diplomatic tactic of marrying the daughters of chieftains and petty kings whose commercial enterprises brought him the wealth mentioned in 1 Kings 10. He no doubt gave daughters as well as receiving them, paying no attention to the unhappiness the dislocations produced.

Internally Israel was witnessing the break-up of tribal structures as more and more Israelites were uprooted and assigned, perhaps only as supervisors, to work places in the newly rebuilt cities. They could no longer enjoy life among their kindred, but must contribute to Solomon's glory and his enlarged and specialized defense department. 1 Kgs 9:22 says "of the Israelites Solomon made no slaves, they were the soldiers, . . . his officials, his commanders, his captains, and the commanders of his chariotry and cavalry." Locked into the hierarchy of Solomon's regime, they were effectively enslaved without the word, which was probably reserved for those still considered to be foreigners. As the biblical editors saw it, the break-up of God-given tribal structures was the principal sin of the period.

The crossing of an undefined line between good and evil may be seen only in retrospect. Particular sins are easy to identify since adulteries, murders and thefts get attention in any community, but defining a culture as sinful raises a dauntingly broad set of questions. Most of the workers and their wives did what they were required to do, as slaves and wives had always done in Israel, in Canaan before Israel took possession of the land, or in Egypt prior to the Exodus. Today the slogan word would be "freedom." But that would mean fragmentation, as it did with Jeroboam and Rehoboam.

Individual overseers, military captains, and the priests who served the newly built Temple developed skills appropriate to their tasks. In the third epiphany of YHWH to Solomon, however, the shocking message was clear. Solomon's failure to observe what the Lord commanded would result in the division of the kingdom. The historian quotes God: "Since . . . you have not kept my covenant and my statutes . . . I will tear the kingdom from you and give it to your servant" (1 Kgs 11:11).

If the logic appears fuzzy, look again. Solomon had made slaves of free men and women, and soon his "slave" would take most of his kingdom. God, whether appearing in a vision from heaven or approached in the temple, would allow both sin and its consequences to happen. Israel's apparent prosperity was built by workers who were practically slaves. Would the "eye for eye" punishment pattern assert itself before Solomon died?

Before the kingdom was divided, YHWH had "raised up an adversary [Hadad the Edomite] against Solomon" producing the same kind of affliction the Israelites had complained of during the time of the Judges (1 Kgs 11:14). Hadad probably wanted to add prosperous Israelite towns to his kingdom. Israel shared a culture with every state in in western Asia. But a different adversary was emerging from within Solomon's empire. The nation would treat the symptoms rather than the disease.

The watershed of Solomon's reign included the conscious emergence of real sin and the first of its major consequences for Israel. What should we call this reality? Patricia Williams offers the term *"structural sin,"* and theologians have spoken of *"original sin." "Communal sin"* avoids the biological implications of "original" sin and the mechanistic implications of "structural" sin. Instead, the reality of sin is in the interactions of people, where what one person does invites responses from others. A leader like Solomon can take a whole people into sin without either being fully aware of what king and people are doing. His public example was enough to corrupt the national culture. While Solomon and his court enjoyed the fruits of their wealth, many young men did not inherit enough of their family's wealth to establish families of their own. Although the problem of landless youth is not mentioned in Solomon's time, it is likely that many families did not have sufficient wealth to share with more than one son. Others were drafted into the king's service and supposedly reduced to faceless individuals.

The book of Leviticus might label some of it *"unintentional sin."* It is this abstraction that we are trying to define, unspecified acts that stain the fabric of a society or affect its health.[3] Intention is the final step of a mental process that leads to considered harmful action, which we commonly label "crime." Add the observing God and crime becomes sin. From unfocused awareness of angst or annoyance, repeated moments of pain demand focused (left brain) attention, which generally leads to action humans view as intended. Leviticus is charitably gentle in allowing the possibility that many sins were not intended and could be "covered" through ritual action.

Chapters 4–6 in Leviticus list those who commit unintentional sin and some of the ways such sins may be committed. Priests and lay people may accidentally touch uncleanness; an individual may make "rash utterances" or may do "anything that ought not to be done." The whole "camp" or the king may sin without intending to sin. Only in 6:1–7 does the Levitical text mention "deceiving a neighbor" and "swearing falsely"

---

3. See also Lapsley "Unintentional Sins," 160–65. Lapsley is interested in the ill effects on a person's health from an unintentional sin. A community's unintentional sins could affect community health.

when called to account, in which cases unintentionality can no longer be claimed. For other vaguely sinful behavior the text offers ritual sacrifices which are to be brought to the priest and may be scaled to the sinner's economic status: "if you cannot afford two turtledoves or two pigeons, you shall bring . . . one tenth of an ephah of choice flour . . . and the priest shall scoop up a handful of it as its memorial portion, and turn this into smoke on the altar, with the offerings by fire to the Lord" (5:11–12). One assumes that the remainder of the flour was kept by the priests and used for their food. Was this manipulation of people's feeling of guilt a subtle way to support and establish the authority of the priesthood of the second temple? At the time, however, requiring a sin offering for an unintentional or unconscious act made for a sense of the reality of sin and its forgiveness. The person who brought a sin offering to the Temple gave public notice of his sin, but it relieved many individuals of responsibility to live without communal sin.

Dividing the Baby

Solomon's wise "judgment" in the case of the disputed baby should have taught his son Rehoboam how easy it is to slip into *functional sin*. The incident may seem trivial, but for two mothers it was important enough to take to the Israelite supreme court. Each mother had a child, and in the course of getting established at home, one of the neonates died. Both mothers in what was evidently a typical Israelite extended family claimed the surviving infant, and the case was presented to Solomon. Solomon's judgment: bring a sword, cut the baby in half, and give each mother half. (1 Kgs 3:16–28) Naturally the real mother, or the less possessive, withdrew her claim, and the court, Solomon and the people, awarded custody to her. We could label the false claimant a "sinner" but her only action was to make the claim, possibly innocently, though I am sure that every mother who has looked closely at her newborn child will swear that such a claim could not be innocent. Solomon's outrageous proposal would have resulted in the intentional taking of human life, but the two women would each have had to insist on it, and one of them refused to do so.

Rehoboam might have remembered this incident and seen it as a prophetic parable on the fate of the kingdom, but he didn't. Instead he allowed or encouraged the kingdom to divide itself between the haves and the have-nots. Workers, whether Israelite or alien, did not share in the affluence that came to Solomon's court, but were burdened with labor and punished for failing to meet quotas instead of being paid overtime, as we may infer from Jeroboam's challenge to Rehoboam: "Your father made our yoke heavy. Now therefore lighten the hard service of your father and his heavy yoke . . . and we will serve you" (1 Kgs 12:4). Note the structure of a typical bargaining moment.

The division of the kingdom did not separate individual haves from have-nots, but was a political separation between the ten northern tribes who complained of their burdens, and the tribes of Judah and Benjamin who apparently were enjoying privileged status, perhaps as a Yahwist military elite or because they lived near the Temple.

The baby, having divided itself into followers of Jeroboam and Rehoboam, could only exist as twin states. Neither fraction "won," but both survived for two centuries. The stronger child claimed the name Israel, while the Judeans claimed the presence and protection of YHWH's Temple, which was in Judean territory. Jeroboam's Israel developed its strong sense of right and wrong in a series of legal codes based on the experience of receiving Torah at Mount Sinai (see chapter 16) which exiled priests passed on to returning exiles in Jerusalem. In Judah the less extended region sought to preserve a center of holy power in Solomon's temple, which would be tended by priests descended from Zadok.

The problem with *communal sin* is that no one person can be charged with committing it, or of being the sole "cause" of the consequences that follow. From the standpoint of Rehoboam, the kings of the Davidic dynasty, and the Judean people, it was Jeroboam who "caused Israel to sin" by returning the people to their "tents" in place of the Jerusalem Temple. But Rehoboam's insistence on forced labor clearly led to the division into two kingdoms. Thus two claimants to the throne of Solomon forced the division. As in American political campaigns and the partisan discussions between elections, responsibility for division falls on political leaders.

In retrospect we recognize how Solomon's large-scale building and indulgent court life were carried on the backs of ordinary people and how his efforts to please his wives revived the idolatries that should have been eliminated in previous generations. Apparently Jeroboam had seen the labor problem, but he was banished to Egypt for rebellion, ostensibly for something concerning the closing of a wall in Jerusalem, which 1 Kings 11:27 mentions in connection with the introduction of Jeroboam into the narrative. Neither he nor Rehoboam is charged with sin in this part of the narrative, but Jeroboam would be charged with leading Israel into *ritual sin* when he set up the golden calves at Bethel and Dan. In his 1963 commentary on 1 and 2 Kings John Gray comments that the calves were "the places where the spiritual presence of God was visualized, like the ark in the Temple in Jerusalem and the bull-pedestals of Baal-Hadad in Syrian sculpture." Gray suggests that Jeroboam promoted "syncretism between the worship of Yahweh and the Canaanite nature cult, to which the language and imagery of many of the psalms refer."[4]

It is probably not possible to build an empire without committing *structural/communal sin*. Taking shape from the model of the generic family, composed of the male who impregnates, the female who carries and gives birth, and the child who requires lengthy nurture, covenantal structures have been bridges from lone individual men—Cain and his descendants—toward villages, towns, cities, city-states, nations, and empires. There appears to be an inevitable and necessary development from free association of individuals for mutual support to organized social groups with hierarchical structures. Conflict between political parties and war between neighboring cities and states appear unavoidable as one group encroaches on the ideological and geographical territory of another.

4. Gray, *1 and 2 Kings*, 290.

Part 2: Sex and Power Relationships in Some Israelite Stories

We can also sense the increasing dominance of chieftains, judges, priests, and kings during the successive stages of Israel's development with an equivalent subservience on the part of the majority of the people. The Hebrew Scriptures do not give much attention to the structural aspect of these essentially covenantal relationships as more recent "social contract" theorists have done. Instead, in the Deuteronomic literature we read of the political, social, and religious arrangements made by Samson, Eli, Samuel, David, Solomon, Jeroboam, and the rest of the priests, kings, and military leaders with prophets contributing to the concepts that shaped particular patterns. Solomon may have sinned by giving disproportionate attention to temple and palace building, trade and chariots, in today's language "national security," instead of supporting the families of his slaves. All were led to focus attention on the glories of the building in Jerusalem.

Every effort to impose structure on the living body of people by proclaiming decrees and laws from Moses to Josiah was followed not only by disobedience but also by a climate of corruption and abuse that characterizes structural sin.

After Solomon, the northern kingdom, Israel-Ephraim, began to develop the pragmatic and legal aspects of the covenantal paradigm, which are spelled out in the Covenant and Deuteronomic Codes and abbreviated in the second table of the Decalogue. Religious apostasy in Israel-Ephraim, promoted by Ahab's wife Jezebel and challenged by Elijah and repeated by successive kings and priesthoods until the fall of Samaria, is the theme of 1 and 2 Kings. Judah, on the other hand, focused attention on the religion of YHWH as defined in the first table of the Decalogue and set up the offering of proper sacrifices in Solomon's Temple, thus giving priests the power to channel forgiveness for sin broadly to the people.

Thus developed two theological "schools" and two political "parties" which followed separate but interwoven paths until the fall of Samaria to the Assyrians in 720 BCE.[5] *An infection of sin*, stemming chiefly from kings and priests, but sustained by women, including Ahab's Sidonian wife Jezebel and Athaliah who reigned briefly over Judah, *diffused through both kingdoms, but was particularly evident in Israel-Ephraim*.

Three notable prophets, Elijah the Tishbite, his disciple Elisha on whom the spirit of Elijah rested, and Micaiah ben Imlah delivered words from YHWH, denouncing sins of Israelite kings and announcing the downfall of Ahab's regime and the violent death of his wife Jezebel. The historian comments "there was no one like Ahab, who sold himself to do what was evil in the sight of the Lord, urged on by his wife Jezebel. He acted most abominably in going after idols" (1 Kgs 21:25–6).

The brief restoration of Deuteronomic Torah/law in Josiah's time was a public attempt to return to a remembered covenant between YHWH and the whole of Israel; to confess widespread communal sin; and to achieve the political re-unification which the Judean king Hezekiah had intended.

In the more recent history of the western hemisphere three unifying imperial/religious cultures have had their roots in the Hebrew Scriptures. Judaism found political

---

5. Miller, *A history of Ancient Israel and Judah*, 332–39, has established the date for the organization of Samaria as a province of the Assyrian empire.

expression in the state of Israel after existing for two millennia as a Diaspora; Islam expressed itself in a loose culture of mosques tended by mullahs after establishing glorious states and empires in the Middle East, northern Africa and Spain; Christianity's empire centered in Rome, Constantinople, and Alexandria before spreading to Western Europe and the rest of the world. The pattern of social, economic, political, and religious corruption has appeared in the history of each of the daughter cultures.

A Spiritual Infection

Without formulating any "natural law" of corruption, sin or iniquity, one can remark that *sinning appeared at every stage of Israel's life during the millennium of its existence.* Likewise corruption infected the daughter cultures. One may ask what the nature of sin is, and whether corruption is physical, spiritual, or both. That sin belongs to both distinguishable arenas of life is fairly obvious, originating in either intentional thought or unintentional thoughtless impulse, and finding active expression in the material world. The Hebrew, Christian, and Islamic scriptures, and probably all religious writing after the closing of the sacred canons, testify to the enduring pervasiveness and depth of the thing designated by the term "sin." When harm was done and Abel was killed, we persist in believing that a sin occurred both in the thinking and in the act of Cain. "Sin" evidently passed on to Adam's descendants through social viruses—Dawkins' "memes"—so we may speak of a *spiritual infection of sin.*

As children in a schoolroom "catch measles" from one infected child, the citizens of a nation emulate leaders who grow wealthy through the contracts of their corporate enterprises and become careless in their relationships with wives, children and business contacts. An evidence of this low-grade socio-economic *and spiritual* infection is in letters to syndiated column "Annie's Friends" which complain that a husband has begun to view porn on the Internet or buy an increasing number of lottery tickets. Son or daughter has used up an aging parent's resources for his or her luxuries instead of saving them for the intended beneficiary of an estate. Legal redress becomes pointless after the death of the intended beneficiary.

The nineteenth-century theological controversies reviewed in H. Shelton Smith's *Changing Conceptions of Original Sin in American Theology since 1750*[6] demonstrate the development of a liberal consensus that rejected physical and legal mechanisms (imputed guilt) for the transfer of "sin" from fathers to children. The learned teachers of the nineteenth century did tend, however, to agree that "there is in the human mind, a constitutional propensity to sin," but most rejected the idea that the propensity was itself sinful.

We are not inclined, however, as the ancients were, to think of accidental killings or injuries as sin, as when an ox gored a child. Physical acts may or may not be sins. *What makes an act sinful is a sort of perverse intentionality, a crossing of the line between intended good and actual harm.* The human species is still in the experimental process of transcending the natural world and is capable of physical activities that are

---

6. Smith, *Changing Conceptions of Original Sin in American Theology since 1750*, 123.

not considered sinful when animals do them. The goring ox may actually kill, and its owner may be angry and kill it for the good of the community, but both actions are no longer "sins" for people who live in the Judeo-Christian world, whereas the killing of a sacred cow in India may be considered a sin by Hindus. Likewise an animal's or a human's mating is "natural" and a subject for a child's curiosity, scientific investigation, or community management without being considered a sin against God. What activities and thoughts do Muslims today think constitute sinful behavior and are their criteria the same as those of Christians?

Sin has a quality of ambiguity, uncertainty, or contingency that leads from time to time to strong accusations or subjective confessions of sin on one hand and equally strong efforts through law(s) to prevent it on the other. We cannot avoid considering the elemental feeling level which makes immediate judgments: *Sin is "wrong" behavior, when people instantly compare it to "right" behavior.* So when Judah learned that Tamar was pregnant, he assumed that she had done wrong according to community standards, and he or her family demanded punishment immediately. When Tamar presented his seal and the community saw that she had a right to his family's semen, everyone agreed that Judah was the one who had done wrong. It is this community agreement at the feeling level that establishes a common ethic deeper than law.

Many incidents we could mention suggest that *sin is "in the eye of the beholder"* instead of the realm of physical behavior. But this needs further definition. In biblical literature the Ultimate Beholder is God, a Judge who can be called on to support avengers, to make punitive visits to troublesome humans when the troubled pray in the midst of their troubles, and generally to enter human societies to rid them of inequities. However, in personal conflicts both victim and victor can be seen as sinners from their opposing standpoints. The person doing the harm, Cain, and the person to whom the harm was done, Abel, were beholders as well as actors, and either may have seen "sin" in the other's violence. Thus instead of a single transcendent Beholder, we may recognize many beholders who function as the eyes and ears of God and who remember and judge particular vicious acts.

In following chapters we will sketch the development of Hebrew Torah/law from family and community stories, as Israelite priests, prophets, and kings determined to head off the worst abuses of their people by creating a body of law. Why did, or do, legal formulas fail to prevent sinning?

When Albert Einstein insisted that God does not throw dice, or more exactly, that his formulas functioned in all ranges of space-time down to the infinitesimal and most fleeting events, Niels Bohr responded by announcing the discovery of an "uncertainty principle." Bohr declared that in the mysterious world of quantum physics, the observer cannot determine both the location of a particle and its velocity at any instant. In chapter 1 we tacitly assumed that when a theory had passed the tests of E. O. Wilson's *Consilience*, it could be used as a predictor of behavior. In several fields of science, however, theorized formulas do not work in ranges very far beyond the initial observed data. Further, when chemical elements combine to create new entities, the compounds do not function like the elements that compose them, but appear to discover new laws. Neurons operate in the realm of physical biology with its organic molecules and their laws, but override the rules of inorganic chemistry. Groups of neurons take on a life of their own, when they appear to make decisions beyond the simple reflexes of the basic structures. A "new biology," described by Bruce H. Lipton and made available by developments in electron microscopy, is exploring the activities of organelles in the billions of cells that make up the human body.[7] What looks at first like random combining may be following a higher level predictable functioning, as sap rises against gravity to nourish leaves in the crown of a tree. Lipton takes us up the ladder of complexity and declares: "As more complex animals evolved, specialized cells took over the job of monitoring and organizing the flow of the behavior regulating signal molecules. These cells provided a distributed nerve network and central information processor, a brain. The brain's function is to coordinate the dialogue of signal molecules within the community."[8]

When Lipton uses the word "community," he means the animal or human body. It is as if extremely tiny pieces of an imaginary jigsaw puzzle become active in a minuscule realm of geography as active political bodies, not limited to old rules, but finding new rules which enable them to create new and "higher" entities which contend in new and previously unrecognized arenas of reality, such as life and thought.

It may not be stretching an analogy too far to see political and moral entities as subject to unexpected contingencies and uncertainties, which represent choices made by many individuals, and also a society's inability to control the activities of all of its members. Lipton observed similar activity in the sub-microscopic world of living cells, which seemed to act with intentionality. In *The Design of Everyday Things* Donald A. Norman points out: "Much of our knowledge is hidden beneath the surface of our minds, inaccessible to conscious inspection. We discover our knowledge primarily through our actions." Many actions arise from the more or less subconscious realm Freud explored, and may be characterized as sin only when a conscious mind has chosen to do them. The power to make conscious choices and to act intentionally seems to characterize humans, and *only* humans, in a mid range of the scale of realities between the submicroscopic and the cosmic.

Tamar's pregnancy, Samson's pranks, and David's adultery certainly intruded both *predictably and unpredictably* into the social order of the time, but the legalist historians of the scriptures accepted them as part of the inscrutable design of God as well as the free actions of human beings. Assuming the viewpoint of God, they did not label them, but allowed participants (and readers) to judge or confess the cultural realities of sin and good behavior.

After identifying a number of acts as crimes against humans and as sins against God, the ancients have given way to secular moderns who are not convinced that God cares what people do. So today "sin" has become a convenient term for especially egregious crimes, that is, which a current cultural norm disapproves. *Random House*

---

7. Lipton, *The Biology of Belief*.
8. Ibid., 131.

PART 2: Sex and Power Relationships in Some Israelite Stories

Webster's Dictionary lists meanings of sin: "1. transgression of divine law. 2. any act regarded as such a transgression, esp. a willful violation of some religious or moral principle. 3. any reprehensible action; serious fault or offense."

The quotation marks on the word in this book's title indicate that sin's meaning depends on a speaker or writer's intention. *The reality of such "sin" is in both harmful acts and the community's judgment, with God's judgment pronounced by religious speakers.* The result is that people disagree as to whether homosexual behavior, for example, is inherently sinful when no obvious harm occurs. In nineteenth-century America some argued that slavery was inherently sinful, while others saw it as abusive and impractical in a democratic society. Today the problem is distinguishing the voice of God in the multitude of voices that media offer to our minds. Which is a true prophetic voice? And should the others be called "sin?"

The Sin of Mismanagement

Legal formulas are attempts to manage the social, economic, and political lives of people in social bodies. The reality of *communal sin* came into focus in the experiment of Israelite kingship, which attempted to replace the failures of the judges and the priesthood of Eli and his sons. *The malfunction at both ends of the judge/people, or the king/people spectrum may be characterized as a failure of management*, and hence as "sin" from the viewpoint of God, a viewpoint which was made known through prophetic disputation oracles. The modern term "management" serves better than any biblical expression to clarify the nature of the problems to which the biblical historians and God gave their attention.

In the early days priests functioned to connect people to the source of the material blessing of fertility they needed to survive. Using prayers and offerings, early Israelites thanked YHWH for the blessings of children, lambs and grain, and asked for the continuation of the blessings in the year to come. In a sense priests "managed" the people's relationship with the gods, particularly YHWH, but they also managed a number of social relationships more or less successfully, participating in local customary behavior as the covenantal representatives of God.

We might have expected that only individual personal sins should have marred the scene, and community elders with help from local priests or a recognized judge could have judged these. Observing the military and political weakness of tribal leadership and the corruption of the priesthood, however, Samuel reluctantly anointed Saul and later David as rulers over YHWH's people with a view to their being instruments for saving the people "from the hand of their enemies all around" (1 Sam 10:1). When Samuel called the people to Mizpah to witness the public installation of Saul as king, he "told the people the rights and duties [the opportunities and responsibilities] of the kingship, and he laid it up before the Lord." The king's relationship with the people was essentially covenantal when the people shouted, "Long live the king!" (1 Sam 10:24–25). King *and* people agreed on the arrangement and established a shaky structure in which the king was expected to serve as highest human judge and lead the people in protecting themselves from aggressive neighbors. His function was to be managerial, the promotion of general welfare. Failure in either judging or protecting function would be personal sin, possibly unintentional. But to see the whole of sin in the king's failure is to ignore any responsibility on the part of the people. In modern democracies with representatives elected by the people, functional sin begins with failure to vote for representatives, and moves on to buying influence on those elected.

To understand this responsibility—or the sins—of *both* king and people we can look at the mechanism of brain operation in which thought moves to action. Or to parody Holmes Rolston's question, how do *can, may, and will* morph into *decide* and *do*? The basic mechanism appears to be the electro-chemical activity of *many* neurons, which manage in a not yet fully known way to hold memories, map the world, plot schemes for anticipated activity, and finally launch that activity.[9] The actual chemicals and the locales in the brain are of little consequence for this aspect of the theory, but a process of linking, grouping or "summing" the action of neurons appears significant.

The body's cells of perception, as in the skin, ears or eyes, respond and act in clusters—never alone. The more cells responding to photons of light, or the more rapid the sequence of receiving photons, for instance, the more intense is the sensation, and at some identifiable intensity the brain directs muscles to close the eyes to protect the receiving neurons. This simple mechanism of amassing sensory information acts throughout the tissues of all forms of animal life. Plants show little of the mechanism that leads an animal to act, but amass the sugars and starches created by photosynthesis to extend roots and branches. Their growth gives evidence of more than mere three-dimensional "being"; the result may be characterized as plant dynamics. Coordinated stimuli lead to active responses that may be characterized as animal dynamics. Social structures behave in much the same way with observers amassing information and agents or agencies fulfilling decisions.

The human brain has an additional capability of initiating responses to imagined situations, not only to external stimuli but also to self generated thoughts, most clearly when the body is at rest or the mind is not occupied with other activity. My brother, Professor Frank B. Gailey, who taught biology at Berea College in Kentucky for a number of years, explained this process to me in conversation, and I neglected to ask him to cite other authorities. When the process functions, it is probable that neurons connect with other neurons in transactions like the joining of sperm and egg or the linking of states in a nation in a way similar to the master covenantal paradigm. In each case the result is more than the originating elements, a step up the ladder of complexity.

In thought the human is capable of mapping the world, that is, seeing entities not only one item at a time, but in their relationships to each other. With thought, the human can note obstacles and plot paths around them before taking steps. The process is akin to God's creation of order out of chaos, and it enables every human to exist as a functioning Self, Soul, or Person, potentially creative or destructive. Self-generated

---

9. Ashbrook, *The Mind and the Mind of God*. Charts on pp. 8, 17, 45, 54, 88, and 90 map four regions of the brain, showing how each region contributes through alternating modes toward a convergence of processing systems.

PART 2: Sex and Power Relationships in Some Israelite Stories

thoughts rise above stimulus and response mechanisms and enable people to plan and create their niches in the four-dimensional puzzle that is the cosmos.

The serpent's questions to the first woman and the "sin" lurking at Cain's door may be characterized as self-generated thoughts, but the first biblical reference to such thoughts is in the evil "inclination of the thoughts" of mankind prior to the flood (Gen 6:8, NRSV; "imagination" RSV). Thinking is done in individual brains, but when it is expressed in cultural language it becomes public property, ideas in effect being "summed," assembled, or even mobilized for mass behavior. "Revolutions," such as the American in 1776 or the Russian in 1918 are the result of public sharing of ideas similar to decision making of individuals. Whether the decisive action of an individual or a group should be called a "sin" remains a subject for discussion.

A transaction of "proposal" [stimulus] and acceptance [response] sets up a conventional marriage commitment. Similarly, an interaction of command and obedience between military leader and troops is essential to war-making. Likewise churches and crusades result from the covenantal coupling of priest figures with bodies of believers. Modern corporations and political bureaucracies work through similar hierarchical structures. *Sometimes sin is in the real harm done by individuals who are consciously or subliminally led into it as members of groups.*[10] As Solomon said in his prayer, "there is no one who does not sin." *Sin is cultural and communal as well as personal and structural.* However, abstract structures like corporations and states do not sin; they are only paths in the cultural world that people have created and follow.

Two States: Two Minds

When Rehoboam rejected Jeroboam's demand for a more favorable labor contract, the representatives of ten tribes responded with one mind and returned to their tribal homes in a major secession (1 Kgs 12:16). Jerusalem could keep Solomon's temple for visiting YHWH or for YHWH's visits, and the people of Israel would visit the shrines where priests would minister before calf images of Baal on their behalf. The people of Judah would continue a Yahwist form of worship while their kindred in the north would address God (*'elohim*) as Baal, "master," or "husband." Probably the people of neither kingdom used the language patterns exclusively.

Although there were differences between the two kingdoms during the two centuries of their separation, their real diversity was in theological and ethical nuance, not in the use of man-made images or royal successions. Both Ephraim and Judah thought of themselves as "Israel." Jerusalem followed right brain awe and faith in the supremely holy YHWH, and believed in a God who forgave sins, while Samaria, the new political capital of the northern kingdom, became the center from which Jeroboam's successors launched their efforts to create a political empire greater than Solomon's. "Ahab the Israelite" was notable enough to merit a place on Shalmaneser's victory stele in

---

10. Rissolatti, "Mirrors in the Mind," 54–61, for a report on a new development in neuroscience which will explain the imitative behavior of young children. In my opinion the mechanism may be extended to explain much group behavior. Examples of group behavior range from the movement of schools of fish to mob action.

Nineveh.[11] But Ahab is remembered by the biblical historians for allowing his wife to seize Naboth's vineyard through a perversion of customary law (1 Kings 21), and for his wife's support of hundreds of priests of Baal whose role was to support the expansion of the Israelite kingdom (1 Kgs 18:20–46).

A Comprehensive Look at Sin for Today

It is tempting to follow the conflict between the Baal-like kings of Israel and the prophets YHWH sent to reprove them, but it is perhaps more important to see how the kings of Israel-Ephraim adopted left brain pragmatic thinking in contrast to the right brain mystical thinking of Israel-Judah's prophets. Both can be seen not as "proven" knowledge of God but as expressions of faith in a Power beyond the grasp of humans.

In the course of our "Natural History of Sin" we will refer to the two modes of thinking identified by James Ashbook, and return finally to the deep questions that persist in our time.

In the 1901 Gifford Lecture, *The Varieties of Religious Experience*, William James opened the way to a scientific approach to religion for the twentieth century, and a century later Charles Taylor revisited the subject in a second Gifford Lecture which continues a thematic approach to religion and also affirms the importance of sin as an essential aspect of religion in the twenty-first century as James had done for the twentieth. Between the two Gifford lectures Reinhold Niebuhr declared in 1934:

> The sense of sin is peculiarly the product of religious imagination, as the critics of religion quite rightly maintain. . . . The consciousness of sin has no meaning to the mind of modernity because in modern secularism reality is merely a flux of temporal events. In prophetic religion this flux is both a revelation and a veiling of the eternal creative principle and will. Every finite event points to something beyond itself in two directions, to a source from which it sprigs and an end to which it moves. Prophetic religion believes, in other words, in a God who is both the creator and the fulfillment of life.[12]

In fact, sin may be considered "a moving target" like the human immunodeficiency virus (HIV) which "is constantly changing its genetic makeup . . . and also . . . because the proteins of the virus surface are actually moving themselves."[13] Instead of genes and proteins, think of *memes*, and try to pin them down by prescribing laws or moral injunctions. The problem of stopping "sin" is not one of attacking a social entity in the world, such as a neighbor nation, but of resisting the movement of ideas embodied in people who are seen either as criminals and enemies of an ideal social order or as moral beings who intend behavior that will result in good for them, but fail to achieve it.

It would be interesting to read of the way the sins of some of Israel's neighbors were dealt with, such as the Philistines in the time of Samson or the Syrians in the

---

11. Pritchard, *Ancient Near Eastern Texts Relating to the Old Testament*, 279.
12. Neibuhr, *An Interpretation of Christian Ethics*, 65–66.
13. Alice, "The Man Who Could Beat Aids," 46.

PART 2: Sex and Power Relationships in Some Israelite Stories

time of Ahab and Elisha, but no literary reports for them have been preserved. An alternate "neighbor" for whom records exist is in the accounts of the conflict between Spanish conquistadors and the Aztec kingdom in the heart of what is now Mexico. Montezuma's people served a "goddess of filth," the Lady Tlazolteotl, whose function was to "accept all the filth of sin to herself" and thus to offer absolution. The ritual required all sins to be confessed orally to the priest, and the ritual could be performed only once, after which the sinner was expected to live without sin. It was customary to wait as long as possible before observing the ritual.[14] Thus Aztecs and Spaniards could agree on an awareness of the reality of sin and the need for a form of atonement.

A comprehensive look at reality has to include sin along with the realities of sex and war. Sex and war have a predominantly physical reality in our experience, while we sense sin as deeply rooted in thought, though it is expressed in the material world. In every age thought about behavior includes a sense that some Higher Power or group of personal powers may be watching. Hence we continue to think and write about the sins of politicians and religious figures.

What is to be done with this cluster of realities? How is the individual to manage the temptation to do harm or to indulge greed, anger or lust in what we think of as sin? How should kings, councils, and gatherings of ordinary people prevent or limit sinning? How can individuals, families and social groups, *including churches*, escape the corruptions of *our* time?

At least two answers can be found in the Hebrew Scriptures. First, Deuteronomic Torah/law and history (Deuteronomy through 2 Kings) feature the struggle of prophets from Moses on to turn Israel-Ephraim toward the building of a structure of God-devised right behavior in a community under law. Their work was merged after the fall of Samaria with the Yahwist/Judean mystical stream that relied on the presence of and words from God in Solomon's temple.

Second, the Chronicler's work (Ezra, Nehemiah, and the books of Chronicles), together with the priestly portions of the Pentateuch, concentrates on the worship of YHWH with prescribed rituals in the holy Jerusalem temple and relies on the political governance of the Davidic dynasty. Both are systematic efforts to relate redemptively to the mix of personal and social good and evil. Israel's prophets challenged the dynasties of Israel-Ephraim and Israel-Judah together with the hereditary priests of both kingdoms in spontaneous oracles announcing, "thus saith the Lord." Hosea, Micah, Jeremiah, and both Isaiahs brought God's words of forgiveness and restoration to the distressed human race.

What legacies from the Hebrew Scriptures present themselves for the realities of life in today's world? Two patterns present themselves, now frequently in secular instead of religious language:

(1) Physically punish the criminals of society who refuse to abide by laws against murder, rape, theft and deceptive business practices. Declare and wage war

---

14. Burland, *The Aztecs: Gods and Fate in Ancient Mexico*, 106–7.

against "rogue" states or groups like Al-Qaida, which threaten to destroy the carefully built economic structures of international trade.

(2) Find ways to *forgive the burden of debt* for shelter and food, which underpaid workers bought in a "market" operated for the benefit of lenders and investors. Explore new ways of forgiving international obligations imposed on third world states that can only offer raw or partially processed materials in unequal exchanges to meet their needs.

Reflective thinking has led us to recognize the realities of human selves, tribes, nations, the cosmos, and the Reality we call "God." Using metaphorical abstractions, we also recognize past and future, matter and spirit, faith and knowledge, good and evil, pain and pleasure, plus *sin, virtue and forgiveness* as intangible aspects of a single amazing but flawed reality. Sin is bad human behavior, defined by its damaging effects on individuals as members of groups whose goals should be healthy interactive life.

Belatedly we are beginning to realize the futility of the path of violent punishment to bring about better behavior, personal, communal, national, and global. Violent punishment, whether in war or individual execution is also bad behavior—or "sin"—that needs to be eliminated from the rules for a civilized social order.

15

How Innocent Anxiety Morphs into Guilt

IN THE THIRD CHAPTER of Genesis the transition from innocence to guilty shame occurs almost instantaneously on a single day when "the eyes of both [man and woman] were opened, and they knew that they were naked." As we look back with deeper understanding of the so-called primitive mind, we can sense a millennium-long expansion of the circumstances that provoked feelings of guilt and awareness of sin. We could also survey the multiplication of prophetic and legal prescripts during the historic period to deal with new circumstances. How did the human race as exemplified in Israel move from the innocence of simple opinions or insights that certain acts were "wrong" to writing laws that prescribed punishment for behavior that disregarded standards of morality? How did some behavior that apparently was not characterized as sin in earlier times come to be in that category?

In the previous chapter we recognized that in spite of uncertainty about the nature of sin, its reality could hardly be questioned. Even if some thoughtful people are inclined to consider crime a more appropriate category for what others call sin, there remains a nagging feeling that a Power higher than the police is watching and judging. When someone, a politician or an unscrupulous businessperson, "gets by," our anger flares and we think or say, "They'll get it in the end."

Reflecting on his All-seeing, All-knowing God, the poet of Psalm 139 concludes with two prayers:

> O that you would kill the wicked, O God
> and that the bloodthirsty would depart from me . . .
> Search me, O God, and know my heart;
> test me and know my thoughts.
> See if there is any wicked way in me.
> and lead me in the way everlasting (Ps. 139:19, 23–24).

How is it that humans have matched belief in the reality of sin with belief in a judging and punishing God?

In chapter 16 we will consider how Israel arrived at one of the core ethical commandments, the one forbidding adultery. In this chapter we trace an underlying "slippery slope" from early innocence to later guilt. The term was current during 2003 in newspaper editorials opposing marriage of gay couples. This superstitious theory was that legalizing the mutual commitment of two people of the same sex would "destroy" the bonds of family life. From the standpoint of the biblical historians some of their ancestors thought themselves "not guilty," while their neighbors risked God's vengeance for relatively innocent behavior. The word "innocent" is both a term used in judging legal guilt and etymologically the negation of "nocent," which means "doing harm or having a tendency to harm." Consider how the participants, the historians *and God* felt about some early incidents of Israel's history, noting how humans may have learned that they could harm other people, and thus have "sinned."

Outside the Garden of Innocence

Except for newborn infants and very young children, innocence and guilt are relative: some people appear more innocent than others. An initial loss of innocence occurs when a child begins to see herself as she is observed by a parent or some other adult. Armand M. Nicholi, Jr. retells two incidents from Freud's childhood that related to his need to be famous. "An old peasant woman had prophesied to my mother . . . that she had given the world a great man." But when he was seven or eight years old young Sigmund accidentally urinated on the floor in his parents' bedroom. "His father exploded in anger and commented that the boy would never amount to anything. This embarrassment haunted Freud for years and recurred in his dreams."[1] Thus Freud's loss of innocence reflected his parents' contrary appraisals of his future. Through his father's eyes he suddenly saw himself as no longer innocent. In her 1997 book *Healing the Broken Heart: Sin, Alienation, and the Gift of Grace*, Susan L. Nelson calls this rejection by parents and other people in the child's world "refusals." The psychological trauma can last a lifetime.

With the dawning of *self*-consciousness the transparency in the child's communication with the people around her becomes cloudy, and her parents can no longer read all her thoughts.[2] In spite of popular Freudian theory there is nothing particularly sexual in the earliest loss of innocence. Instead the child begins to assume ownership of her thoughts and to reserve some of them for herself just as she knows that some clothes are hers and others are her mother's. The wearing of clothes by human beings from the Garden of Eden to the present day remains an apt metaphor for our loss of innocence. Knowing or suspecting that we have done what our parents would probably disapprove, we attempt to hide the evidence and cover ourselves from scrutiny.

Without telling us what the descendants of the first couple felt, the storytellers (designated J, E, D, P by scholars) relate experiences of good and evil outside the garden. Apparently without forethought Cain killed Abel, but even though marked for survival, he was afraid that his act would be avenged. Genesis lets us imagine how Cain

---

1. Nicholi, *The Question of God*, 117.

2. In Chapter 19 we will refer more extensively to the Erikson-Kivnick study which supports the observation my wife made when our daughter was three or four years old.

felt when he left the community of his brothers and sisters. We can imagine how anyone who has single-handedly killed another person may feel: angry, but regretting the loss of a brother. Always looking over his shoulder as he passed his kindred, Cain must have wondered if they also were angry or a bit frightened of him. Even if he thought, "He had it coming!" Cain could forever wonder if anyone would truly be his friend.[3]

Cain was not alone in his regret. "The wickedness of humankind was great in the earth . . . and the Lord was sorry that he had made humankind" (Gen 6:5–6). Apparently the Creator was distressed, and destroyed almost all life in the great flood later, with no expressed emotion, the inhabitants of Babel found themselves unable to communicate with each other or finish building their tower. The Israelite historian saw in that situation an irate God who acted to confuse human speech so that the people could not build their lofty tower to heaven. The people may have had trouble moving from Steven Pinker's "mentalese" to coherent talk.

As the narrative of biblical history narrowed, the patriarchs and their neighbors all appear to have been anxious for their safety but without any clearly defined sense of guilt, sexual or otherwise, in their stratagems. Neither Abimelech nor Abraham knew the other's thoughts when Abraham directed Sarah to set up her tent in Abimelech's compound. But when God approached Abimelech at night regarding Abraham's wife, Abimelech could reasonably ask, "will you destroy an innocent people?" Questioning Abraham's innocence, he accused his guest of shameful behavior, of doing "things that ought not to be done." "What were you thinking of that you did this thing?" he asked in Genesis 20:8–10, but events did not establish the guilt of either man.

Jacob and his mother Rebekah *were* guilty of deceiving Isaac in the matter of the blessing intended for Esau, and Laban and Jacob were each guilty of hard bargaining in their sharing of the wealth that accrued to the developing tribe in Harran. Both Yahwist and Elohist traditions tell stories of poorly concealed deceit which gradually edged Jacob's family away from his father-in-law's. Each could accuse the other when they finally parted company. The final deceit was Rachel's, as she refused to allow her father to search her seat on the camel's saddle in which she had hidden their household gods, saying "Let not my lord be angry that I cannot rise before you, for the way of women is upon me" (Gen 31:35). Genesis leaves to our imaginations other fears and anxieties these heroic figures may have felt. Did Rachel's heart beat a little faster as she refused her father's questioning search?

Joseph's brothers may have *felt* guilty about their treatment of him, but they admitted their "sin" only years later when they were faced with an Egyptian official who claimed to have caught one of them stealing his cup. The essence of superstition may be in the way an early wrong action haunts the guilty one with fear of some final retribution whose connection is only apparent to the guilty party.

Israelites suffering under the oppression of a Pharaoh prior to the exodus from Egypt do not appear to have been guilty of much of anything, nor of being haunted by guilt. At least we do not read about any crimes they were committing until the young

---

3. The *Intelligence Report* of the Southern Poverty Law Center quotes a letter from accused murderer David Nikos Pillatos, ". . . I killed him and I liked it."

Moses intervened in a fight between two men and repeated Cain's act of manslaughter. Any guilt they felt for petty injuries to each other was probably passed over just as Joseph's brothers repressed their feelings.

Nevertheless they may have felt uneasy as well as oppressed when the treatment from Pharaoh's overseers became harsher. As the grandchildren of Jacob recalled the kind treatment they had received when the Pharaoh honored them as Joseph's kindred, they could not help wondering if God had forsaken them and was now punishing them. Had they done anything to deserve the change in official attitude? Had each adult lost childhood innocence or was God extending punishment for the sins of the fathers? And why did Pharaoh order their innocent infants to be killed?

Thus from the start of Abram's journey to the time of the Exodus an apparent innocence covered deceit and the guilt that accumulated through several generations, but God and the reporting historians remembered. The history of Israel can be seen either as a series of human experiments or as a single Great Experiment. God had created creatures that could think up all sorts of trickery, and God was seeing, remembering, and evaluating how his humans behaved. Bondage to Egyptian taskmasters brought a painful suspicion that something was wrong in the life of Hebrew slaves who were now required to make bricks without straw and kill their offspring.

Just before their departure from Egypt, God sent a special word to the children of Israel. They were told to perform a ritual so that God would pass by them on a particular night and no plague would destroy them: "take some of the blood [of the unblemished lamb or goat they would be eating] and put it on the two doorposts and the lintel of the houses" (Exod 12:7). The ritual served to distinguish the enslaved guilty from the oppressing guilty.[4] The enslaved would be "covered" by the ritual marking. The descendants of Abraham, Isaac, and Jacob were to take no chances that the "destroyer" would see them as guilty. Their parents' unpunished crimes had sent Joseph to slavery in Egypt. In the preparations for the exodus their communal guilt could be dealt with ritually and the tribes would be saved.

At the Mountain

Shortly after YHWH engineered their expulsion from Egypt, newly reborn Israel waited near a smoking, quaking mountain, while Moses received two tablets as reported in Exodus 19–20 and 34:1, one of which, according to tradition, contained four basic rules for the future worship of YHWH, and the other, commands for human relationships. According to Exodus 32, however, while Moses was still on the mountain receiving the commands from God, the frightened people asked Aaron to "make gods, who shall go before us," and Aaron directed them to take off their jewelry so that he could "form it in a mold." The historian suggests what they were thinking: God had appeared and spoken to Moses; now both God and Moses had disappeared; and the people acted in near panic.

---

4. Credit for this distinction belongs to Professor Kenneth Bailey whose comments have appeared from time to time in *The Presbyterian Outlook*.

New leadership would be needed. When Moses came down from the mountain and saw the golden calf the people were worshipping, he threw down the tablets God had written, physically breaking the commands of God. As a result of their "great sin" three hundred people died at the hands of Levites loyal to Moses and YHWH, and others faced instant death if YHWH were ever to be among them. Instead God visited the tent of Moses, and talked with him before giving him a second set of commands on Mount. Sinai. These are spelled out in Exodus 34, a scripture scholars call a 'ritual Decalogue' because it calls for festivals instead of ethical behavior.

In a proclamation before announcing these rules for worship YHWH described himself to Moses as "a God merciful and gracious, slow to anger and abounding in steadfast love and faithfulness, keeping steadfast love for the thousandth generation, forgiving iniquity and transgression and sin yet by no means clearing the guilty, but visiting the iniquity of the parents upon the children and the children's children, to the third and the fourth generation" (Exod 34:6–7).

There is a striking ambivalence in this self-description of God, which teeters on the line between forgiveness and punishment. It is almost as if YHWH couldn't decide whether to spank or hug his favorite son. The focus shifts in one sentence from the mercy and grace of God to the human guilt of iniquity.

In the "Decalogue" of Exodus 34 YHWH's covenant with Israel is exclusive, like love in marriage. Adulterous relationships with other gods are forbidden. Although joining of two sexes is needed to generate children, the jealousy of God will not abide a variety of other mixings. Israelite men must not mate with the women of the land nor worship their gods. Rest and work must not be mixed: "even in plowing time and in harvest time you shall rest." "You shall not offer the blood of my sacrifice with leaven." "The best of the first fruits . . . you shall bring to the house of YHWH." "You shall not boil a kid in its mother's milk." "Their daughters . . . will make your sons prostitute themselves to their gods."[5]

The concern of these rules was not to preserve the bond between husband and wife, but to strengthen the weaker link between Israelite men and the jealous god YHWH. Sex within the conventional social structure of the tribe was no problem. Sex with an outsider, a woman who does not worship the only god, opens the door to iniquity and sin: "for when they prostitute themselves to their gods and sacrifice to their gods, someone among them will invite you, and you will eat of the sacrifice. And you will take wives from among them for your sons, and their daughters ... will make your sons also prostitute themselves to their gods" (Exod 34:15–16).

Strictly speaking, this was not a law but a warning anticipating the dangerous situation that would confront Israelite men when they would be tempted to eat unclean sacrificial meat (pork?) and have sex with unbelieving women. No matter how beautiful the women or tasty the meat, the temptation must be resisted pre-emptively, since it would lead not only to lusting after gods other than YHWH, but to an exposure to the dangerous liminal area between a living God and non-gods.

---

5. Exodus 34:21, 25–26, 16. Deuteronomy 9:6–29 retells the story of Israel's stubborn rebellions, but omits the sexual events at Shittim.

The events at Sinai introduced the revolutionary concept of order under law to the Hebrew ex-slaves who were to become a nation, and later two nations. At that moment a band of Jacob's descendants saw themselves not as Pharaoh had seen them, as slaves subject to his command, but as YHWH was seeing them, a people destined to be guided by the conditions of Torah. But almost immediately a by-product of this concept was rebellion against the leadership of Moses, a guilty liaison with an alien god or goddess, and the initial breaking of commands from God. Like the child's loss of transparency to her parents, the history of Israel began with this right brain look at themselves.

We should note that "this moment" is not fixed in conventional chronological history, since the information found in Exodus was crystallized in the post-exilic period when priests reviewed the early stories and located the introduction of law to the legendary experiences of Israel in the wilderness between Egypt and Canaan. No direct external confirmation of the life and work of Moses has been preserved. We will consider probable origins of the legal material in the next chapter, but in principle there could be an awakening of conscience for any people at any time. It is that experience which Israel's writers located at the mountain.

Incident at Shittim

The retired anthropologist Mary Douglas and a group of bible scholars have re-examined the work of the exilic and post-exilic priests, particularly the books of Leviticus and Numbers. Their studies include chapters 25–40 of Exodus which tell how the Israelites constructed the Ark of the Covenant and the Tabernacle after receiving the commandments. The book of Leviticus describes the offerings and rituals that were to be made in the Tabernacle, and the book of Numbers reports how God prepared the twelve tribes and the priestly tribe of Levi to start their campaign to wrest the promised land from its inhabitants. At this point we are concerned only with an encounter they had with the women of Moab/Midian.

"While Israel was staying at Shittim, the people began to have sexual relations with the women of Moab" (Num 25:1). As God had anticipated, the Moabite women invited the visitors "to the sacrifices of their gods, and the people ate and bowed down to their gods." If there had not been a specific directive against sharing ritual meals with friendly natives, it might have been an innocent pleasure. But "the Lord's anger was kindled against Israel" and Moses was told to "take the chiefs of the people and impale them in the sun before the Lord." Moses directed the people's judges to kill any of the people who had "yoked themselves to the Baal of Peor" (Num 25:1–5).

The incident at Shittim reached a climax when "one of the Israelites came and brought a Midianite woman into his family in the sight of Moses and . . . the whole congregation of the Israelites." Phinehas, grandson of Aaron, went after the man and woman "into the tent, and pierced the two of them, the Israelite and the woman, through the belly" (Num 25:6–9). With that the plague was stopped.

PART 3: A Natural History of Biblical "Sin"

How quickly the people had forgotten the commands Moses had received! Or should we say that the "seven year itch" is such a part of human experience that two spare Hebrew words, practically all the Decalogue has to say about sex, are not enough to control the biological urge when people who have been limited to familiar patterns of kinship for mates are suddenly confronted with new opportunities for expression. Perhaps the men simply ignored the rule forbidding intermarriage with the natives, thinking that the Moabite women were prostitutes. We can only probe our own experience of the tension between biology and culture, and wonder how we might have acted. Hearing a student's report of a dormitory "gang banging," the teacher wonders what he might have done in that dorm. In the incident at Shittim we glimpse the way some Israelites behaved when they were offered a new combination of sexual and religious experiences—young women dancing in worship of a pagan god or goddess at a harvest feast.

Festivals and Sex

A dialogue between Hannah and Penninah, to which the historian alludes in 1 Samuel 1:5, could clarify the way a person's worry becomes a guilty feeling. We can imagine the two women discussing why Hannah had no children. Had the Lord closed her womb because she had not bathed herself properly? Should she have tried a sexual technique practiced by the Canananites? Was it somehow a mistake *not* to have one of the pagan teraphim in their home? Or was she too prudish to respond to her husband during the harvest festival? The traditions did not recall these very personal thoughts, but left them to our imagination.

Although the amount of sexual license at harvest festivals may have been exaggerated in the imaginative retelling of Israel's history by the pre- and post-exilic historians and prophets, they suggest that whenever Israelites had contact with Canaanites, they were tempted to indulge in sexual orgies while they were worshipping at the shrine of an alien god. The sin at Shittim, however, was in the worship of the "other god," the god Baal and/or his consort. No physical harm was done until the plague began to spread, but YHWH had been slighted.

Nevertheless, every contact with holiness, whether at an altar to YHWH or in the person of a holy man or woman, could engender an uneasiness of possible guilt, as modern ministers recognize when people make veiled confessions of sin to a minister seatmate on a plane. When the son of the woman at Zarephath became ill, she asked the prophet Elijah, "What have you against me . . . You have come to me to bring my sin to remembrance, and to cause the death of my son!" (1 Kgs 17:18). She could have asked, as many still do, "What have I done to deserve this?"

We instinctively identify with the experiences of these men and women. In the incident at Shittim we recognize God's requirement not of justice but of purity, and we understand that the God the Israelites believed in had feelings like ours. As pre-adolescent children our initial innocent feelings of delight at our excretions gave way to disgust at their uncleanness. Later we overcame our shame at the thought of physical contact with another's sexual organs when we began to experience the attractions of sex, while our elders were advising us to go slow with physical contact.

From God's Perspective: Disgust

Steven Pinker has pointed us to the way the mind uses metaphors based on the physical structure of the three dimensional world. In *How the Mind Works* he illustrates his "computational theory of mind" and prints several graphic figures which can be seen in more than one way, depending on what subliminal assumptions a viewer brings to perception. Using metaphors, human thought can "handle" abstractions and watch ideas "grow" and develop. We are capable of "flights" of fancy, and can choose the career "path" we will follow. We can "rise above" earthly affairs, and imagine the world from God's point of view. Reading, Pinker I had the "feeling"—almost tangible—that he could have "moved" into the "realm" of theology, but he "stopped" before he got to that. His discussion of the pervasive sense of verticality in human language could have led him to explain why the concepts of God, righteousness and heaven are "above" and "beyond" human thinking and behavior. No wonder Moses had to climb to the top of a secluded mountain, physically above his people, to hear and understand God's words! Word from God seems to have come to Moses, the prophets, modern scientists, poets and theologians in what Pinker calls "mentalese," an inner intuition or visual image that is a precursor to spoken language. Holmes Rolston refers to Noam Chomsky's "deep grammar" for the "neural transmission of ideas" and the "bewildering variety in thousands of human languages" in which we observe "the free assignment of meanings . . . not preset by human biology."[6] In abstract thought we approach a godlike perception of the way the world works, seeing principles, patterns or structures that we understand as operating below the surfaces of the material world. For human beings our skins conceal incredible but necessary processes. We can begin to understand our dysfunction as we approach God's point of view. So initial anxiety at contact with a holy God has morphed into a view of ourselves as God has seen us, profane and far from holy.

At the beginning of the biblical story God pronounced his creation "good," but quickly regretted what "He" had done. What God saw from his lofty point of view was crude and disgusting. In anger God dumped a cleansing flood on almost all of it, effectively flushing the human toilet.

Then, when bad behavior continued to erupt, God began a series of experimental treatments, some of which would hurt. So, there is a place for physical pain in the economy of God. It alerts an organism to an injury or an illness in the body, and calls for measures to restore feelings of well being. Physical injury requires healing, and much healing occurs as resources from within the body are delivered to the site of the pain. Disgust, guilt and shame are socio-spiritual analogues to physical pain. A person can experience them after doing physical, mental or spiritual harm to another. Our attention turns inward to a past action that we were not satisfied was appropriate.

---

6. Rolston, *Genes, Genesis and God*, 171.

PART 3: A Natural History of Biblical "Sin"

A lingering anxiety reminds us of that past and calls for a revised pattern of behavior when similar circumstances arise. Moderns call that anxiety conscience.[7]

Cries for Help

Repeatedly in Egypt and in the period of the Judges the Israelites cried for help when foreign tribes or states oppressed them, but as occasions for these prayers the historians report only the people's apostasies, which did no physical harm. The Israelites felt pain at what their enemies were doing to them, and wondered superstitiously why God did not rescue them. Deuteronomic and priestly historians explained that the raids by foreign tribes which seized stores of grain and wine and young goats were a consequence of the way the tribes resorted to altars to "Baal and the Astartes" (Judg 2:13).

When and how did sexual acts engender feelings of outrage and guilt in Israel? How did people begin to see human behavior from the point of view of God? Most of the stories we are considering do not give attention to physically damaging sexual relationships. As far as we can tell, there was nothing abnormal, degrading or brutal in the couplings of Judah and Tamar, Samson and Delilah, Hannah and Elkanah, David and Bath-Sheba or with the couple at Shittim. It is probable that when Shechem took Dinah it was what today would be called statutory rape, but her brothers treated the event as an insult to the family's integrity. The women who visited the shrine at Shiloh were probably seduced by Eli's sons, rather than raped, and though *we* may consider their behavior sinful, the Israelite public was only mildly disturbed. The people were angrier when the young priests insisted on the best pieces of meat. Eli appears as a failing old man, unable to control his sons, and the people thought he should have done better. It was only when prophetic voices brought a parental God's viewpoint to the attention of the people that relative innocence changed into guilt.

Seeing Behavior as Moral

David had to visualize a man physically taking his neighbor's lamb before he could see his relatively innocent desire for an afternoon of sex as theft and adultery. Here another of Pinker's ideas is useful. In writing about the mind's use of categories he distinguishes between "crisp" and "fuzzy" thinking. The four curt negative commands of the second table of the Sinai commands appear clearly defined: theft is theft; adultery is adultery; murder is murder. But in a life situation individuals may see the same act as either, both, or neither. Recall Nathan's analogy of theft for David's adultery. David did not think of himself as guilty of either theft or murder. At the time he knew Bath-Sheba was another man's wife, he could ignore that fact or take the chance she would not get pregnant. His attention was entirely directed to the anticipated sexual pleasure; he was oblivious to other aspects of the situation and its consequences. Such fuzzy thinking is the bane of categorical imperatives. Yet the human mind is haunted by the viewpoint of God. From that vantage point colors and shadings merge and we discern

7. See Sigmund Freud, *Civilization and its Discontents*.

figures, however fuzzily defined. Individuals stand out from their fellows as either strong or weak, good or bad, friends or enemies, pure or defiled, innocent or guilty.[8] It is in the light of some such worldview that guilt and sin are ordinarily defined.

The mind's capacity for assuming another's viewpoint makes possible the self-judgment we call guilt. The enemy also has feelings. God's viewpoint comprehends the feelings of both the actor and the one receiving the action. Guilt appears as a refinement of feeling that cannot be denied. Positive feelings come naturally when we have succeeded in doing what we intended, as when a child is happy with a drawing she has made, or when a candidate wins an election. Negative feelings arise out of the frustration of intentions or out of a realization that one has done what he did not really want to do.

Ongoing studies of the brain's activity suggest that the trigger of violent activity is in the so-called "lizard" brain, the hippocampus, while more reflective thinking centers in the medial prefrontal cortex. Our lizard brains are wired to "act first and talk later," but civilization tells us to practice the discipline of thinking before acting. James B. Ashbrook, in the work we will cite in chapter 19, calls attention to the working of two sections of the anterior (prefrontal) brain, which process its "output." The right lobe participates in impressionistic input and responds holistically, while the left communicates rationally and with conceptual language as well as with directions for actions. Humans can talk about their inner experiences and invent words for guilt, sin, and God, while their brains are working during and after physical activity. Rational thinking labels our feelings, and proceeds to judge the rightness or wrongness of our actions.

In the next chapters we will see how the concept of sin entered the legal system of Israel, and was transformed into a formal ethic. This transformation was Israel's ethical contribution to the western world. But first we will consider how stories were used to create laws.

---

8. See chapter 19 for fuller development of these apparent dichotomies.

16

From Family Stories to the Adultery Commandment

According to the Hebrew scriptures YHWH God gave laws, including the eighth commandment, to guide Israelite society. After the book of Genesis, the Pentateuch includes at least four recognizable packets of laws that were either handed down at the top of a mountain in the Sinai peninsula or delivered *viva voce* to Moses in conferences with God in the "tent of meeting." Church teaching has continued to think of Torah as the monolithic law of Moses, more exactly as two tablets of stone. Initially presented as ten commandments in Exodus 20:1–17, and followed by detailed laws in the remainder of the book of Exodus, an evolution in the forms, phrasing and substance of many of the laws can be detected.

Traditionally the Levites and priests of Israel, particularly the sons of Aaron, and later the sons of Zadok, were custodians of Mosaic law. Journeying from the Sinai wilderness toward the land promised to the fathers, the Levites shouldered the Ark of the Covenant, which contained the two tablets, and apparently delivered it to the shrine at Shiloh. A Deuteronomic tradition reports that Moses had delivered the book of the law to Joshua with instructions to "keep it in his mouth" and meditate on it day and night.

On his deathbed King David is reported to have declared in Deuteronomic language:

> I have kept the ways of the Lord,
>   and have not wickedly departed from my God.
> For all his ordinances were before me,
>   and from his statutes I did not turn aside,
> I was blameless before him,
>   and kept myself from guilt.
> Therefore the Lord has recompensed me according
> to my righteousness,
>   according to my cleanness in his sight (2 Sam 22:22–25).

Then he charged his son Solomon with language YHWH had used to Joshua,[1] "Be strong, be courageous and keep the charge of the Lord your God, walking in his ways and keeping his statutes, his commandments, his ordinances, and his testimonies, as it is written in the law of Moses, so that you may prosper in all that you (the northern kingdom) do and wherever you turn" (1 Kgs 2:2–3).

The historian, who added the last chapters of David's life and wrote what David should have said, clearly believed or intended his readers to believe that David knew and obeyed the whole legal corpus from the time of Moses. However, the stories of David's life indicate that no one used collected law to pass judgment on Saul, David or their sons. Stories of the Ark in 1 Samuel do not mention the Decalogue. The occasional prophet preached YHWH's requirements in increasing detail through several centuries, without mentioning the stone tablets. The people of the northern kingdom (Ephraim) and of southern Judah responded guiltily to the preaching of their men of God just as Americans have turned out to hear, repent and be converted by Jonathon Edwards, Billy Sunday, and Billy Graham.

Today, however, we can trace broad stages or plateaus on which the Israelites managed sexuality and power and wrote laws during the historical periods reported in the Hebrew Scriptures. From the early stories of patriarchal life to the legislation of the second temple, we can distinguish three initiatives through which people dealt with problems that related to sexuality, sex, and other power relationships such as slavery, war, economic and political affairs, a "bottom up" understanding of religion.

"Good and Evil" Relationships in the Story Stage

It appears that the impulse to verbalize the rules for successful living arose out of the experience of distress when "The Israelites did what was evil in the sight of the Lord." (Judg 4:7) From the relationships between individuals in families, like Cain and Abel, Isaac and Ishmael, and Jacob and Esau expressions of pain and moral distress led to talk in families instead of violent action, perhaps in the form of a story told by one of the parties to a dispute. The public initiative which resulted from the telling of such a story—as must have occurred when Tamar's pregnancy was noticed—led to an elder's wise suggestion and an oral consensus which can be termed a second initiative by the community to calm the angry expressions of feelings. Later, formulaic words of advice accumulated in the memories of the people and their leaders. Finally these incidents and judgments were recorded as scripture.[2] In this chapter we will investigate how the prohibition against adultery became fixed in the Torah/law of Israel, with the result that it remains a fixture in Judaism, Christianity and Islam.

The three initiatives correspond roughly to stages of the developing culture characterized in Jay W. Marshall's anthropological approach to biblical law.[3] Marshall

---

1. Deuteronomy 31:23: "Be strong."

2. William Johnstone cites current opinion that, "the Decalogue reaches back, not to one single event in Israel's remote past but to the long threefold tradition of Israelite theology shaped by prophets, priests, and wise men" (The 'Ten Commandments': Some Recent Interpretations," 453–62).

3. Marshall, *Israel and the Book of the Covenant*, 10.

lists eight different types of legal systems from a self-redress system through several types of third party mediation to a state level legal system, as distinguished by K. S. Newman, *Law and Economic Organization*. But for our purpose I reserve the term law for written forms.

For Marshall, "law" functioned in the "maximal decision making unit," i.e., first in the extended family or segmentary society; then in the tribe or chiefdom; and finally in the organized state. Since law can be defined "as principles of social control abstracted from the decisions of legal authorities in a society (such as judges, headmen, fathers, tribunals, or councils of elders)," what I speak of as "custom" is included in Marshall's inclusive term "law," and identifies the first initiative.

The starting point is immediately after the fifth day of creation in the book of Genesis. It begins with people and their simplest experiences. Every infant distinguishes people from things,[4] and relates to them in a way different from relating to fuzzy dolls. Likewise members of the human species strongly identify with other people and distinguish themselves from other animate and inanimate entities.

In the earliest "family" stage of movement toward Israelite laws we observe socially acceptable and unacceptable behavior between males and females. An agreement between a man and a woman creates a quasi-legal, covenantal, and emotional bond as well as a physical union even without any formal verbalizing or documentation. "Marriage"[5] emerged out of many experiences that satisfied the need for stability within the family, to meet demands for justice when commitments failed, and to keep some sense of order and civility in the community. Slavery emerged when males "owned" males and females who were not considered wives or sexual partners, but were expected to do whatever a master required. Marshall reports: "In a survey of food collector societies, Newman found that the common legal conflicts concerned the distribution of food, unsatisfactory gifts, murder of someone within the social group and occasionally theft. However, the most prominent legal disputes involved gender relationships. The usual topics were adultery and the failure to satisfy a marriage agreement. In a neutralized society, these cases are usually settled by self-redress."[6]

Three of the Decalogue's four briefest commands can be identified as concerns of hunter-gatherers long before the transhumance culture we see in Genesis. Also, the common terms—man, woman, family, child, tribe, and god—evolved to meet the need of humankind to identify the personal roles that had to be fitted into a worldview for early groups of people.

Genesis begins with two brief descriptions of a worldview for Israel, and even credits the first man with naming what he could observe. Already, long before villages, or the city that Enoch built (Genesis 4:17), couples bonded together and men

---

4. Steven Pinker discusses the child's developing awareness at length in a chapter, "Good Ideas," (*How the Mind Works*, 317).

5. Biblical Hebrew does not include the term, but expresses the idea through verbs drawn from the male's actions of "owning" (*ba'al*) and "taking."

6. Marshall, *Israel and the Book of the Covenant*, 51. I would have omitted the repeated word "legal" in the statement, since I think disputes occurred without being referred to "laws."

protected their wives and children from capture or other sexual unions. Genesis reports that early humans chose wives and begot children, lived in tents, farmed, and managed livestock in an orderly social economy.

But Genesis reveals an underlying feeling that a transcendent Creator was not pleased with some human activities. As the biblical stories show, the inhabitants of Canaan and newly arrived Israelites believed that adultery was a bad thing, even when it resulted in the birth of a healthy child. Everyman could feel that his exclusive right to impregnate his wife had been violated—an experience that defiled the wife and was unjust for the husband. The latter's violent response of murderous revenge destabilized the natural order of procreation and threatened the life of more than one member of the community.

Steven Pinker reminds us that the word adultery is related to the word adulterate.[7] The Hebrew word is used to refer to adulterous relationships and has no cognates in related languages. Its meaning must be inferred from its uses in the prophetic literature and in the verses from Proverbs 6 that we discussed earlier, in chapter 1.

Seen as a physical act, adultery represented the introduction of an improper substance into an otherwise pure vessel, seminal fluid into a woman's vagina from a male who was not her husband. At least in patriarchal times if not earlier the corrupting of his wife's reproductive organs angered the cuckolded husband. In the Levitical laws forbidden sexual relationships are unholy. Thus biblical laws, which focus on the physical act as well as the marriage relationship, also give attention to the relationship with a holy God.

Seen as a breach of relationship, adultery could be described as a "sin" because the Israelites felt that God was interested in the mutual or covenantal relationships between human creatures. When Abimelech talked with God in his dream, he was told that he had been prevented from sinning because of God's interest in the web of human relationships in the Gerar area. He had innocently taken Abraham's *wife*, not his sister, into his harem (Gen 20:3–7). Imagine an ancient harem as a cluster of tents not as rooms in one building. On the other hand, YHWH would approve Joseph's handling of his relationships in Egypt, including the way he avoided the entanglement proposed by Potiphar's wife. Joseph's God did not want the social roles to be confused.

Thus the biblical movement toward a nation with laws began with the stories of the patriarchal families and their relationships with the people of the land toward which they had been directed. For them learning was not so much by divine revelation as by human discovery. People made mistakes, and they and their children learned from those mistakes, and the community elders remembered the way mistakes were corrected. Joseph, at least, sensing God's way, understood how to behave in a culture without formal laws. In the Elohist traditions of the Tetrateuch, (the Pentateuch without Deuteronomy) prophetic insight is not limited to the ancestors of Israel, but includes such neighbors as Balaam and Abimelech. In the Yahwist

---

7. Pinker, *How the Mind Works*, 491.

Part 3: A Natural History of Biblical "Sin"

tradition of Genesis 12, however, the Pharaoh who kept Sarai in his harem, and the Yahwist editor, superstitiously believed that she was the cause or occasion for plagues that afflicted his household.

In this oral stage the traditions give attention to the cultural relationships and the feelings that accompanied them, glossing over the underlying physical behavior, of course with the exception of Lot's daughters. The early stories only occasionally pay attention to word from YHWH/God. Sarai/Sarah is told she will have the hoped-for son. She and Abram/Abraham retire to their (or her) tent, and in due time Isaac is born. Only in the written, legal stage will the physical accompaniments of sex, like uncovered nakedness (Lev 18:6–18) be seen behind closed doors.

Thoughtful Israelites, reflecting on the stories, saw patterns of behavior that they could either approve or disapprove. And they believed that YHWH "felt" the same way about human behavior. As late as the gang rape of the Levite's concubine in Gibeah, for example, a group of Israelite tribal leaders could say to each other, "We just don't do that in YHWH's Israel" (Judg 19:30, freely translated). Isn't this the germ of self-government that God intended in the creation of free human beings?

Even though Judah's neighbors felt that no father should have sexual relations with his daughter-in-law, they did not believe that either he or Tamar deserved to die, so the twins Perez and Zerah were allowed to live and become significant persons in Israel. In fact neither Judah nor Tamar had physically harmed anyone, and no clearly formulated law existed for her case. Judah had ignored a social custom (Hebrew "way") that was strongly supported by his tribe, and had treated his daughter-in-law with disrespect, effectively consigning her to an unproductive life and ultimate death. In spite of the fact that Judah and Tamar had shared in what was considered an incestuous act, the elders who gathered at the gate of justice heard the evidence and decided that neither should be punished (See Gen 38).

The roots of human thinking about behavior are in these either/or, *Yes* or *No* responses to daily experiences of relationships with people and things. The right brain decides immediately to "fight or flee" when a person senses a threat to survival or serious harm. The left-brain guides the decision in the form of a law.

The Moral Center of the Pentateuch

When the latest editors assembled materials for the five books of the Pentateuch, the Torah, they began with what scholars designate as "J and E" traditions and the Alexandrian Greek translators named "Genesis." They completed the project with Deuteronomy (D), "the second law" which recapitulated the giving of the law at the mountain in the wilderness of Sinai. Although Genesis and Exodus are built from Yahwist (J) and Elohist (E) traditions, the first four books of the Bible were edited and to a large extent completed by exilic and post-exilic priests (P). They tell an incomplete, imperfectly remembered story of the ancestry, birth and early childhood of Israel in which Hebrew people journeyed from Mesopotamia by way of Canaan into Egypt and then to the east bank of the Jordan River. The moral center of that story was at Mount

Sinai (or Horeb) when YHWH presented Israel with the Ten Commandments, which are recorded in Exodus 20 (P's version) and Deuteronomy 5 (D's version).

Thus Genesis and the account of the sons of Jacob in Egypt leads up to the moment when YHWH proclaimed Torah in an isolated region between Egypt and Canaan to that selected family, by then grown to twelve tribes. On the other side of this mountain top experience the congregation of Israel would spend forty years being prepared to assume life in the land that YHWH had promised to the forefathers. Israel's behavior would forever be judged in the light of the revelation of Torah.

John Rawls has developed the idea of an overlapping consensus between holders of reasonable comprehensive doctrines as a means to the unity and stability of a well-ordered society.[8] In the case of Judah and Tamar it was not doctrine but a situational moral judgment for which a consensus was needed. The more legalistic of the community may have demanded a severe punishment, but those with concern for the growth of the tribe under the leadership of Judah saw the pregnancy as an opportunity, and ascribed it to the specific intention of inscrutable YHWH.

When Joseph's brothers sold him to slave traders, their consensus ignored the implicit commitment to the good of every member of the family, and it was not until they stood before an "Egyptian" who asked questions about the family, that they remembered what they had done. With that memory refreshed the sons and grandsons of Jacob could understand the justice of Joseph's questions about the family's welfare. They would be replaced by the new generation who would receive the revelation of Israel's Torah/law.

Community Oversight and an "Israelite" Consensus

In addition to recalling YHWH's lawgiving at Sinai, Israelite elders needed to gather from time to time to decide what to do in such cases as Tamar's pregnancy or the rape of the Levite's concubine, so special convocations of representative men from a number of tribes were called to make decisions. The precedents set by such gatherings mark the beginnings of the formal law that the priest-historians (probably the Levites of Israel-Ephraim) ascribed to conversations between YHWH and Moses. These precedents tended toward punishments inflicted on the "guilty," but the deliberations showed considerable sensitivity toward more or less innocent participants.

As long as Joshua lived he was the recognized successor to Moses to whom people could bring their problems, but after his death leadership fell to local individuals who were recognized as "judges." Community oversight of problems within the tribes and the common defense of tribes were organized by these individuals, called into action by visiting messenger/angels or directly by YHWH. The resulting actions taken by small and large groups of tribes led to a developing sense of "all Israel" led by Judges for the common defense and for common ways of dealing with internal problems.

Eli failed to manage his sons, and when Samuel grew old, and *his* sons "took bribes and perverted justice," the people asked for a king, in effect asking for someone other

---

8. See "The Idea of an Overlapping Consensus" in Rawls: *Political Liberalism*, 133–172.

than the priest to be the arbiter of justice. Samuel had anointed a Benjamite named Saul as king and also wrote a list of "the rights and duties of the kingship; and he laid it up before the Lord." (1 Sam 10:25) It is not likely that Samuel's written covenant between king and people contained the Deuteronomic provision (17:17) which says the king "must not acquire many wives for himself, or else his heart will turn away," but it might have included the prohibition of sexual relationships with the people of the land, which is a part of the Ritual Decalogue in Exodus 34:15–16.

Apparently no laws were written until Samuel drew up that contract with the first king. This, in spite of the sequence in the book of Exodus which places the proclamation of "all these words" in Exodus 20 and the detailed provisions of the Covenant Code (Exod 21–23) together as one covenant-making ceremony at mount Sinai.[9] The events of Exodus 31–34 (J) appear as a second covenant making between YHWH and Moses, which included the rules of the Ritual Decalogue. Brevard Childs correctly sees these as parallel traditions of covenant making preserved in the kingdoms of Ephraim and Judah, but he does not attempt to date the writing of either E or J traditions. Instead he concludes that a "JE redactor introduced the legal traditions contained in the Book of the Covenant into the wilderness narrative," and the same redactor introduced "the tablet motif of a covenant restoration into J's account" with God dictating and Moses writing the words of the covenant on the tablets.[10] Therefore we cannot date or locate the oral origins of either tradition except to recognize that both claim to go back to Moses. Obviously they have been modified in transmission and finally written in the sequence we find in the book of Exodus. So the document Samuel laid up before the Lord probably concerned only possible abuses of the king's authority such as the people had experienced with Eli's sons. Since the injured party customarily avenged adultery, no provision forbidding it appeared in either the Covenant Code or in Samuel's rules for the kingship.

Nathan confronted David with the community's need for justice when he told the story of the rich man's appropriation of his neighbor's ewe lamb, and with that insight David saw that he had sinned when he took Uriah's wife. The king realized that YHWH was not only a supporter of his military prowess, but also a God who demands *hesed*, the fulfillment of covenantal commitments. His sin would not be defined as the breaking of two of ten commands, but as a damaging of the social fabric of an Israel in the process of arriving at its permanent structure of authority. At the end of the book of Judges and in 1 Samuel the people had hungered for an authority figure, a "head of state" who would judge justly. David had seemed to satisfy that need but in committing adultery and covering that with murder, the king had failed his people. Nathan did not need to say that YHWH was not pleased.

---

9. Alan W. Jenks excludes both Decalogue and Covenant Code from consideration as E material "for lack of both external and internal evidence" (*The Elohist and North Israelite Traditions*, 47).

10. Childs, *The Book of Exodus*, 608. Below we will mention Coote's prima facie case that the Elohist supplemented a Judean (J) history to support the revolution of Jeroboam against Rehoboam and that Jeroboam authorized the preparation of the Covenant Code.

From Family Stories to the Adultery Commandment

Developing an Israelite consensus about sexual and power relationships represents the second stage we are observing, a stage that overlapped the stage of family and tribal customs. Everybody knew that YHWH disapproved of marriage with non-Israelite women and that any breach of a marriage would bring unhappy consequences within the kingdom. The failure of the monarchy to establish justice within the king's house would require the writing of YHWH's laws by priests.

Issuing Commands and Forming "Laws"

"Of making many *laws* there is no end," the wise preacher might have written in the twelfth chapter of Ecclesiastes. The Sumerians began the third stage of the story by formalizing laws many centuries before we see them in Israel, and each year new law books are added to the shelves of lawyers and courthouses in the "civilized" nations of the world. Shortly after members of the human species discovered that they could put meaningful marks on handy materials, wood, stone, clay, or papyrus, to tally things they possessed and exchanged, humans began to identify *to whom various items belonged and how they were traded*. The recording of trades and ownership led to laws and histories. Laws may have been the earliest texts to be written, but histories came to be written to honor the memory of heroic leaders whose victories established the stages of developing civilization.

Israelites remembered both ethical and religious rules for their exchanges by way of the Torah/teaching of their elders and priests. In the story stage of Israel's development, which clearly preceded the stage of written law, village elders were loosely responsible for justice concerns in what Marshall calls "family law." Priests took care of the purity of the community in its meetings with God by insisting on unblemished sacrifices.

The linguistic form in which both quasi-legal judgments and directions for sacrifices were given to worshippers appears to have been the verbal imperative: "Bring your first-fruits," "Don't make idols," "Stone the guilty one," "Give her back to her father."

Thus direct commands originated in the form familiar to us in the unconditioned negative and positive commandments of the Decalogue, and are intelligible as the orders of Authority, passed on from God by acolytes.[11]

In what may be called the consensus stage of Israel's life, local elders, chiefs, or priests were the authorities whose judgments (Hebrew *mishpatim*) became the core of community consensus. Though this chapter is particularly interested in the eighth of the commandments, "don't commit adultery," its pre-emptive prohibition probably did not find expression at this stage. Judgments would have been issued only after a crime. The command's two Hebrew words summarize and reinforce a bit of proverbial / moral wisdom, not a legal judgment made by elders and chiefs. It is better to call it a

---

11. Marshall, *Israel and the Book of the Covenant*, 123, cites E. Gerstenberger ("Covenant and Commandment," 38–51) and J. Blenkinsopp (*Wisdom and Law in the Old Testament* 81), as arguing convincingly for similarities between apodictic law and family wisdom sayings.

"rule" since it instructs members of a community and does not include recommendations for punishment.

On the sketchy path from early innocence to later guilt a category of true laws can be distinguished in the Pentateuch. These were formed as judgments and statutes, or in modern terms, "case laws." These probably originated when elders heard both sides of a quarrel and questioned witnesses before coming to a decision of guilt or innocence regarding individuals' violation of each other through various forms of murder, theft, adultery, or verbal abuse. We noted Newman's list of common "legal" conflicts in food collector societies, and recognize that they continue to occupy the lower courts today. When altercations occurred over women, cattle or the lines that separated one field from another, elders or priests "judged," issuing opinions, which people would agree, were just. Incidents were remembered, and at some point priests began to incorporate these cases along with instructions for worship, citing Moses as the traditional intermediary who declared the oldest judgments.

In contrast to direct commands that can stand alone, conditional or circumstantial laws usually begin with "if" or "when," and detail a particular activity that the community, *including* YHWH/God, found unacceptable. They may conclude with a direct command. For example: "*When* a man seduces a virgin who is not engaged to be married, and lies with her, he *shall give* the bride price for her and make her his wife. But *if* her father refuses to give her to him, he *shall give* the bride price for virgins" (Exod 22:16, emphasis added).

Behind this double law is no doubt a series of incidents, little stories of luckless daughters who were either forced or seduced into a premature relationship, before families had made the customary arrangement for a proper marriage. In the heat of the moment tempers flared and violence could have led to murder—of either or both of the offending parties. But the community encouraged fathers to tame their anger and accept the unplanned event. Except for the ancestral figures whose stories are connected with some of the laws, names have been forgotten, new families were formed, and grandchildren may not even have been told of the incident. The wives captured by the Benjamites who survived the punishment inflicted upon the tribe in Judges 20–21 have remained anonymous, but the incident was recalled since it concerned the survival of one of the twelve tribes. The story of Dinah is an exception, not only because the incident apparently took place within doors, but because it involved two of Jacob's sons and an interruption to the family's settling in Hivite territory.

Written laws condensed many early incidents into a single formula and set a rule that the majority of the community would agree was the way to deal with any future case. In the "if" or "when" clause of the law we are hearing what has already happened or what might happen. The protasis—the "if clause"—of the conditional sentence tells us the typical situation as an abbreviated history. The apodasis—the rest of the sentence—is guidance for the community's handling of a similar new situation. It may use the direct imperative, "you shall" or a third person (jussive) verb as in the case just mentioned: the accused "shall give."

The rhetorical structure "if, then" is a useful literary device for a variety of human undertakings, including syllogistic logic, "if *p*, then *q*" and the reporting of scientific experimentation, "if the experimenter does . . . then the consequence or result is (or should be)." Here it formulates the decision reached by a community in a case under dispute.

Structuring Sexuality and Power in the Law Codes

Although Moses is given credit for writing all Israelite law, it is likely that the first body of laws, the so-called Ritual Decalogue (Exod 34:10–26), was not written before the JE editor brought together traditions from the Ephraimite and Judean kingdoms.[12] Its only concern with sexuality is that Israelites "shall not make a covenant with the inhabitants of the land" since "you will take wives from among their daughters for your sons, and their daughters who prostitute themselves to their gods will make your sons also prostitute themselves to their gods." With this provision intermarriage within a tribe or between kindred tribes became a customary unifying "law" of the early Israelite confederacy. Other aspects of the covenant initiated at Sinai/Horeb came to require families to visit altars tended by YHWH's priests three times a year, and to avoid impure features of the worship of other gods. The writing of the Ritual Decalogue must be later, perhaps by a century or so, than the familial agreements that linked tribes together as Israel. The only recollection of these earliest agreements is preserved in the legends of Jacob's family and his descendants. But instead of gathering regularly, Jacob's sons were sending to Egypt for grain and marrying the daughters of their neighbors, actions that the biblical editors neglected to call sinful for Judah and Joseph.

After the return from Egypt to Canaan and Joshua's initial victories the only unifying structures were the temporary defensive groupings of tribes for battles led by judges, the use of the ephod to decide on military tactics, the widely understood requirement to gather in worship three times a year and the reminders that YHWH was displeased with adulterous worship.

Efforts at structuring a nation of tribes were in the early "Covenant Code" (E and JE) and in the later "Deuteronomic Code" (D), both of which introduced concerns for interpersonal justice in addition to reminding Israelites of the three yearly festivals. The later priestly legislation (P and H) of Leviticus was sometimes concerned with justice, but more firmly required the holiness of the community around the post exilic Jerusalem temple.[13]

The overriding principle of the Covenant Code is stated in apodictic (direct command) form by God through Moses, as the most Senior Member of the covenanting community's tribal leaders: "You shall not pervert the justice due to your poor in their

---

12. John van Seters promoted this idea in papers before the Society of Biblical Literature and Exegesis, and in his book *The Life of Moses: the Yahwist as Historian in Exodus-Numbers*.

13. Jacob Milgrom suggests that the four legal "sources" of the Pentateuch "can be considered as two: JE leading to D, and P leading to H." ("The Changing Concept of Holiness," 66).

PART 3: A Natural History of Biblical "Sin"

lawsuits. Keep far from a false charge, and do not kill the innocent and those in the right, for I will not acquit the guilty" (Exod 23:6–7).

People are obligated to show equal concern for the welfare of women and men, except that "when a man sells his daughter as a slave, she shall not go out as the male slaves do." Instead: "If she does not please her master, who designated her for himself, then he shall let her be redeemed, he shall have no right to sell her to a foreign people, since he has dealt unfairly with her. If he designates her for his son, he shall deal with her as with a daughter. If he takes another wife to himself, he shall not diminish the food, clothing or marital rights of the first wife. And if he does not do these three things for her, she shall go out without debt, without payment of money" (Exod 21:7–11).

These "judgments" established the rights of a woman whose relationship was of lower order than the formally married wife, in effect establishing a legitimate polygyny in Israel, designed to keep every Israelite within the extending circle of tribal life. This law serves incidentally as recognition of the legitimacy of every member of Jacob's family and those of other affluent landowners. Patriarchal landholders and their sons were to own and protect all the women of the Israelite extended family; male slaves might also belong in the family/tribe, but they could not take a wife away to freedom. It is worth noting that the female slave may be treated as nearly equal to a son: "he shall deal with her as with a daughter" (Exod 21:9).

The Covenant Code also details what should be done with the family of a male slave who has earned his freedom after serving the maximum six-year term:

> if he comes in single, he shall go out single; if he comes in married then his wife shall go out with him. If his master gives him a wife and she bears him sons or daughters, the wife and her children shall be her master's and he shall go out alone. But if he chooses to remain with his master and declares his love for his wife and children, then his master shall bring him before God [or "judges"]. He shall be brought to the door or the door post, and his master shall pierce his ear with an awl; and he shall serve for life" (Exod 21:3–6).

The Code thus prescribed family sized covenants within The Covenant, but made no provision for the freed slave to purchase his wife. The only way for him to demonstrate his loving commitment to his wife was to remain in slavery with her. She remained the property of her master, and her husband became a permanent serf.

The Covenant Code imposes the judgments of the first section of the code (21:2—22:17)[14] at a level of authority above the family—God speaking through Moses, but not yet at the national level. Marshall concludes, "the legal system reflected in BC [the Covenant Code] would seem to be that of a paramount chieftainship" which is distinguished from chieftainship by "the existence of administrative and legal levels below the chief, rather than the chief being responsible for all adjudication."[15] These laws represent a level of structure broader than the tribe and belong to an intermediate time when Israel was beginning to differentiate itself from its tribal roots. It is possible

---

14. Childs, *The Book of Exodus*, 455.
15. Marshall, *Israel and the Book of the Covenant*, 174–75.

that the Covenant Code was in the hands of the judges Jehoshaphat appointed with instructions not to pervert justice, show partiality, or take bribes as they visited tribal settings (2 Chr 19:1–8).

The laws of the first section of the Covenant Code contribute little to our understanding of sin and guilt. The behavior endorsed is ordinary and relatively innocent, supporting the cohesion of extended families within a society that allowed the institution of slavery. The laws are intended to limit social abuses, not physical abuse. Since the laws of the code were directed toward the owners of slaves, only affluent males could break them. Nevertheless, by the middle of the ninth century BCE Israelite social order saw some female slaves as wives, and the male slave as a (seven year) temporary employee with the possibility of becoming a very junior member of the family/tribal enterprise.

2 Chronicles 17 reports that the priests Elishama and Jehoram "taught in Judah, having the book of the law of the Lord with them." Both Israels had evidently developed a culture of cities by the time of Ahab and Jehoshaphat, with affluent citizens who could respond appropriately to the written word, at least when it was presented in the hands of a Levitical priest. The Chronicler's information is biased to show Judah in a good light. The level of authority was no longer the extended family or the tribe but the coalition of tribes.

Other interesting laws in the Covenant Code are property oriented: harm to slaves, male or female, should be paid for according to the principle of *talion*, "like for like" (Exod 21:20–27). The father of a seduced virgin is entitled to her value as a bride (Exod 22:16–17). It is obvious that these rules are regulating economics, not sexuality. In these laws, however, we see a dawning awareness of the personhood of women and children as well as male slaves in Israelite society, possibly stemming from the memory of depersonalizing Egyptian slavery or awareness of the practices of affluent Canaanite city dwellers dispossessed by Israel. Exodus 21:10–11 includes a comprehensive formula—"food, clothing, or [and] marital rights"—for the first wife who must share her home with another woman.

In the YHWH, possibly Judean, section of the Code (Exod 22:18—23:19) God distinguishes between innocence and guilt and oversees the judgments made by human beings, refusing to permit the wicked to be declared righteous. Although the Covenant Code as a whole is primarily concerned with family custom and tribal law, it may have been completed by the northern kingdom's Jeroboam I or, more likely, the southern kingdom's Jehoshaphat, both of whom needed the support of divine endorsement. One wonders if the two kingdoms developed essentially similar parallel codes during the two hundred years between Jeroboam I and Hezekiah, perhaps by a sort of verbal osmosis through the political barrier between them, each of which claimed to be Israel.

The cult of YHWH, which, according to Marshall, "does not appear to be the central focus of the society reflected in BC" (the Covenant Code), could have provided an overarching unity to the three legal levels (family, tribe, and kingdom) because it sanctifies the authority of the uppermost level, possibly only in Judah, Only in references

PART 3: A Natural History of Biblical "Sin"

to YHWH is there explicit identification of a Power higher than the paramount chief. That Power addresses the Israelites directly in the second person, "You shall not wrong or oppress a resident alien, for you were aliens in the land of Egypt" (22:21). Feasts and offerings presented to God would have had a unifying function because they communicate loyalty to the larger social group and help maintain balance within the economic system. This summary drawn from Jay W. Marshall's *Israel and the Book of the Covenant,* provides a sense of the historical and sociological context for the transition from a loose confederation of tribes to the ongoing process of creating a nation.[16]

Adultery is not mentioned in the Covenant Code. At the time the code was written the cuckolded husband was still allowed to avenge a wife's infidelity himself without guilt, and probably with his neighbors' approval. The Covenant Code established the distinction between righteousness and iniquity for Israel, which was already recognizable in the good and evil stories of Genesis. YHWH's requirement of justice had applied only to the covenantal family relationships within the tribes God had selected for the revelation of Torah/law. Political Israel, however, seems to have developed rapidly in this period, but religious Israel continued to press for the authority of YHWH who could support tribal and national structures.

A Comprehensive Program for a Nation

"The Book of the Law" contained in Deuteronomy, whose appearance and publication can be dated with reasonable assurance to 621 BCE when workers restoring the Temple found it and brought it to king Josiah, marks *the third stage of law development*. It expands the treatment of many of the laws and rules found in the Covenant Code. However, it also states the Ten Commandments, adds the *Shema* and makes the whole a hortatory oration by Moses just before the Israelites crossed the Jordan River. Chapters 12–26, sometimes called the Deuteronomic Code, include prescriptions for worship and for government. The principal concerns of the code's religious rules are that the nation Israel should avoid (1) the worship of any God but YHWH, and (2) the forms by which other gods were worshipped. Also positively, (3) offerings should be brought to the place YHWH would choose for his Name, and (4) the festivals of the Ritual Decalogue and Covenant Code should be observed *joyfully* (Deut 12:7).

The Deuteronomic Code (D, seventh century BCE) is heavily economic and somewhat political, but also touches sexuality. Evidently as time went by features not specifically covered earlier called for new rules: Did a rape occur in a town where a virgin's cries for help could be heard, or in the open country, and was she engaged? (Deut 22:23–29). Sons born to the unloved wife must be treated fairly, even to granting a double portion of the inheritance to a firstborn (21:15). Calum Carmichael's observation that this law evokes memories of Jacob and Esau[17] points to a recognition of the need for a better distribution of the family estate than was customary in the patriarchal period. To avoid family feuds every son should have a share.

---

16. Ibid., 176.
17. Carmichael, "A Strange Sequence of Rules: Leviticus 19:20–27," 182–205.

From Family Stories to the Adultery Commandment

The case of a newly married young man drafted into military service is a new problem. Deut. 20:5-9 lists several reasons for sending such a young man "back to his house": "he might die in the battle and another would dedicate [his house]" or "he might die in the battle and *another* marry [his wife]," or "he might cause the heart of his comrades to melt like his own." Not mentioned is the motivation to replace one generation of fighting men with the next, but evidently the nation valued every family's firstborn son enough to give the newly married time to produce an heir. The lineage of firstborns no doubt maintained councils of elders before the establishment of the kingship.

The most interesting of the Deuteronomic laws revive ancient concerns for the purity of the community. Whereas in the Ritual Decalogue men were forbidden to marry the women of surrounding non-Israelite tribes, in Deuteronomy 21:10-14 a man who desires a beautiful captive may "bring her home" where she "shall shave her head, pare her nails, discard her captive's garb and remain . . . for a month, mourning her father and mother" before he goes in to her to "be her husband." The month's delay allowed time to discover that she was not pregnant, and thus prove that she was pure and that her child would be Israelite. It is not likely that the month was intended to give the captive woman a chance to get acquainted with the man and the rest of his family. If, on the other hand, "a man marries a woman, but after going in to her, he dislikes her and makes up charges against her . . . saying, 'when I lay with her, I did not find evidence of her virginity,'" then the father can provide "evidence, the cloth, before the elders of the town." [Does this suggest that marriages were scheduled to follow immediately after a menstrual period?]

The slandering husband is to be fined and required to keep her as his wife with no possibility of divorce. If the charges were true, the woman was to be stoned in front of her father's house to "purge the evil from Israel" (22:13-21). The child must be certified to be the husband's, not some foreign slave's or of another member of the father-in-law's family.

Among the miscellaneous rules (Deut 21:22—25:18) which we would classify as neither specifically religious nor political we find a few laws against mixing "two kinds" repeated from the Covenant Code, but the strong prohibition of intermarriage with indigenous people has disappeared. Exclusions from the "assembly" are now from within the Israelite community of tribes, specifically "one whose testicles are crushed or whose penis is cut off," as well as "those born of an illicit union." Third generation Edomites may be admitted to the "congregation" because "they are your kin," but Ammonites and Moabites, "even to the tenth generation" shall not be admitted. The reader recalls that these latter tribes originated from Lot's incestuous relationship with his daughters, who carried a perpetual taint of impurity. These laws assert YHWH's great concern for the purity of the nation. A contaminated bloodline from before Abraham could be detected in Ammonites, but Israel was not yet ready to recognize kinship with Ammon or Moab. It appears, however, that these foreigners moved freely, perhaps as traders or craftsmen, in Israelite cities.

Part 3: A Natural History of Biblical "Sin"

The only law in the Pentateuch which enforces the eighth commandment is found in Deuteronomy 22:22: "If a man is caught lying with the wife of another man, both of them shall die, the man who lay with the woman as well as the woman. So you shall purge the evil from Israel." Immediately following come are refinements. Two conditions must be met for the community to authorize the stoning: the young woman should be "engaged to be married" and the encounter occurred "in the town," "the young woman because she did not cry for help in the town and the man because he violated his neighbor's wife" (Deut 22:23–24). But if the incident occurred "in the open country": "You shall do nothing to the young woman; the young woman has not committed an offense punishable by death, because this case is like that of someone who attacks and murders his neighbor. Since he found her in the open country, the engaged woman may have cried for help, but there was no one to rescue her" (22:26–7).

Since it was not clear that the woman willingly cooperated in adultery, only the man who attacked her was to be stoned. Her testimony that she was attacked set her free. The situation was not precisely adultery; it was rape, perhaps adultery on the part of the rapist, as we might say.

In this complex of rules the motivation has shifted slightly from an injustice committed against the husband to abuse of the security and purity of women in town and country. For wives to be insecure in Israel was an "evil" that must be eliminated. Hence the ancient custom of avenging wrong by killing the wrongdoer was preserved and made into Israelite law. Anthony Phillips concluded that Israel's treatment of adultery as a crime was unique in the ancient world.[18]

The rules of the Holiness Code of Leviticus would take the concern for the purity of women one step further, focusing on the behavior of male and female family members living in the same house, as may not have been the case in patriarchal tents: "None of you shall approach anyone near of kin to uncover nakedness: I am the Lord. You shall not uncover the nakedness of your father, which is the nakedness of your mother; she is your mother, you shall not uncover her nakedness" (Lev 18:6–7).

One final situation gained a place in Deuteronomy:

> Suppose a man enters into marriage with a woman, but she does not please him because he finds something objectionable about her, and he writes her a certificate of divorce, puts it in her hand, and sends her out of his house, she then leaves his house and goes off to become another man's wife. Then suppose the second man dislikes her, writes her a bill of divorce, … her first husband is not permitted to take her again to be his wife after she has been defiled, for that would be abhorrent to the Lord, and you shall not bring guilt on the land that the Lord your God is giving you (24:1–4).

A number of points are worth mentioning in these rulings. The "something objectionable" is not defined, but is accepted on the husband's word. Divorce has become an established possibility, with public documentation, and is granted by the man to a wife who does not please him. Although the divorcee is then technically free, it is assumed

---

18. Phillips, "Another Look at Adultery," 3–25.

she will become the wife of another man, not a prostitute. There is no mention of her second marriage being adulterous, or that semen from the first husband has tainted her. However, only women can be "defiled" through their liaisons; men can take more than one wife or visit prostitutes, and nothing is said about male purity. Finally, we cannot tell whether the woman or her father's family arranged her second marriage, but she has evidently reached nearly equal status with men in the community, probably like that of the relatively affluent widow Abigail, whom we characterized as an "independent woman," and whom David married near Hebron. YHWH's watchful eye evidently approved the arrangements for economic support of the divorcee, but disallowed finding it with her first husband. Presumably that would involve a forbidden mixing of semen or confusion as to the paternity of a child.

Deuteronomy thus refined the economic laws of the Covenant Code and added a new emphasis on the holiness which YHWH required of Israel, while providing a comprehensive program or constitution for a purified remnant of Israel after the fall of Samaria (720 BCE) and a quarter century before Jerusalem fell to the Babylonians in 586 BCE.[19] The anger felt by a man toward his adulterous wife becomes a horror, which is linked to YHWH's anger and disgust toward people who visit the defiled and defiling shrines of "another" god.

In the code's canonical form underlying principles were applied to the realities of life in Jerusalem, Judah and any of the territories of other tribes that could demonstrate allegiance to YHWH. The code of Deuteronomy established compassionate standards for a wounded nation, but continued to provide for the execution of adulterers as well as the daughter whose father could not prove her virginity (22:20–21). The most disturbing feature of this code for western progressives is that execution is called for at all. On June 25, 2008 the United States Supreme Court, in a controversial ruling, struck down a Louisiana law that allowed rapists to be executed if their victims are children. Will the Supreme Court legalize further limitations to the death penalty in future rulings?

Remodeling a Dormant Decalogue

The events at Sinai introduced the revolutionary concept of moral order under law to the Hebrew ex-slaves who were to become a nation, and later two nations. At that moment a band of Jacob's descendants saw themselves not as Pharaoh had seen them, as slaves subject to his command, but as YHWH was seeing them, a people destined be free to be guided by the conditions of Torah as YHWH's servants. But almost immediately by-products of this insight were rebellion against the leadership of Moses, a guilty liaison with alien deities and the initial breaking of commands from God, sins that transgressed laws given by YHWH. The most profound insight emerging from the Ten Commandments is that God has given humans the capability to disobey as

---

19. Other Possible dates have been established by Miller and Hayes in *A History of Ancient Israel and Judah*, 337, 416.

well as obey every one of the commands.[20] Like the child's loss of transparency to her parents, the turning point in the history of all humans begins with this right brain look at ourselves.

Note that no one moment can be fixed in conventional chronological history for this insight, since the information found in Exodus was crystallized in the post-exilic period when priests reviewed the earlier information and located the introduction of law to the legendary experiences of Israel in the wilderness between Egypt and Canaan. No extra-biblical confirmation of the life and work of Moses has been preserved. We will consider probable origins of the legal material in the next chapter, but in principle there could be an awakening of conscience at any time. It is that experience which Israel's writers located at the mountain.

Laws were not enough: the experimental procedures of each of the three stages failed the profound moral sense YHWH imposed on the descendants of Jacob. In the family traditions of the first stage custom permitted a husband to murder his wife's lover. The community consensus stage lacked a coherent system of enforcement. And in the Deuteronomic stage laws that had appeared to be firmly established needed amendments to meet new conditions that had not been thought about earlier. Laws had not solved all problems.

What principles should guide the handling of a really new situation? How were people who lived in established towns to follow a specific rule promulgated in the desert? How well did people understand God's words? Where were the two stone tablets that carried the precious words from YHWH when Nathan confronted David?

The early chapters of 1 Samuel tell how the Ark, which contained the two tablets from Sinai and symbolized YHWH's presence, had been taken into battle to support Israel in its war against the Philistines. Captured by the Philistines and later returned to an Israelite farm, the Ark was brought to Jerusalem and installed with joyous ceremony in a tent in the City of David when David successfully united Judah with the tribes of Saul's kingdom. During the period from the making of the Ark to its arrival in Jerusalem, its only apparent value was to support Israelite warriors. Were Israelites aware of the full message or importance of its tablets, or did they think of it as a golden calf, a totem or token of the God who had led the people out of Egypt? Sexual and other social problems were being handled ad hoc by patriarchal chiefs, judges, priests, Levites, seers, and prophets without reference to the commands the Ark was supposed to contain. Until Saul, David, and Solomon "there was no king in Israel," and the structuring commands from God were apparently out of sight. But a deep-rooted sense of right and wrong persisted in responsible Israelites, and the sense found expression in prophetic indictments.

Scholars have tried to reconstruct the exact language of the two tablets from Sinai, and many agree that neither Exodus 20 nor Deuteronomy 5 can be considered their original form. It may even be questioned whether precisely ten commands were brought to people at the foot of the mountain, since only in Exodus 34:38 are we told

---

20. Credit for this insight belongs to Kim Shinkoskey, with whom I exchanged drafts of our biblical studies by email.

From Family Stories to the Adultery Commandment

that Moses "wrote on the [second set of] tablets the words of the covenant, the *ten* commandments."

At the end of Deuteronomy (31:24–27) Moses is reported to have given an undefined "book of the law" to the Levites who carried the Ark with instructions to "put it beside the ark of the covenant" where it would remain as a "witness" against Israel.

Since we cannot be certain what wordings were actually original, it is possible that oral forms of YHWH's commandments were all the people heard from their priests and Levites. Hosea referred to five of them in his indictment against the inhabitants of the land:

> There is no faithfulness or loyalty,
>   and no knowledge of God in the land.
> Swearing, lying, and murder,
>   and stealing and adultery break out;
>   bloodshed follows bloodshed.
> Therefore the land mourns (Hos 4:1–3).

The "knowledge of God" (poetically parallel to "faithfulness" and *hesed*) can just as easily refer to healthy human relationships as to obedience to divine commands, as John Calvin suggests in the opening chapter of his *Institutes of the Christian Religion*, when he declares that the "sum of our wisdom . . . is comprised of . . . the knowledge of God and of ourselves."[21]

Did Hosea recall the core ethical prohibitions from a sleeping Decalogue or did his words inspire the writing of ethical rules prior to the formal publication of the Decalogue in Deuteronomy? Alan W. Jenks quotes James M. Ward: "we cannot be at all sure that Hosea is making references to the Decalogue in 4:2, since the literary parallels are not precise enough to make that determination."[22] Nevertheless swearing, lying, murder, stealing, and adultery were certainly not YHWH's way.

A century later the prophet Jeremiah, perhaps recalling Hosea's words or the book of the law rediscovered in the Temple,, in his sermon at the gate of the Jerusalem temple asked: "Here you are trusting in deceptive words to no avail. Will you steal, murder, commit adultery, swear falsely, make offerings to Ba'al, and go after other gods that you have not known, and then come and stand before me in this house, which is called by my name, and say, 'We are safe!' only to go on doing all these abominations?" (Jer 7:8–9).

The Decalogue appears to have lain dormant, first in the Ark, and later in Solomon's Temple; while sacrifices were offered, prayers for help were voiced, praises were sung, and from time to time the hope for victory was pinned on its symbolism of the warrior God YHWH.

An oral tradition of the commandments must have circulated in several different forms until the time of Josiah, including a core minimum of four ethical commands. Brought back into public hearing by eighth-century Hosea and again by the prophet

---

21. Calvin, *Institutes of the Christian Religion*, 23.
22. Jenks, *The Elohist and North Israelite Traditions*, 114.

Jeremiah at about the same time as scribes were using the Decalogue to introduce the Deuteronomic revision of practical law, ethical commands could not alone rekindle the flame of devotion to YHWH. Jeremiah knew that the words on the old stones would not work magic. They must be internalized and related to God's direct word to individuals: "The days are coming, says the Lord, when I will make a new covenant with the house of Judah . . . I will put my law within them, and I will write on their hearts, and I will be their God, and they shall be my people . . . I will forgive their iniquity, and remember their sin no more" (Jer 31:31–33, 34).

Deuteronomy was written to bring Israel's laws up to date after the fall of Samaria. Its author(s) revised and updated the laws Hezekiah's scribes had brought together out of the two kingdoms. But laws to improve on laws were not enough: What principles should guide the handling of a really new situation? How were people living in established towns and cities to follow a set of specific laws supposedly promulgated in the desert? How well did people understand God's words? Deuteronomy's author reached back to the fabled appearance of law for Israel, to the moment of revelation when YHWH gave a succinct summary of religious and ethical principles to Moses.

With its original simplicity lost, the Decalogue of Deuteronomy 5:6–21 appears to be a refurbishing of God's commanding principles to undergird the practical code of chapters 12–26. In particular, the tenth command does not forbid overt behavior as most of the commands do, but forbids *coveting* "your neighbor's wife and *desiring* "your neighbor's house, or field, or male or female slave, or ox, or donkey, or anything that belongs to your neighbor." The Deuteronomic Decalogue looks below the surface of the behavior judged by Hosea and Jeremiah, and the prime author of Deuteronomy applied the whole Decalogue as a preface to the code for the remnant of Israel. Its internalizing does not deal with specific situations as the laws of the Covenant Code had done, though it does extract a few specific terms, "ox, ass" from those familiar directives. Instead it attempts what modern scientists do when they formulate a natural law after making a series of observations which describe the way a process works or is presumed to work.

In Deuteronomy the Decalogue defines *the ideal Israelite* as one who will *not* do certain things, but who *will* do others. He won't kill, commit adultery, steal, witness falsely, or covet no matter what situations arise. He *will* worship YHWH appropriately, that is, without needing an image to hold his attention. He *will* do his work six days and rest on the seventh, and he *will* honor his father and mother. Specific situations have faded into the background as Israelites were called to hear what God wanted from them.

Perhaps this is what God intended Moses to understand and communicate to the people waiting by the smoking mountain. But Moses and his successors would have to deal with murders, adulteries, deceits and thefts. When Israelite priests collected the first laws for their people, they intended to put brakes on hotheaded action in an attempt to give time to think of a suitable response to a disturbing development. Written laws codified what elders had done for generations, channeling anger into constructive decisions. The sermonic sections of the Book of Deuteronomy follow the model set by judges, focusing on the "Now" moment of conscious turning from past failures to the making of decisions about the next step to take. In the oration Moses contrasts "then" with "now," as he retold stories of early faulty behavior in the wilderness and sketched commandments for life in Canaan:

> The Lord our God made a covenant with *us* at Horeb
> *Not with our ancestors* did the Lord make this covenant,
> *but with us, who are all of us here alive today.*
> I am the Lord your God who brought you out of the land of Egypt
> you shall have no other gods before me . . .
> You shall not murder,
> Neither shall you commit adultery.
> (Deut 5:2, 6–7, 17–18, emphasis added)

Being alive today means better behavior is still possible.

It appears that the writer(s) of Deuteronomy felt the need for a more comprehensive and simpler word from God than appeared in the specifics of the law codes. They remembered Moses and the legendary account of receiving words directly from God. The words of the original tablets, lost to public view, could provide a summary preface to what was intended as a definitive legal code for the Judean kingdom after the fall of Samaria, or for any day thereafter. After lying dormant for generations, the ethical code awoke to challenge Jews and their successors in exile to live in the presence of YHWH/God. The commands of the Decalogue could thus embody a faith and an ethic that transcends historical situations and does not specify sanctions for disobedience. At the heart of its ethic "thou shalt not commit adultery" is second only to "thou shalt not kill," and is morally equivalent to "thou shalt not steal" or "thou shalt not bear false witness."[23] The adultery commandment remains a fixture in ethical imperatives around the world today. The Deuteronomic Decalogue is more church than state with the commands being heard as coming from God.

In shifting from cases and their details Israelite lawgivers not only set forth an ethic which used the apodictic form familiar in the commands of senior members of the community, but lifted nebulous "law" from the pragmatic solution of specific social problems to the statement of what has been called "the moral law." More recently the ethicist Paul Kurtz has catalogued what he calls "the common moral decencies" in a list that is equivalent to the core principles of the Decalogue.[24] Kurtz lists more than the core principles of Deuteronomy 5, but seriously objects to making them the absolutely authoritative word of the unseen God of Moses' time. His list covers much the same ground as the Deuteronomic Decalogue and brings them from Newman's quasi-legal issues observed among hunter gatherers into the twenty-first century, thus tending to confirm the universality of a common human ethic. So the writers of Deuteronomy

---

23. Two papers that suggest the idea of an evolving set of laws: Walter Gross, "Wandelbares Gesetz—unwandelbarer Dekalog?" suggests that while laws have changed over time it is questionable whether the Decalogue suffered essential change; Frank-Lothar Hossfeld, "Der Dekalog: Seine spaeten Fassungen, der original Komposition und seine Forstufen" offers a "biography of the Decalogue."

24. Kurtz, *Forbidden Fruit*, 80–96.

Part 3: A Natural History of Biblical "Sin"

sent Jews into exile with a reasonably clear understanding of the law and ethic that both Israel-Ephraim and Israel-Judah, *and their neighbors,* had disobeyed. Torah, law plus ethic, has testified against the behavior of believers in one God from before the days of King Josiah. It continues to speak to sensitive minds in the twenty-first century.

Vision: a Happy People

The Ten Commandments, including the eighth, were intended to challenge the people of Judah to think more deeply than their obligation to obey the specific laws of the codes that had developed through the centuries between Moses and Josiah. The laws were originally formulated by the community to protect the people's sexual and family arrangements, as well as their work situations and their protection from neighbors who threatened to take God's gift of land from them. Deuteronomy envisioned a people at work in the haven YHWH had given, individuals and family groups sharing products of their labors and enjoying the pleasures associated with each of the overlapping areas of community life. If the people would remember the weekly Sabbath and the annual festivals, and obey all the commands, their future would be life instead of death.

Though the author-editors of Deuteronomy were aware of external threats to the happiness of Israel and dealt with them, they gave considerable attention to internal threats to its happy functioning. For Israel's still mostly patriarchal society, the chief problem in the area of sexuality was adultery, the invasion of a man's private relationship with his wife. Thus sexual impurity, a prime evil, needed to be purged from the nation along with a variety of forms of injustice, including the fair treatment of male and female workers in the family enterprise.

The Decalogue lifted these concerns from the level of social relationships to a perspective in which God forbade some behaviors while others were commended and recommended. After the first four commandments, which portrayed God as a nonmaterial Spirit to whom worship and obedience are due, the remaining six commands laid down principles by which behavioral problems could be solved. None of them called for execution or punishment. Instead they anticipated that a happy citizenry would worship and obey YHWH.

Nonetheless, the Decalogue failed, or at least was not effective widely enough; Jeremiah's preaching did not turn enough hearts to avert the fall of Jerusalem and the seventy-year exile from the holy city. But some remembered the advice of Jeremiah and the words of the great prophets of the eighth century BCE; priests recalled the sermon of Moses, and the people hoped for forgiveness and the end of the Exile.

The Exile ended, at least for Jews who returned to Jerusalem, and through the decrees of Cyrus, Artaxerxes, and Darius the temple was rebuilt, Jerusalem's walls were rebuilt, and revised forms of worship were established, including prayers of confession and rituals to assure the people that they were forgiven. Judaism took the form of what may be called a "church" in the secular world of the Persian Empire. But troubling events continued, and the books of Nehemiah and Ezra report several times of failure and national confession. Would people look to God for rescue or develop church structures to meet the need for a coherent society?

17

From "Unclean Lips" to Confessions of Sin

When the prophet Isaiah had his vision of the superlatively holy Lord in the Temple, he declared, "I am lost, for I am a man of unclean lips, and I live among a people of unclean lips" (Isa 6:5). Why unclean lips? How was the prophet rendered so unclean that in the presence of the Holy One of Israel he felt destroyed? What was the problem that he and his people shared? Was it a form of guilt shared by other prophets? In Jeremiah 6:2 the later prophet used the word translated "lost" to describe unoccupied Jerusalem as a peaceful pasture for sheep. People who had formerly lived and sinned in Jerusalem were no longer in the city of YHWH's temple.

Isaiah's metaphor for sinfulness was accentuated when one of the seraphs touched his lips with a live coal from the altar, but the full explanation would be reserved for the writing of exilic and post-exilic priests. The mission to which Isaiah was commissioned was prophetic speech to an insensitive people:

> Make the mind of this people dull,
> and stop their ears,
> and shut their eyes.
> so that they may not look with their eyes,
> and listen with their ears.
> and comprehend with their minds,
> and turn and be healed (Isa 6:10).

Because the word he is to speak comes from the Holy One of Israel, the prophet's lips must be cleansed by symbolic fire, while the people are called to ritually

> Wash yourselves; make yourselves clean;
> remove the evil of your doings from before my eyes;
> cease to do evil; learn to do good;
> seek justice, rescue the oppressed.
> defend the orphan, plead for the widow (Isa 1:16–17).

Both prophet and people needed a cleansing. A little later the prophet described Jerusalem as God saw it from Solomon's Temple:

> How the faithful city
> has become a whore!
> She that was full of justice,
> righteousness lodged in her—
> but now murderers!
> Tell the innocent how fortunate they are,
> for they shall eat the fruit of their labors.
> Woe to the guilty! How
> unfortunate they are,
> for what their hands have
> done shall be done to them (Isa 3:10–11).

The prophet voices and shares God's loathing for many of his fellow citizens. Though some may be innocent and would have no reason to fear a holy God, others had turned aside to whoredom, murder and abuse of the poor. The people are wallowing in a variety of corrupt and corrupting practices. Washing can remove blood from the hands that bring offerings during solemn assemblies, but YHWH will not bless guilty thieves, murderers, and adulterers without a radical change of behavior.

Corporately guilty, all have been tainted with sin. The prophet must help his people see their sins and turn from them. The other prophets of the eighth century BCE, Amos, Hosea, and Micah, all voiced indictments for the sins of Israel-Ephraim and Israel-Judah , and called for repentance and return. Micah, however, speaks as a faithful Judean:

> But as for me, I will look to the Lord,
> I will wait for the God of my salvation;
> my God will hear me.
> Do not rejoice over me, O my enemy;
> when I fall, I shall rise;
> when I sit in darkness
> the Lord will be a light to me,
> I must bear the indignation of the Lord,
> because I have sinned against him,
> until he takes my side
> and executes judgment for me (Mic 7:7–9).

The eighth century prophets saw injustice as corruption of the good behavior YHWH required, and Isaiah confessed the injustices and corruption of his people as his own uncleanness as he stood in the Temple, but Micah could trust in the faithfulness of YHWH to correct believers without destroying them all. Isaiah could begin his prophetic ministry after the symbolic cleansing of the live coal against his lips.

Children as Signs of a Twofold Future

Facing the threat of war with Syria or invasion from Assyria, Isaiah pointed king Ahaz to two children about to be born. One is the child of a nameless "young woman" whose son would be known as "God with us" (Hebrew *immanu-el*, Isa 7:14). For the other child YHWH instructed the prophet to write *Maher-shalal-hash-baz* "The spoil speeds, the prey hastens" (NRSV translation of Isaiah 8:1; free translation: "Let's get it over with quickly, so we can get on with our lives") on a tablet as the name for his anticipated son, whose birth and childhood would herald Judah's relief from the threatening war.

The message of the first child was that responsible Judeans need not put off innocent and normal family relationships for fear of foreign threats, even though the people are deeply defiled. Those guilty of neglecting widows and orphans, "rebels and sinners, shall be destroyed together . . . but if you are willing and obedient, you shall eat the good of the land." (1:19, 28) Isaiah sees and speaks not of sexual but of economic oppression, though he stigmatizes the finery and perfumes of wealthy women. In the coming days the haughty will be humbled. However, God is, and will continue to be present with his people:

> See, I am laying in Zion a foundation stone,
> a tested stone,
> a precious cornerstone, a sure foundation:
> "One who trusts will not panic."
> Then I will make justice the line
> and righteousness the plummet;
> hail will sweep away the refuge of lies,
> and waters will overwhelm the shelter.
> Then your covenant with death will be annulled,
> and your agreement with Sheol will not stand . . .
> (Isa 28:16–17).

Military preparations and alliances, a "covenant with death," were not YHWH's way to defend Jersualem. Panicky arrogance against the Assyrians was one more affront to the Holy One of Israel. In Isaiah's day Samaria fell to the Assyrian army, but Jerusalem was saved by a miraculous pestilence that wiped out most of the enemy at its gates.[1] So the Lord had decided to give Jerusalem more time, not because the daughter of Zion was more just than Samaria, but because YHWH had chosen to stretch God's mystical "outspread wings" over Zion (Isa 8:8). The Assyrian invader's fires would cleanse the people, but a remnant would return to normal lives of righteous behavior and the rituals of the Temple.

Worship Practices of Women

A century later the prophet Jeremiah announced that God was not bound to the Temple, and that, like the priests' Ark in Eli's day, the king's temple would not save the remnant of Israel. The persistent defiling of Jerusalem and its environs was about to fill YHWH with such disgust that God would no longer protect the city (Jer 7).

Susan Ackerman has called attention to Judahite women's continuing worship of a female deity whom she identifies as "a syncretistic deity whose character incorporates

---

1. The lifting of the siege of Jerusalem is recounted at length in Isaiah 36–39 and variant forms of the story in 2 Kings 18–20 and 2 Chronicles 32.

From "Unclean Lips" to Confessions of Sin

aspects of west Semitic Astarte and east Semitic Ishtar."[2] Linked with this "Queen of Heaven" was a young male fertility god Tammuz, mentioned in Ezekiel 8, who courted and married her, but, like Baal in the agricultural cycle of Ugarit, was believed to have died at the end of the hot summer season and was restored to activity in the following spring. In his visionary tour of the Jerusalem temple, Ezekiel saw women weeping for the dead god just as their Canaanite predecessors had done. In Canaanite mythology the recurrently virgin goddess Anat had journeyed to the underworld to restore her consort to life, and the women wept to support the effort of the goddess to bring her male partner back into full power as the year began anew with the winter rains. The "god" Rachel stole from Laban's family, and the images and altars Solomon set up for his foreign wives probably all represented this deity, who was known by different local names. For Israelite women the superstitious prayers to Asherah that had brought the miraculous return of spring fertility could be expected to do so each year as late as the time of Jeremiah and Ezekiel.

Sandra Scham includes photographs of "The Lost Goddess of Israel," large breasted female figures with "pillar" bodies, which are believed to represent the goddess Asherah mentioned in 1 Kings 15:12 / 2 Chronicles 15:63.[3] Mary Douglas has connected the dots, relating the practices of women in the worship of the Queen of Heaven to the rebellion of Israel. Using her analysis of matching sections of the artfully designed book of Numbers, Douglas sees Moses' sister Miriam as a metaphor for Israel. In Numbers 12 Miriam and Aaron conspire to rebel against and claim equal authority with Moses, while on the opposite side of the book's ring structure, in Numbers 25, Cozbi, the daughter of a Midianite chieftain, was executed by Phinehas, Aaron's grandson, for openly having intercourse with an unnamed Israelite man. Their execution completes the report of Israel's introduction to sexual/religious sin at Shittim.[4]

Seeing a symbolic connection between the two chapters, Douglas points out "the danger of religious apostasy was at the top of the priestly agenda. Israel's temptations to religious syncretism, the frenzied attacks on kings for false religion, and the filth imputed to foreign cults, these supply enough explanation of why Miriam was silenced."[5] Appropriately, a would be a prophetic voice had been silenced long before Isaiah and Jeremiah, as Israel developed a rational understanding of good and evil behaviors in place of less rational disgust.

The silencing of Miriam may also be seen as an aspect of the power struggle between orthodox Yahwist and alien heretical priesthoods and the Ephraimite kings and queens the latter supported. Although the connection is not explicitly stated, Miriam

---

2. *Under Every Green Tree: Popular Religion in Sixth-Century Judah* [Harvard Semitic Monographs, 46]. (Scholars Press, Atlanta, Georgia, 1992), "And the Women Make Cakes for the Queen of Heaven," Jeremiah 7 and 44, pp. 4–35.

3. *Archaeology*, March/April, 2005. pp. 36–40.

4. To understand Douglas' reasoning read her study of the elaborate "ring" structure of the book of Numbers, which spells out her study of defilement in the book of Numbers, "Sister of Moses, Queen of Heaven," *In the Wilderness* (Sheffield, 1993), pp. 199ff. See also "Incident at Shittim" in chapter 15.

5. Douglas, *In the Wilderness*, 203.

and Aaron represent female and male priests. Apparently women "priests" assisted the women who prayed to variously named female deities. The Chronicler lists the wives and concubines of Israelite kings but, Mary Douglas suggests, effectively silences them by reporting only the number of sons and daughters they bore. In 2 Kings, on the other hand, Jezebel, Athaliah, Jehosheba, and other women have significant roles in the history, acting for either good or evil beside the men. In Numbers 12 Miriam is afflicted with leprosy after joining with Aaron in criticizing Moses for marrying a Cushite woman. Both siblings of Moses are told that YHWH speaks with their brother "face to face," not in riddles or dreams (Num 12:8). The Numbers narrative echoes the prophetic account of power struggles within the royal households. After the exile priestly custodians of God's laws would seek to control the common people's lives in a Judean "church" in a territory ruled by a foreign emperor.

The women's rituals were not only superficially different from the official religion of the Temple; they preserved a way of thinking about God, or, more accurately at the time, the family of deities who ruled important aspects of the world. The superstitious common religion of the ancient world never really surrendered to the One God who had made YHWH's Self known to Moses. It simply went underground, and was preserved by women to support them in their peculiarly female needs. There could be no reconciling the two views, and the debate between politically correct priest-prophets and the "people of the land" did not end even when the Temple was destroyed.

Is there nothing good that can be said for the faith of the women? Can superstition be one path toward a proper faith? The persistence of superstition indicates that women needed more then they received from YHWH or YHWH's priests. Whatever the reality of the experiences of Hosea's wife, the prophet managed some sort of reconciliation with her and her children that did not spread more widely until the end of the exile, and then only in principle through the poetry of the Second Isaiah and the priestly practice of rebuke in place of punishment.

Disgust as a Basis for an Ethic of Holiness

Whatever date we give to the writing of particular biblical laws, some of them appear to express very ancient feelings of disgust and fear which shaped the social and religious world of the ancient Near East. Among these were prohibitions against eating certain "unclean" animals and fowl, touching blood, or decaying meat, and what M. H. Lovelace calls "reversals of the natural."[6] It is not clear why YHWH considered the wearing of clothes proper to the opposite sex to be "abhorrent" (NRSV), but the decree against it is absolute even though this abnormality is not labeled sinful. Disgust and fear are so deeply embedded in the human psyche that people seldom explain their superstitious feelings of revulsion.

According to Leviticus 18:22–23 YHWH is just as disgusted with men's homosexual relationships as "He" is with men or women who have sexual relationships with

---

6. Lovelace cites Deuteronomy 22.5 as the only sexual "reversal" but mentions three proverbs for ethical reversals (Lovelace, "Abomination" 13).

an animal. Except for the fact that these words are found in a long list of direct commands of YHWH, we could consider them to be the opinion of the Israelite male community or its priests. Such sexual experiments were obviously repugnant to most Israelites, and the word from YHWH ascribes a similar repugnance to God, but does not characterize them as sins or mention any consequent harm. Along with sacrificing a child to Molech and approaching a woman during her menstrual cycle, they are so abnormal or unnatural that Israelites *must not* do them. Why then was the unnatural rite of circumcision required for every male? Zipporah's comment, "Truly you are a bridegroom of blood to me!" (Exod 4:25) when she circumcised the son of Moses suggests that YHWH sometimes demanded the unnatural.

The priests may have thought (and taught) that the forbidden actions did real harm to the post-exilic community, as the historians believed worshipping a Canaanite deity was connected with foreign invasions during the time of the Judges. God's word to Moses had lifted them from ethical to religious faults. It is not that people *cannot* do them. Men can have anal intercourse with other men as well as with women. In Israelite society they *may not* do so without being ostracized or executed. Under YHWH's command they *should* or *must not*. Mary Douglas suggests that some of these rules express God's concern that his people avoid intentional defilement, but it may be that many men, especially physically large ones, have a deep fear of being seen before other men as weak or effeminate.

No doubt the Israelite community thought these irregular behaviors were sinful as well as disgusting even before they became a part of the prohibitions of Leviticus, and people who knew of such activity, probably wondered how anyone could behave in such a disgusting way. However, the gay men and lesbian women of our time, and probably those of ancient Israel, *do not share* the disgust of the community, and obviously find pleasure in their relationships. In a study of *Risky Sex* Dwayne C. Turner explains the patterns of some unsafe homosexual encounters as "unambiguously spontaneous. Additionally, they were all in a state of heightened arousal, and each found the unsafe event more pleasurable; but after the fact, they expressed grievous remorse for having put themselves in such a risky situation."[7] YHWH may have seemed homophobic to people in post-exilic Judea, but the God we know in Jesus Christ values mutually satisfying relationships and strong loving commitments. When commitments include heterosexual relationships we think God approves, but because of our disgust with some aspects of homosexual relationships, biblical moralists and their followers believe God disapproves them. It is sad that public opinion and popular religion have superstitiously laid the burden of "sin" on them. A friend who died of complications from AIDS never confessed to being gay, but spoke frequently about his sinful life. He recommitted himself to Roman Catholic worship in the final years of his life, but never seemed to find peace of mind. Disgust can morph either into a community's vicious intolerance or a church's loving acceptance of "abnormal" relationships.

---

7. Turner, *Risky Sex*, 110.

PART 3: A Natural History of Biblical "Sin"

The Levitical recapitulation of some of the Decalogue's commands (see the next chapter for a look at Leviticus 19) tends to confirm the idea that irregular sexual relationships are not inherently sinful by suggesting an atoning sacrifice to forgive a man who has had sexual relationships with another's man's female slave. Also it adds a command prohibiting "making" a man's daughter into a prostitute. Surely God does not consider the family's economic benefit to be worth the defilement imposed on any young woman (Lev 19:20–22). The bald prohibition in 19:29 carries no sanctions against prostituting a daughter, but explains that to do so would prostitute the land. Verse 30 inexplicably connects the prohibition with Sabbath observance and reverence for the land.

The Unknowing Poor

What is important in considering the movement from innocence to guilt is not which functionary spoke for God, but which voice was believed and what the message was. As children look to parents and their peers to see what behavior is appropriate, so the members of Israelite tribes listened to the words of priests and prophets for guidance in moments of uncertainty. People are always somewhere between not knowing and the knowing which we should more properly call belief. We believe that we and most of our fellow humans know right from wrong. As children we believe we can distinguish good tastes from bad until an elder says "I like it," and we actually try the new dish. Then comes a time of uncertainty: which "good" to choose? Uncertainty perplexes us at every fork in the paths we can barely see in the jungle of civilized life. In a strange city all streets look alike and the tourist cannot find his way back to his hotel without the help of map or knowledgeable guide. Letters to newspaper editors reflect the wide range of strong opinions on moral and ethical issues.

A little more than a century after Isaiah, the prophet Jeremiah raised his voice, sometimes speaking as himself, and at other times speaking for God. A contemporary of king Josiah, Jeremiah saw the sins of his people and their unavoidable consequences. He saw a dangerous corruption at the heart of his people, which could only be remedied by a surgical act like the circumcision of the male foreskin, for he saw his people going "after Baals," like an adulterous wife who "on every high hill and under every green tree sprawled and played the whore" (Jer 2:20).

This vivid picture reflects what must have been moments of disorienting spring (or fall) fever in Judean and Ephraimite society, when, possibly at the time of the full moon, or at one of the annual festivals, women forgot their husbands and men forgot their wives in not quite innocent abandon like the tales of midsummer revels from northern Europe.[8] Eli's sons had misled some women before Samuel's reforms. The prophets Jeremiah and Ezekiel described Judah's waywardness in terms that evoke the sad experience of Hosea's Gomer. She bore children whom Hosea named "Jezreel," "Not-Pitied," and "Not-my-People," publicly proclaiming a link between adulterous unions and the corrupted faith of Israel's northern kingdom. Whether the children

---

8. Note Jeremiah 3:1,13,20,23; 4:30; 13:25–27; 22:20–23; 23:13–14; 30:14.

were really Hosea's and symbolically named, or, as I suggest, the result of adulterous unions, is not material at this point. A reading between the lines of Hosea 1–4 indicates that some adulteries were real in Israelite society.

Jeremiah's concern was the way Jerusalem and Judah had forsaken the God who had brought them out of Egypt to "a plentiful land to eat its fruits and its good things." His message was laced with imagery of family life, which evidently reflected the indulgent life that surrounded the late seventh- and early-sixth-century prophets, but reminded his hearers of Yahweh's way. His metaphors link spiritual to physical adultery.

The distinction between the "unknowing poor" and the rich who presumably had seen and heard of the written law found in the temple in Josiah's time marks the last stage of the path from innocence to guilt. In Jeremiah 7 the prophet lists six of the actions forbidden by the Decalogue. After the publication of the Book of the Law in Josiah's eighteenth year, the leaders and people of Judah could no longer plead ignorance, even when Jeremiah could speak (ironically?) of the lying pen of the scribes.

Whether most of the people knew the laws of Moses or not, many were aware that it was wrong to have sexual relations with anyone not a husband or wife, even when it happened as part of the celebration of an annual festival dedicated to YHWH, Baal or the Queen of Heaven. Jeremiah, like Hosea, saw that yielding to the impulse of passion at an altar dedicated to a life-saving Asherah was a sin. Only YHWH, the God of creation, had a right to be worshipped. And YHWH approved sexual relations only within marriage.

The publication of the Book of the Law in the eighteenth year of Josiah's reign presumably should have led to the removal of "all the abominations that were seen in the land of Judah and in Jerusalem" and had produced a widespread awareness of sin and guilt. Like some adolescent conversion experiences, that "revival" was incomplete and quickly forgotten, but it evidently engaged the attention of many Judeans. Nevertheless the building consensus for right living had reached an ethical milestone.

A Period of Sensitive Self-Examination

The fall of Jerusalem brought a wave of soul-searching for Judeans, soon to be known as Jews, whether they were taken to Babylon or remained in the environs of Jerusalem. An unnamed poet sang the laments of the lonely "city that was once full of people," speaking first *about* Judah and Jerusalem as seen by God:

> Judah has gone into exile with suffering
> and hard servitude;
> she lives now among the nations,
> and finds no resting place;
> her pursuers have all overtaken her
> in the midst of her distress.
>
> . . .
>
> Jerusalem sinned grievously,
> so she has become a mockery;
> all who honored her despise her,

PART 3: A Natural History of Biblical "Sin"

> for they have seen her nakedness;
> she herself groans,
> and turns her face away.
> ...
> Her uncleanness was in her skirts;
> she took no thought of her future;
> her downfall was appalling,
> with none to comfort her.
> Then Jerusalem confesses her sin, telling her story to any who will listen:
> The Lord is in the right,
> for I rebelled against his word;
> ...
> I called to my lovers
> but they deceived me;
> my priests and elders
> perished in the city
> while seeking food
> to revive their strength
> ...
> You have made us filth and rubbish
> among the peoples.
> Finally the poet explains Jerusalem's fate:
> It was for the sins of her prophets
> and the iniquities of her priests,
> who shed the blood of the righteous
> in the midst of her.
> Blindly they wandered through the streets,
> so defiled with blood
> that no one was able
> to touch their garments.[9]

We cannot tell how literally to take the metaphors of this lament, but we can recognize the genuine distress of the exiles and the feeling of community guilt the poem expresses. Apparently the poem refers either to the actual brutality of rape or at least to the menstrual bleeding of women as the material iniquity that led to their enslavement in Babylon. Had the women been guilty of inviting rape, or is the poet referring to the bringing in of alien worship by the whole community? The poet confesses the reality of Judah's unfaithfulness to YHWH together with the violence of her prophets and priests. No one was completely innocent. As an adulterous wife and her lover could be punished, so an unfaithful nation should have expected YHWH's wrath.

In Babylon with the first deportation of Judean leaders, twenty four years after the reform led by king Josiah's priests, the prophet Ezekiel saw contrasting visions. On the one hand he saw "four living creatures" moving with wheels "gleaming with beryl" up to a dome which was "something like a throne, and above the throne was something that seemed like a human form." On the other hand he saw the people of Jerusalem still committing abominations in the temple "to drive [YHWH] from [His]

9. Lamentations 1:3, 8–9, 18–19; 3:25; 4:13–14.

sanctuary." He also saw two sisters, Oholah ("her tent," Samaria) and Oholibah ("*the* tent is in her," Jerusalem), playing the whore and lusting after Assyrian warriors, governors and commanders, "all of them handsome young men." The names translated: "her tent" and "a tent is in her," perhaps reflect the way prostitutes welcomed their clients. Ezekiel 23 thus provides details of the physical and spiritual adulteries only hinted at in Lamentations.

Ezekiel turned away from the vision of abominations in disgust, but paused to discuss with the Lord the proverb: "The parents have eaten sour grapes, and the children's teeth are set on edge." In God's eyes "it is only the person who sins that shall die . . . A child shall not suffer for the iniquity of a parent, nor a parent for the iniquity of a child." (Ez 18:2, 20 NEB) The prophet saw another puzzling irregularity. More and more during that half century Judeans began to wonder if their personal sins were responsible for the catastrophe that had occurred to the city of Jerusalem. Strangely, after the destruction of New York's twin towers on September 11, 2001 no similar widespread soul searching occurred in American church or state.[10]

The biblical narratives, however, under the influence of prophetic preaching charge the kings and the whole people with guilt, while the laws urged individual self-examination and confession. William Johnstone[11] points out that in the exilic writings "Leviticus legislates for the [unfaithfulness of the] individual; in Chronicles the unfaithfulness is corporate and compounded generation by generation."

Thus in the long slide from innocence to guilt it was the poets and prophets who were most aware of the people's guilt, while the people were suffering the indignities of deportation and loss of home and identity. No longer a "people whose God is YHWH," the exiles could mourn with the words of Psalm 137:

> By the waters of Babylon,
> there we sat down and there we wept
> when we remembered Zion.
> . . .
> For there our captors
> asked us for songs.
> and our tormentors asked for mirth, saying,
> "Sing us one of the songs of Zion!"
> How could we sing the Lord's song
> in a foreign land?

Is Guilt Necessary?

We have traced the movement of ancient Israelites from relative innocence to their deep guilt as they were taken from their homes into exile. Guilt began with patriarchs who acted thoughtlessly, was publicly shared with community elders, tribal chiefs and kings, and finally returned to haunt individuals in exile. With Moses and his succes-

---

10. Soul searching has occurred after two atomic bombs were dropped on cities of Japan.
11. Johnstone "The Use of Leviticus in Chronicles," 247.

Part 3: A Natural History of Biblical "Sin"

sors to guide their thinking, Jews in exile understood from their experiences how they had strayed from the path of rightness and holiness. As a people called into covenant relationships with God and each other, they had fallen short both in their commitment to YHWH, who had chosen them, and to their wives, husbands and children. They could only interpret the loss of Jerusalem and its Temple as evidence of YHWH's total displeasure. Sensitive Judeans understood that they were all at fault.

Must we follow the path from innocence to guilt in our time? Contemporary prophetic voices like William Bennett or Martin Luther King Jr. have proclaimed the traditional values of faithfulness, justice, and virtue. We continue to read Paul's letter to the Romans in our churches and measure our virtue against his reading of the ancient scriptures: "Therefore you have no excuse, whoever you are, when you judge others; for in passing judgment on another you condemn yourself, because you, the judge, are doing the very same things" (Rom 2:1). Like the prophets of Israel and first-century Jews and Gentiles, some people believe our society is wholly corrupt. It seems that everyone has disobeyed some rule, and we are all doomed to go into exile together. And even if a Job here or there protests his innocence, will he be forced to go into exile with the rest of society?

Exile was not Isaiah's lot, but he could not protest his innocence. Earlier prophets of the eighth century BCE had spoken of specific transgressions:

> Father and son go in to the same girl,
> so that my holy name is profaned. (Amos 2:7)
> ... your daughters play the whore,
> and your daughters-in-law commit adultery.
> I will not punish your daughters when they play the whore,
> nor your daughters-in-law when they commit adultery;
> for the men themselves go aside with whores,
> and sacrifice with temple prostitutes;
> thus a people without understanding comes to ruin.
> (Hos 4:13–14)

So also, as a prophet of Holy YHWH, Isaiah could not bear to take on his purified lips the words to describe the corruption of his people, which is one form of what Patricia Williams calls "structural sin,"[12] in this case the materialist memes of an indulgent society. Would his people feel the guilt the prophet felt? It would be more than a century before the shock of exile and the destruction of the temple woke the people to their sin.

Is guilt necessary? In the grand scheme of things why were prophets like Isaiah and law-givers like Moses obliged to prod people about their "sins?" Is there something about the way God made the world that demands a humbling recognition of human failure? Or, in a perspective that has no place for God, are sin and guilt simply dark blotches on canvasses novelists like Dostoyevsky and playwrights like Tennessee Williams prepare for the delight of connoisseurs of literature? Crimes and sins certainly make for interesting contrasts in the comedies and tragedies we tell each other,

---

12. Williams, *Doing without Adam and Eve*, 174.

whether part of Holy Scripture or of secular literature. But a question remains as an aspect of existential *angst*: Is the guilt we feel a step toward a possible learning experience?

It is a thesis of this study that stories are told and laws are formulated to help us discover our feelings about injuries humans suffer at the hands of other people or from the world itself. Just as physical pain alerts an individual to a need for healing, so social pressure alerts one to consider what's wrong. Asking, "How does what is not possible for animals become possible for humans?" Holmes Rolston III observes, "Human mental and cultural development somehow generates a possibility space for ethics, which emerges where none was before."[13] That possibility space is first of all in the mind of an individual who can perceive himself or herself as an actor in a drama involving other people. Noting the consequences of current or past actions, the internal spectator—a god figure—may share a gut reaction of pain or pleasure at what one observes *one Self* doing to another Self.

Richard Dawkins coined the word "meme" for what might be called the software of the social brain, i.e., the conscious and unconscious ordering of responses to new experiences that grows out of previous experiences. Patrick Miller writes that "the Psalter and Deuteronomy are the books of Scripture that most explicitly set within the community of faith a *cultural memory* that finds its identity and guides its life."[14]

Sometimes we actually *feel with* another, and share in the pain of the other. That possibility space has been called conscience, a "knowing with" another, and may suggest different, more consciously directed behavior for new encounters. The youth who revisits the girl with whom he had last year's summer romance cannot forget her question, "Why did you come back?" as he forsakes her. Laws are an expression of the conscience of the community and an effort to reduce people's ethical feelings to rules. They serve to focus attention on the guilt or pleasure that results from our actions toward our friends and neighbors.

Feelings Lead to Confessions of Sin but No Definitions

In rereading the Hebrew Scriptures one discovers no definition of "sin." Instead, one finds confessions of sin. David's "I have sinned," is one, and Lamentations 1:18, "I have rebelled against his word," is another. Two Psalms, in particular, are vehicles for the private and public confession of sin. Having seen himself or herself from God's point of view, the Psalmist, traditionally David, reverts to transparency:

> Then I acknowledged my sin to you,
> and I did not hide my iniquity (32:5).
> For I know my transgressions,
> and my sin is ever before me.
> Against you, and you alone, have I sinned,
> and done what is evil in your sight (51:4).

---

13. Rolston, *Genes*, p. 227.
14. Miller, *Israelite Religion and Biblical Theology*, 331.

PART 3: A Natural History of Biblical "Sin"

Neither of these confessions is explicitly sexual, though they are commonly thought to be David's. Every pastor hears confessions of adultery, premarital sex or lust, often the only sin confessed by a burdened soul. Instead of definitions of sin the Hebrew Scriptures give us the confessions of a few ancient sinners and words of *generalized confession* available to worshippers in the second Temple and to users of the scriptures and prayer books today.

What lies on the path beyond the confession of sin? The first of the Songs of Ascents puts it this way:

> If you, O Lord, should mark iniquities,
> Lord, who could stand?
> But there is forgiveness with you,
> so that you may be revered (Ps 130:3-4).

The Hebrew Scriptures answer: hope for forgiveness and restoration to community with God.

18

Afterthoughts: Sin and Forgiveness in Retrospect

The either/or-ness of Deuteronomy and the Decalogue does not satisfy everyone, and afterthoughts often arise when we think we have settled on a plan. To put the personal ahead of the ethical, in writing this series of thoughts I found myself cycling through brief periods of concentrated writing at my computer, thinking at the end of each burst that what I had written was "very good" and deserved to stay for the final show and tell. Before daylight the next morning, however, I would find myself lying in bed thinking instead of sleeping. Almost daily a fresh insight called for revising or supplementing what was already supposed to be "in the can." I came to think of these insights as gifts from God, and at the same time the fruit of a brain's activity in deep sleep, or perhaps a necessary converting from Pinker's "fuzzy" mentalese to "crisp" professional expression. In the leisure of retirement this cycling between meditation and writing was not frustrating but strangely exhilarating. I felt inspired. Will the ideas in this study inspire readers to return to the Hebrew Scriptures for fresh understanding of God's way?

Did the successive prophets and editors of the scripture and the theologians who followed have something of that experience? Priests transformed ancient superstitions into concepts of imageless Deity and ways of stabilizing community. Prophets correcting priests, Deuteronomy improving on Exodus tradition; Leviticus improving on Deuteronomy; Numbers organizing the tribal "Sons of Israel" into military companies, the Gospels fulfilling the Law and the Prophets. We, like post-exilic redactors, value these paradoxical afterthoughts. Although each new contributor felt that it was time to close the canon of interpretation, has there not always been a continuing need for fresh interpreting? For explaining insights to an evolving community of faith, as Rabbis, pastors and teachers, and new prophetic voices have always done.

According to the first chapter of Deuteronomy, when the Israelites had reached the eastern side of the Jordan in Moab, "Moses undertook to expound the law." The frightening experience of receiving the law at the mountain had failed. Evidently the people had forgotten what they had heard, or simply ignored it during the forty years

PART 3: A Natural History of Biblical "Sin"

in the Sinai wilderness.[1] How could they be expected to remember all the accumulating details God had given Moses when they would soon be scattered from Dan to Beersheba?

The high priest Hilkiah, who rediscovered the laws in the temple's treasure box during Josiah's reign, felt just like Moses when his secretary read from the dusty book. The discovery provoked a new set of afterthoughts, and the king called for the septennial reading of Torah. Moses had told the priests, almost as an afterthought at the end of Deuteronomy, to read the Torah in the hearing of the assembled people "in the scheduled year of remission" (2 Kgs 22–23). Would the people respond so that God would avert the threatening armies from northeast and southwest? Jeremiah hoped so and repeatedly YHWH addressed his people: "Reform the whole pattern of your conduct, so that I may dwell with you in this place. Do not put your trust in that lie: "This is Yahweh's temple, Yahweh's temple, Yahweh's temple!' No! Only if you reform your whole pattern of conduct—if you really behave justly toward another, no longer oppress the alien, the orphan, and the widow [nor shed innocent blood in this place], nor follow other gods to your own hurt—only then can I dwell with you"[2]

That brief revival of piety did not last, and within thirty-five years Jerusalem and its Temple were destroyed. An unknown priest who survived the slaughter of leaders described in the last chapter of 2 Kings must have carried much of the book of Deuteronomy into exile in Babylon after the fall of Jerusalem. He recalled that Moses had given a written copy of the law to the children of Levi to carry in the Ark of the Covenant into Canaan and now he and a few other priests would carry on that ancient tradition in a foreign land. In a day when few written documents existed the people would learn from these exilic priests "to fear the Lord . . . to observe diligently all the words of this [no longer oral] Torah" (Deut 31:9–13). Thoughts that came to the minds of priests and people in Babylon would accumulate and be written into the Torah.

"The Second Law" and Prophetic Insight

Jeremiah appeared in the Temple one day a few years after the publication of the law book. It was at the beginning of the reign of Zedekiah and he was wearing a wooden yoke to announce that no nation, not even Judah and Jerusalem, would escape being swallowed up by the Babylonian empire. Unseen YHWH seated between the cherubim of Solomon's Temple would not lift a finger to save the building. King Zedekiah should bow to the might of Nebuchadnezzar and live (Jer 27:12–13).

Hananiah opposed his brother prophet, breaking Jeremiah's yoke and announcing "Thus says the Lord . . . I have broken the yoke of the king of Babylon . . . within two years I will bring back to this place all the vessels of the Lord's house." Apparently silenced, Jeremiah "went his way," and the rituals of sacrifice in the "den-of-thieves"—house-of-prayer—went on. But "sometime after," a second word for Hananiah came

---

1. We will look at Douglas, *In the Wilderness: the Doctrine of Defilement in the Book of Numbers.*
2. Jeremiah 7:3–7, as translated by John Bright (*Jeremiah*, 52).

to him: "Within this year you will be dead, because you have spoken rebellion against the Lord."

Second thoughts are not an unfamiliar experience for people, and they could emerge after a confrontation with threatening danger. The intelligent mind is capable of reviewing experience and evaluating it at leisure: some who risked their lives had died; others and those who fled lived and learned, perhaps to pass on their experience to others. Jeremiah's experience included time in a pit prison, where he lived and learned. He could declare that when the word of the prophet who prophesies peace "comes true, then it will be known that the Lord has truly sent the prophet" (Jer 28:9). This sounds very much like the way scientific theories are floated and tested: a thoughtful observer considers a series of experiences, then plots a path from a present situation like those he has examined toward a projected one that appears to fit the pattern he has seen. Having chosen and taken the path of his theory, the experimenting observer awaits results. If it comes out as projected, the prediction is treated as true. When more than one person is involved, as was the case with Judah in the time of Jeremiah, the group may decide on a path through a variety of interactions, many of which we can observe in the stories from the scriptures. Social and religious experiments are similar in many ways to those of the science laboratory; and in the minds of the wise they can produce ethical theory and lead to practical politics.

For its time Deuteronomy, the "second law," had collected and codified the ethical and religious theory of half a millennium of the teaching by priests and prophets.

Ascribed to an aging Moses, it reviewed the experimenting of Israel's wilderness experience and had seemed to settle the need for final answers to all questions of behavior for the remnant of Israel after the fall of Samaria. It provided detailed legislation for practical affairs *and* a small group of ethical principles—six of the Ten Commandments—to guide future social behavior. We are not concerned here with the four commands of its theological theory, though its authors put the concept of One Invisible God first in the Decalogue. They had completed *their* meditation by introducing the absolute commands of the Decalogue into the Book of Deuteronomy before presenting their revision of the Covenant Code. Very clearly they and Jeremiah saw sin as rebellion against the word from YHWH.

> Do not follow other gods . . . because the Lord your God,
> who is present with you is a jealous God. (Deut 6:14–16)
> I brought you into a plentiful land
>   to eat its fruits and its good things.
> But when you entered you defiled my land,
>   and made my heritage an abomination. (Jer 2:7)

A Future with Hope

Deuteronomic thinking was right in a variety ways, but it was too rigid and inflexible to meet the needs of people in changing real life situations. The exile would be just such a situation. In Deuteronomy, the writer of Moses' addresses had laid out a way

Part 3: A Natural History of Biblical "Sin"

of life for a settled nation with only one center of worship and ethics. People must choose between life and death, or more exactly, they must obey the whole set of laws or die. The Deuteronomic Moses had also told them: "You must utterly destroy [the] seven nations mightier and more numerous than you" (Deut. 7:1–2). They were to purify the land, settle in it, and gather periodically to worship YHWH "in the place that the Lord your God will choose out of all your tribes as his habitation to put his name there" (12:4). This afterthought condemned Israel-Ephraim for its apostasy from Solomon's temple and its failure to eliminate native Canaanites from the midst of the northern tribes. When Jerusalem was attacked, Judeans thought they must resist, but in 586 BCE it was not possible to defend their sanctuary or their homes. Sacrifices in the Temple, the prayers of the priests, and scattered obedience to God's commands had not worked and could not be carried on in Babylon. All that was left was a book to study.

In his meditations Jeremiah saw a different way. The Temple would be destroyed, but new words from God were coming. Those who survived could continue to live. In his letter to those already in Babylon, who had been deported eleven years before the destruction of the Temple, Jeremiah urged the people to try the new path as he wrote: "Build houses and live in them; plant gardens and eat what they produce. Take wives and have sons and daughters; take wives for your sons, and give your daughters in marriage, that they may bear sons and daughters, multiply there, and do not decrease. But seek the welfare of the city where I have sent you into exile, and pray to the Lord on its behalf, for in its welfare you will find your welfare" (Jer 29:5–7).

The viability of the future Israel/Judea would depend on marriages, husbands and wives, sons and daughters—in short, normal community activity with sexuality producing an increasing population—whether in Egypt, Babylon, or Judea. Israel's way of life was taking a new turn, and many exiles followed it. A mini-Israel or several mini-Israels could survive in Babylon. Every family's home could be a house of prayer for the welfare of any city where Jews found themselves.

George Wesley Buchanan contrasts "activist ethics" with a "passive ethics" in Israel's history: "If Israelites were free from sin, they could attack with confidence any nation with only a small, poorly armed troop, because the Lord went forth with them to battle."[3] A "theology in action" had worked in Joshua's time and in David's time, but as Jerusalem fell it was time for the Jewish exiles to rethink their relationships if they were to survive as a people. Jeremiah's counsel included a promise from God: "Only when Babylon's seventy years are completed will I visit you, and I will fulfill to you my promise and bring you back to this place. For surely I know the plans for your welfare and not for harm, to give you a future with hope (Jer 29:10–11).

"Babylon's seventy years," were like "the iniquity of the Amorites" which was not yet full when YHWH told Abram his descendants would be "alien slaves in a land that is not theirs" (Gen 15:13–18).

---

3. Buchanan, *The Consequences of Covenant*, 2.

Afterthoughts: Sin and Forgiveness in Retrospect

So Jeremiah interpreted the exile as corrective discipline for the disobedience of Israel's slaveholders who "took back . . . male and female slaves, whom you had set free . . . and you brought them again into subjection to be your slaves" (Jer 34:13–17).[4] Jews in Babylon or still in the environs of Jerusalem must not be idle during the exile, but they must give up war and dreams of empire. Normal sexual activity and the building of families would maintain a national identity ready for the day of release. "On that day" not only would the exiles be free, but previously enslaved Israelites who were still held by their masters would or should be freed. Jews in exile would repeat the story of the exodus from Egypt.

A New Temple to Ensure the People's Holiness

Priests in exile, now unemployed, were not satisfied with simply settling in houses and having babies. Having brought the sacred writings from the Temple in Jerusalem to Babylon, they intensified their meditations on the words from God, and began a new round of writing. These custodians of the ancient Torah recalled the period of wandering in the wilderness and recaptured the insights that came from the tent of meeting where God spoke directly to Moses. They recounted the building of a tabernacle where pure sacrifices could be offered for the people (Exodus 25–31). It is noteworthy that both Israelites and "strangers" (*gerim*) were "entitled to the benefits of . . . purification and the protection of the local city of refuge."[5] However, any who "are unclean but do not purify themselves . . . shall be cut off from the assembly, for they have defiled the sanctuary of the Lord" (Num 19:20).

In her study of defilement in the Book of Numbers Mary Douglas[6] recognizes that we "know too little about post-exilic Israel," but as an anthropologist she notes a strong political bias in the book of Numbers. She suggests that some priestly editors may have been left in Israel during the exile, and would have protested "against the appropriation of the Covenant for a small section of the descendants of Jacob," those descended from Judah. Douglas writes that she "could never develop or defend an independent conclusion about the probable dating of Numbers or Leviticus" but with Jacob Milgrom sees some parts of Leviticus and Numbers as "very, very old."

At first the returning exiles refused dealings with the "idolatrous foreigners" whom the Assyrians had settled in Samaria, but they were evidently persuaded to "share the cult" with the "stranger" (*ger*) who claimed descent from Jacob. "He has the right to offer sacrifice and he can have atonement made for his unintentional sins (Num 22–30). It follows that the rules of ritual uncleanness must apply to him because he is entitled to approach the tabernacle." As Mary Douglas says, "Numbers makes sense as an attack on the [returnees'] policy against intermarriage, and particularly as a rebuke to the definition of Israel as consisting only of those who had been in Babylon."

---

4. Ibid., 9, "The national debt."

5. Douglas, *In the Wilderness*, xvi. Also note Douglas' analysis of the purification rung of the remarkable ladder structure of Numbers in chapters 15, 18, and 19 of the book (150).

6. Ibid., xviii–xix.

Part 3: A Natural History of Biblical "Sin"

In her study Douglas sees the remnants of Israel-Ephraim as claiming a place in the restoration of Israel, and explains the conflict in Nehemiah and Ezra as a result of the mixing of the survivors of the two Israels. She also sees the book of Numbers as a series of story sections, which carry the history forward interwoven with law sections, and which impose insights from a timeless world with which every inhabitant must deal.

The result was a new set of writings we call priestly (P) and a special group of them known as the Holiness Code ("H," Lev 17–26). These writings emphasized God's requirement of holiness as well as justice. They became part of the Pentateuch, which became a preface to the historical "Prophets" section of the Hebrew Scriptures.

As the priests were inspired to review the history, others attempted one more explanation of the situation into which the Jewish people had been plunged. With the prophet Isaiah, they remembered that the Promised Land had been "planted with choice vines . . . on a very fertile hill" (Isa 5:1–2). The "beloved"—either YHWH or his chosen people—had expected a harvest of good grapes, but instead the vineyard had only yielded wild grapes. What had happened in the years leading up to the exile had been a repetition of the story of the first couple in the legendary Garden of Eden. Their land had vomited them out because they had not observed the laws of healthy life. In *Civilization and its Discontents* Sigmund Freud writes prophetically of the human "capability to destroy itself" and confesses that he has no consolation to offer his fellow revolutionary believers. In his view the prevailing super-ego in any epoch offers a therapeutic ethic that promises healing but actually results in neurosis.[7]

The "second law" (Deuteronomy) had been a stage in the ongoing process of revelation and discovery its author(s) had hoped that exhortations from the mouth of Moses would bring stability and holiness to the Israelite nation. The priestly book of Numbers recalls the path of life and death that had brought the people from Egypt to the land God had promised. In moments when God made His presence known, marvelous events could take place, but the generation of slaves released from Egypt had been frightened by reports of mighty cities in the Promised Land, and had refused to do without their idols.

Now the return from Babylon would be a new journey from an oppressive empire to the Promised Land and offer a cure for the spiritual neurosis. Isaiah 40–55, "second Isaiah," written about the same time as P, develops the theme of a second Exodus at some length. People could see it as they read between the lines of the new writing.

Instead of focusing on issues of ethical behavior the priests undertook the task of preparing for the worship of YHWH in the holy setting of a rebuilt temple. Their studies led them to write about the tabernacle in the wilderness, which had preceded Shiloh, Solomon's Temple and the sanctuaries at Bethel and Dan.

Having written of the impure worship in Solomon's temple, the priest-prophet Ezekiel also wrote a vision of a new temple, complete with measurements, set "on a very high mountain" in the land of Israel (Ez 40–48). The rebuilt sanctuary, was to be staffed by divinely authorized priests, where unblemished sacrifices would "be

---

7. Freud, *Civilization and its Discontents*, 767–802.

acceptable on your behalf as atonement for you" (Lev 1:4). Rituals are spelled out in the first nine chapters of Leviticus along with the arrangements for inaugurating an Aaronic priesthood.

Interwoven among the narratives of Numbers are a number of commands requiring the separation of unclean persons from the holy camp in the wilderness and rituals for their full restoration to the common life, many of which include washing with water. This priestly journal of the wilderness wandering includes background for several rules through which the Israelites were supposed to manage sexual problems. However, the incident at Shittim shows that not every breach of holiness could be atoned for either by sacrifice, purging, or washings. God himself brought a plague in Israel that consumed twenty-four thousand (Num 25:9).

Purifying Rituals

The priest scribes recalled the ancient ritual of the "water of bitterness" to determine if a wife has been unfaithful. They transcribed it into law in full detail in Numbers 5:11–31. As we noted above, this custom combined ancient religious fear of the divine presence with civilized justice, delaying a husband's angry murder of his wife until the community could determine her guilt. The accusation, for which no witness could be found to testify, was that the woman had gone "astray" and "defiled herself." And the verdict was: "The [accusing] man shall be free from iniquity, but the woman shall bear her iniquity" (Num 5:31). The rule assumes the probable guilt of a woman who could not or would not name a lover, but through a ritual God could determine the truth. The rule made no provision for punishing a man who falsely accused his wife, perhaps because the community concluded that the child of a woman who survived unharmed, must be the husband's. He would bear the shame of having made a false accusation, and she would have no iniquity to bear.

The Levitical stories and legislation thus represent a return to what the priestly scribes believed was God's original intention for Israel following their exodus from Egypt. Old taboos would be revived and enforced. As Deuteronomy had indicated, Israel was to have been a people worshipping YHWH at the place where "YHWH" would dwell. The real presence of YHWH would not, however, be limited to four marks (YHWH) on stone, but would be an enveloping spirit, like cloud or fire, which could not be limited to Ark or Tabernacle or city or world. That Spirit both demanded and provided cleansing, and the priestly scribes aimed to help the exiles returning to Jerusalem to live as YHWH's holy community.

Some Muslims, practicing Shariah law today, have dispensed with the water of bitterness and concluded that an unmarried woman's pregnancy was proof enough for her execution by stoning. Have they not heard the gentle voice of the Spirit?

Relief from uncleanness and defilement—spiritual as evidenced by physical— may be understood either through the dietary rules in Leviticus 11, through the treatment of ailments of the skin or house walls in Leviticus 13–14, or through treatment of bodily discharges in Leviticus 15, but our main concern is the "defilement" which must be atoned for through the rules Leviticus 12 lays down for the woman who bears a child. The mother of a male child shall be "ceremonially unclean seven days; as at the time of her menstruation," and after the circumcision of her son on the eighth day, her uncleanness continues for thirty-three more days. During the full forty days "she shall not touch any holy thing, or come into the sanctuary." For a female child the period of uncleanness is twice as long, totaling eighty days. The ritual period atones for the defiling power of flowing blood, not for any ethical guilt.

The NRSV translators added the word "ceremonially" to clarify the sacramental character of the flowing blood associated with menstruation and childbirth. "Purify" in older translations carries the same meaning, which is a kind of physical forgiveness for the "sin" of sexual activity, which is not an ordinary transgression, but a human venturing into the liminal zone where life is created.[8]

Since "the life of the flesh is in the blood" (Lev 17:11), blood is particularly holy and at the same time polluting. If anyone slaughters an animal "and does not bring it to the tent of meeting, to present it as an offering to the Lord . . . he shall be held guilty of bloodshed . . . he shall be cut off from the people" (17:3–4). It is not clear how the priests expected families to apply this rule when they were resettled in Jerusalem, but the rule could operate either to keep families in close relationship with the priests and the rebuilt temple, or to exclude them altogether. Because the woman's monthly cycle involved a flow of blood, and was connected with the creation of new life, members of her family must avoid touching her or anything she has touched (Lev 15:19–24). If her "uncleanness" continued longer than normal, she must remain apart for seven days, and present two small birds as sin and burnt offerings for atonement before the Lord (Lev 15:19–30).

As the priests wrote in Leviticus, all aspects of family and community life must evince a quality of holiness purer than the defilement that both surrounded it and emerged from within it as bodily discharges. Just as the rebuilt temple must be kept more holy than the city around it, the families that were to live in Jerusalem must evidence more holiness than those further away from the earthly residence of the Holy God. The book of Leviticus spells out how that holiness could be achieved. Only certain foods, "clean" animals and fowl, may be eaten by a people aspiring to holiness. If clothes, persons or houses become defiled, even inadvertently, they must be purified through appropriate rituals. Chapters 11, 13–15 of Leviticus deal specifically with this aspect of personal and family systems, while chapter 12 provided the ritual for the purification of women after childbirth, i.e., in physical sexuality. Leviticus 15:2–18 directs the man to wash thoroughly after a discharge or an emission "from his member" in a ritual similar to that for the menstrual woman. In addition chapter 18 spells out ways men may avoid defilement by not approaching "anyone near of kin to uncover nakedness" (18:6).

Thus Judean priests labored to develop a left brain/mind strategy to ensure the purity of Jews returning to a Jerusalem that would center on a rebuilt Temple.

---

8. Douglas, *In the Wilderness*, 15.

Afterthoughts: Sin and Forgiveness in Retrospect

The modern world recognizes the value of cleanliness, but generally does not make a religious fetish or taboo about it. For Jews in exile, however, holiness-defilement was a spiritual power, the extension of God's life creating nature, safely approachable only through rituals for cleansing as prescribed in the book of Leviticus.[9] Few actions are clearly identified as sins in either Deuteronomy or Leviticus, but readers could, and perhaps still can, recognize our own need for cleansing *and* forgiveness as we see ourselves against the laws. Living in a secular world with its duties to employers and families does not obviate the need for refreshed access to the presence of God. In public worship and/or private meditation anyone can and should enter the zone of God's holiness.

Revitalizing the Ethical Decalogue

The heart of Leviticus is its recapitulation in chapter 19 of parts of the Decalogue, but its most penetrating commands are additions to the other forms of the Decalogue:

> You shall not hate in your heart anyone of your kin;
> you shall reprove your neighbor, or you will incur guilt yourself.
> You shall not take vengeance or bear a grudge against any of your people,
> but you shall love your neighbor as yourself.
> *I am the Lord* (Lev 19:17–18).

The immediate context for this second great commandment is a sermonic litany on personal holiness for "all the congregation of the people of Israel" which includes a chanted response to a series of God's commands:

> You shall be holy,
> *for I the Lord your God am holy.*
> You shall each revere your mother and father,
> and you shall keep my sabbaths;
> *I am the Lord your God.*
> Do not turn to idols or make cast images for yourselves.
> *I am the Lord your God* (Lev 19:2–4).

Perhaps in this chapter we have the first recorded instance of a congregation actually hearing and responding to the Commandments. But interwoven with the original ten are a wide variety of additional prohibitions, many of them oriented to practical rather then religious affairs. The sermonic ritual gives directions for the "sacrifice for health" (NRSV: "of well being," Hebrew: *zebah shelamim*), which is to be eaten on the day it is offered (vss. 5–8) and directions for leaving gleanings at harvest time (vss. 9–10), before the congregation repeats God's word, "*I am the Lord your God.*"

The litany continues with commands forbidding stealing, false dealing, lying, and swearing falsely by God's name (verses 11–12), but it omits the adultery command. Then after the response come commands related to stealing (don't defraud, don't keep a laborer's wages until morning) and commands forbidding the abuse of the deaf or blind in verses 13–14. The litany continues to the end of the chapter with a wide variety

---

9. Douglas and Milgrom, "The Changing Concept of Holiness," 65–66.

Part 3: A Natural History of Biblical "Sin"

of commands, touching on forms of injustice, the breeding of two kinds of animals (ass and horse?) and kinds of garments, and six or seven commands in verses 32–36, regarding respect for the aged and the alien in the land as well as the trading partner who has no measuring devices to determine length, weight or quantity. Each group is followed by the response: "I am the Lord your God."

Instead of the command forbidding adultery the sermonette deals specifically (in verses 20–22) with the practical problem of a man having sexual relations with another man's slave. Obviously executing the two of them would rob the owner of his slave "since she has not been freed." The solution to this problematic ethical situation of near adultery is for the man to "bring a guilt offering for himself to the Lord. And the priest shall make atonement for him . . . for his sin that he committed, and the sin that he committed shall be forgiven him."

Thus Leviticus deals with a not uncommon failure of practical life, perhaps for the first time in Israel's legal systems identifying a sexual crime as sin. At the same time the commandment is linked with God's recipe for forgiveness—a ritual. What the priests of exilic Judah saw was that commands exhorting to holiness must be supplemented by rituals that assured forgiveness for unholiness. Both God and the injured owner of the abused slave woman must be satisfied not with vengeance, but with a forgiving ritual. The slave and the slave's owner are required by the general command not to "bear a grudge" or "hate anyone of your kin," though the injured person may (and should) *reprove* the guilty party. Forgiveness is called upon to replace anger; *the ritual accomplishes atonement* in the sight of God, and the guilty man is permitted or encouraged to come to the sanctuary. Nothing is actually done to repay the slave's owner, perhaps on the theory that with the birth of an unplanned child his household will gain an additional slave. The slave woman's feelings of joy at a birth or anger at the abuse are totally ignored. The exilic writer of Leviticus has imposed his ideas of effective rituals on the legendary travels of Israel in the Sinai wilderness. Ritual serves as a liminal area or border permitting passage from unholy to holy ground. Bobby Alexander would characterize the passage as social as well as spiritual change.[10] The concept of forgiveness through ritual belongs to exilic or post-exilic thinking.

The other command in the chapter forbids profaning a daughter by "making her a prostitute." Here also the woman had as yet no right to have feelings. It is not clear whether any purifying ritual could accomplish the "covering" atonement for this obviously sinful decision. Nor is it clear whether making her a prostitute was accomplished by incestuous intercourse, by failing to provide food and shelter, or by selling her to an early form of brothel. Such cases were not to be permitted among the members of the congregation to be established in the holy city.

I note, however, that Leviticus does not call for executing either the father or the prostitute daughter. Was this ambivalence because the community (and God?) could see some social benefit in prostitution? With some diffidence I suggest two possible benefits the priests might have had in mind: (1) even prostitutes could bear healthy

---

10. Alexander, *Victor Turner Revisited*, 129.

children who would augment the lower ranks of the population, that is, slaves and those more distant from the holy Temple; (2) prostitutes, "the oldest profession," have always served the sexual requirements of otherwise unsatisfied men who would therefore not resort to adultery or rape.[11] Exilic priests apparently saw no way to change human nature, and God did not usually move quickly to right the wrongs that vexed a social order, having delayed the return to Canaan four generations (or four hundred years), "for the iniquity of the Amorites is not yet complete" (Gen 15:13–16) before bringing Israel into Canaan. Forgiving rituals would provide for the increase of a population needed to live in outer rings around the city while they served the holy God.

Nevertheless, the writer of Leviticus 20 and 21 does provide for execution of the most blatant offenders against the holiness of the congregation, including a series of sexual offenses in verses 10–16 of chapter 20. For a man's adultery with the wife of his neighbor "both shall be put to death." Likewise when men commit the offense of intercourse with women members of the household, a father's wife or a daughter-in-law, for example, "both of them shall be put to death." And only in this brief list of offenses that merit the death penalty is there mention of a man lying with another man "as with a woman" or having sexual relations with an animal, or for that matter, "if a woman approaches any animal and has sexual relations with it, you shall kill the woman and the animal." Is the principle for these executions an ancient superstition about infectious unholiness? Or do the rules imply a requirement that every possibility for procreation must be exploited? Perhaps the priests sensed that social prohibitions were too limited to be effective—a wife cannot easily trust her husband after his affair—once they had been breached. It seems that even in the literary work that urges holiness most intensely what is socially good for the whole people is predominant. No man or woman is exempt from the obligation to use the "vessel" productively. Unproductive individuals, no matter how "holy," do not build a holy community in the midst of a world of unholy defilement.

The Decalogue has exploded into sets of specifics. The possibilities for sinning have multiplied. This multiplication of afterthoughts continued in the rules relating to sexuality in the rabbinical Mishnah and the Justinian and later Codes as well as the current efforts to install definitions of the beginning of life and of marriage in the laws of the United States. Perhaps the writers intended public reading of the commands by a cantor with the congregation supplying the voice of God. Also the miscellaneous character of the specific cases included in the chapter suggests that the priest or cantor who led the litany was free to include commands appropriate to seasons, situations or occasions rather than slavishly following a written book. Instead of adhering to the strict count of ten commands, Leviticus 19 appears to have adapted a liturgical pattern already seen in the curses and "Amen" responses of Deuteronomy 27:11–26. Later, free litanies of all kinds have become familiar in prayer books and worship services of the Judeo-Christian tradition, and possibly of the Islamic tradition. Through such a ritual Jews would be reminded to avoid a variety of sinful patterns of behavior,

---

11. Ackerman, *A Natural History of Love*, 18–21, 39, 41, 77, 89 for references to prostitutes and courtesans in classical Greece and Rome and the Victorian age in England and Europe.

including those in which a possible contact with dangerous holiness must be respected and avoided. YHWH's holy presence would be lethal to the impure who approached too closely.

We may find the laws of Leviticus and their modern equivalents unnecessarily tedious until it is our lot to be involved in a question of morality. Then, as President Clinton discovered, law books are searched and personal behavior is scrutinized to discover whether a sinful crime or a criminal sin has been committed. Everyone wants to know exactly what happened, whether it fitted a written law, and if it did, what the proper punishment should be. Often, however, the religious remedy designed a way to reprove and forgive, and suggested bypassing the conventional punishment.

Designing "Churches"

The exilic priests were probably unaware that they were designing synagogues that would develop for Greek speakers during the centuries before the Common Era and the Christian churches that would come later. While Ezekiel's interest was in the shape of the building where God's spirit could rest, the writers of Leviticus designed ways to assure the quality of the congregation. They were convinced that God had destroyed the state that centered in the temple in Jerusalem because of the sins of its people and their leaders. Corruptions of their enemies had penetrated to the innermost room of the sanctuary, as Ezekiel had seen. The new temple would remain a quiet, secluded sanctuary, later to be seen as "a house of prayer"[12] where only the most thoroughly purified priest(s) would minister, but the Spirit of Holiness would spread outward, with diminished intensity, beyond the frames and curtains of the tabernacle/temple (Exod 26–27).

Instead of citizens of a state, the surviving and purified Jews would be a congregation (Hebrew *qahal*) of individuals (Hebrew *'ish'ish*) who would present their offerings to fulfill vows or as free will thanks to YHWH (Lev 22:17–19). Thank Cyrus for making this transition possible! While maintaining political control over all parts of their vast empire, Persian emperors released Jews from their stay in Babylon, sent them back to Jerusalem, appointed a Jew as governor and supported the rebuilding of a temple in Jerusalem. See Haggai, Ezra, and Nehemiah for the history.

With imperial authorization to rebuild the temple Jews had the rudiments of "church"—a gathering of believers, a building, a priesthood, the essential prayer of confession, and orderly rituals to bring atonement/covering for the sins confessed. In the replacement for Solomon's Temple, they would be able to set up a socio-religious order parallel to the larger state, exercising religion in place of politics. The gathering of God's people in Jerusalem should not oppose or compete with successive empires, but should follow Isaiah's passive ethic of trust in the promised presence of God. Exilic and post-exilic experimental "churches" would give congregations psalms of praise and confession of sin to voice.

---

12. See Mt. 21:13; Mk. 11:17; and Luke. 19:46.

In *The Consequences of Covenant* George Wesley Buchanan distinguishes between the activist ethic of the Israelite conquest under Joshua and the passive message of Isaiah to Ahaz, "take heed, be quiet, do not fear, and do not let your heart be faint because of these two smoldering stumps of firebrands . . . Rezin . . . and the son of Remaliah" (Isa 7:4–5). Churches may be seen as an ad hoc creation of an alternative social order by people who have lost control of the secular government under which they live.

Ultimately, however, the concept of a kingdom of God would develop. The gatherings of Jews in Babylon, Alexandria and Jerusalem grew into a pseudo-state, the child of the marriage of Gentile political order and Semitic faith in a personal Creator-Redeemer. It is not impossible that the origins of Israel's twelve-tribe confederation should be traced to the marriage of Indo-European (Hittite, Philistine) political models, leagues of cities, with the tribal/familial (rural) models of the Hebrew Scriptures. Augustine's "City of God," transmuted into the Holy Roman Empire, would one day replace the mighty Roman Empire. It is not likely that the exilic prophets and priests saw that far ahead, but with the permission of Persian emperors they laid the groundwork for the dual church/state confrontations that continue to the present day.

The Paradox of Forgiveness

What the priests did see was the possibility of turning the commandments from negatives to reinforcing positives, of treating the guilty person with love instead of anger, of reproving and including the wayward, instead of punishing and excluding. They had learned a lesson in the exile, and taught their people what they had learned. In revitalizing the Decalogue the priests calmly and quietly called attention to an ethic *between* angry, retaliatory judgment and placid acceptance of abuse: "You shall not hate in your heart anyone of your kin; you shall reprove your neighbor, or you will incur guilt yourself. You shall not take vengeance or bear a grudge against any of your people, but you shall love your neighbor as yourself." (Lev 19:17–18) The new structure for society was to be a marriage of fatherly correction and motherly nurture. The only fault in this program is that apparently at the time, it was conceived not for Jews to use with Gentiles, but only for the restored and mixed community in and around Jerusalem.[13]

The keyword is "reprove," which is used primarily in the causative stem of the Hebrew root *YKH* with various meanings relating to convincing, deciding, judging, correcting, and rebuking. It is Isaiah's word for the triumph of YHWH's benign judgment between nations from the future Zion: "He shall *arbitrate* for many peoples; they shall beat their swords into plowshares . . ." as the NRSV translates the vision which copyists claimed for both Isaiah (2:4) and Micah (4:3).

Centuries before Jesus advised his followers to "love your enemies" prophets had sensed the powerful enigma of forgiveness, which could almost magically change anger into love. In their afterthoughts the exilic priests injected the idea of reproof between the alternatives of hate-for-enemy and love-for-self. The prophetic vision

---

13. See the tales of Jonah and Esther in chapter 24.

PART 3: A Natural History of Biblical "Sin"

pointed to possibilities inherent in the ancient Torah, understood not as a punitive law but as a teaching device for the creation of a peaceful world. Nations would come to Zion not for plunder or to enslave its citizens, but to learn the way of forgiveness and peace. It is not clear which prophet originated the vision, or that it is truly pre-exilic, but it has the broad perspective that sees history's movements at a glance.

The book of Isaiah as a whole moves from addressing pre-exilic leaders with words of judgment to comforting the Jewish exiles, but the change of focus can happen with people of any era. A person intent on the rape of a particular woman, as Amnon appears to have been with his beautiful sister Tamar, cannot stop his headlong lust without turning his attention to a higher good such as the happiness of the woman. Animal awareness of prey can be replaced by the human awareness that a Just and Holy Power may be seeing and pointing to a better way. Conversion from bad to good behavior seldom comes, however, without some crisis, a sickness, or a near death experience, which reminds of one's own mortality and the frailty of the other person. It is in that awareness that the paradoxical power of forgiveness expresses itself.

Understanding the Exile's Meaning

Modern interest has been in the application of this paradoxical idea to family life, but as the exile came to an end, the idea extended into national life, just as earlier personal experiences affected the stages of Israelite development. Covenants at every level are the result of conversations—verbal or nonverbal exchanges—in which individuals come to terms about their giving and receiving. Recall the discussion in chapter 6 about Jacob's relationships with the families of his father and uncle. Sexual relationships are only a small part of living. What is important is the way two individuals or groups who have misunderstood and injured each other can become reconciled by mutual forgiveness.

As we have seen in the stories out of early Israelite history, the chief "sins" were not about sexual purity. The sexual affairs of Judah, Shechem, Samson, and David, unconventional as they were, were not the cause of the deaths that followed. Instead they were features of a complex web of life and death relationships. What appeared evil from one point of view could appear good in a broader perspective. We may judge that it was wrong for the first Tamar to become pregnant by her father-in-law. Leviticus 20:14, not yet in tune with the reproof of 19:18, declared, "both of them shall be put to death; they have committed perversion, their blood is upon them." Yet apparently that union was accepted by God and it produced an ancestor of King David and also of Jesus the son of Mary. The social meme, which called for punitive treatment, was set aside by a community feeling that it was not right to execute a man who had been tricked into doing what he should have done, to provide a husband for an obviously fertile young woman. A higher duty to the God of life transcended the social rule.

David's "sin" involved adultery and murder, but after losing the child of her illicit union, Bath-Sheba bore Solomon. Because of the blood on his hands David was not allowed to build a house for YHWH, but Bath-Sheba's son could celebrate the Temple's completion and enjoy the blessings YHWH showered on him. Amnon brought serious trouble into David's family and the only apparent good that emerged was that two rivals to Solomon were publicly disqualified. What in retrospective judgment may be considered sins had mixed effects on the course of biblical history. Divine intervention through the prophet Nathan brought attention to a wrong, and God *reproved* David with the death of Bath-Sheba's first son. Forgiveness continued a sequence of events of more value to the nation than an immediate execution of David.

So the Exile could be seen as a major reproof, not of individual sins, but of the climate of sin which had led Israelite and Judean kings and nobles to dream of leading an empire onto the world stage. As "Servant of the Lord" Israel had not brought forth the light of justice to the nations (Isa 42:1, 3; 49) nor raised up the fallen tribes of Israel. But through the miracle of God's forgiveness Torah (NRSV "a teaching") would

> Go out from me [the Servant, a manifestation of YHWH],
>   and my justice [*can, may or will be*] for a light to the peoples.
> I will bring near my deliverance swiftly,
>   my salvation has gone out
>   and my arms will rule the peoples;
> the coastlands wait for me,
>   and for my arm they hope (Isa 51:4–5).

The NRSV translates the Hebrew verbs in this stanza as determined futures, "*will be*" etc., but we need to remember that "can," "may," and "might" are also possible. At this point in the text there is no verb "to be," but the theology of a determining God has led the English translators to insert one, making "salvation" solely the work of a manifestation of God. I prefer to see the glorious future as a possibility that may be created by God, the Servant and other humans working together.

The afterthoughts of Isaiah 40–55 do not entirely relinquish dreams of empire, but another afterthought inserted in the poem about the work of the Messiah assigns its human leadership to Cyrus, armed, anointed and called by name,

> whose right hand I have grasped
>   to subdue nations before him
>   and strip kings of their robes,
>   to open doors before him (45:1)

Cyrus *did* authorize the remnant of Jews to return to Jerusalem and there rebuild a house of prayer for YHWH. James D. Smart argues that the references to Cyrus in Isaiah 44:28 and 45:1 are fulfillment intrusions into the poet's magnificent vision of the Messiah's work.[14] Apparently the editors and some recent interpreters considered the Cyrus decree of Ezra 1:1 as a legitimate justification for including "Cyrus" in the poem. But they were nearsighted. Other interpreters including Philip and Luke in Acts 8 and the New Testament church recognized Jesus as the "fulfillment" of Isaiah's prophecy. So the life, death, and resurrection of the man from Nazareth remain the most significant manifestation of God in human life to this day.

---

14. Smart, *History and Theology in Second Isaiah*, 120–34.

Part 4

Using the Hebrew Scriptures Today

19

The Civilized Jigsaw Puzzle

Any person living in the modern or "postmodern" age is bound to feel moments of wistful longing for the simplicities of some ancient golden age or Garden of Eden. Or we'd ask for yet one more manifestation of God while we are occupied with the necessities of getting dressed for work, worship, recreation, or purchasing food for the family. The difference between Eden and life outside the garden is this human need to impose some sort of ideal order on the world in which we find ourselves. The image of a complex multidimensional jigsaw puzzle with pieces of indeterminate shape that we attempt to put together can characterize our efforts at culture for our "civilized" lives. The biblical metaphor of the "straight and narrow way" in ancient cities or the metaphor of trajectories of orbiting bodies in space might also serve to visualize the ideal in the midst of the real. In *Reason, Faith, and Revolution: Reflections on the God Debate*, Terry Eagleton observes that whereas medieval Christendom saw itself as a unity of culture and civilization, in the postmodern period religious faith has proved powerless to emancipate the dispossessed, and "has not the slightest interest in doing so. With the advent of modernity," Eagleton writes, "culture and civilization were progressively riven apart. Faith was driven increasingly into the private domain, or into the realm of everyday culture, as political sovereignty passed into the hands of the secular state."[1]

Instead of a complete set of neatly shaped pieces, we are handed disjointed fragments by our parents and teachers together with an evident assignment to fit them together in a coherent way. Some order, a succession of hours in a day with things to do, not necessarily ideal, is required in our lives. By planning with other members of our family we can make the best of each day. Will what we do be good or bad?

If we could only find ourselves out of our world's noisy streets in a heavenly choir robed and singing one of the parts of Bach's "Passion according to St. Matthew" or Schiller's "Alle Menschen werden Bruedern" set to music in Beethoven's Ninth Symphony, we could smell the smoke of incense, and, stepping outside the temple, see

---

1. Eagleton, *Reason, Faith, and Revolution*, 165–66.

and feel the stones of quiet streets, admire the buildings of the heavenly city, and taste the fruits of its gardens.

Several problems come to mind when we return from this daydream to the realities of our present life. For one thing, our fantasy did not include very many people, or if it did it was limited to family members and a small number of like minded friends who were briefly "saved" from the turmoil of the world we know. Obviously there were members of the chorus, a few soloists, and certainly the members of an orchestra. None of the voices could be discordant. All would flawlessly follow the musical score and the directions from the Greatest of Conductors. The choices, which led to this Heaven of our dream, had all been made, and nothing remained for creative argument, discussion, or contention. Even the selected music was preprogrammed, and our rehearsals went smoothly and without undue effort to master the scores.

Once made, the decision to reunite East and West Germany could be celebrated with a concert in which Leonard Bernstein conducted Beethoven's Ninth Symphony with a mixed chorus left us with no further decisions and we could spend our days and evenings experiencing the joys of new music written by composers whose lives would follow ours.

Of course, in addition to the Conductor, chorus, soloists and orchestra, the dream should have included an audience of non-singers whose assignments may have included other performing arts, such as telling histories, acting in plays and writing poetry or working at the crafts of carpentry, plumbing and electrical wiring. And the audience probably would include Wall Street financiers relaxing from the management of investments that might benefit their clients and improve the health and welfare of third world nations. When these workers laid down their tools and shut down their computers, what would keep them from voicing the joy of the human race brought together by the Spirit of God?

Will a similar Decision one day bring together Palestinians and Israelis as their Common Humanity agrees to diverse forms of worship of One God instead of the preservation of separate Jewish and Palestinian nations in the region that cannot yet properly be called a "Holy Land."

Many remnants of materiality remain in this heaven to make possible the spiritual activities of the souls who participate in it. Singing requires the inhaling and exhaling of material air, unless we imagine a totally mental alternative, such as conductors have mastered when they study a new score, or as Picasso contemplated the bombing of the Spanish town of Guernica before he painted his masterpiece.

A serious problem is how or where to fit the uncountable entities of our present life into the heaven of our dreams. Adam Gopnik quotes a comment by the realist-idealist G. K. Chesterton about one of the entities of the modern world: "a city [London] is, properly speaking, more poetic even than a countryside, for while nature is a chaos of unconscious forces, a city is a chaos of conscious ones."[2] It is this chaos of forces, natural, cultural, and religious that we humans are trying to put together like a jigsaw puzzle.

2. Gopnik, "The Back of the World," 54.

Commonly people think the wasted discards of our present world are assigned to the care of the Devil and his angels in a region of fire and brimstone. After spending their days walking the streets of our great cities and their nights huddled under cardboard shelters, wrapped in cast off coats, some hope to find themselves in imagined happy homes and gardens while others fear that they will be rewarded with hell for sins they had not been able to avoid committing. In his novel *The Great Divorce*, however, C. S. Lewis pictures hell as a city from which anyone can take the bus to heaven, but most people do not. Many of today's discards resign themselves to living on the street, looking for the labor that provides enough money for a fast meal, a bottle of cheap wine and a cigarette before a lonely sleep ends the day. Many cities do not provide adequate facilities for the discarded to answer nature's calls. Heaven and hell are simply the infinite extension of life in the here and now, wonderful for some and miserable for others.

A recent article in *Scientific American* describes how "shanty towns, favelas and *jhopadpattis* turn out to be places of surprising innovation."[3] An unregistered 400 to 900 million people live an orderly and productive life in third world countries.

Ancient Israelites did not dream of heaven or hell, but hoped for a time when every "man" could rest after his day's work under his "vine and fig tree," sleep with his wife or concubine and see children and grandchildren growing up undisturbed by wars and rumors of wars. Before Satan began his testing, Job saw to it that every ritual proper to God was performed for the whole family so that they would all walk the "blameless and upright" life he had chosen for them.

Persisting Choices

Every personal relationship, whether with God or fellow humans, involves choices between either/or possibilities. No matter how complex the situation, a choice may be considered in its simplest form as occurring in the mind of a personal being who reduces the possibilities to two: "this" or "that." This is the case because one apple or piece of meat engages the attention at a time, and the choice is between it and any of the others we noticed on the plate. It is also the case since every pollinated acorn is fated either to rot on the ground and die, or sprout and make a tree. In the supermarket of life I make choices *for* what pleases me, or *against* what I don't like, and ignore the rest. That is, until another person is either physically present or contemplated for an evening or weekend rendezvous. Then the likes and dislikes of that "other" complicate the picture. Which movie would she like? What menu should I prepare? Give *him/her* the choice!

Dichotomies seem to characterize both the objects to be chosen and the paths to reach them. But nowhere in modern life do we have a right to speak of a simple dichotomy. The shelves in the supermarket are loaded with too many enticing products. "Yes" and "no," however, persist in appearing as the alternatives to all questions, with "maybe" hedging the bets and postponing the choice. Following the pattern of

---

3. Neuwirth, "Global Bazaar," 56.

simplifying complex decisions by making one decision at a time, the early Israelites used the mysterious "ephod" held by a priest, which Robert Alter describes as a "binary device," to decide whether to fight today or not.[4] When David brought supplies to his bothers as they faced the giant Goliath indecisively, he did not wait for a priest to cast the sacred lot, but told Saul, "Your servant will go and fight with this Philistine." And having decided, he faced the Philistine with his bag of pebbles and sling.

The Benjamite Saul, however, postponed giving the promised daughter to David, and instead gave his older daughter Merab to Adriel the Meholathite, whose loyalty, we presume, Saul could count on. He feared that the hero from Judean Bethlehem would take the kingship, so he directed David to serve as armor bearer for his son Jonathan, until he could no longer withhold Michal from David. As we noted, both Jonathan and Michal joyfully said "yes" to David while David fought Philistines with Jonathan.

The path of *love* between two people can be seen as an interwoven series of choices through friendship, longing, intimacy, and companionship defined for the Greeks by the four words mentioned in chapter 4. And, as we will elaborate in chapter 21 but on an opposing trajectory, tribes and nations move toward *war* through recognizing and choosing potential enemies. In place of love's longing, fear, anger, or hate become the habitual attitude toward the stranger, and sooner or later violent conflict—war— "breaks out." The pieces, large or small, of our imagined puzzle seem either to attract or attack each other. On the continuum of time the "now" moments of Moses' address in Deuteronomy occur when choices must be made.

Some choices may be seen as the crossing of not too imaginary lines between zones of good and evil, times of birth or death, or regions of wholeness and of chaos. From the days of Abraham, Isaac, Jacob, the Judges, Saul, and David, the kings of Israel and Judah, the choice was for border wars to establish the limits of a chief's control. Since then and to the present day wars have been the preferred means for the growth of nations. How else could or can political forms grow and survive?

A Fresh World View

The conceptual four-dimensional puzzle, with its pieces linking and being linked through covenantal transactions, offers a fresh frame for the discussion of sex, war, and sin. In a major TIME essay (June 25, 2007) Columnist Joe Klein proposed a pattern for the synergistic, mutually reinforcing issues facing the electorate in the 2008 election in which "they fit together like the pieces of a jigsaw puzzle." Four of his five issues were *challenges to service*: Foreign Policy and National Security, Universal Health Care, Education, and National Service. They all, also including Energy Independence, require a fair matching of adult giving with adult receiving, which is fundamental to the paradigm sketched in chapter 2. Givers can choose whether to give or not; receivers may choose whether to ask or take without asking. Klein did not mention God, but he described the inaugural oratory of President George W. Bush's second term as "fool-

---

4. Alter, *The David Story*, 142).

ishly messianic." Klein's essay offered a less expansive prophetic view, with the United States working to solve current international problems as well as its domestic ones.

In an editorial by syndicated columnist George Will, appearing in the Hendersonville Times News, found "reassuring continuity" and David Brooks saw "a new way of nation building" in the bridging of foreign policy from the Bush administration to the Obama administration. Noting that "it is impossible to draw neat lines between security, democratization, and development efforts," Brooks cited Secretary of State Condoleezza Rice as calling for a transformational diplomacy, which Secretary of Defense Robert Gates would see as using "integrated federal agencies to help locals improve the quality and responsiveness of governments." The Covenantal Paradigm of chapter 5 provides an abstract scheme for the smooth working of a government with the social equivalent of feedback mechanisms harnessing the personal energies of individuals and groups.

Consider the mapping of the pieces that make up the puzzle. Ordinarily the pieces of a jigsaw puzzle have shapes fixed by the manufacturer. To discover the God-intended picture believers need only fit together all the pieces as the biblical Manufacturer intended. Intelligently designed, we and our predestined mate, two of the "pieces," must find each other, compare our "fit" with that of other possible mates, fend off rivals, and settle into our sexual and economic corner of the larger picture. The resulting family would probably increase the number of pieces in the Great Jigsaw Puzzle into the next generation, whose members have no choice but to continue the process of finding right partners. Thus the stories of Genesis are followed by the Exodus experience, the wandering through the Sinai wilderness and the settlement of twelve tribes to replace the inhabitants of the Promised Land.

Or consider the experience of David and Jonathan, two ambitious young men who could each see themselves as the "right" successor to Saul, but who managed to temper ambition and together fight the Philistine enemy with reasonable success. Through their covenant with each other in a sacramental exchange of Jonathon's tools of war and David's skill with weapons (1 Sam 18:1–5) they forged the beginnings of a permanent bonding of the tribes of Judah and Benjamin. Though the two tribes experienced disproportionate growth, Israelites could remember that together they had led the way to a briefly united Israel.

On the scale of tribe and territory today's pieces are families, tribes, churches, corporations, and nations; each necessarily required to fit with other social entities in an ongoing actual world. In an ideal narrative, peaceful and constructive interchanges would shape the larger pieces through treaties or the transactions of a market place, while wars have been uniformly destructive when political leaders attempted to force the marriage of a dominating people with a not yet subservient body of enemies. The goal of wars has been the building of political "houses" on land whose resources could be exploited to benefit the victors.[5]

5. My daughter Landen Gailey lent me *Coercion and its Fallout* by Murray Sidman, cited above, after this chapter had taken its tentative shape, but it must be mentioned here for its thorough analysis of "This Coercive World," 15–24.

Part 4: Using the Hebrew Scriptures Today

The biblical story of David's relationships with Michal and Abigail exemplify the way in which puzzle pieces, strongly joined at the personal level, served at the same time to join tribal entities—people and lands—to form the kingdom of Israel. Rather than forcibly cut pieces, a refreshed world view sees living individuals and groups of individuals, aggregating together and *gently shaping each other* to create new and larger configurations and a previously incompletely imagined picture.

This interweaving of distinct individual units in relationships with the larger groupings appears to characterize all existence, not just all life. We need only mention that the simplest organic molecules are "made" of inorganic atoms, joined in stable but internally energetic configurations. And recent explorations at the cosmic level have found the Milky Way absorbing small neighboring galaxies with their individual stars.[6] At every level, including the psychological, social, and spiritual the covenantal principle appears to function. Some agreement or congruence between dissimilar elements is required even when larger and wider groupings are created. Creation, whether by God, plants, animals, or humankind involves this joining of entities not exactly like each other to produce expected (and unexpected!) new entities.

In biblical times the significant new entity was the confederation that identified itself as "Israel." Perhaps artificially defined as twelve tribal units named for sons of Jacob, it appears to have become an entity as a result of the need of "servants" of YHWH to present a united front against tribes who resisted losing their land to YHWH's Israel. The Baal identified as Dagon appears to have been the principal opponent to YHWH before the time of David, but Baal's political achievement was a five-city confederation which was linked more strongly than the YHWH tribes under Saul.

Remaining on the map a century later as Israel-Ephraim and Israel-Judah, two "YHWH [*is*] God" kingdoms contended with Syrian and Egyptian neighbors instead of developing healthy trade relationships. Meanwhile leaders of the two Israels corrupted themselves with ideas of domination over the "pieces" in the neighborhood. As an entity, Israel fragmented and its fragments began to reassemble themselves under both internal and external pressures. In the end eastern empires enslaved both Israels.

Size, Efficiency and Quality

Today the principal bone of contention in the Middle East is over the luxuries with which westerners indulge themselves and the necessities which inhabitants of much of the world lack. Conflict over food and shelter appeared as early as the sons of Noah when Canaan the son of Ham was condemned to serve his brothers (Gen 9:25–27). Later, Isaiah's accusing woe was to "those who join house to house, who add field to field until there is room for no one but you" (Isa 5:8). The prophet depicted an early form of homelessness. Today homelessness arises as the affluent have built large mansions that use vast quantities of fuel for heating and air conditioning but pay the servers in restaurants and fast food establishments so little that they need help in paying for utilities and medical care.

---

6. Ibata and Gibson, "The Ghosts of Galaxies Past," 40–45.

The modern world has believed that growth was good, that the bigger a corporation could grow the more efficient its services would be. National governments aspired to be big and powerful in order to protect the little people of failing states from the abuse of dictators. "Big oil" and "Big Energy" promised "Ready Kilowatts" to power homes, farms and businesses, trusting that not every customer would make massive demands on generating capacity at the same time. Similarly, life and health insurance systems hope to pay promised benefits spaced over time instead of all at once.

Churches forbade efforts to limit population growth either by contraception or abortion, believing that God intended "chosen" people to multiply without limit. But at the same time a younger generation discovered the gratification of sex without the responsibility of caring for a child, and the luxury of attending mega churches which invited attendance at weekly mass entertainment and little else. The intended good of taking the gospel to the largest number of people was lost in a mass "feel good" message, though many who had never faced the challenge of the life, death, and resurrection of Jesus Christ were satisfied that they were relating properly to God, and would not be among the lost souls in a final climactic Judgment.

For some what was lost was a sense of quality and meaning in their present lives. "Quality time" with children, spouses, and friends was reduced to a minimum when both husband and wife, or live-in partners reconnected after being separated during many hours of the week. How many children sit happily with parents in the services of the mega churches? Perhaps a "mid week manna" serves to bring families into the larger fellowship of the church, and thus tries to satisfy the need for communal life. But for many people life remains segmented into shrinking times of work, recreation, school, and religion.

The ideal life has never been reached. Instead the human race has managed to survive with imperfection in contrast to an idealized perfection we would like to create—enough food for everyone, freedom to explore other worlds, to invent new devices for travel and communication, and an *un*forced cooperation of all peoples in civilized community.

Crossing Lines

In the traditional world view that we see in the books of Judges, Samuel, and Kings a contentious crossing of the lines between hostile communities intending violent domination can be seen as failed efforts to discover what the Greeks called a golden mean, a perfect shape that takes the eye gracefully to a space between extremes, and balances contending forces.[7]

As successors to Moses the post-exilic Jewish community of the second temple found its way *through reproof to forgiveness* for the nation's previous sin, as faithful Jews and a reconstituted priesthood performed rituals in a "holy" community. Returning

---

7. Mathematicians have explored a variety of algebraic analogies for an understanding of the forces that operate in the natural and cultural regions of the world, but we do not have space for the first steps in the math.

PART 4: Using the Hebrew Scriptures Today

exiles believed they had succeeded in finding a peaceful life in Jerusalem. The line between enslaved corruption and free holiness had been crossed, or so it seemed.

Lines exist, at least in people's minds if not on the ground between the adult political schoolboys who lead nations. The lines mark apparent dichotomies. On each side we think we see real people, but what we actually see are real people or groups clothed in abstractions, which become the uniforms for contending forces:

EVIL vs. GOOD
"Evil Empire" vs. "free people"
warriors vs. peaceniks
attackers vs. defenders
sinfulness vs. righteousness
corruption vs. purity
abomination vs. holiness
pain vs. pleasure
injury vs. wholeness
"SIN" vs. not-sin (*hesed?*)

Abstractions are the identifying uniforms people wear as they move about on the playing field as kindred or aliens, righteous or unholy, conquering or joining with other people in meaningful relationships. In church and state people join in teams, parties, or cliques often looking around for opponents against whom to test their strengths. But sometimes individuals and groups of humans find joy in joining strength with strength in an intentionally productive enterprise like marriage.

YHWH's New Way

During the exile YHWH's priests looked again at the patriarchal stories, and began to reject the drawing of sharp lines which are often so narrow that they appear as a pencil line on a piece of paper or the knife edge that balances a pair of scales. The rituals of chapters 4 and 5 of Leviticus interjected a middle term between the extremes of innocence and guilt: "If the whole congregation of Israel errs unintentionally, and the matter escapes the notice of the assembly . . . when the sin that they have committed becomes known, the assembly shall offer a bull . . . for a sin offering" (Leviticus 4:13–14) thus providing the third way that Sidman finds in carefully designed positive reinforcement. As a thoroughgoing behaviorist, Sidman observes, "Positive reinforcement works and coercion is dangerous."[8]

In the post-exilic temple (if not already in Solomon's) a person who was ready to move out of adolescent guilt into mature responsibility could find a way through forgiveness rituals for unintended sin, especially through the elaborate ritual of the Day of Atonement, spelled out in Leviticus 16, when the two sons of Aaron died after they had drawn near YHWH without following proper ritual protocol. So, when one

---

8. Sidman, *Coercion*, 213.

was guilty of hating "anyone of your kin," *reproof* and *forgiveness* could restore a sense of lawful *order* to the community, and of *belonging* to the guilty person.

The covenantal paradigm is not static: forward and upward movement between the polar extremes of abusive and submissive behavior is always possible in the scheme, whether it is thought to be ordered by God or emerges through the choices of humans.

The Christian message of good news adopted the modification laid out in Leviticus, *offering forgiveness* through confession of sins *and reinstatement* in community through rituals of baptism and a communal Lord's Supper. Jews observe "high holy days" annually, using the ancient ritual of the Day of Atonement (Yom Kippur), and Muslims likewise fast for the month-long period of Ramadan seeking similar purification and reinstatement in their communities of faith. The three persisting monotheistic ethical religions are thus discovering that they share what John Dewey called *A Common Faith*.

The strengths that define an ideal model of personal development can be over exercised or underused. Eating food provides strength for normal living: eating too much produces obesity, too little is starvation. Reproving a person who has strayed from the ideal path can lead from bad to good behavior or it can be understood as coercive punishment and lead to resentment and further bad behavior. Sidman reports successes in a federally funded project to pay prisoners to learn elementary skills of reading, writing, and calculating, which opened up new possibilities for life after their release.[9] In Leviticus 19:17 the command to reprove one's neighbor is followed by the alternative, "or [*if you fail to reprove*] you will incur guilt yourself." The path between heavy punishment and ignoring bad behavior is narrow and treading it calls for sensitive caution.

Scientifically minded Levitical priests set the path of reproof in the time dimension:

past bad behavior → REPROOF → intended good behavior

Deuteronomy had already focused on "this day," the briefest of moments poised between past and future:

past failures → NOW → future successes

Both Deuteronomy and Leviticus present the wandering in the Sinai wilderness as the crucial time of Israel's decision making, each "now" being a moment for reproof. Both books contemplate possibilities for better choices for the times in which they were written and published.

In today's world the third way has been explored through the psycho-social analysis of the two Eriksons and Helen Kivnick.[10] Their analysis focuses on the integrating functions of the mind and characterizes human behavior in a range of developmental categories which exemplify:

gullibility—**PATH BETWEEN**—distrust

---

9. Ibid., 224–27.
10. Erikson, *Vital Involvment in Old Age*, 36–45.

Part 4: Using the Hebrew Scriptures Today

↓

maladaptation—**strength**—malignancy

↓

impotence—**healthy interactivity**—domination

Charts spell out the maladaptive and malignant extremes for each of the eight stages of a human life. The most interesting aspect of the Erikson charts is the cultivation of an individual's developing relationships to surrounding people: *trust* in infancy; *autonomy* in early childhood; *initiative* and *industry* in play and school ages; *identity* in adolescence; *intimacy* and *love* in young adulthood; *generativity* in adulthood; and wise *integrity* in old age.

In the introduction to his father's *Thesaurus of English Words and Phrases*, John L. Roget discusses whether he should have included a third column between the two which list the correlative terms that exist in language. Roget notes that "giving" as a middle term is opposed to both "receiving" and "taking." He notes that sometimes "the intermediate word is properly the standard with which each of the extremes is compared." I consider that to be the case with the eight "strengths" in the Erikson-Kivnick scheme of human development. It is not necessary to revise the covenantal paradigm of chapter 5 to take a set of middle terms into account, since the comparative forms, "stronger" and "weaker," serve to fill the gaps between the superlatives "strongest" and "weakest."

In spite of his strength Samson's behavior was not adapted to good relations with his Philistine neighbors even though they accepted him as a marriage partner to one of their daughters. Instead of a healthy interactivity between families, we saw Samson's adolescent attempts to dominate his wary but friendly neighbors. At every turn this Israelite judge crossed lines of *in*civility.

A letter to the Editor of the Transylvania Times comments that the public "Trust Meter" has taken "another plunge" in the wake of the failure of "government" to keep America safe from terrorists.[11] Some meters are designed to measure the operation of motors, and in a society the trust motor operates to harness the energies available to individuals to a dynamic of useful work and profitable exchanges. After the trust between Samson and his Philistine wife took a plunge with his refusal to divulge the secret of his power, the motor of friendly trading and normal community life stalled.

A little later in the biblical history Eli serves as an example of impotence: he did not correct his sons, and he allowed the Ark to be taken into battle where it was lost. But since the biblical historians did not characterize either domination or impotence as sinful, we would do well to leave that judgment to God.

Two Gods in the Garden?

But this sets up a new dichotomy: Which God? In the second and third chapters of Genesis the newly created man and woman became aware of two voices that offered

---

11. January 4, 2010, after passengers on a Delta flight to Detroit overpowered a fellow passenger attempting to set off a bomb.

guidance for their behavior. One god-figure directed, "You may freely eat of every tree of the garden, but of the tree of the knowledge of good and evil you shall not eat, for in the day you eat of it you shall surely die." A little later another figure raised a question: "Did [*that other*] God say 'You shall not eat of any tree in the garden?'" and suggested that the other god-figure "knows that when you eat of it your eyes will be opened, and you will be like God, knowing good and evil." The man and the woman appear as innocent and naïve as any three year old who believes everything an older child says—at least until what one says is in conflict with what another says.

Were there two gods in the mythical Garden of Eden? Or am I correct in recognizing two apparently contrary voices that the childlike man and woman were still learning to distinguish in the confusing world in which they found themselves? One voice drew an imaginary line that encircled a tree with forbidden fruit; the other suggested that knowledge and nourishment were within reach on the other side of that line. Both voices have continued to speak in the minds of humans, using "sin" language for people brought up in churches, but suggesting careful analysis of behavior for those outside of religious teaching.

In the opening chapter of the book *Forbidden Fruit* Paul Kurtz[12] discusses "Living Outside Eden" and declares that the theistic moral systems of Roman Catholicism, Orthodox Judaism, fundamentalist Protestantism, and absolutist Islam are "rooted in arbitrary and fallacious ground." As opposed to a *transcendental theistic morality*, Kurtz proposes a "*humanistic ethics*, based on man's own perception of good and evil."[13] It should be evident to the reader that I also see a humanistic ethic in the development of biblical law. The ethics Kurtz espouses "seek[s] to develop mature individuals capable of ethical deliberation . . . not based on unquestioning obedience to a code but on an affirmative responsible process of ethical inquiry." Right! But we who believe in God are sure that God requires us to behave ethically.

Two value systems are subtly suggested in the biblical story: On the one hand is the value of restricted and guided learning, and on the other the value of free and experimental learning, which dares to question authority and find out for oneself. Suppose instead of tasting the fruit of the tree in the middle of the garden, the woman of the story had told her husband what the serpent had said, and the two of them had waited to ask God why he had restricted their diet. *If they had only asked,* the God who commanded might have given them a short talk about good and evil, not in abstract language but in story form as John R. Erickson has done in his Hank the Cowdog stories. These portray a character whose behavior "might be summed up in a paraphrase of the apostle Paul: 'That which I do, I should not, and that which I should not, I do—all the time.'"[14] Then God might have told them that they were ready to move from the Eriksons' stage of infantile innocence into a fuller understanding of

---

12. Kurtz, "Ethics of Humanism," 21–22.

13. Ibid., 18–19.

14. The November 6, 2006 issue of *The Presbyterian Outlook* reports John R. Erickson's surprise at children's delight in his stories about this character.

the difference between good and evil. But like any infant, the human race needed both an experience of sin's reality and an interpretation of it to develop a system of values.

In the garden story, as in much of human life, interpretation yielded meaning *after* or in the light of experience. In our four-dimensional world interpretation and meaning grow out of personal experience, or out of others' experience told in stories. The value system disclosed in words from the Lord God implied and established a loose but intelligible structure of right and wrong for the human race, while the discoveries of the couple in the garden could lead them to create a value system for themselves and their progeny. *Both experience and interpretation are required in a value system.* Such has been the genius not only of the Creator portrayed in biblical stories, but also of the living forms produced in the cosmos and observed by scientists. Understanding the underpinnings of value systems may come through the voice of Authority, but more adequately through understanding the experiences of living people. Michael Shermer, whose column "Skeptic" has appeared in *Scientific American*, has argued in *The Science of Good and Evil*[15] that moral emotions evolved like other emotions such as hunger and sexual appetite.

Lest the reader think I am returning to polytheism in contemplating this reduction to either/or value systems, the worst that can be said is that I am flirting with Zoroastrian light/dark, good/evil dualism that seems to have been an unspecified philosophical frame for *every* ancient religion and the cultural legends associated with them. The process of integrating the dualism of experience and interpretation may be considered, however, as the working together of the two hemispheres of the brain, or of two "minds" as James B. Ashbrook has suggested. Until the eleventh century, experience and explanation had commingled, he writes, citing Augustine's harmony achieved by the opposition of contraries, and the development of the dialectical method by Anselm and Abelard. "Aquinas aspired to unify faith and reason into One Mind of God."[16]

Seeing the World with God and/or Science

The left brain/mind analyzes and interprets experience abstractly and objectively; the right brain perceives and experiences the world subjectively in its external concreteness. Responding to the latter, the whole person tends to make immediate decisions while the left brain wants time to "think it over." The left brain also constructs a mental picture, or as we now believe, a mental moving picture of the world as it has developed prior to the NOW moment, and a second, imagined picture, or series of pictures, of possible next and future shapes of the world. The science of the mind's activity is developing rapidly, and my use of "right" and "left" brains will no doubt appear naïve or simplistic, but the experience of "second thoughts" is real.

Neither set of pictures can pretend to be complete: the historical picture because observations are inherently limited to one's standpoint, and the futurist picture

---

15. Shermer, "Free to Chose," 32.
16 Ashbrook, *The Human Mind and the Mind of God*, 196.

The Civilized Jigsaw Puzzle

because unknown and unanticipated forces have in the past upset our best projections. The religious view has always ascribed this ambiguity to an inscrutable but all-powerful God, who can see from outside the puzzle. The scientific mind, seeing from within the puzzle and having designed experiments to test theories, looks forward to the results of its schemes and intends to integrate them into its developing world view. Individually we all look for a meaningful arrangement of the pieces of the puzzle that we can fit into our section of the broader picture. Even if we do not compose music, write novels, or build skyscrapers, we awake each morning to arrange the available pieces in a pattern that we and our community will like.

The daily arrangement of "pieces" mentally manages a great many minor routines that in practice seldom call attention to themselves, but may have previously been thought about as discrete actions. One puts on shoes and ties shoelaces automatically while one's mind can project significant plans and sets them into memory for specific moments in a busy schedule. As chores are done, the thoughtful observer recognizes that everything is composed of elementary bits that will find their way through the processes of life into new situations where their energies will find new uses.

Atoms of carbon, hydrogen, and oxygen come together under the sun's radiant energy in trees to produce fruits, which are brought to markets to feed a hungry population. Lipton's new biology follows the energies through digestive processes into forms that animals and humans organize for the building of homes, churches, businesses, and political structures. The human observer sees much of it, and believes either that a divine Mind is pleased with the processes or that the processes themselves can be said to be happy when they cycle through their lowest levels of quantum tension. However, no atom, particle of space or quantum wave-particle has been observed at a temperature of absolute zero activity. Instead, the inscrutable God and/or God's mysterious creation keep challenging us to see further into steps not yet taken. Inner energies call us to awake, eliminate wastes, find nourishment, and do something creative every day.

The revised paradigm rejects the idea of a God designed picture to be put together by people or by God, as if people and other entities were to be assembled like the parts of a child's swing set. Instead, in a post-modern theistic version of the paradigm, God may be seen as the active Creator of both space and its actively creating inhabitants. Humans can be and should be creative.

Because in our experience time is always moving, the only lasting solidity is in the three dimensional residue of past activity available for study and analysis. The cosmos, including all its entities, from the smallest to the greatest, is being created moment by "now" moment. In spite of seeming to be relatively permanent fixtures in the world, stars, atoms, and persons all contribute to the creative process, working together with an inscrutable God.

Living creatures, including human beings, contribute bits of design and their execution, shaping the pieces of the always-unfinished jigsaw puzzle. Antagonistic entities—predator/prey—are evidently inherent in the process of such a creation. Some pieces destroy ("waste" in street language) other pieces, or find their meaning by surviving for a time and contributing to the ongoing process. Their happiness, success, or biblical "glory" is to be felt in the warmth of good relationships in the here and now. In the renewed paradigm the "vital involvement" of every human being is needed at every stage.[17] Neither individuals nor the larger picture are static.

So, Moses, the prophets, Jesus and other religious teachers have always directed followers to give care to anyone and anything. Care giving and receiving are the dynamic means by which pieces find their "fit." Failures in early efforts to fit can be forgiven, sometimes through rituals that function by salving the sting of failure. Surviving pieces may go on to try for improved fittings.

The Erikson-Kivnick study presents the details of some twentieth-century individual case histories that illustrate the meaningful fitting together of pieces. Ashbrook uses two great churches, Hagia Sophia and Chartres Cathedral, to explain how medieval individuals fitted themselves into the large pictures of mystical eastern and pragmatic western church traditions. His abstract structural analysis examines the working of human minds and suggests a parallel in the working of the Mind of God. In the following paragraph he rejects the coercive form of the paradigm and invites readers to think and work in the light of a cooperative paradigm: "The cognitive precariousness of western reality, and of our theological assumptions as well, can no longer be obscured. At best, cognitive extremes create unnecessary difficulties, at worst they are dysfunctional. In our present ecocultural and ecological crises we are, paradoxically, colliding with an incredibly finite and amazingly infinite universe. Instead of the previously dominating competitive, abstract, principled, rational, and independent strategy the human situation calls for a more inclusive, cooperative, concrete, relational, and interdependent strategy."[18]

Superstitions: Ancient and Modern

As I have read, reread, and thought about the biblical stories I have frequently thought that I was seeing superstition instead of faith in action. Superstition may be defined as seeing a faulty or wrong paradigm in a situation and then acting in terms of the dynamics inherent in that paradigm instead of one which better understands the actual forces.

The decisions of the kings at Gilead Heights, which we will consider in chapter 20, are a good example. Ahab's decision to go into battle was made in the belief that God had decided the outcome of his effort to win back the town the Syrians had taken. All that was needed was for him to be assured of God's intention and then to launch an attack, which would be supported by the forces led by Jehoshaphat, and also by the God YHWH who, Judeans believed, resided in Solomon's temple. To persuade the Judean king to be a part of the coalition of the willing, Ahab had to get a concurring word from YHWH (1 Kgs 22:5–12). The prophet Micaiah saw that the real target of the battle was not the town but the Syrian king, or from the point of view of the Syrians the Israelite king, and he tried to warn Ahab that he would die in the battle. As

17. The allusion to the Erickson-Kivnick study is intended.
18. Ashbrook, *The Human Mind*, 326.

it turned out, Micaiah had seen correctly and the unanimous vote of Ahab's prophets was wrong. A superstitious belief in hearing a word from God authorizing him to marshal a superior military force brought Ahab to death and his country to defeat.

In *Coercion and its Fallout* Sidman analyzes a wide variety of coercive behaviors and argues that although some coercion is inevitable, positive reinforcement enables people of all ages to control their own behavior, whether they are children, teenagers, or adults managing a household or the affairs of a nation.

In Madeleine Albright's account of the ambivalence of her husband after he announced that he was asking for a divorce, apparently Joe Albright had made up his mind, but then returned to persuade his wife that she should agree to his no fault decision. Failing that, he decided to let his marriage depend on whether he received a Pulitzer Prize. In the end it was the Pulitzer committee that "decided" the fate of their marriage. As commonly understood superstition is belief in and following the guidance of a false god. In the Albright family Joe followed the guidance of his right brain irrational impulse instead of heeding the calm and rational arguments of the future Secretary of State.[19]

As an architect of a restored Kosovo, Albright challenged a cheering crowd of returned refugees in the central square of Pristina with a better paradigm: "Democracy cannot be built on revenge. If we are to have a true victory in Kosovo, it cannot be a victory of Albanians over Serbs or NATO over Serbs. It must be a victory of those who believe in the rights of the individual over those who do not."[20]

After visiting the Serb orthodox monastery of Gracanica, where the mood was fearful and bitter, and hearing world leaders speak in the stadium of Sarajevo, Albright concluded that her "belief that America can use force legitimately and wisely in support of important diplomatic goals short of all out war" had been justified. The combination of a minimal use of reproving force with a clear diplomatic goal of re-integrating two distinct political and religious cultures seemed to work in the Balkans.

Structurally, the old paradigm in which powers contended for dominance can be transformed into a new paradigm with powers integrating their resources in the building of an entity that would probably subordinate the names of contending leaders in the service of the little people of both contenders. Ahab, a king ambitious for his own glory, had to be forcefully removed from the border territory between Israel and Syria in order for the two peoples to share in peaceful trade. No easier solution to the problems of the fragmented Middle East will be found in today's world, but once the "kings" have been removed, the problem of restoring responsible partnerships should be solved as people find that they and their neighbors have similar wants and needs.

There is nothing holy about irrational choices even though they are often made in the name of the "honor" of an autonomous state, the "legacy" of a leader, or the will of God. Every party to these debates believes in the rightness and justice of their cause and tends toward actions to shape their surroundings to fit that theory. Instead

---

19. Albright, *Madam Secretary*, 96–97.
20. Ibid., 417.

of relying on a conflict-causing or violence-provoking word from a supernatural being, the rational mind relies on its best understanding of processes in a world of many realities. The Creator of those realities waits with us for the completion of the experiments God and we have undertaken as we hear a new message from God.

In the new form of the paradigm godlike Justice, Virtue, and Truth are available guides to fitting our pieces into the jigsaw puzzle of life, better guides than our imperfect understanding of a Holy Power visiting from outside our world. In turning toward the virtues set forth in the Hebrew Decalogue, the echoing teachings of Jesus, and the wisdom of the Spirit of God we may find that we have not only glimpsed the larger picture, found the middle path between extremes, and understood a fresh Word from the God whose Spirit permeates the world, but have reshaped ourselves and some of our fellow humans. In the process we may expect to find forgiveness for our sins and a reconciliation in which some enemies have become our friends. Together we shall have enjoyed a bit of heaven on earth.

20

The Sustaining of Healthy Families

Under the heading "Americans Love Marriage, But Why?" TIME Magazine's John Cloud pointed out "51% of women are now living without spouse."[1] However, he went on to write, "More than 90% of women have married eventually in every generation for which records exist." After mentioning a grim statistic from a 2006 book by Bella Depaulo that showed "being married was associated with a [minuscule] 0.115 point increase in life satisfaction on a 0 to 10 scale," Cloud concludes that it is freedom that makes us healthy and happy, not bonds of marriage." So, we may legitimately inquire if the gender/sexual version of our master paradigm can work for today's families.

Christophe Andre's minimal formula for happiness lists food and shelter and "ties to other people," but does not mention marriage. Cloud's editorial focused on women and their happiness or discontent, but in our study of stories from the Hebrew scriptures and our observations of life today we can see that both men and women have been willing to be tied into relationships involving sexual, economic and legal aspects, not just once but repeatedly.

The original whimsical bundle of themes with which I started, sex, sexuality, and sin has spilled over into the broader perspectives of nature, culture, and religion. Whether we are theologians attempting to describe the relationships the Creator intended or biologists visualizing a cultural "possibility space" for ethics and religion as they emerged from vibrating matter, we confront the problem of finding meaningful language to describe and analyze the familiar and familial structures in which we "live and move and have our being."

Factors Making for a Good Marriage

As we explored the significance of several biblical stories and the laws derived from the sexual and other empirical observations and the teaching of a particular ancient people, we began with a look at some situations in which no formal laws played a part. In the story of Tamar's seduction of her father-in-law we noted that an informal

1. Cloud, "Americans Love Marriage, But Why?," 56.

covenantal relationship had been established that promised her several benefits: (1) food and shelter, (2) the "seed" of the patriarch's family, and (3) a socially secure setting. In return she was expected to produce sons and daughters to build the "father's house," and ultimately the clan, tribe, and nation. As we saw, the fulfillment of Tamar's commitment was delayed through Judah's negligence, but was finally achieved through her clever deception. Overall, it appeared that God was pleased.

Did you notice when you read that paragraph that the order of the factors was reversed in the statement of Tamar's obligations? Judah's family had promised food, shelter, and "seed" to Tamar, but she promised to bear children first of all. When her marriages to the first two sons failed to produce the high priority heir to a principal share of the family's estate, Judah withheld the food & shelter and the family's seed by sending her back to her parents. The socially supportive setting simply did not materialize.

Traditional Christian wedding ceremonies give first place to the third factor, at some length, leaving seed for the next generation in last place: "Our Saviour has declared that a man shall leave his father and mother and cleave unto his wife. By His apostles, He has instructed those who enter into this relation (3) to cherish a mutual esteem and love, to bear with each other's infirmities and weaknesses, to comfort each other in sickness, trouble and sorrow, (1) in honesty and industry to provide for each other, and for their household, in temporal things ... and (2) to live together as the heirs of life."[2]

Note how priorities changed as people moved into the modern world. In the ancient and modern worlds, however, it was and is primarily the secular community that has managed marriages. The modern state insists on registering the intention of young couples to experience intimate sexual relations just as the patriarchal father restricted access to his maturing daughters and delayed arranging for a wife for his sons until he was ready to grant them a partial independence from the father's house. The biblical stories we have examined amply illustrate the roots of the modern secular state in the practices of ancient households. The word household is an adequate translation of the Hebrew "father's house" (*beth ab*), which defines the units in clans and tribes.

The Basics Must Include Companionship

According to Genesis YHWH was not pleased with the incident that led to the expulsion of the first man and woman from the garden. God pronounced curses on serpent and ground, thus announcing the qualities of the lives that all the creatures would lead in the world outside the garden. Instead of the happy sharing of life in the "Father's house," which was pictured as a garden, the woman could look forward to enmity with the serpent, a great increase in the pangs of childbearing, and subjection to her husband. The man could look forward to the toil and sweat of working the ground all the days of his life. The serpent would be reduced to crawling in the dust. Thus the complementary roles of husband, wife, and undomesticated wild creations

---

2. *The Book of Common Worship*, 183.

were painted in dark colors at the very beginning of the Bible. Men would become slaves to providing bread; women would suffer the pains of bearing children; and the rest of creation would be seen as hostile to the creation of families.

Heard as curses, God's predictions condemned the behavior of three figures in the garden. The serpent was condemned to be the lowest of animals, eating dust and no longer to be a friend of the human family; the woman was condemned to increased pains as she added new members to the family, but would still desire her husband's embrace. And the man: *"Because you have listened to the voice of your wife* and have eaten of the tree . . . *cursed is the ground because of you* . . . by the sweat of your face you shall eat bread until you return to the ground . . . to dust you shall return"* (Gen 3:14–19). A third aspect of family life, verbal exchanges, that might have led to continued enjoyment of the garden, instead brought pain, suffering, weariness, conflict, and sin into the world. In Chapter 14 with Patricia Williams we dismissed the concept of "original sin," and expressed a preference for the term "communal sin." A meme describing socially shared sin offers a better explanation for the human problem than the biological one implicit in the Shorter Catechism.

Seen in terms of psychosocial human development, Genesis 3 illustrates the transition from infantile trust in the goodness of a parental figure to the undertaking of mature responsibility for satisfying the needs of every member of a family. The chapter may also be seen as a stage between animal-like behavior and the memes of adult behavior. Other biblical stories highlight particular relational problems encountered as the human family developed.

Proverbs 31 offers a somewhat happier and brighter picture of the roles of wives and husbands in words King Lemuel learned from his mother. She counseled her son not to give his strength to women who destroy kings, perhaps as David, Amnon, and Solomon had been tainted. Then she declared that a capable wife is "far more precious than jewels . . . She does [her husband] good, not harm, all the days of her life," working wool and flax with willing hands, rising early to provide food for her household, opening her hand to the poor, whose rights her husband has been advised to defend.

> She opens her mouth with wisdom,
> and the teaching of kindness is on her tongue.
> She looks well to the ways of her household,
> and does not eat the bread of idleness.
> Her children rise up and call her happy;
> her husband too, and he praises her:
> "Many women have done excellently,
> but you surpass them all" (Prov 31:26–29).

The idealized woman of Proverbs thus fulfills all three responsibilities of her role as a mother in Israel. She is not a patriarch's slave, but the honored manager of a thriving household. Childbearing is incidental. The happy management of the household appears to be her principal occupation, but she also sets the moral tone for her family with her teaching of kindness (Torah of *hesed*), which is transmitted through her husband to the larger community.

What is missing from the chapter in Proverbs is an equally extended presentation of the husband's role. In the 29th chapter of Job, however, we hear Job recalling his life as the ideal patriarch, who "delivered the poor who cried, and the orphan who had no helper," complementing the wife's role within the household with his administration of justice in the community. Today's adults in many African countries remember such patriarchs, the fathers of extended families who were so respected that heads of less affluent families offered daughters for them to marry in order to share in the economic security and social prestige of a clan.

When the two roles, the wife's and the husband's, are placed side by side, can anything else be said? In Proverbs the husband praises his wife, but what about the deepest sharing of life together? Our sources tell us only the sometimes-superficial details of life of many of the biblical families. In depriving Tamar of the family's "seed" and material support both Judah and Onan failed to provide what at the time was the most important benefit implicit in the family's commitment to her. Judah evidently did not care enough to keep her in intimate contact with his household until the youngest brother would grow to manhood.

The reader will have to indulge a bit of English wordplay at this point, for the third aspect of commitment to family is appropriately called com*pan*ionship. The italicized syllable refers to bread (Latin *panis*, French *pain*). A companion is one who eats with you and *talks with you*. When Judah sent Tamar back to her family, which Israelite custom permitted for failure to satisfy a husband's expectations, he not only withheld food and shelter, but excluded her from the ordinary family gossip, chatter, and companionship a woman would have enjoyed with other women in the preparing of meals, carrying water and washing clothes for the establishment.

We noted Samson's abrupt departure from his bride of one week, and that he did not return with the gift of a kid until the wheat harvest. When he did return he found that his father-in-law had given his bride to his best man. His marriage and his later affairs seem to have been only occasions for sexual intercourse, with overtones of Danite domination over Philistines. Bedroom talk had to do with the secret of his strength, which Samson withheld from his women. As for David's marriage to Michal, there can be little doubt that its failure was partly due to his extended absences fighting Philistines and escaping from Saul.

As far back as humans can remember, we recall the pleasure of preparing meals and eating together. Pre-Israelite Semites no doubt gathered for meals and storytelling while their goats rested. Hebrew and Israelite households, probably clusters of tents in the pre-settlement period, enjoyed preparing food together just as people have always done, but the Bible does not mention the possibility of a common menstrual cycle which Anita Diamant imagined in *The Red Tent*. Instead, in Jacob's family we have two chapters (Gen 29–30) of family squabbling and bargaining, first over Jacob's marriages, and then over which wife or handmaid he would sleep with.

Evidently, Laban and Jacob discussed wages. The two men probably did not discuss the whole range of family affairs with their wives and children, but only rendered judgments when conflicts arose, either approving or rejecting decisions of their subordinates. It seems that neither patriarch paid much attention to the women's household goods until they turned up missing.

The wife of a Christian Nigerian doctor who worked in Saudi Arabia reported that today only men are invited to social evenings with friends; in the twenty-first century many Muslim women can associate and talk only with other women. Companionship, however, is not just another "thing" being exchanged within the family; it is the lifeblood of relationship, which makes the tangible exchanges meaningful.

A lead letter in the newspaper column "Annie's Friends" from a wife of a little more than a year reports that her "great guy" has lost interest in sex, still thinks the relationship is great, but doesn't think he needs to talk with his doctor or counselor. This complaint may be traced to the increasing complexity of our lives in which sex is crowded into the moments between changing into nightclothes and going to sleep. Making sex an obligatory part of a busy schedule, however, fails to provide a spontaneous conversational balance among the essentials of the healthy family. Today career responsibilities, which are the modern equivalent of pastoral and agricultural work, tend to dominate our lives, infecting male/female roles with the ancient master/slave pattern seen in biblical stories.

It is this dominating to inferior relationship that Cloud's article "Are Gay Relationships Different?" addresses. Like heterosexual couples in the twentieth century, more or less released from patriarchal patterns, he declares gay and lesbian couples are learning and can teach new and better ways to manage the social aspect of family life. After therapy intended to help "repair" a failing relationship, Cloud reports that he and his male partner are now friends instead of the antagonists they were, but should not have been, when they were together. He goes on to suggest that "heterosexual relationships may have a great deal to learn from homosexual relationships."[3] However, heterosexual couples have been learning to become friends both with or without sexual intimacy in new ways during the twentieth and twenty-first centuries. We will explore some of them in chapter 22.

A young woman's letter to Billy Graham complains that her boyfriend "refuses to even talk about" marriage. In response Graham tells her that marriage is "important, because it includes the one thing that you'll never be able to have in your present arrangement—namely, commitment."[4] As I read Graham's response, I realized that the best translation for the Hebrew word *hesed* is, in many settings, the English word "commitment." Certainly better than NRSV's bland "kindness" in Proverbs 31; "commitment" says it all.

---

3. Cloud, "Are Gay Relationships Different?," 80.
4. TIMES-NEWS, 8/3/10.

PART 4: Using the Hebrew Scriptures Today

Choosing YHWH's New Way

The climate of the conversations within the Laban-Jacob household appears to have varied from cool to irritable; and it was seldom companionable. Only in the book of Ruth do we overhear genuinely loving conversations. When Naomi urged her two daughters-in-law to remain in Moab, Orpah chose to return to her family while Ruth determined to go with her mother-in-law to the Judean highland at Bethlehem. The two women schemed an appeal to a kinsman named Boaz for a place in his extended family. They could challenge him to fulfill an unwritten commitment to restore a plot of land to a possible descendant to whom it would belong, if Moabitess Ruth could have a Judean child.

We are told of the public redemption of the land, certified by a ritual of handing over a shoe in the presence of the elders of Bethlehem with the utterance of the language of the transaction that also announced the forthcoming marriage of Ruth to Boaz. But we can also overhear the conversation that took place near a heap of grain in the chill of the night after Ruth "came stealthily and uncovered his feet, and lay down." Ruth's talk with Boaz concerned Israelite family values:

> At midnight the man was startled, and turned over, and there, lying at his feet, was a woman! He said, "Who are you?" And she answered, "I am Ruth, your servant, spread your cloak over your servant, for you are next of kin." He said, "May you be blessed by the Lord, my daughter, this last instance of your loyalty [Hebrew *hesed*] is better than the first, you have not gone after young men, whether poor or rich. And now, my daughter, do not be afraid, I will do for you all that you ask, for all the assembly of my people know that you are a worthy woman" (Ruth 3:8–11).

Sexuality, but not necessarily sex, was clearly present. Sex was secondary to concern for material support, shelter and sustenance, and serious talk, however we enumerate the commitments in marriage. The value system visible in the story is at a transition between independent patriarchal families and villages managed by a council of elders. The overriding concern of both Ruth and Boaz was to maintain both *justice* and *purity* in the relationship that Ruth and her mother-in-law proposed. If Ruth had lured Boaz into a sexual affair, which apparently was not uncommon during the nights in the field at harvest time, their honor would have been tainted as was Judah and Tamar's. Instead both Boaz and Ruth could face the community without scandal. More importantly, they could build their family with mutual respect and shared values. Perhaps Boaz recalled the experience of Judah and Tamar. Beyond sustenance and sex he offered Ruth and Naomi the comfort of a wholesome household.

It would be a mistake to treat the coming together of Ruth and Boaz as purely secular, for both recognized an overriding influence of YHWH. Naomi had read her experience as an indication that "the Lord has turned against me" (1:13), but later she learned that the barley was ripe for harvest in Bethlehem. Ruth seized the opportunity and committed herself to go wherever Naomi went, to lodge where Naomi lodged, and said,

> Your people shall be my people,
> and your God my God . . .
> May the Lord [YHWH] do thus and so to me . . .
> if even death parts me from you! (1:17)

Her oath was genuine Israelite; and would be matched by the word of Boaz, "As the Lord lives, I will act as next-of-kin for you" (3:13). Israelite covenanting before YHWH was more religious than secular in patriarchal times, at least as the storytellers remembered it. Though the covenant of a Moabite man and woman might have expressed an equal determination to stay married until death, it would have been in the name of the god Chemosh. Were average Moabite marriages as healthy as those of Israelites?

The marriage covenant between Ruth and Boaz seems idealized for a time characterized by tribal conflicts: YHWH is portrayed as an Israelite's companion in battles against enemies but also as the supporter of private and personal relationships. In Ruth's day Israelites and Moabites had laid down their arms, and Boaz and his household could harvest their grain peacefully while YHWH could smile in anticipation of the birth of Ruth's son.

Healthy and Unhealthy Families

In addition to marking the change from youth to adult responsibility the word "marriage serves as a metaphor for "family," as women frequently speak of "my marriage." Recent political discussion and Congressional action has centered on a "Defense of Marriage Act" (DOMA), while our need has really been to understand what makes for vital families.

The "Defense of Marriage Act," signed into law by President Clinton in 1996, has two effects: (1) No political subdivision "need treat a relationship between persons of the same sex as a marriage" and (2) "the Federal Government may not treat same-sex relationships as marriage for any purpose, even if concluded or recognized by one of the states."[5] Both provisions preclude the filing of joint income tax returns and many other economic benefits for unmarried couples, whether same sex or heterosexual.

Modeled on laws against interracial marriages, which have now been struck down by the Supreme Court, DOMA sets up legal barriers to the public functioning of mutually beneficial relationships between private individuals who intend to establish family-like establishments, effectively forbidding the use of the term "marriage" for application to many of the benefits of marriage. For no biological reason the law forbids legal and economic relationships to otherwise healthy individuals. It "defends" marriage from a specter— an imaginary object of dread or disgust—and uses the power of the state to support an irrational fear held by a segment of the population.

---

5. Wikipedia, "Defense of Marriage Act."

Part 4: Using the Hebrew Scriptures Today

So, the "Defense of Marriage Act" missed an appropriate target in 1996 and failed to help some people to family health. The post-exilic Jewish priests were nearer the mark when they forbade sexual contacts within families. Amnon should have sensed that the rape of his sister would not maintain healthy relationships in David's family. And why was it necessary that the author of Leviticus 18 should list all the family members whose nakedness a man was forbidden to uncover? That rule would make up for some people's lack of common sense.

What distinguishes healthy from unhealthy families? As with good and evil, strength and weakness, truth and falsehood, we dare not oversimplify. Nothing in life is a bald alternative between two extremes, the best versus the worst. Always, it seems, values can be scaled as better or worse, stronger or weaker, more or less truthful, seen from some intermediate stance on a continuum that extends in two directions. In the modern world the science-minded define scales with numerical values: "On a scale of 1 to 10, how bad was your pain last night?" the doctor asks. The answer gives the doctor a rough idea where the patient fits on the twin scales of physical and emotional feeling. In the ancient world households were often so large that many different relationships were going on at the same time, so "getting along" was often more important than anything else.

The *quality of family life* can be estimated by considering how all its members enjoy the benefits of the commitments of the marriage vow or relationship. Israelite men and women measured sexual fulfillment by counting the number of sons produced, but today it is a personal matter for discussion with counselors who can advise couples with problems. Ancient couples, however, probably found sexual fulfillment at about the same level as their physical health with its occasional indigestions, headaches, colds, or major illnesses. Normalcy in all three areas varies from individual to individual, and the discussion of anything human opens an almost infinite set of possible comparisons.

The material health of a household (and of a community!) might be measured by the relative affluence enjoyed by *each* of its members, not by the wealth vested in its patriarch. The biblical record shows a wide range of the benefits enjoyed by individual members of large extended families. When Isaac prepared to give the wealth he had accumulated to only one of his two sons, for whatever reason, he introduced an unhealthy divisive feature into the family that threatened to cut Jacob off from sharing the future management of the household and ranch. And prior to Jacob's departure from Paddan-Aram, Laban's sons apparently forced a similar division between Jacob and themselves. Jacob's conversations with Laban's sons had apparently concerned only his "pay" or share of the young goats that would be produced each year. Some would be consumed as the family's food, but it was Jacob's accumulation of wealth that disturbed Rebekah's brothers.

Happiness is not arrived at through measurement of relative affluence or political power, but by the quality of the companionship between the members of the extended family. The sharing of day-to-day decision-making is as important as the sharing of bread and meat. Family meals are ideal times for "touching base" and coordinating the material aspects of life. Every member should have a voice, even the youngest. By that measure David and Michal apparently score very low. But then as now, moments of successful discussion were probably rare, resulting in low levels of family health. Conversations within families too often lack honesty and trust. Reports of much poor family health today can be seen in the daily newspaper columns of "Annie's Friends" and "Dear Abby."

Family Health in Community: Flow

This chapter was at first I titled "creating healthy families" because we tend to assume that the way things begin can determine the path to be followed. Get married in a beautiful, spiritual setting, and we will live happily ever after! However, it should be obvious that creating a healthy family is a "work in progress," not an instantaneous achievement accomplished by a wedding ceremony. The three or four commitments of ancient people remain basic for the ongoing happiness and health of today's families. Whatever ceremonies took place in ancient times, today's religious ceremonies and the counseling that precedes many of them are trying to offer constructive guidance for maintaining family health.

The secret of maintaining the health of family and community is to give attention to the law of all relationships, which is the way covenants function. Covenants work through a balancing process of giving and receiving, also of questioning and responding. If a marriage is to work, this balancing must operate both before and after the religious or legal ceremony or ceremonies customary in western societies. Families must be intelligently designed, to some extent by God, but more significantly with the mediation of secular and religious members of the community, who recognize and approve a couple's path through the stages of love in chapter 5. As we have seen, in the biblical stories from creation onward, God is as much interested in the secular side, which guides people into common sense behavior, as in the religious side which points attention to the holiness of the relationship. The legal prohibition of same sex marriage denies the awareness of holiness to many couples, while casual "shacking up" has the same effect.

The family is a basic social structure analogous to the physical body, since it consists of functioning parts that both receive and expend the energies that pass through it every day. On a larger scale, communities of families, formed into villages, clans, tribes, nations, businesses, corporations, and even larger groups of nations, all appear to operate by the basic "covenantal" paradigm, when humans speak and write about their lives.

Preparation for the new family begins from the births of the two individuals who will appear before the licensing clerk and the minister. Early lessons are in the patterns of parents' affectionate conduct of their lives and the gentle verbal expressions of their decision-making and commitment to the good of the family. In ancient Israel it was the Naomis, the mothers or mothers-in-law, who guided sons and daughters into marriage.

Part 4: Using the Hebrew Scriptures Today

Today public ceremony and pastoral counseling can help to point the way. A counseling session with bride and groom should clarify the three responsibilities of each partner to the other, and point out that the responsibilities will continue for the rest of their lives. It may also point out that the responsibilities—and the benefits—of the marriage will affect the welfare of the children and of the whole community.

A marriage or an unmarried relationship is always a work in progress, which must follow the path of *hesed*, the faithful fulfilling of promises and agreements made by both partners. The best antonym of *hesed* may be "sin," and sins occur in every family, but the mature way laid out in Leviticus 19 provides for gentle rebuke and forgiveness. Perfection is elusive, but companionship and the determination to talk quietly and to stay together can bring healing. God or the whole human—mind, body, spirit—needs time for healing. Pray for time and the patience to work quietly through problems.

How important is companionship? David Brooks declares, "happiness isn't really produced by conscious accomplishments. Happiness is a measure of how thickly the unconscious parts of our minds are intertwined with other people and with activities. Happiness is determined by how much information and affection flows through us covertly every day and year." His statement follows the fictionalized mental life of "Harold and Erica" from before birth to their maturity as a happily married couple attending a lecture by a neuroscientist, who saw things differently, as he no longer thought of himself as a lone agent, who made certain choices and established certain alliances with colleagues and friends. "Now," the fictional scientist declared, "I believe we inherit a great river of knowledge, a flow of patterns coming from many sources. The information that comes from deep in the evolutionary past we call genetics. The information passed along from hundreds of years ago we call culture. The information passed along from decades ago we call family, and the information offered months ago we call education. But it is all information that flows through us. The brain is adapted to the river of knowledge and exists only as a [self conscious] creature in that river."[6]

What keeps a family or a community healthy? Today the secular answer is a normal flow of the energies that keep a variety of systems working. Normal? Not too much and not too little, as we are told that to stay healthy one must eat enough and not too little.

Too much leads to indigestion and obesity; too little can lead to starvation. Thoughtfully selected food provides the necessary energy, which is transformed into healthy activity, physical mental, and spiritual. The human brain is a natural device for managing the conversion of food energy into people and their practices. After digestion the residue must be disposed of for the body to remain healthy. Excrement, in turn, can be used in natural processors, which produce more food. Life in the Garden of Eden could have showed the way.

---

6. Brooks, "Social Animal," 26–32. The bracketed: "self conscious" is my way of abbreviating the remainder of the paragraph.

The Sustaining of Healthy Families

The secret of healthy life is *behind*, *under*, or *in* the flow of the spiritual interactions that we participate in. Energies come from an ultimate source, which the religious identify as God while the secular describe as a fantastically energetic cosmos. Early humans identified the energies as residing in animal and human shapes and forms, but moderns can understand how important is the harmonious talking and working together of the members of one great extended family.

21

Creating and Sustaining Cultural Entities

To the probing minds of the exilic priests who wrote the first chapter of Genesis, perhaps to be considered early scientists, the original creation of living entities appeared to have occurred in three stages or phases. The first phase, which may or may not have been a "beginning," appeared to have been a "wind from God" which "swept over the face of the waters." Metaphorically, it is as if a Personal Being awakened from sleep, took a deep breath, and sneezed powerfully enough to disturb the surrounding "formless void and darkness." This first phase in God's metaphorical awakening concluded with an opening of eyes to distinguish light from darkness and the unveiling or discovery of the forces in the surrounding chaos and the beginning of thought processes.

Creatio ex nihilo (creation out of nothing) may impose an unnecessary ontology—the creation of space and light—on the personal experience of awaking in the dark. In what appears to be the theory of the priestly writers a wind disturbed a dark chaos before a personal God spoke the first creative word. Those who believe in an eternally existing personal God are forced to recognize the existence of parallel "stuff" as Patricia Williams calls the scientists' imagined "soup." However, one can imagine God as awaking from sleep to begin the work of creating the cosmos, but Genesis does not explain what was there or why God started the creation.

The second phase began with a command that the light assemble itself into discernible entities, with suns, moons, and stars coming into focus. Having awakened, the Creator *designed* orderly night and day for the remaining steps of this phase. The third and final phase of creation was the enjoyment of achievement, when God rested and "saw everything he had made, and indeed it was very good" (Gen 1:31).

A Paradigm of Creative Mind

This left brain analysis of the working Mind's creative actions serves as pattern for the six-days' "work" outlined in Genesis 1 and also for many human enterprises, which may be analyzed into the aspects of discovering, designing, and achieving. The Divine Imaginer with metaphorical voice called for "all-at-once" action and achieved the reality of "day one." This impressionistic all-at-once-ness is what James B. Ashbrook has characterized as the "right brain" experience of a worshipper in the Hagia Sophia of Constantinople.[1] The casual tourist who visits the church/mosque/museum in Istanbul may not care how the building was made by left brain directed labor; it is simply there to be experienced as a moment of right brain awe. In some such moment "God said, 'Let there be light,' and there was light. And God saw that the light was good; and God separated the light from the darkness. God called the light Day, and the darkness he called Night. And there was evening and there was morning, the first day" (Gen 1:3–5).

The story exilic priests told as the creative designing of a Personal God is now being told by scientists without the personal commands but with no less awe at the process and the achieved design with its systems within systems.[2] A thoughtful modern theology could well have inserted a modal auxiliary verb in the statement: "God *could distinguish* the light from the darkness." Discovery surveys the world around the mind and is left brain language for what the right brain experiences as insight or revelation.

Left-brain designing then selects from available materials, plans possible experiments, plots procedures and strategies, and selects one to try. Achieving (or failing to achieve) is the result of the person's discovering materials, designing forms, and creating as tangible reality what was heretofore only in the mind. Is this not what the priests perceived as God's creative activity?

Instead of developing a philosophical category labeled "ontology" biblical writers identified certain elemental entities that were created during the earliest imaginable activity of the personal entity who they identified as "[YHWH] God." The entities, night, day, sun, stars, etc., served as pegs in the frame for God's further creations of the second and successive days. After their "creation" animate entities, plants, animals, and humans began the constructive and destructive activity of history.

When the first man and woman tasted the fruit that God had forbidden, the human race left the comfortable world of innocence and entered a world of human relationships where thought and voiced word could lead to creative action like God's, *if they were to survive.* The world we know has become a cultural world, a world of good and evil, right and wrong, and the possibility of choice between them. Choices enable us to create cultural as well as material "things," which we can see, talk about, or talk with.

Achieved reality may be judged good or bad according to the success or failure of the intended design. Created realities may be judged good or bad when they exercise their installed powers to produce constructive or destructive effects on other entities.

In this worldview a near infinite number of creatures, entities, or "things" present themselves as being shaped from the materials of a supposed original creation. At the same time created entities can also create. For example, some modern left-brains

---

1. Ashbrook's discussion of human brains is summarized on Table 3 (46) and in chapters 4–6 in *The Human Mind and the Mind of God*.
2. See Sagan, *The Varieties of Scientific Experience: a Personal View of the Search for God*; and Barrow, *The Book of Nothing: Vacuums, Voids, and the Latest Ideas About the Origins of the Universe*.

believe that the human species evolved or was created from species of larger apes such as the chimpanzees, just as the familiar family pets evolved or were domesticated from species like the tigers and wolves which exist in the wild today.

Our mammalian ancestors were able to function with input and output from both hemispheres of their brains without any evident internal conflict.[3] Humans, likewise, learned to manage right and left legs for standing upright and walking. Conflict among sub-humans was customarily managed in ways that anticipated the covenantal relationships of modern humans.

Analogous to the human experiment but without using the word "mind," John D. Barrow presents an overview of recent cosmological speculative developments.[4] Barrow has enjoyed "dealing with entire universes on paper," demonstrating that mathematicians can create simulations of possible universes, one of the simplest of which corresponds with our expanding universe. The math describes both large scale and small scale features we can observe, including life forms and humans but does not venture a Personal God in our niche of time.

The human mind does not, and cannot, *know* how its creative efforts will turn out. It is also conceivable that God did not and could not know what God's cosmos and its creatures would do after God paused to rest on the seventh day. For exilic priestly "scientists" who wrote the P sections of Genesis, however, the outcome of the original creative acts was good, a perfect finished creation, which we see as the vitally changing realm of nature, with human minds becoming conscious of it.

We may judge, however, from the Yahwist account that YHWH was extremely disappointed, frustrated, and displeased with the human race between creation and the flood, and that the biblical writers believed that the development of God's grand experiment was less than perfectly successful. Once minds were given the power to co-create physical and cultural entities some results were imperfect. The second section of this book reviewed accounts of some human experiments reported in the Hebrew Scriptures, some reasonably successful and many we judge to have been imperfect. Now we turn briefly to several cultural entities that the Hebrew Scriptures tell us we co-created with God *or* that the secular view says have emerged from the mindless creativity that some modern thinkers have imagined in place of God.

Cultural Entities

In our experience cultural entities are absolutely unique in Creation, appearing only during the second half of the sixth day, after "living creatures," or as anthropologists see the appearance of hominids and true humans. Without mentioning minds, either those of the earliest humankind or those of the priestly writers themselves, God ordered a creature metaphorically figured like God's Self and designed to have dominion over everything else God had made. The modern scientific "big picture" recognizes the

---

3. Julian Jaynes introduced the idea of the segmented brain and mind in *The Origin of Consiousness in the Breakdown of the Bicameral Mind.*

4. Barrow, *The Book of Nothing*, 166–92.

emergence of beings similar to the higher animals, but markedly dissimilar in surprising ways. In the modern worldview we see ourselves as persons, capable of mentally transcending the limitations flesh imposes on animals. The enigma is our acute consciousness of the time dimension in the complex jigsaw puzzle of life. Like the first Adam and his mate we would prefer not to die after eating the enticing fruit of our childhood garden. We imagine that we can swallow some newly created concoction or inject stem cells into our veins and postpone death. Without the limitations imposed by a creating God or evolving nature, our cells might live on indefinitely, possibly even forever! It seems, however, that biological parents must give way to the lives of their offspring, as cell vitality cycles through beginning, maturing, decline, and death.

Every cultural entity, like natural objects, exists not only in three dimensions but also in a measurable duration, which in our experience includes beginnings and endings. Time is thus quite properly one of the "dimensions" of every object, plant, animal and human. In this respect there is little difference between natural and cultural entities. What distinguishes cultural from natural entities is the intrusion of Selves, capable of generating existences which can survey the material world in all four of its dimensions, and in the previously unimaginable dimensions recently proposed by cosmologists.

Using language, minds have the capacity to manage materials and thus to create new entities, both material and cultural. When Socrates, in Book Ten of Plato's *Republic*, contemplated this human capacity, he thought that entities existed as ideas in permanent conceptual forms, perhaps waiting to be realized materially. They could be actualized by the work of craftsmen who could build beds, cities, and temples. When the Hebrew priests contemplated this capacity, they saw that men could beget and women could bear new people like themselves who could be named as members of a "father's house" and tribe. Practically, both Greek and Hebrew minds worked to produce very similar material and cultural entities: beds and children, identified through the distinctive vocabularies of the two languages.

To create a cultural entity one needs to proceed as God is said to have done in the left brain/mind second chapter of Genesis (2:7):

1. Begin by discovering available raw materials:
   The Lord God formed man ['adham] from the dust of the ground

2. Find ways to fit or shape the materials into a workable design:
   formed man . . .

3. Actualize the chosen design in space with the expectation that it will endure for a time:
   and breathed into his nostrils the breath of life and the man became a living being.

Creation continued with the appearance of human families, Adam and Eve and two named sons, Cain and Abel, followed by a succession of descendants. Like animals and plants natural descendants are not clones, but new and unique individuals, and when humans appear they are not only individually unique, but have the capability of naming the creatures of their world. That is, they have the capability to create new identities in addition to those produced through procreation. They can invent beds, tools, and political forms, many of which Plato could not contemplate, but might have considered as pre-existing for human discovery.

The scientist who makes a telescope or microscope or a nuclear weapon fits materials into a new and previously unimagined shape, in some ways similar to what science's "nature" or the theologians' "God" did in creating humans. Human thought, language, and developed skill have created new cultural entities. Thought—imagining, meditative, or questioning thought—is the parent of new ideas and things. It follows the creative pattern just as God is reported to have done.

Israel as a Cultural Entity

It is beyond the scope of this book to investigate the creation and maintenance of modern states, empires, corporations, business associations, and churches but this chapter will include a parenthetical look at the roles of members of the modern entity known as the "committee" before we look at an attempt to redeem a small part of the ancient kingdom of Israel and the creative diplomacy of Secretary of State Madeleine Albright.

According to the scriptures the concept and will to create "a great nation" arose in the mind of God and was first manifested in the word that came to Abram, "Go from your country . . . I will make of you a great nation" (Gen 12:1–2). The repeated command to the first man and to Noah "be fruitful and multiply on the earth" may have implied the making of a nation, or a "people" (Gen 1:28; 9:7). God's further commands effectively transferred a part of the responsibility for discovering the materials of nationhood and designing its shape to members of the race descended from Noah and Abram/Abraham.

Abram and his successor tribal groups found and acquired the materials needed for their culture by taking possession of land and its products as they made babies. The pattern of discovery and acquisition, design, execution is implicit in Genesis and the rest of biblical history, as the ancient notables found mates, begot/bore children and found/protected homes for them.

Twin strategies of population increase and land acquisition were tribal customs from earliest times. From the moment Jacob wrestled with a "man," traditionally recognized as God, before crossing the Jabbok he received the name "Israel," and became the prototype of an entity which no longer envisioned itself as the man Jacob, but as a God-generated people of one lineage. With land acquisition came the opportunity to assimilate slaves, domesticated and "foreign," which, though contrary to Mosaic policy, became the norm. Thus Yahwist theory and pagan practice were intertwined in Israelite life. Yahwists strictly forbade assimilation with foreigners, while Elohist practice made a place for state approved slavery in households.

Successive generations contributed both to the increase of population and to the laws ordering political design. Small imperfections, or disconnections, appeared in nearly every generation. Jacob and Esau, for example, were not able to function peaceably in one household, and their conflict anticipated the two kingdoms of Israel and Edom, which would be at war with each other during the time of Saul (1 Sam 14:47).

Implicit and obvious dualisms pervade the Hebrew Scriptures. These may be interpreted as the working of two mindsets in the life and thinking—the history and theology—of the twin kingdoms of Israel and Judah, their predecessors, and also in the spiritual successors of the people we identify as Jews. It is possible to apply the logic of Ashbrook's comparison of eastern and western Christendom to the prophetic section (*nebiyim*) of the Hebrew Scriptures. The strangeness of the achieved reality has always been a feeling for necessary unity—one people under One God—in spite of the deep divisions that have been manifest in Israel, Judaism, Christendom, Islam, and whatever identifying designation will succeed our present war torn world. At the end of Solomon's reign the division between Ephraim-Israel and Judah-Israel became permanent, but not without a sense that a physico-spiritual entity—a true Israel—had been fractured.

Kings on Middle Eastern Mountains

The adolescent boys' game "King on the Mountain" is both a model for and a preparation for the adult establishing of economic or political entities, such as businesses or corporations. Individually, teenage boys (no girls in my day) attempt to hold onto the highest spot on the playground; each king owns the mountain until two or three others pull him down and a ringleader replaces him.

Biblical references to sacred "high places" give vague identification to particular geographical settings that were the objects of the tribal conquests of parts of the land God promised Abraham and his descendants. These centers were where patriarchs and priests conducted worship rituals for families intent on meeting with a traditional local god (who might be identified with YHWH but might also be recognized as one of the female deities mentioned in the early chapters of Judges). "Judges," with the help of "angels," priests and other religious figures, successfully controlled sections of Canaan centered on "high places" before Israel became fully united. After the early patriarchs, judges supported by priest-figures were the first "kings" on the Israelite mountains.

Beginning with the ministry of Samuel and for about half a millennium, the designing of the Israelite state was taken from priests and judges by prophets and kings. These pairs of leaders, mostly men but like boys, worked as minds in tandem: priests or prophets *speaking* to and for God with messages intended to shape the kingdom, and the judges or kings *acting* to build a governing hierarchy to activate structures and defensive programs. In the Israelite southern kingdom a Davidic dynasty maintained a fortress-like complex of palace and temple on the hill known as Zion, while the northern kingdom absorbed and lost neighboring tribal chieftainships in an effort to build an empire centered on the hill of Samaria. Israel-Judah clung to a defensive posture centered in Solomon's Temple, while Israel-Ephraim produced laws for the assertive regulation of ordinary human relationships. Relationship with God in the

PART 4: Using the Hebrew Scriptures Today

south tended toward an emphasis on purity and holiness, while in the northern kingdom justice between individuals and tribal groups dominated national thinking.

Continual designing and redesigning marked progress in both kingdoms, perhaps more in the northern kingdom, where dynasty replaced dynasty, prophetic figures came and went, and laws were modified to accommodate new situations during the two hundred years of their separate existence. The problem of a titular head of the southern Judean state was solved by the providential survival of David's descendants through some four hundred years into the exile and beyond, and, in expectation, to the dawn of the Christian era. Kings functioned as executives in the embodying of ancient states, and repeatedly in the Deuteronomic history are credited with warring against other kings. A war between Jeroboam and Rehoboam was aborted in 1 Kings 12:21–24 at the "word of God [which] came to Shemaiah the man of God." Seers, priests, and prophets were occasionally consulted to learn if particular military actions met God's approval, as we noted in the establishment of the early kingdom under Saul, Jonathan, and David.

Practicing Canaanite Kingship

Once established on a mountain, however briefly, a king did more than hold his position and honor the god who owned the mountain. The Israelite king Ahab learned from his wife the way other kings managed their privileges and responsibilities. When he married Jezebel, the daughter of Israel's western neighbor King Ethbaal of the Sidonians, Ahab built a house in Samaria for the worship of the Sidonian Baal, and followed his wife's advice in the ways of Canaanite kingship. Jezebel saw to it that Ahab's kingdom was staffed with four hundred and fifty prophets of Baal, who could call upon Baal in times of national emergency. The day came when the prophet Elijah confronted Jezebel's Baal prophets in a contest to offer sacrifice as a prayer for rain at the site of the ancient altar on Mount Carmel. Elijah's prayer was answered and it is reported that he slaughtered the Baal prophets before fleeing to the mount of God for a renewal of his prophetic vision. Afterwards, "Ahab told Jezebel all that Elijah had done, and how he had killed all the prophets with the sword" (1 Kgs 19:1).

The war with Israel's eastern neighbor Benhadad of Syria ("Aram" in NRSV) began when Ahab refused to continue to pay tribute which at first consisted of silver, gold, and the "fairest wives and children" of his household. Consulting with his elders, Ahab was advised by "a certain prophet" to make a stand, and the Syrians were defeated (1 Kgs 20).

Relaxing between his responsibilities on the western and eastern fronts of his kingdom, like David before he noticed Bath Sheba, Ahab noticed and wanted a Jezreelite vineyard that belonged to a man named Naboth. When Ahab asked Naboth to sell him his vineyard, Naboth refused, saying "The Lord forbid that I should give you my ancestral inheritance" (1 Kgs 21:3). The story continues: when Jezebel asked why her husband was sullen and depressed and not eating, Ahab told her that Naboth had refused his offer. At that, "Jezebel said to him, 'Do you now govern Israel? Get up, eat some food, and be cheerful; I will give you the vineyard of Naboth the Jezreelite'" (1 Kgs 21:7).

How Jezebel got Naboth's vineyard for her husband is a lesson in the corruption of what should have been a good government. Using the king's name and seal, she wrote letters to the elders of Jezreel: "Proclaim a fast, and seat Naboth at the head of the assembly; seat two scoundrels opposite him, and have them bring a charge against him, saying 'You have cursed God and the king.' Then take him out, and stone him to death." It was all technically legitimate whether Israel-Ephraim had such a recorded law or not: two witnesses, not just one, and a charge of blasphemy. In the persisting popular superstition of the day no delay for formal judging would be called for. Cursing God was to curse the Supreme Entity to whom everybody appealed for righting ordinary wrongs. The people carried out the execution; the king claimed the vineyard. But the prophet Elijah visited Ahab with a message of coming disaster and the end of his dynasty.

A Parenthesis about Committees

Modern committees in business, church or state have adopted the paradigm of creative mind, usually unconsciously, by assigning the three functions of ancient priests, prophets and kings to individuals for give and take within the group. Like Israel's priests, a committee's secretary or "clerk" retains the group's memory of actions that worked or didn't work and records decisions in the form of "minutes." A chairman is the "king" who states and delegates into action what the committee decides. While the secretary-priest's role is to look to the past, the prophetic looking-to-the-future role belongs to every member of a committee. Ideally every committee member should function as an ancient prophet with alert mental eyes anticipating possible failure as well as success. An incident in 2 Kings 22 illustrates the way an Israelite royal council worked.

When the king of Israel (Ahab) asked Judah's king (Jehoshaphat) to join forces and retake an Israelite city from the Syrians (about 851 BCE), Ahab gathered four hundred prophets and asked, "Shall I go to battle against Ramoth-Gilead or shall I refrain?" (1 Kgs 22:6). This had been the yes or no question customarily asked of God through a seer or a priest carrying the Ephod. But when Jehoshaphat was not satisfied with the unanimous affirmative response of Ahab's prophets, the kings were reminded that they had not heard from Micaiah ben Imlah. Called on to speak to the issue and advised by the messengers to favor the planned battle, Micaiah first assured the two kings that they would triumph against the Syrians, but then he told how he had seen God planning the death of Ahab. "And the Lord said, 'who will entice Ahab, so that he may go up and fall at Ramoth-Gilead?' Then one said one thing and another said another, until a spirit came forward and stood before the Lord, saying, 'I will entice him.' 'How?' the Lord asked him. He replied, 'I will go out and be a lying spirit in the mouth of all his prophets.' Then the Lord [the divine Executive] said, 'You are to entice him, and you shall succeed; go out and do it'" (1 Kgs 22:19–23).

The picture of God with his group of spirits mirrors the decision making process of ancient kings and is similar to the way the parts of our human brains collaborate in coming to a decision to act. The way parliaments make decisions is similar. Students of the mind no longer think of a single decision making center in the brain marked "self," but of at least two regions, one of which, like Ahab, is *itching to act* in the presence of an existential threat or opportunity, and the other is inclined to deliberate over *how to achieve* the desired result. In the battle for Ramoth Gilead the two kings achieved a momentary unanimity, a single "mind" and a briefly reunited Israel against an aggressive Syria. Using the available troops, the two kings tried, but failed to achieve a step toward an Israelite empire.

Attempting the Redemption of an Israelite City

Ramoth-Gilead was a strategic border city like the Golan Heights today on a road known as "the kings' highway" between the states of Israel and Syria. Its name can be translated as "Gilead Heights,"[5] and it could defend the road between Samaria or Jerusalem and Damascus for either state. So, holding Gilead Heights was both a matter of pride for Israel's Ahab and a defensive measure against further encroachments by Syria, and later Assyria, into Israelite territory. Jehoshaphat's Judean state was being asked to support the effort to redeem the captured fortress city from the king of Damascus.

In the brief agreement with Jehoshaphat Ahab may have intended not only to redeem Ramoth-Gilead from the Syrians, but to bring together the two Israelite kingdoms in a joint effort to re-create an Israelite empire with himself as its king. Ahab would thus have restored Israel to its former glory under Solomon. How much of this scheme was shared with Jehoshaphat we are not told, but it must have been in Ahab's mind. Jehoshaphat probably agreed to support Ahab's effort because he could see that after taking Ramoth-Gilead the Syrians would want Samaria and then Jerusalem.

Contests between Owners of Cities

The biblical and other histories of the ancient empires picture ancient wars as large-scale chess games with left-brain kings masterminding the contests between their soldiers, and left-brain priests or prophets calculating the odds of success, always as if their people were expendable pawns. Land and its wealth provided the material setting for battles as well as the victors' prize. People and their capabilities provided the recruits for the building of families, tribes, armies, kingdoms and empires. Kings served as deputies for the gods who were the real masterminds, presumed to be designing cities, states and empires. The king's role was to focus the people's attention on a task for a particular moment.

The Syrian king Ben Hadad is not named in chapter 22 of 1 Kings, but we know that he had directed the taking of Ramoth-Gilead, and actively participated in the

---

5. In Hebrew grammar the construct state for "heights" anticipates the name of an owner, in this case the ancestor Gilead who had claimed the geographical feature and established the first city.

battle along with the soldier who wounded Ahab. Earlier (1 Kgs 20) what could have begun as a friendly exchange of "gifts" to build an alliance between the two kings had turned into a game of extortion with Ben Hadad receiving both money and the city of Ramoth Gilead. Ben Hadad was the human "owner" of Damascus (Syria), just as Jehoshaphat was owner of Jerusalem (Judah). Samaria (Israel) belonged to Ahab.[6] YHWH decided to eliminate Ahab in the battle.

Earlier Ahab's marriage to the daughter of the Sidonian king had cemented a trading and political partnership with Israel's rival to the west. The people thought of their kings as sustainers as well as owners of each kingdom. Everyone realized, however, that Judah really belonged to the god YHWH who had brought it into being; Israel belonged to "*Elohim*," designated "Baal" (husband or owner) by Jezebel; Syria belonged to its god. When the three kings were at war it was as deputies on behalf of the Real Owners. The Real Owners had allowed representations of themselves to be kept in sacred temples and assigned deputies to protect the territories with their people, while the kingdoms were "protected" by their gods. This Grand Chess Game was—and still is—being played on the board we know as the Middle East.

Agreeing to Word from God

We remember that prophets with "words," priests with ephods, or seers with visions, brought word from God to kings and people. The mysterious shaping and delivery of word from God is similar to the "aha!" of scientific discovery, or to the result of a mind's visualizing a solution to a relational problem posed for a committee, cabinet meeting, or parliament. A single person may grasp the solution, but it remains useless unless others agree.

After writing about her diplomatic efforts to bring peace instead of war to Kosovo in the Balkans, Madeleine Albright, with President Clinton's support, tried her diplomatic skill on a solution to the Israeli/Palestinian problem. Concluding her "memoir,"[7] she lists four lessons "connected to the goal of building—not an American Empire—a more integrated, stable, and democratic world, with increased security for all who respect the interests and rights of others."

First on her list of lessons was the hope that foreign policy be described not as "a debate between Wilsonian idealists and geopolitical realists. In our era, no President or Secretary of State could manage events without combining the two." Second, "we need to obtain adequate resources for our international operations and programs, . . . generous funding for the armed forces, but [also] what we spend to advance our overseas interests by other means." Third was support for democratic practices overseas, and fourth "it is vital for America to find the right role for itself." The similarity of the

---

6. The Hebrew Scriptures regularly identify the ancient kingdoms by the names of the cities in which their owner-gods were supposed to reside. The NRSV translators prefer the ancient geographical term "Aram" for territory belonging to the modern state of Syria whose capitol is still Damascus.

7. Albright, *Madam Secretary*, 505.

PART 4: Using the Hebrew Scriptures Today

process of assembling materials, deciding on design, and accomplishing achievement we sketched for the early chapters of Genesis should be apparent.

It may help to understand ancient and modern wars when we recognize an apparent deputizing of political leaders by unseen but real "gods." Ancient empires embodied the dominating spirits of their gods in their deputized kings. Modern empires and corporations embody the philosophies of their presidents, prime ministers, and CEOs.

The American democracy has its God, though there is conceptual conflict about the nature of our God. Missing in modern American, ancient Israelite and modern Israeli political designs has often been an assenting and thoughtful will of the people who actually fight the battles. It seems no one asked the people of Gilead Heights if they wanted to be taken into the Syrian kingdom or redeemed for Israel by Ahab and Jehoshaphat. Solomon had not asked the towns of Naphtali if they wanted to be traded to Hiram of Tyre. It is still not practicable to secure unanimous consent of the inhabitants of cities to choose which deputy of a larger political-economic-religious entity they will support. Elections in democratic nations are attempts to reach agreement, and recently have left sizable minorities dissenting. Individuals are nevertheless forced to fill the ranks of the armies that "defend" their cities and countries, and many do so willingly, believing in the rightness of their causes. Citizen armies often choose to fight for their homes, believing that not to fight would mean the total loss of everything of value to them. Or soldiers loyal to their chief can be roused to a battle against a rival chief whose ideology they have come to hate or fear. Nevertheless, wars are more than contests between kings. In the contests between social and cultural entities the people are the real owners as well as the embodiment of complex sets of values that are expressed in the propaganda and public "spin" which inspire their jihad, crusade, or struggle. None of this rationale was preserved in the biblical account of events in 851 BCE.

In her memoir *Madam Secretary* Madeleine Albright tells how as a child she witnessed the efforts of Eduard Benes and Jan Masaryk to rebuild a democratic Czechoslovakia after World War II. Located between the democracies of Western Europe and the communist governments of Eastern Europe, "Benes put the best face on this by calling his country a bridge between East and West, partly belonging to both," she writes, but "Masaryk thought little of this image, saying to England's King George VI, 'Horses walk over bridges and often litter them with droppings.'"

Ahab's effort to build an empire had succeeded for a while but failed to survive his death. As it turned out, Ahab decided to disguise himself as a foot soldier in the battle and persuaded Jehoshaphat to wear his royal regalia, hoping that he would escape death on the battlefield. Jehoshaphat agreed, but when the Syrians recognized that he was not Ahab, they turned aside and accidentally wounded the Israelite king. Ahab bled to death in his chariot, dying just as Micaiah had predicted.

His death was the cost of Israel's attempted redemption of Ramoth-Gilead. Ahab and Israel are commemorated on an Assyrian stele that listed the kings and states hostile to the great empire to the east.[8] In the ninth century BCE the Assyrians had just begun to expand *their* empire westward toward Syria, Israel, and Egypt.

In Isaiah's time Jerusalem and Samaria were the cities the empire builders fought over. Judean Hezekiah had begun to play the empire building game, but 2 Kings 18:9-11 tells how king Shalmaneser of Assyria "came up against Samaria, besieged it . . . and carried the Israelites away to Assyria." A few years later it was Jerusalem's turn to be besieged by deputies of the king of Assyria.[9] Jerusalem and Hezekiah survived that siege, but the Babylonians took the last king of Judah into captivity in 586 BCE and left Jerusalem and its temple in ruins.[10]

After seventy years of exile the living remnant of Israel was authorized to return to Jerusalem by the Persian emperor Cyrus. Re-forming as a statelike church, the Judean community saw itself as privileged to rebuild the temple in Jerusalem, chastened but still faithful to its original calling from Egypt. After 515 BCE a core group of Jews accepted their role as custodians of the mystery and sacred writings of YHWH.

Using War or Talk to Build

David and his successors should have learned from Abigail's surrender of Nabal's establishment that slaughtering "enemies" is not the way to build a peaceful state. But as we noted David continued the policy of giving independent settlers only one choice: either contribute supplies or be massacred. When David "served" the Philistine king Achish, he could report deceptively that he had raided "the Negeb of Judah" or "the Negeb of the Kenites" and he was careful to leave "neither man nor woman alive to be brought back to Gath, thinking 'They might tell about us.'" (1 Sam 27:5–12) Thus David concealed his developing ambition to build an Israel of united tribal groups. In fact he encouraged his followers to look to him for leadership, which could have remained that of one tribe, Judah instead of Benjamin, but expanded to include the twelve tribes of biblical tradition.

The cultural entity we think of as ancient Israel was more a theological concept than an actual historical kingdom or empire. As long as it existed on Canaanite land, it was flawed by persisting divisions as prophets voiced criticisms of royal decisions. As a concept it was believed to exist in the mind of God and was imperfectly shared in the minds of priests, prophets, judges, kings, ordinary men, women, and children. Its earthly reality consisted mostly of descendants of Abram/Abraham, but it also incorporated many people whose connections to Abram were very slender, often as the wives, children, or slaves of those fictively descended from the patriarch. The person of the king was the focal embodiment of the national identity. As with every living body,

---

8. "Ahab, the Israelite" and his successor "Jehu, son of Omri" are listed with other kings defeated by Shalmaneser III in a text translated in Pritchard, *Ancient Near Eastern Texts*, 279–80.

9. Sections of Isaiah 36–39, 2 Kings 18–20 and 2 Chronicles 42 are almost word for word parallel accounts.

10. Miller and Hayes, *A History of Ancient Israel and Judah*, 412–15 gives details of the Judean rebellion and the fall of Jerusalem.

PART 4: Using the Hebrew Scriptures Today

Israel felt the need to separate itself from its neighbor nations by destroying "enemies," while at the same time converting some of those enemies into slaves.

However, neither the divisions within the people nor defensive contact with greedy neighbors were what the prophetic historians called "sin." These Yahwist chroniclers of past glories and shame frequently made a point of describing the reigns of Ephraim-Israel's kings as the way laid out by Jeroboam, son of Nebat, "who made Israel to sin." In their eyes his sin was focusing worship on the golden Baal calves at Bethel and Dan instead of the imageless YHWH in Jerusalem. More realistically and with the prophets, however, we see the sin of king and people—Israelite, Judean, Syrian, Assyrian—as the greedy building of "kingdom," always wider than the inherited one. To that end kings focused on the path of war against their nearest neighbors. Both Ben Hadad of Damascus and Ahab of Samaria focused attention on the border city of Gilead Heights, but the Syrian took it first, incorporating it into his expanding kingdom.

In the battle to retake Gilead Heights Ahab lost his life (in 851 BCE), and Jehoshaphat returned to Jerusalem to build a state governed by Israelite laws that were the basis for the reforms of King Hezekiah. Ahab's dream of an imperial kingdom was not realized when he chose the path of war instead of more peaceful natural growth with Gilead Heights as a trading link with Damascus. Like Laban who allowed Jacob to launch his sons into semi-independent tribes, the Syrian king Ben Hadad and the Judean king Jehoshaphat might have allowed Gilead Heights to choose its trading partners without being politically a part of either kingdom. The fighting to own the border city we may recognize as a sin of greed for both empire builders.

After the exile, the exiles' dream of an empire with its capital in Jerusalem was transmuted into building a "church," which the Persians were willing to incorporate in their empire. Nehemiah's creation of Jerusalem with its rebuilt temple was something like the ancient walled city-states of pre-Israelite Canaan. The concept and reality of a true "kingdom of God" would have to wait. Sin, in the case of the Israelite states and the ancient and modern empires, may properly be seen as the forced empire building that ignores the slow and methodical—covenantal—joining of people in individual and group trading and social relationships. This is the only way to forgiveness and reconciliation between political bodies and a clue to the possible solution of today's conflict between Israel and the Palestinian people. In chapter 22 trading can be seen as mutual care giving and receiving of care, but under Israelite and Judean kings attempts at nation building involved war-making.

22

Caregivers *Not* Anonymous

THE HEBREW SCRIPTURES TELL of a journey that led to the birth of a people and of the adventures of the founding ancestors of ancient Israel. Unlike the story of Odysseus/Ulysses the journey of Abram/Abraham and Sarai/Sarah was over land. Instead of the perils of a trackless sea the ancestors of Israel followed paths that people—and animals—had trodden and marked for others to follow. Ancient epic journeys began from places where people had already lived, and the migrant looked forward to "a place that he was to receive as an inheritance," as a New Testament author put it (Heb 11:8). Along the way Israel's ancestors, like the builders of Athens, Rome, Ur, and Babylon, had to work out relationships with those who already lived there. How was Abram to know if "this" was to be the place for his heirs? And how would they relate to or displace people who already lived in the new area? Would his descendants find ways to live with the survivors of an initial conquest?

If the principal distinction of Israel's story is the character of the unseen God who guided Abram/Abraham, a second distinction is the way the biblical patriarchs had to find mates who would share in the procreation and birthing of the new generations to come after them. The Hebrew scriptures give us highlights, good and evil, of these stories, naming names for fame or infamy, and calling attention from time to time when heroic figures "did *hesed*" or else did what could be called "sin."

Modern and postmodern humans have discovered the story of Everyman, the ordinary "Joe" who is born, grows up to find a job and raise a family before he retires and fades away noticed only in the obituary published in the local paper at his family's expense. Developmental psychology traces his/her story as one of care giving by parents in childhood and care receiving in old age. In between however, life is an un-heroic tale of struggles to settle on a career, find a mate, earn a living, take part in the community's larger life and possibly accomplish something his/her family can be proud of.

For many young men and women in the twentieth and twenty-first centuries America has plotted a path of wars that led to no victorious conquest of subject peoples. Instead our wars have led to the overthrowing of dictatorial rulers, but no real peace. How can we do better the next time we feel threatened?

Crossing Lines in the Risky Human Journey

As we read the ancient tales we can imagine ourselves and our leaders as latter day heroes, living in the midst of a new generation, hearing the voice of God calling to new stages of the risky journey. The same powerful God calls our names in the silence of our minds, and we begin without knowing where the journey will take us or what adventures we will meet. All we know at the outset is that others have heard and responded, and have found that God was with them providing for personal needs and assigning responsibilities as well as offering challenging opportunities. We may think of ourselves as the young Samuel, obeying his mother Hannah, serving God with the priest Eli, and taking over the old priest's leadership of Israel. Or we may think of ourselves as Samson's mother, raising a son whose unusual strength enabled him to do whatever would weaken alien neighbors.

Or we may think of ourselves as Jacob leaving home not so much to find and marry the bride God intended, but to escape murderous conflict with a brother. Isaac and Ishmael were saved from early death to take up opportunities and responsibilities to establish footholds for their future tribes. Like ancient patriarchs our feet cross unmarked boundaries not only between geographical regions, but also from threatening dangers into regions of promise. Our steps often take us into very ordinary settings, where like Jacob who came to Laban's door asking to be a servant, we are married and must provide for a family. Perhaps we wait like Rachel and Leah for the attention of the hero who will see one of us as the wife he has been sent to find.

In the domestic life of Laban's household the daily caring was highly personal as women shared meals, drew water from nearby wells, and came and went in their quarters. Likewise Laban's shepherd sons and Jacob's met from time to time to share rocky sheepfolds at night and went separate ways to range over a rugged landscape to find forage for their flocks. The implicit promise between the two families was to share resources for which every member toiled and from which they could all make withdrawals.

The underlying danger was the human tendency to claim "turf," which set up contests for land and its resources and products. Within the newly blended family the interface between former strangers was hardly noticed as gossip was exchanged among the women, and food was served by mothers and maidservants to hungry children and weary men, when the latter brought the products of the field indoors.

Only when issues of control arise do people become aware of the reality of the interface, of the fact that two or more members of a family may confront each other with hostility instead of friendship. Such was evidently the case when Cain confronted Abel over some forgotten issue of control. Jacob's wives handled the interface between them by bargaining for the right to sleep with Jacob, thus *sharing control* over his procreative power. The father of twelve sons did not need to assert his power to manage the household as long as smaller matters were handled amicably through little covenantal exchanges.

The business of the family was to "be fruitful and multiply" and as long as its members were fairly fed, housed and cared for, no conflicts need have arisen. The process of growing up, however, introduced a different form of interface, that within age cohorts with their varying needs and potential responsibilities.

Care Giving in Families and Between Strangers

An individual's life is marked not only by many face-to-face situations, but by some remarkable shifts in the movement of the services which are rendered between parent and child, brother and sister, husband and wife. No clear lines of demarcation appear between childhood and adulthood or between mature adulthood and senility, but the care of young children and of aging or ailing adults is quite different from life between these extremes. *Every* person is both a receiver and a giver of care at almost any moment in a lifetime, but very young children and ailing adults need and usually receive far more care than they can give in return. In contrast, maturity is marked by the expectation that the care returned should be more or less equal to what has been received.

Youth and old age are transitional times during which the shifting of responsibility for care is particularly noticeable. Young people expect and are expected to assume more responsibility to give as they mature, and they tend to avoid asking for help—financial in modern times—once they get jobs. With increasing strength and responsibility they can carry burdens that children cannot. From time to time the local newspapers report unusual projects of high school students who spend time with elders in nursing homes or with children in play school.

Toward the end of life mature responsibility gives way to receiving care, for which the only returns may be expressions of thanks. Biblical narratives make little mention of times of transition and generally ignore infancy and extreme old age. The laws of the Pentateuch and the stories of the Hebrew Scriptures are concerned with adult responsibilities and the problems of trust and mistrust.

The stories of Genesis are particularly conscious of the problems ancient people had when they came face to face with a stranger. As Abram/Abraham journeyed into Canaan/Palestine he must have met many people, but Genesis tells only of a small number of significant meetings with strangers. The writers give us few clues as to how travelers handled differences of language, but apparently migrants have always found ways of communicating and exchanging basic information about themselves and their needs. Like dogs who sniff each other and wag friendly tails, Abraham welcomed a traveling stranger with the offer of rest and a meal. As they ate, the stranger and his companions learned that Abraham did not have an heir, and they assured him that he could expect one. They could no doubt see the size of his family group, and he could sense that the three men posed no threat to him, so the principal exchange between them in Genesis 18 was personal information.

Not all the stories of travelers were as civil. In Genesis 19 two "angels" were met with hostility and violence when they arrived in Sodom. Further communication and friendly relationship were impossible. The crude effort to overpower the visitors led to tragedy for most of the inhabitants of Sodom.

When Abraham's family began to make contact with the inhabitants of Canaan, he and Isaac met households—groups of people not yet numerous enough to be considered tribal communities—and they also developed their households into small communities. Because populations increase and people are no longer personally acquainted with the children of distant kin, the relationship between kin and not-kin approaches anonymity. Thus Jacob and his sons, whose institutional structures centered in a patriarch, began to meet other groups as strangers instead of distant kin. If they remembered the early links, such as the story of Lot's incestuous begetting of Ben-ammi, it was to condemn Ammonites as impure and not suitable for covenantal relationships. After many more generations only the exilic priests could trace the family connections of the "foreign" neighbors of Israel. During the period of the Judges the kinship links had already begun to be forgotten. The biblical record, however, focuses on identifiable Israelite heroes like David, Gideon, and Samson, and the matching Philistine leaders Goliath and Achish, but loses sight of many other individuals. Approaching anonymity, most aliens were simply "the Philistines," "the Midianites," or "the king of Syria."

Contrasting with the biblical account of Abram's migration and the return of his descendants from Egypt, George Mendenhall, in *The Tenth Generation* and others have argued that the early Israelites were a servant class who rebelled and left the fortified cities of Canaan and their outlying fields to establish a culture of villages in the hill country. If true, the rebels adopted the legendary stories of Abram, Isaac, and Jacob and focused on the exodus experience as their history. The story's power to unite the YHWH tribes is demonstrated in the largely historical account of David. In that time Abigail's husband Nabal thought himself independent, so that although he appears in the record as a descendant of Caleb, he is not described as either Israelite or Philistine. Nabal cared only for *his* establishment; David's men could go hungry. Nabal's wife introduced David to a better, more caring way when she led her servants with food for his outlaw followers. Perhaps as a result David encouraged his followers to choose local women as wives and settle in the area loosely held by Philistines and other tribes.

A Lost Chord and many Unfinished Symphonies

With the loss of conscious kinship came a "don't care" feeling between Israelites and their neighbors. Samson, for instance, could without feeling kill thirty Philistine men to get their outer garments to pay his debt to the guests at his wedding. And when Solomon felt the impulse to build the Temple, he didn't take the time to train Israelites to do the work, but hired skilled stone masons from Tyre, probably reducing Ephraimites to the more menial tasks, as "hewers of wood and drawers of water" like the Gibeonites with whom Joshua had made an enslaving treaty (Joshua 9).

During David's flight from Saul, he "served" the Philistine lord Achish, by raiding Geshurites, Girzites, and Amalekites, ordering his men to leave neither man nor woman alive so that he could report to Achish that he was raiding settlements friendly to Israel, when he brought him the plunder (1 Sam 27).

However, David's heart could be touched with honor or political acumen if not with love. When he might have killed his father-in-law, sleeping in a cave in the wilderness of Ziph, David showed something of a caring spirit (1 Sam 26). But we remember that he forced Michal to leave the husband who loved her. On balance David appears to have been more ruthless than caring.

What did Tamar think when Amnon asked her to prepare a meal for him? Were other women of the household asked to prepare such meals so that she felt flattered that her brother had noticed her? Or was it an opportunity to break an otherwise dull routine?

Like other young women in a royal household, Tamar could look forward to being "given" in marriage, and to sharing the ecstasies and disappointments of an Israelite woman's life. Responding to the request from Amnon, Tamar was crossing from the first movement of the symphony of her life and was ready for the slow movement of meal preparation toward the triumphant chords of a finale never written.

Ending or Repairing a Damaged Relationship

As in many situations today it is easy to charge one person, the "other woman," with destroying a marriage, or to blame some situation, the demands of a job, internet porn, or military duty in a foreign war. Too often blame is fixed on one or the other partner in a marriage, and the pattern of mutual care giving falls apart. With or without counseling the couple is in and out of divorce court. The final movement of the symphony is never completed.

Both in culture and nature a relationship will be set aside and replaced with another if it does not work out. A developing fetus ends as a stillbirth, and the couple tries again. In an orchard one tree bears tasteless fruit and the caretaker cuts it down. Jacob and Laban persisted for twenty years before giving up on their repeated efforts to make a permanent covenant with each other. Finally, to avoid physical harm to their children and grandchildren the two men agreed to separate peacefully, and Jacob returned to Canaan to repair the damaged relationship with his brother Esau. When he could not renew warmth in that relationship, Jacob and his sons undertook to relate to chiefs and tribes who inhabited Canaan, thus making a fresh start on the intended stage, while Esau moved to Edom.

Earlier Abram/Abraham could only watch while his wife expelled the Egyptian slave girl Hagar and his first-born son. Biblical historians ignore Ishmael's story, but Muslims trace their religion and culture to Abraham through him. All Abraham could do was to give Hagar some bread and a skin of water "for the boy." Sarai may not have cared for Ishmael and Hagar, but Abram did not want his son to die (Gen 21:8–21).

Actually a covenantal relationship can never be completely set aside, for it is a matter of the whole person, body-spirit-mind-soul-and-self, which connects with another's spirit-mind-soul-and-self when the bodies are no longer near each other. Saying "I never want to see you again" cannot erase an *image in the mind*, which may be the most appropriate translation for biblical "heart." Also when we say, "Keep in touch" we are speaking metaphorically of the communication of souls often achieved by telephone, e-mail or written messages.

In this sense children are never divorced from parents, wives can never be completely separated from husbands, nor husbands from wives. Saint Augustine did not forget the woman and the son she bore for him. Even if all physical contact has ended, the spirit-mind-soul-and-self of each retains memories of the joys and sorrows of the relationship that refuse to be completely erased. Some sweetness and/or bitterness of a caring relationship, even the most trivial or short-lived, can be recalled.

Without forgiveness for "sins" memory can be painful, and anger that has developed into hate may persist as long as one lives. Divorce need not be painful but often is a sad attempt to end a sequence of unpleasant experiences that neither partner will forgive or forget. Nevertheless an adult who suffered abuse as a child may recall moments of joy with a drunken and abusive father. The "Dear Abby" columns of the newspapers regularly respond to letters from people who suffered in relationships they felt had damaged them. As one reads the daily paper, one quickly thinks of the lack of care in several sad family situations of acquaintances. Likewise, victory in battle or defeat in war are regularly recalled by caring patriots, and can be analyzed for faults in foreign policy.

A kind of separation which may, but does not, require forgiveness takes place when business or war forces a partner or parent to be away from home for more than the working hours of the day or night. "Man—or child—does not live by bread alone." It is not just word from God that an individual's soul needs. When a father must leave home every Monday morning to sell his company's product, he hurts—unintentionally—the spirit of his young daughter. When military duty requires a Marine to spend months in a foreign country instead of being a present father to his children and a husband to his wife, the damaged and damaging effects accumulate. The wonderful chord once heard by every member of the family cannot be found on the keys or in the pipes of the organ. Often the damaged resort to damaging other people in the web of their relationships.

Should all of these separations be called "sin"? Although the damage they do to the fabric of a family is very similar to a willful desertion, we do not think of such forced separations as personal sins. Neither did the biblical authors of the stories of Samson and David and their brides. But willful desertion or repudiation of a relationship deserves to be called sin, whether there has been a marriage or not. When Amnon raped his sister Tamar and then failed to get his father's approval of a marriage to her, we have every reason to declare that he sinned. Even after the rape Amnon might have "comforted her" as Shechem had done with Dinah, and asked her father to give her to him in marriage. In 2 Samuel 13:12–13 during the rape, Tamar pleaded "I beg you, speak to the king, for he will not withhold me from you." The spirit of David's daughter would have been damaged, but she and the family could have forgiven the crime, *if he had asked*. As it was, a flame of unhealthy anger spread into the family and into the kingdom, and two of David's sons eliminated each other as possible heirs to his throne. Absalom fled from Israelite territory after ordering the murder of Amnon (2 Sam 13:23–38).

Amnon did not voice any promise to respect Tamar's person when he asked his father to send her to prepare a meal for him, but his subsequent behavior involved a breach of the trust family members expect of each other. His attention was on the intended rape, not the meal, and Tamar was forever *dis*honored.

YHWH did not ignore these human "sins," but did not act immediately to punish or even to restrain those who committed them. Instead the consequences of the human activities were lying in wait to snare the culprits. Sometimes, however, a guilty person changes course, repents and is forgiven.

Thus, in theory damaged covenantal relationships may at any time be reinvigorated *if there is a will* to be reconciled, but the will on one side must be met with the will of the other. Even if there was no will to reestablish intimate family relationship, the separating orbits of Ishmael and Isaac, of Jacob and Laban, and of Jacob and Esau continued fruitfully without violence, as long as neither attempted to dominate the other. The art of civilization is to plot orbits that will not collide. Or, in the image of the jigsaw puzzle, it is to allow every adjacent piece flexibly and without friction or distortion to take its shape with nearby pieces. Can civilization survive without awareness of God's oversight and offer of forgiveness?

Divorce, Remarriage and the Common Good

Maintaining families in ancient times was largely a matter of expecting/requiring every person to assume his or her share of the three responsibilities that make for the healthy family discussed in chapter 20. Exceptions arose, and as we saw in Deuteronomy 24:1–4, the wise writers provided an early "no fault" divorce for the man whose wife did not please him. Torah/law does not spell out acceptable causes for the divorce nor ask how the wife did not please her husband. If she failed, the marriage was simply terminated and she was free to marry again. It is interesting but not very significant that the law recognizes the possibility that she might not please a second husband. Her failure to please is not treated as sin, and the only provision added to the law is that she was defiled (doubly?) and was not to be returned to her first husband.

Moses, the God-authorized deliverer of the Torah's laws, did not consider the possibility that a husband might not please a wife. What the Israelite law did was to formalize some separations that the community recognized as needed for the common good. In that divorce law the Israelite community initiated a care giving concern for family relationships that could be healthy because they would be nurtured in new settings. Mature Israelites made legal room for terminating a man's marriage with a woman he disliked or who was not a virgin, or simply because he wanted to end the marriage.

Until the development of No Fault Divorce in the United States it was assumed when husband and wife wished to separate that one or the other was seriously at fault. In the 1950s and 60's Presbyterian ministers occasionally made discreet inquiries about the previous marriage of a divorced woman who wished to receive the blessing of the church in a new marriage. The unexpressed question for the church was "had she sinned?" A registering county clerk wanted to know only whether the previous marriage had been properly terminated, and in many states if results of a required blood test had been submitted. The caring community and the pastor could then commend the couple for the decision to create a fresh and responsible family unit whose benefits may be summarized in the words "care receiving" which are always linked to "care giving."

Blended Families and Chaste Love

Fairly recently a new and much needed term has been introduced for the members of a family which brings together the children born to previous marriages or relationships.

I first learned of the term "blended families" after performing a wedding ceremony for a man and a woman both of whom had children. Three young children took part in the ceremony and I emphasized that they were becoming a new and special family. The term could also be applied when an older couple with adult children are joined in marriage, though often the adult children may have little to do with each other and are only glad that Mother or Father has found a companion to share their declining years. A new movement has been added to the yet unfinished symphony of care giving love.

Should we practice the "Don't Ask, Don't Tell" policy of the military when an older man and woman travel and room together at an Elderhostel program or choose to share an apartment in an eldercare facility, but do not identify themselves as husband and wife?

What should they be called? Is "significant other" the best we can do? What *do* they tell their children? Terms used for illicit relationships, such as "lover" or "paramour" are not appropriate for two people who have committed themselves to care for each other, but who wish to keep their estates unencumbered. My copy of Roget's *Thesaurus* does not list a noun I find appropriate. Either the situation had not come to general notice or was being ignored. "Partner" is broad enough and vague enough to include the business aspects of managing budgets and property as well as the more intimate personal relationships, but it does not identify a legal status for a family as "marriage" does. (How important is the legal status of couples who share life publicly in a stable community and choose to be known by first and last names?)

The rule adopted by the U.S. military forces for homosexual couples unfortunately contravenes the normal public sharing of awareness and joy that a relationship has been established. It denigrates the reality of genuine caring love between two people who happen to be of the same sex. By defining the homosexual relationship as "sin," some churches circumscribe one application of the second great commandment of the gospel, in effect decreeing that there is a narrow limit to proper expressions of love between responsible intelligent adults. Do we need a word other than "marriage" for their relationship?

Incidentally, the Roman Catholic priesthood and members of monastic orders have voluntarily taken vows of permanent celibacy. The Catholic rule is a conscious limiting of acceptable expressions of a priest's social relationships to the purely spiritual. The Catholic sets up a "higher" love, which priests often indicate by wearing a wedding band, in effect telling the world of their dedication to Christ and his church. One who takes the vow of celibacy, however, is free to offer a wide range of physical and spiritual care giving, including the care and nurture of children, the sick and the aged. Institutions established by monastic orders or by not-for-profit groups of citizens actually create family like settings where the "clients" can blend into new forms of community. It is not necessary to note that such communities can have the same internal relationship problems as any other group. In supporting war and capital punishment churches have effectively rejected the command of Jesus to "love your enemy," but that calls for more discussion than belongs here.

A temporary pledge of celibacy by youth pursuing education for specialized careers in religion, medicine, law, or research is commendable, since it eliminates the distractions of sexual and family relationships. A caring community, however, should be prepared to adapt its provision of financial support for those who "just can't wait" or who have difficulty keeping sexual relationships out of the program of layered schooling.

To summarize this sketchy look at a few of the novel relationships with which people are experimenting, it appears that (1) new forms of "relationship" are proliferating in the late twentieth and early twenty-first centuries; (2) the new forms call for new definitions of "family" and/or new terminology for the new forms of "marriage"; (3) though new forms are unfamiliar, they are expressions of the basic covenantal structure of giving and receiving; (4) the primary one-to-one relationship remains fundamental: two "persons" of not absolutely equal capabilities can and do relate to each other in brief or extended time frames; (5) two morally equal but socially distinct persons must be free to live together; (6) any relationship exists in a context of other similar relationships, in which distinct roles are nevertheless identifiable: men can relate as husbands or "fathers"; women can relate as wives; children are receivers of care; fathers are similar in some respects to mothers and vice versa; brothers likewise to sisters; elders may find themselves filling a variety of familiar roles; and can be analyzed in the familiar terms. Jesus' story of the prodigal son updated the story of Jacob for the first century CE, and both stories remain instructive for use in the twenty-first century

Caregivers Not Anonymous?

The public always wants to know whether private intimacies of a marriage are going well. Mothers, grandmothers and friends demand to be told if prospects for a little one are good. The magazines arrayed next to the checkout line tell us how the notable couples of our entertainment world are managing their relationships. The affairs of a President are more newsworthy than the massacre of thousands of people in an African country. Privacy seems to be a thing of the past.

There is thus a real tension between public curiosity and the private pleasure (or pain) of a relationship, which begins with the first shy expressions of interest between two people. Acquaintances are certain to tease the adolescent boy or girl who cannot hide the new feelings. A blush or the brightening of eyes is enough to tell friends of that interest. Older friends or parents may comment approvingly or ask if the youth knows what is going on. A young unmarried minister or a single newcomer in a small town is watched closely! Older "steady" couples who have not yet decided to marry are also observed.

Covenantal relationships are basic to human life. The diagram in chapter 5 does not show the multitude of real relationships, but every "person" is the center of a wide interconnected network. The tensions and pressures of being the subject of "gossip" can lead to notoriety, fame, or paranoia. The "don't ask, don't tell" rule is impractical. Every individual needs the freedom to risk exposure of honest feeling, but not of every detail of an incipient or failing relationship. Nonetheless communities have an interest in helping to avoid unhealthy relationships.

In the care giving and care receiving aspects of relationships there is no room for total anonymity. Unfortunately, in modern western cultures with their complex systems of public health, education, private charity, insurance, and banking. Rules for the maintenance of privacy for those who receive care are needed, especially in financial transfers. But the professional behavior of doctors, teachers, ministers and loan administrators must be open to public scrutiny and review. So whenever service is rendered, the person giving the service customarily identifies himself or herself if only as "Nurse" or "Officer." A conscious patient being transported in an ambulance is both customarily and necessarily accompanied by an identified caregiver. And her anxious husband sitting in the passenger seat recognizes that both he and the driver play roles as caregivers. However brief the time spent in the giving and receiving of care, it is necessarily personal. No machine can take the place of a human hand on a fevered brow.

Losing the Personal Touch?

Transparency in political and public life is essential. Advertising by ambiguously identified groups corrupts the care giving process. Since the actions of councils, legislatures, parliaments, presidents, and courts of law purport to provide care for the whole citizenry (and also for visitors from abroad?), procedures should be declared fully and clearly. But in moving from the public plan to the individual caregiver there is a danger of losing the personal touch.[1] Every public officer from legislator, judge, business executive to floor sweeper must personally take responsibility for some actions of the social organism of which he or she is *never* an insignificant part.

Two systems for specialized medical care are currently getting attention in the articles and editorials of American newspapers and news magazines. The better established is Hospice. A letter to the *Transylvania Times* (November 24, 2008) is appropriately titled "Hospice: An Oasis at the End of the Road." I can heartily support the writer's testimony about the care she and her husband received before he "died peacefully in our home with loved ones at his bedside." When my wife was diagnosed at age 83 with terminal leukemia, representatives of Hospice came to our home and we received personal care that covered physical needs and our need for sensitive attention to our spirits. Death came so quietly that I was not sure when it occurred.

Another letter in the same newspaper argues that "private, for profit insurance has no place in health care" and supports that assertion by listing the advantages of a "single payer system based on Medicare." Businesses might not be required to provide insurance for their employees in the universal system the letter writer advocates, but should contribute to a general fund to help employees whose payroll tax payments would "be progressive, based on income, but will be considerably less than the cost of private coverage today." An advantage not mentioned in the letter is the freedom to call upon your private physician for care, which is normally highly personal. It is not necessary to lose the personal touch. Under the single payer system that many of us hoped for, every one should expect to *know* a care-giving doctor.

Bargaining for Quality Care

Specific benefits may and should be adequate and kept private—between the doctor and the patient's family—so that the dignity of the recipient is preserved through careful choice of language. The word "welfare" has been so corrupted that responsible people are looking for ways to remove the taint of "unearned" benefits from public provision for the needs of people willing and able to work, as well as those like children not capable of working.

For a start we need to recognize that the benefits of Social Security, Medicare and Medicaid should be entitlements from a vast insurance program into which every working person has contributed *premium payments*, not "taxes." The medical coverage we look for should be financed in such a way that even the lowest paid worker will know that he or she has paid into the system out of earned income. Then when a service is needed, the recipient can say "I paid into the system, and now I am receiving the service I need." Of course, children and those unable to work would share in a national program, but to call such a socialist system "Communist" abuses the spirit of the system.

---

1. Israel's requirement that two witnesses testify publicly to a crime should have been applied to captured "enemy combatants." As it now appears the public has been denied testimony that might have been available at the time of their capture.

PART 4: Using the Hebrew Scriptures Today

An Elderhostel visitor to Finland was directed to the nearest clinic on a Sunday afternoon after arriving with a burst eardrum; she received both the initial attention and the care of a trained specialist, and was asked to pay less than ten dollars for each visit. The national health care system collected a small fee from a foreign patient, but paid the doctors their salaries to be available to meet anyone's need. There was no question of eligibility when the need was obvious. The Finnish system worked like the ideal covenantal transaction: "Ask and you shall receive."

Non-governmental organizations (NGO's) like Habitat for Humanity and Planned Parenthood have become prominent as they offer constructive help in many areas of the world, but we do not have space to describe them.

When Jacob reached the vicinity of his uncle Laban's establishment in Harran, he found a well and three flocks of sheep waiting to be watered, until Laban's daughter Rachel arrived with her father's sheep. When she arrived, Jacob did two things. He rolled the large stone away from the top of the well, and he kissed Rachel. Rolling the stone away was the task of a servant and might not be done without the chief's permission, which came implicitly through the chief's daughter, when Rachel recognized Jacob as eligible kin. Jacob immediately offered himself as a servant and later bargained for tending part of the family flock with a specified share of the new lambs. Thus Jacob asked for and received income and some of the developing wealth of the enterprise.

It was set up with a simple conversation, when Laban said to Jacob: "Because you are my kinsman, should you therefore serve me for nothing? Tell me, what shall your wages be?" Now Laban had two daughters . . . Leah's eyes were lovely, and Rachel was graceful and beautiful. Jacob loved Rachel so he said, "I will serve you seven years for your younger daughter Rachel" (Gen 21:15–18).

After that initial business agreement two full chapters of Genesis tell how the two men bargained for the next twenty years over the care giving which Jacob owed to the household and what the establishment owed to him. Genesis also tells how Laban's daughters bargained with each other to build Jacob's family. Even though there were many bargains during the years Jacob stayed with his uncle's family, I would like to believe that Jacob fulfilled each one until it was replaced with a new one—in spite of being deceived with his first bride.

Every bargaining situation balances feelings of trust and mistrust as two individuals (or groups) seek to agree on the terms for the exchange of goods and services. Genuine trust between people is almost never mentioned in the Hebrew Scriptures. One exception is in the depiction of the capable wife in Proverbs 31, whose husband praises her as a trustworthy business partner. The statement does not mention sexual faithfulness, but indicates that her children "call her happy."

Instead of putting complete trust in people, Israelites called upon God when those with whom they bargained might prove untrustworthy. The wavy lines with arrow points in our second diagram or chapter 5 can represent expressed feelings of trust, but unfortunately only rarely should the solid lines of material transactions between people be printed without any gaps. An undercurrent of mistrust and broken relationships seems to pervade all human affairs, even while individuals reach out to relate to others who they hope can be trusted.

Erik H. Erikson, Joan M. Erikson, and Helen Q. Kivnick approach their treatment of old age with the observation that vital involvement depends on a balancing between a sense of trust and a contrary sense of mistrust, which begins in infancy and continues through all eight of the psychosocial stages of life.[2] The biblical view, which focuses on adult relationships, calls for responsible risk on the side of trust with the tentative suppression of mistrust and the reservation of retaliation for failure to fulfill a responsibility, preferably left to God.

Today even in western countries much bargaining is still face to face between individuals, and the process has come to concern a multitude of specialized business, political, and personal affairs. The settings for bargaining are anywhere and any time two or more people meet, and include any of the means of communication. All that is necessary is that the stronger person becomes aware of a weaker person's need and expresses a willingness to meet that need.

Prisons are unlikely places to seek for care, but a recent essay by Jenny McBride in the publication *Hospitality* of Atlanta's Open Door Community voices the complaint of inmates in Georgia's prison system: "They treat us like animals, like caged dogs. They take our self-respect, beat down our self esteem and then expect us to go out and be civilized."[3] Prisoners are always the weaker in that system, but guards seldom show any willingness to meet the need to empower them to return to the outside culture.

Such covenantal bargaining—quid pro quo—is the master paradigm of human culture. The forms it can take are infinite, many being invented each day in our complex world. It should be noted that the designation "stronger" is not a fixed quality for either person in a bargaining situation, as the shifting of power in the relationship between David and Jonathan illustrates. It often turns out that a wife is stronger in many respects than the husband she thought was an epitome of strength.

Today economically powerful merchants seek relatively weaker customers through advertising. Grocery chains issue semi-personal plastic cards offering discounted prices on many items to identify and establish a special relationship with regular customers, thus seeking to create a sort of family relationship of mutual care giving. Banks and insurance companies advertise the family character of their relationship with clientele, but clerks and bank tellers—and computerized transactions—easily remain anonymous. The consequence in modern societies is a wide range of nearly depersonalized contacts for small services. In the last quarter of 2008 the failure of trust in financial transactions relating to mortgages brought on an international crisis in the monetary system for which no one person could be blamed.

Advertising seeks the customer and the customer seeks the business, but both must use the truth of honest communication to work for *relational quality* as well as the delivery of goods and services. Over time what matters is the quality, not the

---

2. Erikson, *Vital Involvement in Old Age*, 33. Note also the many references to both trust and mistrust in the index of *Vital Involvement*.

3. McBride, "Prison Madness," 4.

quantity of the care giving service. Incidentally, attending to quality is the cure for boredom in any job, and the value of the service can be measured in terms of the quality of the personal attention given to the partner in a transaction.

Murray Sidman proposes that typical coercive police practice be abrogated, wildly impractical as it may seem, with police officers taught to offer *positive reinforcement* to people who slow down and stop at intersections instead of always watching for speeders and other violators of laws. Once such a policy becomes established, he argues, "Police cars would signal not fear and apprehension but anticipation of friendly and rewarding encounters, welcome signs that everything is all right . . . We might see a reestablishment of public trust and confidence in our protective institutions."[4]

Overcoming the deep anonymity of modern life is one of the unsolved problems of our time. Many moderns hesitate to do more than ask directions from a stranger. We are socially and spiritually cut off from other individuals on the streets of New York (or in elevators anywhere!) even when our bodies may accidentally collide. As for offering helpful care we know that ninety-nine of a hundred people would pass by our prone bodies on a city sidewalk, just as priest and Levite did in the story Jesus told. Priests and Levites could excuse themselves, having assumed an obligation to serve a holy God in a temple from which all unseemliness was barred. To fulfill their obligation to God, the two traveling clergymen naturally avoided contact with a wounded man. The Samaritan had no such inhibition; he knew he was already considered ritually polluted.

Care-giving in the Stages of Life

We are accustomed to think of infancy as a stage when nature and culture expect mothers to provide a vast amount of care for the developing human. And we know that some adolescents resent the excessive attention they receive from their parents, as they undertake to live their own lives. In adulthood mature men and women provide care in varying degrees for each other and for the members of their families and communities, but most of us are not prepared to be cared for in illness and old age.

Erik Erikson and his two colleagues introduce *Vital Involvement in Old Age* with a survey of eight "Psychosocial Stages of Life" and chart their adaptive strengths together with maladaptive and malignant tendencies that may be observed in people at each stage.[5] The authors emphasize taking care as the major concern for infancy, adulthood and old age: "So now, at last, we come to the adult reality in the world in which generativity within the cross-generational setting of the technologies and cultures must 'take care' of what is being procreated, produced and created. This vital strength of care (as we have formulated it) is the widening concern for what has been generated by love, necessity, or accident; it overcomes the ambivalence arising with irreversible obligation. Thus care attends to the needs of all that has been generated."[6]

---

4. Sidman, *Coercion*, 235.

5. The two charts are on pages 36 and 45 respectively of *Vital Involvement*.

6. Erikson, *Vital Involvement in Old Age*, 37.

Instead of the command and obedience language of Deuteronomy, the reproof and forgiveness language of Leviticus, or the love language of Jesus, all of which are appropriate for the adults addressed in the Hebrew and Christian scriptures, the Eriksons and Kivnick prefer the functional language of care giving for all the stages of life. It appears that giving and receiving care in more or less equal proportions, though clearly with variations occasioned by the interweaving of other systems, are normal during the productive middle years, while in the early stages and in the final stage of life care receiving outweighs care giving for human beings.

Individuals of any age (or stage) are in a socio-spiritual market place, seeking other individuals as companionable caregivers. Until the mid-twentieth century we assumed that widows, widowers, and other single individuals would limit their relationships to social companionship, but there have always been some who shared living arrangements, care giving, and sexual relations without observing the customary formality of marriage, reasoning (or allowing the community to reason) that since there would not be children to legitimize there would be no need for legal marriage.

Twentieth-century western culture became aware of these situations and has been calling for thoughtful new language and acceptable structures for long-term relationships. Some churches, however, have not been eager to alter the definition of marriage or for the state to grant its privileges to those considered to be "living in sin." Can laws ever be written that do not unduly restrict personal relations?

Unfortunately relatively unstructured living arrangements often fail to provide for an equitable distribution of shared possessions when an arrangement comes to an end. Couples who agree to live together without marrying would do well to indicate in writing how they wish families to distribute household possessions of any value.

"Knowing and Being Known"

It is time for another look at the two diagrams (Chapter 5), the first of which provided a structural image of human covenantal relationships. The double arrows between the three persons in a relationship represented the two way giving and receiving of "goods" and "services" in what could be seen as a market situation in the emerging culture of ancient Israel. The wavy Feynman diagram of verbal bargaining represents the giving and receiving of information preparatory to or accompanying a material transaction. The angled lines represent the religious recognition that "Every generous act of giving, with every perfect gift, is from above, coming down from the Father of lights, with whom there is no variation or shadow due to change," as the New Testament letter of James (1:17) declares. Arrows pointing upward are prayers of thanksgiving or supplication, while those pointing down to the human level represent the tangible thing we pray for.

John Dewey and Arthur F. Bentley discuss this two way street of information sharing in *Knowing and the Known*. The heart of their philosophic work is a chapter entitled "Interaction and Transaction" in which the authors resist the "antique view of self actions which can exist 'in a man's head' in presumed independence of what is observed."[7] Instead they sketch a historic human evolution from a primitive time in which events were visualized as moved by "self action." In place of purely autonomous activity Dewey and Bentley argue that interaction between distinctly autonomous personages, as may be presumed in my first diagram, is an inadequate description of complex human interactions. They insist on a *transactional* view that requires a deeper involvement in the welfare of the "other" in every interaction.

Although the terms can be applied to war making as well as love making, at this point our interest is in what goes on between the minds of participants in a transaction. A male (or female) *notices* and is attracted to another person (of either sex) with the *intention* of achieving a modest transaction. Buying a postage stamp or a bus ticket can be done only when some minimal mental contact occurs. In families a range of communications accompanies a whole range of physical actions from gestures to thoughtful discussions.

At the dining table Father asks, "Who wants a drumstick?" Getting ready for a date, Sue asks her sister, "May I wear your pin tonight?" In addition to *naming* the item or service to be exchanged, relational communication involves a *"knowing"* and a *"being known."* Both participants are known by names that distinguish them from other individuals. Life does not stop with the public creation of families. In a marriage a previously strange person comes into a family and becomes known while coming to know one member of the family in the special relationship.

Classical Hebrew has a three-letter root with two seemingly opposite meanings. On the one hand the verb root *NKR* translates as "regard, recognize," and on the other hand adjectives for "foreign" and "alien" appear to be derived from the same root.[8] It is as if Abram stood by his tent and squinted into the faces of the men who passed his way. Were they travelers like himself, needing water, a meal, and a place to rest for a night or two? Or were they scouts surveying the land to see if their tribe could pass that way without having to do battle with his small family? Moses sent such spies to survey the land before undertaking to enter it. His twelve-man advance party had returned with such a discouraging report that the wandering Israelites did not risk approaching the fortified cities of western Canaan for almost forty years. Joshua sent two men to Jericho on a similar mission.

In the time of the Judges when the Israelites were beginning to be settled, it would be neighboring Amalekites, Midianites, Canaanites, and Philistines who would be the strangers whom Israelites would need to know. Which would be friendly traders supplying needed foodstuffs, and which would be predators intent on taking the grain and young lambs the Israelites intended for the winter? The questions can be phrased another way: Which of the roles played within the family would the stranger fill: Protecting and providing father; nurturing mother; needy child; ambivalent brother; dominating master; or willing servant?

---

7. Dewey, *Knowing and the Known*, 103.

8. Brown, Driver and Briggs, *Hebrew and English Lexicon of the Old Testament* (1907) listed the two meanings of *NKR* as I and II, indicating uncertainty whether one or two roots are involved, perhaps the same uncertainty felt in meeting strangers.

The cognitive component—the enduring product of communication—means that no human relationship is ever completely anonymous. To a greater or lesser degree aspects of individuals and their relationships become known to both parties in the process of development from acquaintanceship to intimacy. Every relationship will have a knowledge component.

One form of this not-anonymous knowing has been called "love," but "care giving" may be the more useful term. A husband is expected to "care" for his wife as he cares for his whole being, body, mind, and soul/self. Parents are responsible for caring for young children, and adults are expected to care for their aging parents. Doctors, dentists, family counselors, teachers, and lawyers, care for their clients, patients, or students in at least two senses. Professionally they offer their services and are paid—a semi-material exchange. Personally, however, the quality of their care is a gift of self, spirit, or soul for which a word of thanks is the only possible return. Caregiving outside the average family may have anonymous beginnings, but persisting relationships do not remain anonymous. The richness of relationship can grow into deep personal love.

When Caregiving Fails

Throughout this study it seems that reality has seldom achieved the beckoning ideal, at least not without the help of God. Tamar bore Judah's twin sons only after her inspired deceit, which God appeared to approve. David ascended the holy hill of Zion, but it was left to his son to build the Temple there, to provide an earthly residence for approving/reproving YHWH. Kings were anointed or claimed their thrones as patriarchal birthright to protect the people from threatening neighbors, but in the end thrones and temples were destroyed when YHWH disapproved the sins of the builders. Whether we look at particular intervals, families, tribes, business enterprises, political movements, nations, or churches, there appears to be degeneration from initiating ideal to corrupted reality. Chords are lost; symphonies are not finished, concert hall performances do not measure up to the concept in the Composer's mind. Even after thinking the creation "very good," God appears to have been disappointed with the human family by the time of Noah. Does the distributed care giving of the twenty-first century also fail? And if we judge so, does that imply God's failure?

A couple pledging eternal care giving love to each other may fail to measure up to their promises. At what point in the range of such failures can anyone declare that a promise has been broken? The simple but unsatisfying answer is that small failures accumulate until they total an unendurable number or cross a line set in the mind of the partner or in a vague community consensus—a common mind expressed in a court's grant of divorce. Like chorales and symphonies, success and failure, righteousness and sin are conceptions of mental imaging which seek an embodiment in reality. People customarily find their footing on the common paths of human activity. A step off the path may be thought of as a "sin" for which an apology and forgiveness are needed.

Many find the relativity of human judgments unsatisfying, and ask priests and prophets for absolute definitions and then return for absolution from the sins they've been taught to confess. It has been too easy to limit the definition of "sin" to the failure to obey the precepts set forth in the biblical teaching of the church, where priests and prophets speak in the name of God. A functional understanding of this universal problem would be particularly satisfying to minds struggling to integrate social and psychological thought with religious tradition.

Consider the keeping and not keeping of promises. The Eriksons and Helen Kivnick write of trust and mistrust instead of the keeping of promises, but in doing so they lay before the reader a psychosocial realm that we may visualize as a spiritual territory whose paths may be owned and controlled by resident or invading human beings. Since the territory is spiritual, it is primarily in the time dimension of our four dimensional world, and can be mapped through the eight stages of an individual life. At each stage "vital involvement" marks a path for adaptive strength and activity, narrowed between maladaptive tendencies on one side and malignant tendencies on the other. When I make a promise to a friend, I lay before him a future but not yet material path that will intersect with his foreseeable path, perhaps to deliver what he is buying from me. If I deliberately do not show up with his purchase, the Eriksons would call that a "malignant" failure rather than a "sin." But if I did not make enough effort, they would call it a "maladaptive" failure. In either case the failure can be forgiven if my friend is willing to accept an apology and the delivery of his purchase.

For adult caring, the Eriksons and Helen Kivnick observed a malignant "rejectivity" leading to stagnation in some of the subjects of their study. The adult who cannot hold a job and expects his wife or girlfriend to provide for his needs is not adapting to the realities of the modern world of business and personal relationships. At the other extreme, a maladaptive over-extension of caregiving generativity can be equally frustrating to a wife who needs to live some parts of her life for herself. Some adults make too few promises while others make too many, instead of making and keeping ones within their capabilities.

There is no place for the word "sin" in the Erikson-Kivnick scheme, only maladaptation or malignancy. The scheme has its roots in the observations of Sigmund Freud and his successors who developed the "scientific" medium of case histories and statistical methods for the study of human behavior. This "science" can be set beside the dramatic stories of biblical characters, non-scientific and sin-laden as they were, without apology, for both are part of our human heritage. The biblical situations are framed in a relgio-ethical scheme of human behavior watched over by God who is "Lord" over human families and tribes.[9] The psychosocial scheme is described and analyzed by specialists in the behavioral and psychological sciences. The two schemes seek to interpret the realities of human experience as it has been observed and reported in two quite different centuries. Much of the biblical scheme is "top down" with the God of the garden of Eden giving orders, while a modern humanist scheme, like the other voice in the garden, lets people decide, "bottom up," what they think is best for their communities, states and nations. People who listen to God may rebel

---

9. In the fourth section of this study it is appropriate to use modern terms for God instead of the Israelite " YHWH."

against His laws, but people who think for themselves may undertake experiments that wound and kill their neighbors. The resulting stories are similar. They offer different terms and explanatory statements as they seek to make sense of human behavior. So modern behavioral analysis is the moral equivalent of the explanation of the law of God ascribed to Moses in the Book of Deuteronomy.

Do we Need Authoritative Instructions?

Ideally the religious view, from where God sits, should observe human behavior and identify right ways as opposed to wrong ways, good ways as opposed to bad ways, and pure ways instead of impure ways. The religious view, however, presupposes a machine like world in which all the parts work properly in only one way. Ancient Israel came to see itself as such an organism, composed of twelve working tribes held together by a specialized Levitical tribe, which communicated God's instructions at pre-exilic annual festival gatherings. Beginning in the Exile scattered Jews in Egypt and Babylon held themselves together in weekly family settings in which selected teachers read from the holy writings of Moses and the Prophets, expecting a restoration to the promised land where a state could be formed out of the newly experienced "churches."

The three great monotheistic religious bodies have continued to maintain the religious view, and its appeal is evident, particularly in Africa, in the twenty-first century. Populations support the weekly worship times in different communities in different ways, but agree on the need to support religious institutions—churches, mosques, synagogues, temples, monastic centers, etc.—together with the persons dedicated to the service of these places. Even an atheistic social order, like the Soviet Union, found a way to institutionalize its faith with a shrine to Lenin, a coterie of ministering priests and a mandatory code of right behavior. Its religious beginnings that called for managed sharing to meet need gave way quickly to the formation of an oppressive state, and the "Union" collapsed through its over-extension.

As we've noted, individuals who support the presence and services of priests and other religious leaders, may neglect or rebel against particular features of the programs of their churches. It seems to make little difference how beneficent the instruction is. Active involvement in the rituals of all religious bodies develops like a life form, beginning small and ending weak, but with peaking strength in midcourse. Some churches label individual failures as "sin," and apply that judgment to erring brothers while other groups undertake special rituals to bring the sinner to confession and a return to good behavior. Verbal guidance appears to work with some people, but others stray from the "straight and narrow." So there seems to be a need for the broad interpretive guidance Moses brought to his followers in Moab before they crossed the Jordan. What else would work?

The Mercy of God-figures

In modern theory authority is granted by people or God to priests, prophets, kings, teachers, doctors, presidents, corporation executives and the like in exchange for the

Part 4: Using the Hebrew Scriptures Today

feeling that one's person, loved ones, and property will be secure, or at least as secure as a human being can expect in a world of contrary forces. Authority may be seen as just another secular covenantal transaction. Deuteronomy's law-giving YHWH and his "people" have the same paired valuation to each other as Plato's philosopher king and his "Republic," a stronger social entity "giving" an intangible "peace" to a petitioner. Both Israelites and Athenians could imagine that they would be secure when or if the contemplated relationship would be heartily and mutually accepted en masse by all three typical figures of the master paradigm: two human figures (or groups) unequally matched in power, plus a mutually accepted god-figure with unquestioned value, power and judgment. The "god-figure" in this image could be a deity or a human with divinely delegated power, such as the "king of kings" in the ancient empires.

The theory has appeared to work—for limited times—when kings, emperors, and dictators have demanded and been given the role of supreme power. Such a historic moment occurred when the Roman world lived through the *Pax Romana* under Caesar Augustus. Another local time of peace occurred after World War II with the reconstruction of Western Europe under the Marshall Plan. What made these situations work was the intelligent use of human powers, inspired by a vision of the covenantal way to peace. In the fourth century of the Christian era the Emperor Constantine called the warring bishops of the growing Christian movement to meet and reach an agreement regarding the person of Christ. The creed they reached, which declared the human Jesus to be one of three Persons representing a supreme God instead of a political football among contending priests, was the basis for centuries of relative peace in western Europe, as the Roman emperors lost their power and church leaders and princes managed islands of security around monasteries and growing cities.

It can be argued that the market places associated with monasteries and cities were more significant in cultivating the emerging civilized culture of Europe than the theology and rituals of the churches, since the care giving paradigm could be applied to the full range of economic life, while the churches emphasized only the individual's path toward a future heaven against a choice for the road to hell. How do today's markets, Wall Street and Main Street for example, measure up in care giving? A population's survival has always depended on mutual care giving between friendly but watchful people.

Theology, philosophy, and history concur in telling us that no structure yet known has achieved a permanently happy or blessed state. Human reality has fallen short of bliss. Plato, however, "considering that the soul is immortal and able to endure every sort of good and every sort of evil," counseled "that we hold fast ever to the heavenly way and follow after justice and virtue always."[10] In a parallel exhortation the author of the New Testament Letter to the Hebrews urges readers: "Therefore, since we are surrounded by so great a cloud of witnesses, let us also lay aside every weight and the sin that clings so closely, and let us run with perseverance the race that is set before us, looking to Jesus the pioneer and perfecter of our faith, who for the sake of the joy that

---

10. Plato, *The Republic*, 277.

was set before him endured the cross, disregarding its shame, and has taken his seat at the right hand of the throne of God" (Heb 12:1–2).

The New Testament and Plato agree in declaring: (1) that *the world is infected* and *afflicted* with "sin" and its results, and (2) that *people may be empowered to persevere* in the heavenly way, hopefully as caregivers for their fellows. An exemplification was seen when Jesus was willing to endure the cross to persevere in the race that is set before us all, or as Socrates was ready to drink the hemlock to teach Athenians the way of peace, or as Moses was ready to die and be buried on an unmarked mountain valley in Moab after delivering his final words to Israel (Deut 33:50; 34:6). Are such examples enough?

Part 5

In the Perspective of Hero Tales

23

Moses and the Name of God: Israel's Hero Tale

At some time in the middle of the second millennium before the Christian era a family of Hebrews found themselves in Egypt, first as welcome guests because one of their number had been able to advise the Pharaoh about stabilizing the production and distribution of grain and cattle through a program of government managed insurance. Joseph, one of the sons of Jacob, had been sold by his brothers to slavery, but through a series of dream interpretations—he was good at those—he rose to be the chief economic adviser in Egypt. His program was simple: every productive year grain farmers would be taxed twenty percent of their crop, and that grain would be stored until the inevitable bad years came when the grain could be sold to people who needed food.

The plan evidently worked; people had food, the managers got rich, and the sons of Jacob kept cattle in the low country beside the Nile. Everybody prospered. But after a while the Egyptians suspected that the Hebrews were doing better than they were, and the new Pharaoh increased the taxes on these aliens and when they couldn't pay he assigned them to labor camps where bricks were being produced for building projects of one of the greatest Pharaohs. The Hebrews weren't being deported back to Canaan, but were treated worse than some Americans want to treat illegal aliens.

One of that Pharaoh's ideas was to reduce their population, and when the hard labor failed to limit the burgeoning population, the king of Egypt said to the Hebrew midwives, "When you act as midwives to the Hebrew women, and see them on the birth stool, if it is a boy, kill him; but if it is a girl, she shall live."

But the midwives did not believe in aborting or killing the children that God had given and did not do as the king of Egypt commanded, so when they were called in to explain why they had not been killing Hebrew boy babies, they said to Pharaoh, "Because the Hebrew women are not like the Egyptian women; they are vigorous and give birth before the midwife comes to them." So the Pharaoh commanded *all* the Hebrews to throw boy babies into the Nile.

That set up the way Moses survived. A Levite woman married to a Levite man just knew that this little boy baby would amount to something. She could not bear to

PART 5: In the Perspective of Hero Tales

throw her baby into the Nile, and when she knew his crying would be noticed she got a papyrus basket, and plastered it with bitumen and pitch, put her child in it and placed it among the reeds on the bank of the river. She stationed his sister a short distance away to see what would happen to him.

Well, I'm sure you remember how the daughter of the Pharaoh came to bathe and found the baby in the reeds, and of course the sister offered to bring her mother to nurse the child for the Pharaoh's daughter. The Pharaoh's daughter thought it would be fun to adopt the boy, and she hired his Hebrew mother to nurse him. When the nursing was finished Moses moved in with Pharaoh's family and got his name, because the Pharaoh's daughter said "I drew him out of the water."

Parenthesis: There is a little mix up on the name of Moses the Egyptian princess probably gave the little boy an Egyptian name that ended like many with the syllable "-mose," which means "son of" usually of a god, as Thutmose means son of Thoth. The mix up is obvious when the Egyptian princess explains that she is giving the name because she "drew" him out of the water, using a Hebrew verb MaSHaH, which can mean "draw out" as women would wash clothes in the shallow waters of the Nile. Do you really think the princess was learning Hebrew from the mother of Moses? Anyway that is the way the Israelites remembered the name of Moses. It is one of the first of the verbal jokes in which Old Testament names have special meaning.

Second parenthesis: Back in the nineteenth century explorers in what is now Iraq found cuneiform "Chronicles Concerning Early Babylonian Kings" and among them was a legend about the great king Sargon in which he tells how his mother conceived him, and bore him in secret. Then in his words, "She set me in a basket of rushes, with bitumen she sealed my lid. She cast me into the river, which rose not over me. The river bore me up and carried me to Akki, the drawer of water. Akki, the drawer of water lifted me out as he dipped his ewer. Akki, the drawer of water, took me as his son (and) reared me." The legend goes on to tell how Akki appointed him as his gardener before the goddess Ishtar granted him her love and led him to rule the early Babylonian empire.[1] In the Akkadian story there is nothing said about the mother of Sargon, why her pregnancy was such a secret or who she was. She was like the mother of Moses, however, in not wanting her son to die before he fulfilled his heroic destiny.

In the second episode of his life Moses is an adult, Egyptian in appearance—he had no doubt started to shave as the Egyptians did and the Hebrews didn't. He must have had the basic Egyptian schooling that would have been given to a son in the Pharaoh's household, but he also knew the story of his birth and childhood.

One day he went out and saw an Egyptian beating one of his kinfolk. After looking this way and that, he killed the Egyptian and hid him in the sand. The next day he saw two Hebrews fighting, and said to the one who was in the wrong, "Why do you strike your fellow Hebrew?" The man replied, "Who made you a ruler & judge over us? Do you mean to kill me as you killed the Egyptian?" So Moses was afraid, and thought, "Surely the thing is known." Sure enough the Pharaoh put out a warrant for the arrest

---

1. See "The Legend of Sargon" in Pritchard, *Ancient Near Eastern Texts*, 119.

of Moses. So Moses fled. Obviously he could not even go back to being the adopted son of Pharaoh's daughter, so he went toward the eastern desert, to a region known as Midian, inhabited by semi-nomadic people who kept goats and got their water from wells in the desert.

Why didn't Moses let down the bucket and draw some water? Well, apparently as a later story indicates, wells in desert areas were not equipped with anything to draw the water. Instead the owner's daughters or a slave had to bring a jug and let it down to bring up water. How many of you remember pictures of beautiful young women clothed in gaily-colored dresses with elegantly shaped jugs from your childhood Sunday school literature? This was not that beautiful, and I wonder why the picture I remember didn't show a rope for the jug handles. Besides a chief's son would expect a slave to do that task.

The girls came home early when they finished watering their goats, and their father asked "How is that you have come back so soon today?" They said, "An Egyptian helped us against the shepherds; he even drew water for us and watered the flock." Where is he? Why did you leave the man? Invite him to break bread' Where were their manners?

Years ago I began to pay attention to the customary behavior these stories reveal. The other story, which has the same pattern, was when Jacob went to find his uncle Laban, and met Rachel where she came to water her family's goats. The two pictures are bucolic, except for the latent hostility between groups of shepherds who have to use the only well for miles around and the social distinctions that separated those who drew water from those for whom it was drawn. This story could be and maybe is one of Joseph Campbell's hero stories.

Nowadays the tour bus is welcome at the well, and the tourists get out, stretch their legs and sample the water as it comes out of an iron pipe. Then they look to see what curios the natives have to sell. Rival shepherds have made their peace and share in the bartering. It is midday and hot, and we are the only crowd, so we get back on the bus and let the locals go back to their siestas.

Moses, we are told "agreed to stay with the man," and he gave him his daughter Zipporah in marriage. In due time she bore a son, and he named him Gershom for he said, "I have been an alien in a foreign land." The first part of that name is 'ger' which is Hebrew for alien. And that is the end of our lesson in foreign customs. But we will have more to say about a special name.

This is not a story that would have appeared in any newspaper, and the only reason I can tell it today is that it has been preserved in a book of the Bible. There is no Egyptian record to identify which Pharaoh was living at the time since the Hebrew woman probably did not know enough Egyptian to remember the name of the Egyptian princess who saved her son. It is still a plausible story that must have happened if not exactly as reported in the book of Exodus, but in some such form. The Hebrews who preserved the story told their children what they remembered the steps that brought Moses to his moments with destiny.

PART 5: In the Perspective of Hero Tales

A moment toward Moses' destiny had occurred when he killed an Egyptian who was beating a Hebrew. At that moment Moses' life began to move from external physical behavior to an internal thought world, as happens regularly in adolescence. A modern psychologist might think that Moses began to indulge an increasing obsession with three things—his birth, his childhood, and the killing of an Egyptian. The Bible has already started this stage of its story with the groaning of the Israelites under their slavery, and says that God "heard their groaning" and remembered his covenant with Abraham, Isaac and Jacob, and "took notice of them." At this juncture two stories come together: "the angel of YHWH appeared to Moses in a flame of fire out of a bush, and Moses looked and the bush was not consumed."

I've given up speculating on the physics and chemistry of a bush which burns and is not consumed, though there have been many theories about that phenomenon. One that appeals to me is that an underground source of methane gas had been kindled by lightning and continued to burn while Moses watched. Incidentally, eight years ago Virginia and I were shown a descendant of that burning bush in the courtyard of St. Catherine's Monastery on one of the mountains in Egypt.

But I'm interested in an equally strange event, which happened in the mind of Moses. First he turned aside to see "this great sight." Then a dialogue between YHWH and Moses began. The voice—as I think, in the mind of Moses—said, "Come closer." And then, "Remove the sandals from your feet for the place on which you are standing is holy ground."

Next the voice said: "I am the God of Abraham, the God of Isaac, and the God of Jacob."

Biblical dialogues allow time for words to sink in, and in this story God let Moses hide his face for fear of looking directly at God. But now God started his current story: "I have observed the misery of my people who are in Egypt; I have heard their cry on account of their taskmasters. Indeed I know their sufferings. I have come down to deliver them from the Egyptians, and to bring them up out of that land to a good and broad land, a land flowing with milk and honey, to the country of the Canaanites, the Hittites, the Amorites, the Perizzites, the Hivites, and the Jebusites." All this information was probably already deeply engraved in the mind of Moses, but it may have been news to him that it was also on the mind of God. God continued to speak in the mind of Moses: "The cry of the Israelites has come to me; I have also seen how the Egyptians oppress them. So come, I will send you to Pharaoh to bring my people out of Egypt."

Now remember that this group of Hebrews wasn't supposed to be in Egypt at all. They were supposed to be settling in the land of Canaan, where God had sent Abraham and Sarai, but where their grandchildren had stepped out of bounds on that playing field and were being penalized in an awkward situation in Egypt. Of course Moses knew the stories about how Joseph's brothers had gotten them all into slavery. So, as he watched the sheep, Moses has been looking forward, wondering what is next? And will there ever be any way to get back to the place where they were supposed to settle?

Moses and the Name of God: Israel's Hero Tale

Moses had two problems with this meeting with God, so he asked: "Why me? *Who am I* that I should go to Pharaoh and bring the Israelites out of Egypt?'" And the answer came back: "I will be with you; and this shall be a sign for you that it is I who sent you; when you have brought the people out of Egypt, you shall worship God on this mountain." Like Moses we ask, "Who is this 'I' who will be with Moses and whose identity Moses can't be sure about until he brings the people to that mountain?"

The dialogue goes on; Moses raises objection number 2, "If I come to the Israelites and say, 'the God of your ancestors has sent me to you' and they ask me, 'What is his name?' what shall I say to them?"

God said to Moses, "I AM WHO I AM." He said further: "Thus shall you say to the Israelites, I AM has sent me to you. YHWH the God of your ancestors, the God of Abraham, the God of Isaac, and the God of Jacob, has sent me to you: This is my name forever, and this is my title for all generations."

There it is: *Moses and the name of God.* Well, most us have been told that this was the moment that launched the Exodus of Israelites from Egypt and started Jews on the path to their place in the world, but it may also be the moment when the Israelites' name for God was born, and when Moses learned that there is more to the world than drawing water out of wells and watching goats for the next meals of a household.

Let me make a personal comment: You are more likely to believe that this story is true if you have had a similar experience, as I had many years ago. What Moses said to God figured in my mental dialogue with God when I faced my call to a career as a minister, so I am sure the dialogue could have happened in the mind of a solitary young adult Moses in the wilderness of Midian. The burning bush had brought his private thinking to a climax.

The dialogue does not spell out a precise picture of a future for Moses any more than it did for me, but it set the stage for an ongoing personal and social drama, which would begin with both right and left halves of the brain carrying out the idea of getting people out of Egypt.

The setting for Moses was his early life as the son of a Hebrew woman and the adopted son of an Egyptian princess. On that stage were Egyptian nobility and Hebrews doing slave labor. And also on the wings of the stage national or tribal gods for many groups.

Somewhere off stage was the mysterious figure of YHWH/God. The consonants, Y H W H, are used in place of the word "Lord" which appears in English bibles where the word "Lord" appears instead of the consonants of YHWH. And you have no doubt heard that the reason is that Jews pronounce the word *adonai*, "Lord," when they read the consonants *Y H W H* instead of the actual name that Moses passed to the Hebrews in Egypt.

Historically Jews began to substitute the title "Lord" for the proper name of God during the Exile in Babylon and it was firmly fixed in the centuries before Christ. It is my opinion that Jews six hundred years after Moses were superstitiously afraid that they would somehow profane the name of God, and thus make God angry. So, as their teachers urged, they just stopped using the name Moses gave to the Israelites.

Part 5: In the Perspective of Hero Tales

We're going to look now at the sacred name. Listen to the way most translations read the verses in the third chapter of Exodus: When Moses looked forward to telling his people that the God of their ancestors had sent him, he knew that they would want to know a little more than that, so he asked "What shall I say to them?"

The enigma is in these few words: "I am who I am" and "I am has sent me." We will return to these words, but first let us continue with the story. God said to Moses, "Thus shall you say to the Israelites, and also, to the Pharaoh: YHWH, the God of our ancestors has met with us; let us now go a three days journey into the wilderness, so that we may sacrifice to YHWH our God."

YHWH goes on: "I know however, that the king of Egypt will not let you go unless compelled by a mighty hand. So I will stretch out my hand and strike Egypt with all my wonders that I will perform in it; after that he will let you go . . . I will bring this people into such favor with the Egyptians that, when you go you will not go empty handed, each woman shall ask her neighbor and any woman living in the neighbor's house for jewelry of silver and of gold, and clothing and you shall put them on your sons and on your daughters; and so you shall plunder the Egyptians."

Moses did go to Pharaoh and did ask for permission to take his people away from their slavery for three days. The Pharaoh or "the King of Egypt" refused, and Moses announced a series of ten plagues. Each plague followed the announcement and the last one concluded with the killing of the first-born Egyptians. At that point the Egyptians were ready to get rid of the Hebrews, who then began their escape from Egypt.

If you've heard reports that this is all a made-up story that got into the Bible by way of the Jews, you still have to explain the people who told the story. How did they come to be? Existence is reality. Jews, Christians, Muslims, Buddhists, atheists, and agnostics all exist and have existed since their earliest ancestors. Many of them have identities that are hard to deny, and stories that trace their development back to heroic events in very early times, and ultimately back to divine and semi-divine persons whose stories, however garbled, kept them alive during their years on earth.

Now you are wondering what all this has to do with the name of God. Okay, let's go back and look at what turned out to be the proper noun 'Yahweh' or the four Hebrew consonants Y H W H. What Moses could tell the people was actually not a proper noun, but a form from a verb that is commonly translated "to be" with the familiar words "I am," or "He is." The living God of Moses and other biblical heroes is better identified by a verb form than by a noun.

Also I think that the English translations, which followed the traditional reading by Jews, Greeks, Latin speakers, and others, missed what the context implied when they translated God's word "I am who I am."

Now that is a perfectly legitimate translation, and it essentially says, "I am God, pay attention to me." Linked with the references to Abraham, Isaac and Jacob, it says I am not a new, strange God. I am the God whose words your ancestors heard in Mesopotamia, and who sent you from there to Canaan and let Joseph be sent as a slave to Egypt to help the Egyptians meet a food crisis before a second Pharaoh began to require you to make bricks without straw. "I am who I am" makes sense when God re-introduces himself to Moses and the Hebrews in Egypt. "I am really the god of the patriarchs. I made things happen for them, and I'll make things happen now."

But there is another possible translation for those four consonants, and it requires only the change of one vowel in the verb a short "a" for a short "e," Instead of hearing the simple declension or stem we call 'qal,' Moses may have understood that God was using a causative stem we call 'hiphil,' "I cause to be what I cause to be." Or in more direct English "I make happen what I make happen." God stands at a moment in time, the way we do, looks backward and forward and declares that new events are going to happen, new entities are going to exist.

At this point the idea of being released from slavery, of enjoying freedom moves from the impulsive right brains of Moses and the Hebrews to the left, "*doing*" brains of all of them, perhaps even in God's left mind. Like an adolescent ready to assume adult responsibility, the Hebrews found that they had no choice but to act. And they did.

It all makes sense in the light of what took place when Moses went to Pharaoh to ask for a few days off to sacrifice to YHWH. When Pharaoh refused it may have seemed to the Egyptians and to hearers of the story that it was Moses who called down ten plagues and became the leader of the Hebrews. But the Bible doesn't put it that way. Over and over when the biblical writers refer to the events, they declare that YHWH exercised his mighty arm and brought the Israelites out of Egypt. Truly it was God, known by ancient Israel as YHWH, who made things happen. However, the Hebrews had to move! That suggests the true meaning of the name that Moses first uttered in answer to a question from the elders perplexed by the announcement he was making.

God was not saying simply "I exist." God was saying, "I am stirring things up." Having allowed a favored group of people to be trapped in Egypt, God was ready to set them back on the track. What was God planning for Moses and the Israelites to do? And how far would that project go?

This is no marble or gold-leafed God shape, idol, or statue that looks like a human, but cannot speak, breathe, or handle a sword. This is a Power who enters into history, an idea in the mind of Moses which he could present to his people in some simple words that would launch the movement back to the holy land and from there into the rest of the world.

You may wonder why most of us do not use the name the way Jehovah's Witnesses do. The answer is simple. The priests who experienced God's second mighty deliverance that brought Jews back from Babylon, Persia, and Egypt and included Gentiles with them, began to be afraid to let the ordinary people use the word, and substituted the word "Lord," "*adonai*," for YHWH.

There was a lot of superstition in the ancient world, and still is today. When scribes began putting marks for vowels in tenth-century Christian era manuscripts people who did not understand their purpose to substitute a safe word for the extremely powerful spoken name of God, Gentiles put together the two words, superimposing vowels on consonants to make "Jehovah." It is easier to explain this to a class of Hebrew students than to English speakers, but take my word for it now.

PART 5: In the Perspective of Hero Tales

So I give Moses credit for sensing God's intention to carry out his plan to settle his people in Canaan. Moses experienced the little dialogue about a name for God, and would pass the consonants of the verb on to the Hebrews in Egypt not in the first person, but in the third person form we read in the Hebrew text, changing the initial *aleph* to *yod*. And that is why I have chosen to write only the four consonants transliterated into the parallel English consonants, to spell them out, and also to pronounce the word the way a few Greek writers wrote it.

God told Moses to take off his sandals because the land was holy. How did Midian become holy? And how would Canaan become holy? My theory is that when the Spirit of God says "I will make happen what I will make happen," it happens. Israelites move and the land where they are going becomes holy wherever the Spirit pauses. The spiritual infects the physical. For the ancient heroes who represented God in the Middle East, whenever they uttered the name of God, their words and the sound of them spread that name into or onto the land they possessed. The reverse of what took place when Cain shed Abel's blood was beginning to happen. Bits of the world were cleansed. What was given to Moses in the desert has continued to infect the earth with holiness in the minds of millions of people.

It is no longer necessary for Ultimate Holiness to be signified by those four Hebrew letters. Instead we are using words for God in Arabic, Greek, Latin, English, French, German, Russian, Chinese, and Hindi and all the rest, and all humans are struggling to give the Sacred a perfect expression in ordinary lives and on the properties where we build our homes.

Religion began to happen with the earliest humans who carefully buried their fathers so that they might be with *their* fathers who were god-figures for them. Those early god-figures lost their particular names, and were known only as "gods" in a variety of languages.

Religious thinkers and writers have pictured the lives and accomplishments, the deaths and failures of human beings in a never-ending variety of ways. The Greek poet Homer told the story of Trojan heroes who defended Troy and Greek heroes who besieged it. He is also credited with tracing the adventures of Odysseus as that hero returned to his home in Ithaca. The Latin poet Virgil celebrated the legendary founder of Rome, the Trojan Aeneas, and traced his voyages across the Mediterranean. These heroes not only attempted to right perceived wrongs done to their kindred but succeeded in establishing new social orders in the ancient Mediterranean world. It happened in Mesopotamia, Egypt, and Canaan before Abraham, Moses, Joshua, the Judges, and the Kings and the prophets.

The Hebrew Scriptures tell of a journey that led to the birth of a people and of the adventures of the founding ancestors of ancient Israel, but Israel's story is distinct in several ways. For one thing the journey of Abram/Abraham and Sarai/Sarah was over land; instead of the natural perils of a trackless sea the ancestors of Israel followed paths which people—and animals—had trodden and marked for others to follow.

Ancient epic journeys began from places where people had already lived, and the migrant looked forward to "a place that he was to receive as an inheritance," as a

Moses and the Name of God: Israel's Hero Tale

New Testament author put it (Hebrews 11:8). Along the way Israel's ancestors, like the builders of Athens, Rome, Ur, and Babylon, had to work out relationships with those who already lived there. How was Abram to know if "this" was to be the place for his heirs? And how would he displace people who already lived in the area? Would his descendants find ways to live with the survivors of an initial conquest?

It seems the early Israelites, particularly in the time of the Judges, used to go into battle shouting the name of their God in an abbreviated form, "Yo!" partly as a prayer for God's help in getting rid of the alien natives of the land, and as it turned out partly to frighten the enemy with their god's power. It worked! At least for a while it worked, until the Philistines decided they could fight as well as those savage Israelites.

It continued to happen when a Jew named Jesus could use the generic word "god" and the title "lord" at the dawn of the Christian era, and his apostle could take the name "Jesus Christ" into the conquered lands of the Roman Empire. But this new name was not that of a savage warrior. Jesus offered forgiveness instead of punishment for the violence between people, and in the name of Jesus people in the Roman world bowed to God and found a submissive peace to replace the *pax Romana*—for a while.

In Egypt and Western Europe Christian priests enclosed bits of land for monasteries dedicated as centers of holiness, and in the Middle East only the Arabic word for God, Allah, carried on the tradition of a holy deity and his community into mosques in northern Africa and Spain. In the new world English settlers set up intentional holy states on the coast of North America and Spanish priests did the same thing in the southwest and much of Central and South America.

All this development started when a name for a particularly active God, or as monotheists believe, for the only real god, was let loose in Egypt to make things happen for an expanding, extending chosen community.

24

More Hero Tales

To trace the path from our stories toward the kingdom of God we pause for a look at Joseph Campbell's book, *The Hero with a Thousand Faces*. The thesis of which is "that myth is the secret opening through which the inexhaustible energies of the cosmos pour into human cultural manifestation."[1]

Campbell traces and analyzes the hero's quest through dozens of mythic stories familiar to readers of the world's literary heritage, and concludes:

> The modern hero, the modern individual who dares to heed the call and seek the mansion of that presence with whom it is our whole destiny to be atoned, cannot, indeed must not, wait for his community to cast off its slough of pride, fear, rationalized avarice, and sanctified misunderstanding. "Live," Nietzsche says, "as though the day were here." It is not society that is to guide and save the creative hero, but precisely the reverse. And so every one of us shares the supreme ordeal—carries the cross of the redeemer—not in the bright moments of his tribe's great victories, but in the silences of his personal despair.[2]

The covenantal paradigm whose operation we have been tracing is like the quest of the hero, who seeks a secular at-one-ment, a joining together of the jagged pieces of living persons in groups through the largely "natural" energies of ordinary life.

Most biblical heroes, like the dozens Campbell notices, emerge from a population in distress, confront the cause of that distress, and successfully overcome it, in effect bringing "salvation" for the sons of Israel in the setting of their times. The possible configurations of these stories are almost infinite, but we can see within the figures a pattern of the hero's experience. Structurally the hero story has essential features of other stories, an initial unhappy situation and the movement toward delivery from it, as the hero approaches the heart of the problem. What makes it mythic is the oversize nature of the problem and the hero's exceptional success or tragic failure in dealing with it.

---

1. Campbell, *The Hero with a Thousand Faces*, 3.
2. Ibid., 362.

Historic and legendary individuals whose socio-ethical roles fitted the elemental paradigm of human relationships led the way. Campbell's heroes perform their labors in mythical or legendary situations, while biblical writers located most of their stories in settings their readers could recognize and identify. Mythical features were regularly historicized, i.e., made to appear more intensely historical than those of many hero tales. Abraham, Jacob, Joseph, Moses, Ruth, Jonah, and Esther are pictured as acting in historical times and places, even though secular historians have found no corroborating evidence of their existence. They nevertheless exemplify virtues significant to Jews and Christians to this day. Those ancient virtues manifested themselves and can be recognized as psychosocial "strengths" which always tread a narrow path of achievement between domination and impotence.

Biblical heroes did not act alone in many of the stories: Abram/Abraham traveled with Sarai/Sarah; Isaac married Rebekah after she was brought by the senior servant from the land from which Abraham had come; Jacob himself sought and found Rachel after traveling alone; Ruth found Boaz after committing herself to accompany Naomi for the rest of her life. Little covenants with women supported the men in their ventures.

The first son of Jacob's favorite wife, Joseph, was born later than the sons of Leah and the two concubines, and appears as a naive adolescent who dreams of superiority over his brothers, and even over his parents. Seen as a rival to his brothers' future greatness, Joseph was packed off to slavery in Egypt where, like Ulysses, he withstood sexual temptation, and was cast into prison in spite of his virtue. As the mythical heroes descended into the nether regions before being helped to return, Joseph was brought out of prison to give the Pharaoh wise advice as to how to save the Egyptian nation from the periodic famines that afflicted them. His adolescent dream of power over his brothers and his parents was fulfilled beyond any imagining as he was reconciled with his family.

During and after the exile Jews and a few converts to Judaism could tell the story of heroic individuals who had met the challenges of the new situation that resulted from their ancestors' sexual, warlike, and sinful behavior. Out of this history emerged the concept of a future shaped by heroic men and women selected not by chance but by a designing God. The seeds of monotheistic theology and ethical religion can be traced to the hiatus between Israel's life early in Canaan and a remnant's evolving development as a faith community in the midst of great empires. That hiatus was bridged by priests who guided Jews returning from foreign slavery to confess the sins of their community and find atonement—a "covering" for sin—through rituals of prayer and sacrifice. For Campbell, however, "atonement" is the bringing together of human spirits who have been separated as a result of abusive actions. Biblical atonement is both process and the result of a sacrificial ritual that "covers" whatever has tainted the sinful community. In the "Confession of '67" Presbyterians are broadening the concept of atonement to include the social reconciliation that emerges from Biblical atonement as sacrificial ritual "covers" whatever has tainted the persons of the sinning community.

Part 5: In the Perspective of Hero Tales

Legendary and historic individuals whose socio-ethical roles fitted the elemental paradigm of human relationships led the way. In chapter 5 named individuals acted as both givers and receivers in the economic paradigm. In chapter 19 the abstract personal figures of the diagram are clothed with the full range of psychosocial strengths as they emerge into our four dimensional world. In this chapter four legendary individuals, whose socio-ethical roles fitted the elemental paradigm of human relationships, led the way as Jews left their Babylonian exile, and set out in a new exodus to resettle the land promised to Abraham, where they would have one more opportunity to fulfill the destiny of being a great nation.

A Missionary Hero

The first figure in this set is heroic, but not for his own people! Unlike the suffering Servant or Queen Esther who endured their trials for exiled Jews, Jonah was called, like a missionary, to preach to the principal enemy of his people. The legend is set at a time when Nineveh was the capital of the great empire that was poised to take the northern kingdom of Israel into slavery and to threaten Hezekiah's capital in Jerusalem. It was to Nineveh, as the tale goes, that Jonah was called to preach. Amos had repeated YHWH's invectives against nearer enemies, Damascus, Gaza, Ashdod, and Tyre, but had done so from the relative security of Samaria or Judean Tekoa, but Jonah must travel to challenge the supreme dragon in Nineveh, capital of the all-conquering Assyrian empire.

Jonah is the perfect example of the hero who refuses his call. Instead of retracing in reverse the steps that led Abraham and Jacob from the east to Canaan, Jonah turned to the Mediterranean and took ship for Tarshish, modern Spain. Threatened with shipwreck like the Greek hero Odysseus, Jonah asked to be thrown overboard so that he might save his shipmates by drowning. God, however, intervened with near supernatural aid, and a monstrous fish swallowed him and returned him to dry land, from which he obeyed a second command from YHWH and proceeded to Nineveh.

"Forty days more, and Nineveh shall be overthrown!" Jonah cried out, probably hoping to see the Assyrians and himself destroyed. But to his dismay "the people of Nineveh believed God; they proclaimed a fast, and everyone, great and small, put on sackcloth." (3:4–5) Even the king of this semi-mythical people, whose name the story teller may not have known or considered important, "removed his robe, covered himself with sackcloth, and sat in ashes." Jonah had assumed a covenantal mission for YHWH, and the Assyrian king and people gave God what He asked for.

Mission accomplished, Jonah was even more distressed. In his anger he asked why YHWH had called him to deliver the message to a people so ready to repent. Like Job, he asked YHWH to end his life, but YHWH responded with a reproving question, "Is it right for you to be angry?"

This angry and rebellious servant who should have been the hero of the tale, made a shelter for himself outside the city and waited to see what would happen. "YHWH God"—the author uses both Judean name and Israelite generic noun—added to the shelter by producing a vine, which was soon attacked by a worm and a hot east wind so that it withered.

YHWH has the last word, which boils down to a rhetorical question: "Should I not be concerned about Nineveh?" The logical answer completes the syllogism: of course the Creator of everything is rightfully concerned for anything God has created, *even if that creature has sinned*. YHWH always has the view from heaven.

God cares, but instead of intervening directly to deliver people from the forces and beings that afflict them, God calls heroes to serve as instruments of deliverance, as teachers of correcting Torah, as negotiators of good will, as prophetic voices, and as the doers of many other helpful tasks. In the larger picture of the Hebrew scriptures Jonah might have seen that the fall of Israel-Ephraim to Assyria would be reproof—not punishment—for Israel's sins. YHWH God also cared about the people of Nineveh whose king had led them into *their* sinning.

Jonah was not the last of the prophets. In 1935 the philosopher John Dewey wrote *A Common Faith*, which argues that a common "religious" view of God is more important for today than the establishing of a particular religion. Instead he recognized what Jonah did not see: "The artist, scientist, citizen, parent, as far as they are actuated by the spirit of their callings, are controlled by the unseen . . . The inherent vice of all intellectual schemes of idealism is that they convert the idealism of action into a system of beliefs about antecedent reality. The character assigned this reality is so different from that which observation and reflection lead to and support that these schemes inevitably glide into alliance with the supernatural."[3]

Jonah may not have wanted the Ninevites to convert and become servants of Israelite YHWH, but their faith only asked forgiveness from an inscrutable God for their sins and deliverance from destruction. Is Jonah the model for many westerners today who would like to see Muslims out of Western Europe, England, and America?

A Heroine with an Attitude

In the latest moments of the exile another representative, a unique Jewish woman, stands out as the savior of her people as they struggled to survive in the Persian Empire. Like the story of Joseph in Genesis, the story of Esther can be construed as a fictional tale in which a not insignificant member of the Hebrew community providentially appeared "for such a time as this" to deliver her people from total destruction. Her story includes remarkable accomplishments with exaggerated results, and links her personal fortune with the long-term well being of the Jews. Her adventurous journey was from obscurity to the royal palace, where she challenged the supreme power of the empire.

Esther was the niece or cousin of a Jew living in Susa, the capital of the Persian Empire. When Vashti, the wife of Ahasuerus (Xerxes), refused to "show the people and the nobles her beauty" at his banquet celebrating the magnificence of his reign, the emperor deposed his queen, and his servants organized a beauty pageant to choose a

3. Dewey, *A Common Faith*, 23–24.

replacement (Esther 1). This meant that when Mordecai entered his niece in the contest, she would spend one night with the emperor to see if she "pleased" him, probably in the full range of pleasures that Scheherazade provided to save her life. As it turned out, Esther was chosen, and became the queen, subject however to the rules governing her position in the royal harem.

As yet only Mordecai knows of Esther's Jewish heritage (and name Hadassah). Mordecai happens to learn of a plot to assassinate the emperor, tells Esther to notify the king, and as a result the would-be assassins are hanged. Meanwhile a palace official named Haman has been promoted to a position of such honor that the king commands people to bow to him at the entrance to the palace. Mordecai refuses to bow to a fellow human and Haman vows to exterminate not only Mordecai but also all Jews in the kingdom.

The storyteller tells us how Esther must proceed to approach the king to intercede for her people's survival, and she finally succeeds in having Haman executed, all according to the "law of the Medes and Persians." When Jews read the book of Esther aloud as they celebrate the feast of Purim, they do so with special relish and hand clapping at the triumph of Esther and Mordecai. "The Jew [Mordecai] was next in rank to King Ahasuerus, and he was powerful among the Jews and popular with his many kindred, for he sought the good of his people and interceded for the welfare of all his descendants" (Esth 10:3).

Aside from the heroic elements in the story our interest is in the way the Persian emperor was bound by the "law of the Medes and Persians." When Vashti refused to come at the king's command, "the king consulted with the [seven] sages who knew the laws (1:13)," and they reported that not only had Vashti done wrong, but also "This very day the noble ladies of Persia and Media who have heard of the queen's behavior will rebel against the king's officials, and there will be no end of contempt and wrath!" (1:18). The biblical pattern of law as regulator of social structure and behavior, but against which it is possible to rebel has been discovered at the highest levels of the Persian court. Persia appears almost as a constitutional monarchy.

In the clarity of life subject to the rigid laws of a foreign power Jews, and even a Persian queen, must pick their way carefully to survive. But the willingness of a queenly savior, an individualist, to risk her life on behalf of the enclave[4] of her people, together with the king's love for her, accomplished the deliverance of Jews throughout the empire. Incidentally, the story refers twice to the extensive and efficient mail system established to hold this increasingly literate empire together and communicate its laws throughout its far-flung provinces. The author of the book of Esther was impressed.

Rebellion was the criminal sin to which the story directs our attention. Neither of the queens nor the emperor are noticed for the possible impurities of their sexual behavior. Living in a harem supervised by eunuchs, both queens had little opportunity for sexual sin. Vashti, however, was guilty of disobeying her husband's command to expose herself and thus set a bad example for other women.

---

4 Mary Douglas, *In the Wilderness*, 44 discusses enclaves as one of four types or "ways in which individuals can organize themselves into a community."

Esther followed court protocol, but intended revenge against the enemies of her people. The possible punishment of a whole people is predicated on the behavior of Mordecai, who disobeyed the king's command to bow before Haman. In retaliation the emperor—the Highest Power and the person nearest to providing a divine perspective on human events mentioned in the book—authorized the Jews to hang the ten sons of Haman and to "defend their lives" and kill "seventy-five thousand of those who hated them" (9:16). The storyteller adds that virtuously the Jews "laid no hands on the plunder."

According to this little book Esther's actions brought economic and political "good" to the Jewish people. Also a more realistic, less mythical, version of the story may have brought them a grudging respect among their neighbors in the Persian Empire. But the revenge Esther launched is far from the Spirit that inspired the story of Jonah. Triumphing heroes are remembered by sympathetic kindred, friends, and acquaintances. But a modern skepticism about details and a Christian ethic properly question whether the God and Father of Jesus Christ could have approved the way the murderous episode reached its climax.

A Deeply Distressed Heroic Figure

The third figure in this series of thought experiments is Job. As pictured in the opening chapters of the book that bears his name, Job lived as an independent patriarch somewhere in the Middle East surrounded by his clan but not out of touch with other clans, whose patriarchal figures would come to visit him in his distress. The problem with which he had to deal came to him, so he made no journey. With God's approval his property and his health were taken from him, and then his friends added to his woes with their advice.

The story begins with a conversation between God and a high level Antagonist whose assignment had apparently been to report the behavior of humans. When God asks if the District Attorney has considered his servant Job, the two agree to set up a test of Job's character, which has thus far appeared to be "blameless and upright." (1:1) The Tempter has authority to strip Job of all his possessions, his security, and his health, and he proceeds to do just that.

In his distress Job rejects his wife's advice to "curse God and die." The book's author considered this a supreme act of rebellion and/or an unforgivable act of impiety. But Job only curses the day of his birth, essentially wishing he had never been born. Since he does not attempt suicide, but only wishes his destiny had been a stillbirth, his wish is no sin.

Patiently Job listens and responds to his friends for thirty-four chapters as they argue that he must have committed some sin. In their statements the friends present the substance of conventional religion as it was understood in the ancient world. Toward the end Job challenges God to respond to *his* questions, and from chapter 38 to the end of the book God and Job discuss the larger issues of God's creative activity in the world. It turns out it is the three friends who need an atoning ritual, since they "have not spoken of me what is right." but when they do as directed, "the Lord accepted Job's prayer" (42:8–9).

In his play, *J.B.*, Archibald McLeish reduces the whirlwind from which God speaks to a modern Job's internalized advice to himself to "blow on the coals of my heart" as he begins his new life after the tragic loss of his family and wealth. In the biblical book, however, Job only confesses:

> I know that you can do all things,
> and that no purpose of yours can be thwarted.
> 'Who is this that hides counsel without knowledge?'
> Therefore I have uttered what I did not understand,
> things too wonderful for me, which I did not know. (42:1–2)

In human circumstances ignorance of the law may not excuse a crime, but it is not a sin to have heard of God only "by the hearing of the ear." When Job recognized God in the whirlwind of chapter 40 he did not die, as the ancient Hebrews superstitiously expected. Instead he only "despised" himself. In this context "despising" meant recognizing how little he understood God, and seeing God meant a nonmaterial image in his mind, essentially an awareness of God's presence. The anger of YHWH is not against Job, but requires his friends, like Jonah's Ninevites, to bring whole burnt offerings that Job will offer as prayers to deal with their "folly." The book dodges questions of the friends' sin, suggesting only that their "folly" was not speaking of YHWH what is right, as Job had done. Nobody is punished, though Job has suffered. His friends have been reproved.

After his prayer for his friends, Job is blessed by the Lord; his brothers and sisters and "all who had known him" visit him in his house and each receives "a piece of money." The writer/editor of the book declares, "in all the land there were no women so beautiful as Job's daughters." Job lives on to see four generations of his descendants before dying "old and full of days" (42:10–15).

Job is not a "suffering servant of YHWH," nor was he clearly related to Abraham. His sufferings do not "cover" anyone's sin. Pointing to many modern examples, William Safire labels him *The First Dissident*. He was simply an exemplary religious man, selected or randomly chosen by God to endure more than what others have suffered. Like the Israelites, others may have had "sins" to confess, but Job heroically maintained his innocence, confessed his ignorance, and survived. As a result his friends could also survive, and his tribe could be saved with a new family. How "orthodox" was his theological thought in the debate with his friends?

An Abused Servant with a Heroic Mission

Among the figures of Israel's historic destiny is one without a name, the "Suffering Servant." The prophet of the exile, commonly called Second Isaiah or Deutero-Isaiah (DI), took a fresh look at his people and their prospects when the Persian king Cyrus took charge of Babylon apparently in a non-violent coup, supported by the priests of Marduk. Their Israelite ancestors had heard the call to the adventure of a nation building experiment, but had displeased YHWH with their idolatries, refused the call and built two nations, each creating a part of the pattern of just and holy life God intended.

When Cyrus began a process of restoring the various idols captured by the Babylonians to their native shrines, this second Isaiah saw the end of YHWH's corrective treatment in the exile and a possible return to Jerusalem for Jews in Babylon. If his people would accept the offer of the Persian emperor and establish a faithful community in Jerusalem, he saw an end to the humiliation of life in Babylon. The whole of Isaiah 40–55 can be read as the proclamation of a Messianic program in which the prophet advances an argument to convince Jews to leave Babylon and return to Jerusalem. This is one aspect of the thesis of Antti Laato's thoughtful study *The Servant of YHWH and Cyrus: a Reinterpretation of the Exilic Messianic Programme in Isaiah 40–55*. Campbell might see the events of the last quarter of the sixth century BCE in terms of the hero myth, while Laato sees the Second Isaiah writing prophetic poetry with obedient Israel as servant of YHWH and potential hero.

Reviewing and interpreting Israel's history in broad strokes, the prophet announces (1) the completion of Israel's period of disciplinary correction for her sins:

> Comfort, O comfort my people,
> says your God.
> Speak tenderly to Jerusalem,
> and cry to her
> that she has served her term,
> that her penalty is paid,
> that she has received from the Lord's hand
> double for all her sins (40:1–2).

and (2) the mission of an obedient "servant of YHWH" to bring justice to the nations:

> Here is my servant, whom I uphold,
> my chosen, in whom my soul delights;
> I have put my spirit upon him;
> he will bring forth justice to the nations (42:1).

The prophet portrays the faithful servant's contribution to the welfare of his people in contrast to the maker of an idol who could just as well burn the wood and warm himself. (44:16) From the womb of disobedient Israel YHWH was calling a faithful Israel "in whom I [YHWH] will be glorified" (49:3,6) and the tribes of Israel will be restored. At the same time the surprising news is that the Servant will be a "light to the nations" (49:5; 51:4), but evidently not a conquering king. In accomplishing his mission the Servant is "despised and rejected," while being "wounded for our transgressions" (53:3,5). Although it evidently was "the will of the Lord to crush him with pain," nevertheless, "through him the will of the Lord shall prosper" (53:10). Writing the words of YHWH, the prophet concludes:

> Therefore I will allot him a portion with the great.
> and he shall divide the spoil with the strong;

> because he poured out himself to death,
> and was numbered with the transgressors;
> yet he bore the sin of many,
> and made intercession for the transgressors. (53:13)

What the prophet heard and saw was to be a near miraculous transformation from pain and rejection to healing and the making righteous not only of the mysterious Servant, but also of the nameless "many" (53:11). Through a humiliating sacrificial offering of the Servant's life for sin YHWH would accomplish his purpose. The exilic priests who glimpsed the miracle of forgiveness for rebellious Israel through ritual were joined by the prophet of the exile who saw the experience of the faithful servant as a sacrificial offering and covering atonement for sin.[5]

Typical features of historic figures appear to be interwoven in the imaginative creation of this figure, such as king Josiah's untimely death when he intervened between Pharaoh Neco's army and the Babylonians at Carchemish (2 Chr 35:20–25). Joseph also, whose brothers sold him into slavery, was such a redemptive ancestor to the most populous of the Israelite tribes. From his prison he rose to save Egypt and his family from seasons of famine, and was able to forgive them and restore the unity of the family of Israel. James D. Smart insists that the references to Cyrus in chapters 44 and 45 are an intrusion after the fact by an annotator, whom I see as one who experienced the return of Jews to Jerusalem.[6]

Understanding the Exile's Meaning

In chapter 20 our interest was in the application of paradoxical forgiveness to individual and family life, but as the exile came to an end, forgiveness extended into national life, as earlier personal experiences affected the stages of Israelite development. Covenantal behaviors at every level are the result of social intercourse—verbal or nonverbal exchanges—in which individuals come to terms about their giving and receiving. Recall the discussion in chapter 6 about Jacob's relationships with the families of his father and uncle. Sexual relationships are only a small part of living. What is important is the way in which two people, tribes, or nations who have misunderstood and injured each other can become reconciled by mutual forgiveness—following the paradigm of granting and receiving.

In the early Israelite stories, the sexual affairs of Judah, Shechem, Samson, and David, unconventional as they were, were not the cause of the deaths that followed. Instead they were features of a complex web of life and death relationships. What appeared evil from one point of view could appear good in a broader perspective. We may judge that it was wrong for the first Tamar to become pregnant by her father-in-law. Leviticus 20:14, not yet in tune with the reproof of Leviticus 19:18, would declare, "both of them shall be put to death; they have committed perversion, their blood is

---

5. In his monograph Laato developed these ideas, but did not make the connection with Levitical forgiveness.

6. Smart, *History and Theology in Second Isaiah*, 120.

upon them." Yet apparently that union was accepted by God and produced an ancestor of King David and also of Jesus the son of Mary. The social meme, which called for punitive treatment, was set aside by a community feeling that it was not right in the sight of God to execute a man who had been tricked into doing what he should have done, to provide a husband for an obviously fertile young woman. A higher duty to the God of life transcended the social rule against incest, perhaps because in this instance the incest was unwitting.

David's sin involved adultery and murder, but after losing the child of her illicit union, Bath Sheba bore Solomon. Because of the blood on his hands David was not allowed to build a house for YHWH, but Bath Sheba's son Solomon could celebrate the Temple's completion and enjoy the blessings YHWH showered on him. Amnon brought serious trouble into David's family and the only apparent good that emerged was that two rivals to Solomon were publicly disqualified. What may be considered sins had mixed effects on the course of biblical history. Divine intervention through the prophet Nathan brought attention to the wrong, and God *reproved* David with the death of Bath Sheba's first son. Forgiveness continued a sequence of events of more value to Israel than an immediate execution of David.

As the rebellious "Servant of the Lord" neither Israel nor its kings and priests had brought forth the light of justice to the nations (Isa 42:1,3; 49) nor raised up the fallen tribes of Israel. Now through the miracle of God's forgiveness, Torah (NRSV "a teaching") would:

> go out from me [YHWH],
> and my justice [can or will][7] be for a light to the peoples.
> I will bring near my deliverance swiftly,
> my salvation has gone out
> and my arms will rule the peoples;
> the coastlands wait for me,
> and for my arm they hope (51:4–5).

The afterthoughts of Isaiah 40–55 do not relinquish dreams of empire, but appear to assign its human leadership to Cyrus, armed, anointed and called by name:

> whose right hand I have grasped
> to subdue nations before him
> and strip kings of their robes,
> to open doors before him . . . (45:1).

With Cyrus managing empire "for the sake of my servant Jacob," the faithful descendants of Abraham could emerge from the structured Persian empire to bring light and salvation to a Gentile world:

> Turn to me and be saved,

---

7. The NRSV translates this stanza as determined futures, "will be" etc., but we should remember that "can," "may," and "might" are also possible. At this point there is no verb in the nominal sentence, but the theology of a determining God has led the English translators to insert one. Of course verbs in past tense represent realized history.

all the ends of the earth!
For I am God, and there is no other. (45:22)

The Servant was rebellious in the past, but now becomes a destined deliverer of the people who had been brought to Babylon in shame, and one who would go forth to serve YHWH "in joy, and be led back in peace." (55:12) Repeatedly, when YHWH's beloved people had rebelled against God's leading and had become mired in corruption, YHWH had reversed the human course with a fresh start, and had waited to see how the chosen humans would carry on the intended plan.

Like Campbell's *Hero with a Thousand Faces*, biblical heroes suffered great afflictions, touched mighty forces, found supernatural aid, and achieved great victories or received great rewards for their faithfulness. If they appear extraordinarily afflicted, it is because the biblical historians contrasted human sin with the ever-present healing Source of their powers.

One More Hero Story

One of the most illuminating of Campbell's hero stories concerns a young prince who, having completed his military studies, set out with the title Prince Fiveweapons to return to his royal father. Advised that the forest through which he must pass was inhabited by an ogre named Sticky-hair, Prince Fiveweapons entered the forest confidently. Challenged by the ogre, the prince used every weapon, but each stuck in the ogre's hair. Frustrated but not daunted, the prince resorted to kicking and beating, but each hand and foot and his own head became stuck in the ogre's sticky hair.

Thus far a reader familiar with Joel Chandler Harris's fable of Br'er Rabbit and the Tar Baby enjoys the caricature of the stubborn political leader who sends his troops into an endless war. The Oriental tale, however, does not end at this point. The ogre begins to think, saying to himself, "This is some lion of a man, some man of noble birth—no mere man! For although he has been caught by an ogre like me, he appears neither to tremble nor to quake! In the time I have harried this road, I have never seen a single man to match him!"

When he asks the youth why he is not afraid, the prince replies, "Ogre, why should I be afraid? For in one life one death is absolutely certain. What's more, I have in my belly a thunderbolt for weapon. If you eat me, you will not be able to digest that weapon. It will tear your insides into tatters and fragments and will kill you. In that case we'll both perish. That's why I'm not afraid!"

Professor Campbell concludes by reminding the reader that Prince Fiveweapons "was referring to the Weapon of Knowledge that was within him. Indeed, this young hero was none other than the Future Buddha in an early incarnation."[8] Instead of hearing the story as the Buddhist legend or an amusing children's fable, we may hear it as a celebration of calm and rational, left brain thinking in the presence of danger. The weapon of rational thought may be seen *either* as God's deepest contribution to

---

8. Campbell, *The Hero with a Thousand Faces*, 79–82.

human survival *or* as the supreme accomplishment of jiggling cosmic energy.[9] Torah, prophetic vision and oracle, supplement the wisdom of the wise in every people, but the believer sees the "outstretched arm" of God acting to fulfill God's design.

It is this wisdom that unites the heroic tales of the Hebrew Scriptures. Joseph's dreams were God's guidance for his people and for Egypt, offering a way forward from distress. Jonah's preaching offered forgiveness to Israel's powerful enemy. Esther's willingness to sacrifice her virtue, offer her life to save her people from a legitimized massacre, and face supreme power cloaked in law, brought respect for YHWH to Gentiles. Job's arguments persisted in rejecting the community verdict of sinful guilt for a relatively innocent family man. Isaiah's prophetic poems promised "good news to the oppressed . . . liberty to the captives, and release to the prisoners. (61:1) Jesus faced his crucifixion with greater understanding than his hero predecessors and gave his life "like a sheep led to the slaughter," as the evangelist Philip explained to a eunuch from Ethiopia, as he gave a name to the suffering servant in Acts 8:35. They all lived by *faith,* as the eleventh chapter of the New Testament essay addressed to Jewish Christians declares.

What can be characterized as cultural experiments emerging from God-inspired minds of individuals or groups, Joseph Campbell calls the hero's adventure. The venture of the Suffering Servant became historical to the eye of faith when followers of Christ wrote the Christian New Testament and identified the Galilean evangelist with the expected Messiah of first-century Judaism. Rituals of baptismal washing and sharing bread and wine assure today's followers of Jesus that sins are forgiven and reconciliation is possible through covenantal giving and receiving of personal care. Are not the essential elements of trust in Supreme Reconciling Power also present in the faith stories of Jewish, Muslim, Buddhist, and other believers?

How much broader is the conception of salvation presented in these stories of transfigured ordinary life than in medieval deathbed confessions motivated by fear of hell! Structural and community sin, however defined, as well as personal guilt are the seedbed from which saving deliverance arises in every generation. One can only marvel at the radical and lasting personal conversions that occur under the simplest and most naive retelling of these stories.

---

9. In his introduction to physics, *Six Easy Pieces*, Richard Feynman uses the term "jiggle" for the perpetual fine scale activity of everything physical.

25

Creatio ex Nihilo, Imago Dei, and Talk with God

Two Latin expressions from medieval theological investigations serve as part of the title for the final questions about the covenantal relationships, practical, personal, and spiritual with which human beings have always been concerned. The third expression is appropriately in simple English.

This epilogue is an "afterthought," or an appendix, to answer questions about belief in God. It is intended for people who were brought up in traditional bible and gospel centered churches and/or who began to ask questions but did not feel inclined to give up their faith. It is not likely to answer a humanist's questions, but it may encourage a reader to ask without fear that you will be packed off to hell or flung into outer space. I do not believe in the popular images of heaven and hell, nor literally in either of the two pictures of creation found in the early chapters of Genesis, but I do believe that God has lodged much wisdom in the Hebrew scriptures for living our present lives.

Our first chapters set out to discuss the three topics, "Sex, War, and Sin" that intrigued me as I reread stories in the book Christians call the Old Testament: the English translations referred repeatedly to "the Lord" (*YHWH* in unvocalized Hebrew), but also to generic "God," not as two entities but as One whose special name had been revealed to ancient Israel. Here is a sketchy picture of God as seen through the lenses of the Hebrew Scriptures and my experience.

The Entity or Being known to ancient Israelites as YHWH God was a central participant in the story of Israel's rise, fall, and restoration as well as in the lives of certain heroic individuals. In addition to telling Israel's story biblical writers and their editors presented fleeting glimpses of actions from the creation of the world to their own times, sometimes designating "God," "YHWH God," or simply "YHWH" as the agent responsible for an activity.

Walter Brueggemann's *Theology of the Old Testament* focuses on Israel's testimonies regarding "Yahweh," as well as the literary embodiments of its testimony regarding the God of ancient Israel. Brueggemann discusses at some length the hiddenness, ambiguity, and character of YHWH and the tension between Israel's core testimony and an interwoven counter testimony which biblical editors preserved. Yet he seldom states his personal faith as distinct from either of Israel's testimonies, except when he proposes a continuing community of interpretation, which may be understood as modern personal and unsolicited testimonies about God. This chapter is one more unsolicited testimony about God.

At some moments I have taken sides, accepting or rejecting elements of the witness of the Hebrew scriptures within the horizon of my reading and thought, but always subject to reconsideration when seemingly contrary ideas loom into focus. This is a "now" statement, incomplete, but of a vital faith. It is not a traditional Southern Presbyterian, Westminster Standards declaration, but I hope will be seen as a benign and healthy growth descended from that tradition. Particularly, I wanted to define "sin" in functional terms, but here the question is whether "God" must also be spoken about in empirical terms, influenced by contemporary science, and beyond conventional creedal statements.

Creation

Chapter 21 began with a look at the two biblical stories of beginnings, and I noted that implicit in Genesis 1:2 is a rejection of the long held idea that God's creative activity began in a total void. Instead, without specifying any pre-existing materials, the biblical story begins with the Voice of a Spirit who could command steps of creative activity. Instead of thinking only of stellar evolution, I believe the metaphor of spoken commands to order chaos is appropriate to speak of our beginnings. Commands are given to beings who can obey them. Who could obey the command, "let there be light?" One traditional answer is "Chaos."

Chaos is *not* nothing. If anything, chaos is the undisciplined activity of too many forces whose potentials conflict into uselessness, as the molecules of a gas in a container do nothing but raise the temperature and resist when pressure is applied. The creating Voice evidently brought some order into what the priestly writer believed to have been an undisciplined activity. We cannot tell whether the Voice or the chaos had prior existence since the authors of Genesis and we were not yet created to confirm the observations of the Spirit.[1]

Like other divine beings who appear on the scenes of beginnings current in the cultures of the ancient world,[2] each with little visible background, the Hebrew YHWH God simply occupied center stage and went to work. As the dramatic story proceeded, props appeared at the Voice's commands. Significantly, cosmologists have recently begun to probe not just space-time after the big bang, but the nature of space-time itself, which is the stage for all cosmic activity, whether of a supreme Personal Being or of emerging material entities and their forces. Such speculations may be mind boggling, but some minds are not content without exploring paradoxical ideas.

---

1. Theoretical physicists are currently exploring the idea that space-time itself was created along with the four recognized fundamental forces of our world.

2. And of the new world discovered by sixteenth-century European explorers.

Part 5: In the Perspective of Hero Tales

In *The Book of Nothing: Vacuums, Voids, and the Latest Ideas about the Origins of the Universe*, John D. Barrow explores not only the mathematical origin and usefulness of the *zero* symbol but also the question of whether the cosmos had a beginning, and whether as a consequence it will have an end. The results of Barrow's serious mathematical calculations are summarized in simplified graphs of four possible curves that plot the size of the cosmos in relation to time. Each drawing recognizes the presently observed expansion of the cosmos as a curve turning upward, but identifies a different point for its beginning, none of which are at the null point of the graph. Barrow describes hypothetical situations for conditions that preceded the expansion, three of which are earlier than the zero point on the time dimension of the curve, which may be understood as negative time. For the reader of Genesis that means that the scientist can offer three possible "beginnings" that are beyond the horizon, none of which can be verified by observations made so far. A fourth curve sets the beginning of the expansion of the cosmos in observable time but does not specify any preceding conditions, which is more or less what the first verses of Genesis portray.[3] Nobody, scientist or religionist, has a completely satisfactory answer to the question about God's origin.

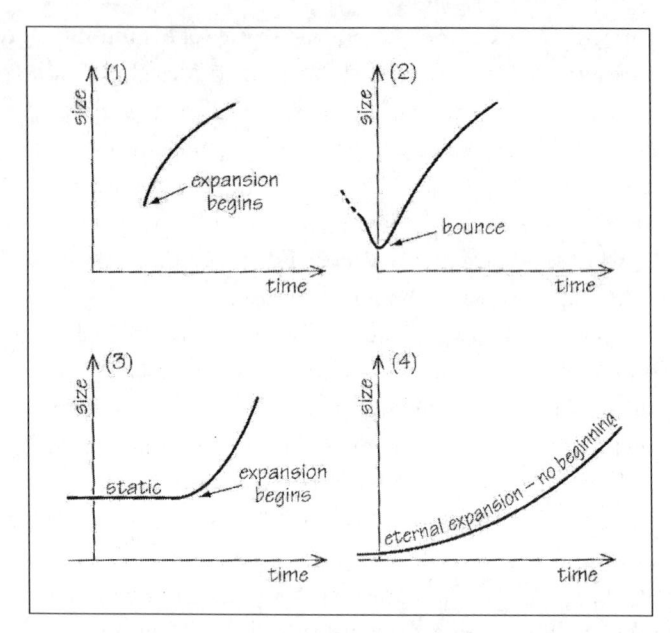

A fundamental question remains in our boggled minds: what had God done before the creation of the cosmos? Or, where was God before the creation of space-time? A "now" implies an actual past and a possible future; is that true also for God? Cosmologists are suggesting that our universe of some forty-two billions of years—as far into space-time as our instruments can probe or as radiation can reach us from the far reaches of space-time—may be only one of many such universes. Scientists are imagining ways of conceptually exploring the possibilities. Would a parallel universe create the same set of atoms from the explosions of supernovas? Are personal and

---

3. Barrow, *The Book of Nothing*, 296f9.6.

Creatio ex Nihilo, Imago Dei, and Talk with God

social as well as material entities emerging in our cosmos or beyond its horizon, by necessity, chance or purpose creating themselves as appears to have happened in the cosmos we know?[4] These questions can be asked by those who believe in a Personal God as well as by those who do not. Barrow retells much of the relevant conceptual development. But where is God when all this is going on?

The idea of creation out of nothing probably originated in ancient Hindu and Buddhist philosophical speculations, which were passed to the western world when the *zero* became a necessary integer for a universally accepted number system. Western thinking, obsessed with the realities of the material world, has difficulty relating to Hindu concepts of non-existence and Nirvana, but speculative thinkers find force fields useful not only in mathematical calculations but in a developing world view.[5]

The question remains: what was happening before the cosmos awoke from the sleep of non-existence or bare material existence, and animate entities discovered the realities and possibilities of the universe in which we live? Did God exist before there was a cosmos?

Instead of asking an ontological question—whether God exists—it now seems preferable to put our questions in pragmatic terms: why do personal beings and physical entities exist and how do they relate to each other? Should we be concerned as to how to relate *to* or *with* an Entity that is or may be immaterial?

Instead of firm answers, whether we approach the questions as believers in the sciences or as religious believers, some of us have no choice but to continue searching for answers to questions about God. Better: how should I seek to improve my relationship with and understanding of an Ultimate Person? Like some writers of the Hebrew scriptures, I am driven by an internal fire to understand the Fire that lighted me.

The Bible, in both its Hebrew and Christian parts, is a story of one people's form of the human quest. Calling themselves "sons of Israel," a peculiar people began with a story of six days of God's creative work followed by one day of rest. Many of us began with that story when parents read or told it in our families and churches, but as we matured we found that some parts of the Story sounded naïve, implausible, and even superstitious. In adolescence I found security and support in the manifestations of the Central Figure of the story. I have seen that Figure in my mind's eye, not in any single manifestation, but through many fleeting glimpses as I followed my calling to study and teach the wisdom of the Hebrew Scriptures with the help of the insights of many colleagues.

The biblical story concerns what the *God Who Acts*[6] did as Abram/Abraham was sent on a heroic quest, and YHWH intervened from time to time both in support of and in opposition to the plans and activities of the people who claimed that He had chosen them. Through the activities of this extended family we get intimations of a Personal Being who allows people to make mistakes, commit sins against each

---

4. Ellis, "Does the Multiverse Really Exist?" 38.
5. In *The Book of Nothing*, John D. Barrow discusses the development of the concept of zero.
6. Appropriately, G. Ernest Wright gave this title to his brief theological essay.

PART 5: In the Perspective of Hero Tales

other, and achieve significant creative actions. Other clusters of humans have told their stories, some of which resemble biblical stories, and we realize that they asked questions similar to ours and found similar answers.

Images or Image?

The images of God projected onto the minds of Bible readers are kaleidoscopic, but can be arranged so as to trace phases of a developing understanding of the Being humans may perceive without seeing physically. Although the material world changes over time, most theologians and believers have declared as an article of faith the unchangeability of the Being represented as Creator. In doing so we acknowledge that we need an ultimate Dependability under the moving picture in our minds, like seeing a house beyond a picket fence from a moving car.

Although the biblical testimony forbids any material representation of God, and modern speculations are limited to verbal and rhetorical descriptions, thoughtful men and women have continued to write creeds for what they have envisioned. Is God changed when we write new descriptions? Hardly! However, although we resist the thought that God is changed by what we think or do, our theologians, scientists, and philosophers are making new statements for new times and contexts. Some of us dare to think that "God" has evolved.[7]

And in spite of ourselves our metaphors, even the most abstract, are based on images. The quanta of modern science can be visualized as both waves and particles, but not one without the other. Mathematics does not help laymen to picture them since we see the two forms as apparently incompatible. Yet in the economy of space-time photons have a calculable mass if not volume.

My imaginary jigsaw puzzle for human activities assumes a viewpoint and at least one theoretical observer outside of space-time, but insists that God is actively at work in the section of the cosmos in which we exist. The problem may be a common human inability to conceive of a non-material entity with the capability of changing material entities, or to reach beyond a cosmos in which nothing is permanent. How can we be sure our thoughts correspond to an Ultimacy beyond our best projections?

The problem may be in the ambiguity of verbal discussions of what we have not seen but may have perceived. Mathematically minded cosmologists may be satisfied with their formulas and graphs which reduce details to simple curved lines, and we might visualize God drawing graphs for formulas that would establish a creation yet to take place in a yet uncreated empty space. Barrow, however, does not allow an empty space, but resorts to his simplifying graphs that represent the effect of recognizable forces.

Using language of twenty-first century cosmologists, Ken Wilber titled a brief essay *A Theory of Everything*, which is what any serious theology attempts. Wilber has room in his grid for a range of human thought from ancient superstition to modern speculative science, economics, philosophy, and theology and their practical

7. See Wright, *The Evolution of God*.

Creatio ex Nihilo, Imago Dei, and Talk with God

expressions in individual and social forms, past, present, and even in hypothetical futures. It is not a depreciation of his work to point out that he does not locate "God" in his grid. Like Solomon's temple, no theology—i.e., talk about God—can contain God. One alternative is to declare that God contains the grid along with other theoretical and material structures. Solomon or the writer who composed his dedicatory prayer appears to have vaguely recognized that possibility, but may have been satisfied with leaving God free to come into the Temple and retire to heaven after visits to the building that Tyrian workers had built.

Parenthetically, one may question whether any worshipper who spent a night in an ancient temple or visited a holy place like Delphi to receive a vision or audition believed he was visiting a resident deity or awaiting a visit from the deity. The meeting, probably with a resident deity, and the message were what was important, not whether the deity came to or lived in the shrine. Theologically the question distinguishes a deity's *immanence* (presence in the world) from *transcendence* (presence beyond the world or in "heaven"). Is there a third alternative? Consider what follows a possibility.

Solomon's prayer of dedication does not necessarily require the actual or continuous presence of God in the Temple in Jerusalem. Instead the Temple resembles an extremely sensitive microphone or telephone terminal that is capable of connecting calls to God from any human situation. It is worth noting that not only Israelites but foreigners who know God's name can make such calls: "Likewise when a foreigner, who is not of your people Israel, comes from a distant land because of your name—for they shall hear of your great name, your mighty hand, and your outstretched arm—when a foreigner comes and prays toward the house, then hear in heaven your dwelling place and do according to all that the foreigner calls to you so that all the peoples of the earth may know your name and fear you" (1 Kgs 8:41–43).

Here "name" means fame, and becomes the ticket for access to YHWH God, or the code to use when the operator asks "Number please?" Solomon's temple was the entrance to a real "not of this world" source of Power, like but unlike the strengths that fight battles, build skyscrapers, and organize corporations. What can we say about this Power? And is it still possible to make such calls?

Dynamic Spirit

Dispensing with material models, I am inclined to follow the wisest of the ancient biblical writers and view God as *nearly immaterial* Spirit, an inescapable entity with *almost no body*:

> Where can I go from your spirit?
> Or where can I flee from your presence?
> If I ascend to heaven, you are there,
> If I make my bed in Sheol, you are there.
> If I take the wings of the morning
> and settle at the farthest limits of the sea,
> even there your hand shall lead me,
> and your right hand shall hold me fast. (Ps 139:7–10)

PART 5: In the Perspective of Hero Tales

In John 3:8 Jesus speaks of the Spirit as wind that "blows where it chooses," and the same gospel begins not with the sneeze I imagined but with a "Word" which "became flesh and dwelt among us" *as a brother*.

What does it mean for a word to become flesh? Olmec and Aztec sculptures like modern comic strip dialogues show little clouds emitted from the mouths of semi divine sculptured figures. Did God's words in Genesis 1 condense into material form as firmament, plants, animals, and humans instead of being written on papyrus or carved on stone? This metaphor must be interpreted to explain a reality beyond the physical, like human speech, without being detached from the Speaker who uttered it.

Created life forms all involved the four elements of early Greek philosophical thought: earth and water for raw inanimate materials, air (which moves leaves, sends storms and also distinguishes the living from dead), and fire (oxidation and reduction) for the essential dynamics of animate life. Today we know/believe[8] that air belongs to the inanimate world, while animate life, like fire, exhibits a level of activity that uses but transcends materiality. Biological and social entities operate in a world that borders *and may be penetrated by* immaterial spirit. In fact, for both scientific and religious exploration and experimentation no clear line can be drawn between the material and the dynamic or "spiritual." What occurs is that thoughts, ideas, and theories are capable of moving mountains by operating from inside ostensibly material beings. Barrow found Newton's laws of motion to be a limiting case of Einstein's relativity theories, and he visualizes force fields instead of atoms of matter in "absolute" vacuums.

Should we similarly visualize human behavior as force fields of intention, activity, and achievement in a material world? In the scriptures most human activity from decision making to material realization appears also, and at the same time, to be God's activity. Often rationalized as God's permission, interwoven personal responsibilities can be distinguished in the telling of the stories. But ambiguity remains throughout. Hebrew patriarchs believed that what they initiated was part of the divine plan or sometimes an aberration from it. They heard God's voice giving guidance and when they were "tuned in" they followed it. Divine impulse became words in human minds, and these in turn moved men and mountains. Ancient legends and heroic tales likewise preserve this ambiguity, pointing to unrealized futures and recalling known pasts. In successive "now" moments of crisis humans and God performed great deeds, apparently together, or *One through many*.

"GOD"

Person ～～～ Person

---

8 We regularly use the word "know" for "believe" when we are talking about experiences we perceive or "feel" but have not actually seen or touched.

Abram, impelled by a divinely spoken word, set out on an arduous journey to settle his family on a western land. Likewise Moses, impelled by a few words associated with a burning bush, returned to Egypt to lead his people to freedom from their slavery. The scriptures tell us that YHWH was the spiritual force that drove these journeys. Having planted the seed of an idea in a selected (or self-selected) human mind, YHWH guided Abram/Abraham to gather to himself the partners who would produce a family and the successive generations of descendants needed for tribal structures to inhabit a promised land. YHWH God was the hidden Designer, like genes and memes in a living organism, of a community structure in which certain core prohibitions would provide the freedom for people to multiply as active co-creators—like creative God but in tangible human forms. Am I right in believing that YHWH's manifestations to Abram/Abraham and his descendants adequately if incompletely represented the God I am seeking?

As the chosen community grew in numbers and diversity, YHWH selected or appeared to select a succession of individuals—patriarchs, priests, judges, tribal chiefs, and kings—and to establish socio-political regimes to manage the biological productivity of available lands and the healthy relationships of people with each other and with their neighbors. Even if leaders selected themselves and competed for political power, the resulting groupings fitted memes of kingship that were common, but evolving, at the time. Gideon for example, rejected the kingship, but could not avoid some aspects of it. His son Abimelech fitted the common pattern too well and was killed (Judg 9). So Israel's political identity awaited better leadership and never evolved onto the full trajectory that God was intending. Was not the God in the shadows involved in all that human activity?

A God with an Active Identity

At a moment reckoned in human time toward the end of the thirteenth century BCE a Voice from a burning bush disclosed *an active verb* form as God's identity: *'eHYeH 'aSHeR 'eHYeH*, "I will be what I will be," or preferably with different vowels, a causative, "I cause what I cause"[9] In either case the words are from a personal entity, perhaps inaudible to any bystander. The Voice's first person pronoun "I" was absorbed into the verb, as is normal in classical Hebrew when one speaks of expected or possible action. No separate pronoun is needed. Some of the sense of urgency is watered down, however, when we tell what "he" said instead of hearing him speak directly of an intended action.

Reporting the moment of insight to his people, Moses replaced the first person prefix of the verb to make the familiar noun *YaHWeH* in the third person form of the verb. The precursor of a human word, the Hebrew name for the God of Israel, had

---

9. Vowels were not added to the consonantal written text until about the tenth century in the common era. With either vowel the verbs may be read, perhaps preferably, as futures of determination "I will ..."

PART 5: In the Perspective of Hero Tales

taken root. This lively verb bore fruit as a noun in the mind of Moses, and thence to his extended family and later to the tribes and kingdom that developed. Many Israelites forgot the verb when they swore by the God designated by the noun, but they were not allowed to forget the Person.

All the while YHWH showed no face or form to those who carried out God's designs, while the people in the Middle East and Europe called God Baal, Astarte, Asherah, Tammuz, Adonis, Zeus, Athena, Dominus, Jesus, 'Allah and hundreds of other names and titles. Rejecting visualizations and the embodiments in statues or statuettes, YHWH accepted or tolerated the political and religious designations "Lord" (*'adonai, kurios*) and "God" (*'elohim, theos*) but was evidently vexed at other terms which designated material images. Patiently (or impatiently?) the God of the shadows spoke with Moses and assumed the character of a strong and benevolent director of human cooperation, instead of captain of a conquering army.

According to Exodus 33:17–23 YHWH granted the nearest thing to a sight of God to Moses alone, after the incident of the golden calf.

Moses asked, "Show me your glory, I pray," and he [YHWH] said, "I will make all my goodness pass before you, and will proclaim before you the name, 'The Lord' [YHWH]; and I will be gracious to whom I will be gracious, and will show mercy on whom I will show mercy. But . . . you cannot see my face; . . . .

The Exodus accounts are consistent: Moses can see something other than God's full face and the words he hears in Exodus 33:19 and 3:14. "I will have mercy," and "I am/will cause to be," signal the creative activity of YHWH for Moses and his people. A sense that YHWH was present remained.

The force of YHWH's presence was felt again in the midnight meeting of Moabite Ruth and Israelite Boaz on a barley-threshing floor, and Ruth and Boaz agreed to a marriage that presaged the succession of Judah's kings and the birth of Jesus.

"YHWH God," the Being credited by Israel with designing, making, sustaining, and correcting the visible world, remains elusive, but an Anglicized successor, "the Lord God," has been deemed to represent the powerful and continuing *source of energies* that have created families, nations, churches with their populations, governments, and the buildings which house their gatherings. Also those energies, even when corrupted, sustain the multinational corporations needed for trade, together with the armies and legislatures capable of defending them. From the earliest moments recorded in many sacred scriptures, deities, including YHWH, have "created" bodies like Israel, using human agents like Moses, Joshua, David, and other heroic figures. Names have been attached to three interwoven entities: the deities, their priestly agents, and the populous bodies they created or assembled.[10] According to the Book of Exodus, however, it was only YHWH who represented God faithfully.

Human agents using human language have led families, tribes, churches, and nations as well as more recent social organizations. In particular Jesus of Nazareth brought together a group of twelve disciples, some women followers, and many

---

10. Virgil's *Aeneid* offers a parallel with a pantheon headed by Jupiter, together with the Roman people and its Senate of elders in the ideal democratic Senatus PopulusQue Romanus.

Creatio ex Nihilo, Imago Dei, and Talk with God

witnesses to his preaching and healing ministry. After his death and resurrection, on the day of the Jewish Pentecost Jesus was acclaimed as "Lord and Christ,"—YHWH and Messiah—and the Christian Church began to establish itself along side of Jewish communities in the Roman Empire.

Jesus, the anointed Messiah (Christ), offered himself as a final manifestation of the God of the Hebrew people, but did not limit himself to Jews. It was Gentiles who joined with Jews to create churches of believers and in the fourth century of the common era declared a faith in God the Father, God the Son and God the Holy Ghost, God in Three Persons, a blessed Trinity.

"Nature" and/or "God"

Today, two concepts are in contention to designate what we are talking about. On the one hand "nature" arose in Greek thought and continues as a general term for researches in the various specialized sciences. On the other hand "God" is identified as the supreme member of a class of entities to whom religious devotion and prayers are addressed.

In The *Body of God* Sallie McFague proposed that the natural world serves as God's body. The marvelous harmony of nature seen in the new world by European explorers was reflected and celebrated in the work of artists and poets who led their followers to a worship of nature. More recently James Ashbrook suggests that the Mind of God functions like two-lobed human brains,[11] whose mutually effective operations have been studied after Freud through the Eriksons, Piaget, Carol Gilligan and others. After considering the contributions of the researchers Ashbrook summarizes: "one becomes a person *only* in one's connectedness." What is true for humans may also be true for God. In a hugely material universe a Personal Entity has come into Active Being, and many human entities have manifested themselves as creators, managers and correctors of other entities. There is no need for worshippers of God and lovers of nature to fight over theories.

Without ever saying so, the Hebrew Scriptures report that God exercised a number of the personal functions we associate otherwise with *homo sapiens*, the "thinking man." Example: God *called* Abram and others promising, "I will make of you a great nation." Also, God became angry and declared:

> For three transgressions of Judah,
> and for four I will not revoke the punishment,
> because they have rejected the law of the Lord,
> and have not kept his statutes (Amos 2:4)
> but added,
> On that day I will raise up the
> booth of David that is fallen,
> and repair its breaches,
> and raise up its ruins,
> and rebuild it as in the days of old. (Amos 9:11)

---

11. Ashbrook, *The Human Mind and the Mind of God*. See his chapter 11, "Concluding an Unscientific Promise."

PART 5: In the Perspective of Hero Tales

The God who *wills not* to be represented with a physical body often preferred to use the minds and voices of human prophets to speak God's words. The pure Spirit of a Personal God found a Voice in the voices of ancient personal entities. The scientists' impersonal cosmos has found a way to work *inside* as well as *outside* the box, through the recognized laws of physics, chemistry, biology, psychology, and anthropology.

Is the Spirit of God as "Holy" (pure and undefiled by the sins of the material world) as we have been told? Only in culture do we think of defilement; in nature the breakdown of physical bodies provides food for other organisms that may look defiling to our cultured minds, but is entirely wholesome to the worms and microbes of our compost piles, septic systems, and lower intestinal tracts. I therefore reject as unwarranted the superstitious distinctions of Leviticus between clean and unclean species of food. It would be better to label substances that actually harm the body, such as arsenic, viral infections, and military projectiles as "unclean."

The holiness of God is in the creation of a community capable of self-purifying, like nature before the "fall." "Sin" is real in the world as we know it, but God is at work within the world, renewing the creation in a wide variety of ways, especially through Jesus, his "many brothers," and God's pervading Spirit. One of the concluding exhortations of the letter to the Hebrews urges: "Pursue peace with everyone, and the holiness without which no one will see the Lord" (Heb 12:14). An unlikely pair in this world, peace and holiness, not genes but memes, makes possible an especially clear glimpse of the true God at work.

Ambivalence

Whether the God hidden in the shadows at the apex of the covenantal paradigm approved or condemned the sum of individual human efforts to achieve intended good was not ambiguous. Significantly, when the prophet Amos spoke for YHWH, he switched from first person pronoun subject, "*I* will not revoke punishment" to a third person subject, "*they* have rejected the law of the Lord," thus identifying the human figures in the ancient setting as rebels. Like Isaiah, the prophet Amos saw humans other than Israel rejecting Torah/law and facing punishment for rebelling. In Amos's day that rebellion included the full circle of seven city states, neighbors of Jerusalem, which was the seat of YHWH's power for the prophet's home town of Tekoa. Without ambiguity the judgments touched every political power within shouting distance. The roaring of the Lion of Judah could be heard over the entire West Semitic world (Amos 1:2).

It was the ambivalence of nations that both accepted and rejected the precious guidance given to Israel for the ancient world that brought judgment on them all. Damascus had "threshed Gilead with threshing sledges of iron," Gaza and Tyre had sent entire communities into exile, handing them over to Edom; Edom had "pursued his brother with the sword, casting off pity"; Ammonites had "ripped open pregnant women in Gilead"; Moab had "burned to lime the bones of the king of Edom"; Judah's closest kin, Israel-Ephraim, had sold the needy for shoes, lain down on garments taken

Creatio ex Nihilo, Imago Dei, and Talk with God

in pledge as father and son went in to the same girl. The specifics applied to every people within sight and hearing, pointing to a common ethic of behavior accepted by all, *but ignored by all.* Summed up as the "Torah of YHWH" in the judgment on Judah, Amos and his hearers—*and we*—share YHWH's anger at the world's non-compliance with a universally acceptable ethic. But our afterthought redirects our anger at *our* guilt, as Amos included his own tribal companions in the condemnations of YHWH.

Amos 9:11 appears literally, however, to revoke the punishment announced in Amos 2. The "booth of David" which has fallen will be raised up, its breaches repaired, "in order that they may possess the remnant of Edom and all the nations that are called by my name" (Amos 9:12). What looks like human ambivalence in YHWH's words as the prophet speaks them is the expression of a broad intention, not just for Judah and Israel, but other nations, some of whom already knew YHWH's name, while others would come to know it. In what sense could Amos see all seven-neighbor nations as subject to YHWH's Torah? Were the idea of One God and the ethics of the Decalogue implicit in the thinking of much of the ancient world, while ancient local deities and their tribal followers contended for increasing dominance over expanding political territories?

The two sides of the prophet's message can be reconciled when we understand that *forgiveness is possible for the chastened wicked who repent,* but a certain ambivalence remains in the divine attitude toward all human actors. When our efforts at harmony seem successful, we believe that God is blessing us and cursing those who oppose us, but our enemies believe God blesses them and curses us. Seeing between the trees in the forest and across the buildings we have built, we glimpse smiles *and* frowns on the face of God. For whom are the smiles and for whom the frowns? God directs both toward us as well as toward our enemies, planting the seeds of thought to be developed into conscience, speech, and repentance in some minds, or continued rebellion in others.

Our enemies have seen events and the approval of the God of the shadows often in a way opposite to ours, seeing our good as their evil, and our evil as their good. The Philistines rejoiced with Dagon in the capture of Israel's container for God, but soon discovered that taking possession of the sacred Ark had another side which brought sickness and death instead of health and happiness, as reported in 1 Samuel 5. How would a Philistine have told that story? Did the God hidden in the shadows rejoice with the Philistines or lament with the Israelites when Samson died? Does the dynamic but inscrutable God rejoice with *every* human achievement, good or bad? What were God's feelings when the first atomic bomb was proved capable of bringing destruction and death to Hiroshima and the end of the war with Japan?

And does the God who made known the name YHWH and accepted prayers in that Name experience the divine equivalent of weeping with our failures and sins? Or is God impassive, as cosmologists perceive the cosmos, without the unvoiced feelings that are the human first response to events? Before the great flood of Genesis 6–9 we read, "The Lord [YHWH] was sorry that he had made humankind on the earth," and a little further, "But Noah found favor in the sight of the Lord." The writer/editor has seen God's ambivalent feelings about an earth that *we* see as partly good but considerably wicked. Are those the feelings of the true and hidden God, who related with Israel as YHWH?

If God grouped similar impressions as humans do in batch processing, only major differences between groups might be detected by a transcendent God, but biblical stories, Torah/law and New Testament insist that every individual as well as nation will be judged. In chapter 18 we saw the paradoxical nature of forgiveness, which condemns past behavior and points the forgiven person to a new "real time" life in the community. The matter is even more complex, since humans see every anticipated good not only as an end, but also as a step toward some further end. A final End, popularly called "Heaven," is almost everywhere visualized as a place where God dwells and from which designs for human affairs flow. However, through our persistent dichotomizing of good and evil in human events, we cannot conceive of only one final Destination, but popularly insist on anticipating "Hell" for those who do evil. This has led *us* to judge behaviors, and to believe that God also judges behavior and rewards or punishes appropriately. The scriptures and events appear loosely to have borne out these judgments, bringing immediate punishment to some and delaying punishment to others. In popular thinking as well as serious theology God appears as the final Judge of all behavior. However, it is possible that God is not concerned with dotting every "i" and crossing every "t" in our essays at good thinking and works, but does care about the ongoing survival and healthy success of all people. Hebrew Sheol welcomed the successful and the failures alike. Success is evidence, not the cause or effect of God's love, but failures also have found peace. Our lives end at death, though memories, like memes, may exist for centuries as another sort of reality.

Am I understanding God correctly when I think that God feels as people feel? And if so, what does that mean? The declarations in *The Book of Confessions*[12] ascribe both wrath and love to God, and clearly understand God as a personal Being. Theologians have argued inconclusively, and the scriptures provide ambiguous answers to the question. Since science has agreed with Hebrew religion that nature and/or God cannot be seen, touched, or sensed as a whole, many who have been "enlightened" can no longer imagine a divine Person with senses and feeling like ours.

Imagination, however, is not so shortsighted. As time duration is surprisingly different in our experience from the dimensions of solid geometry, we may not have exhausted imaginative possibilities for the expression of feelings. Are the attractions and repulsions of love and hate, pleasure and pain, good and evil the evidence of dimensions of a psycho-moral universe or of forces not yet listed along with the forces of physics? When I "fall in love," am I being drawn down a non-material but more than metaphorical, slope toward a resting place similar to the bed on which I sleep at night? In John's Gospel Jesus recognized that when he was lifted up he would draw all people to himself with a force not unlike magnetism. Today's adolescents often find the divine/human Jesus powerfully attractive.

---

12. Part I of *The Constitution of the Presbyterian Church (U.S.A.)*.

Creatio ex Nihilo, Imago Dei, and Talk with God

Is God a Force—or the web of all forces—rather than a Being? Is God acting *in* everything instead of *on* things? The technical name for this is Panentheism. According to Wikipedia the term was first used in 1828 by the German philosopher Karl Christian Friedrich Krause, and later elaborated in the 1940s by the philosopher Charles Hartshorne. We see new growth coming from the inside of plants and children in a way different from the way we build houses.

Does God somehow speak blessing and cursing to people so that what one hears is opposed to what another hears? Or, that what one hears will be heard differently after a few moments of reflection? Condemnation can appear as correction when humans listen long enough to understand God's voice. How do ideas move the resisting masses of personal and social bodies? The ambivalence of feeling must be in the human receptors: We hear what we are prepared to hear; we see what we are prepared to see. One person hears and sees support from God; another sees only obstacles and enemies. One senses existential threats to survival; another knows hope and moves step by step with confidence. The energies of God are available to each as the warmth of the sun reaches creatures from the poles to the Sahara, warming some and stirring cooling breezes for others. The sun's light passes through the vast variety of lenses, which are available to those who asked, sought and found in the covenantal transactions of my earlier chapters.[13]

A Spirit Who Touches Human Spirits

How important is it for us to conceive of God as a personal Being? We and our priests have persisted in addressing prayers to a fatherly Being, and our prophets voice God's judgments like those of human judges. Most humans need some form of god, saint, or angel just as the infant needs parents, teenagers need guides, mature adults need supportive partners for their projects, and the aged and infirm need caregivers. The human need for such godlike supporting figures does not prove the existence of God, but we prefer to pray to a Person whom we can see in our minds, hear in our thoughts, and feel in our guts, instead of pronouncing magical incantations. Instead of *knowing*, we can *believe*, We trust that our faith will be supported not necessarily by material reality but by a compassionate Spirit who touches our spirits and those of our neighbors in our dark as well as in our joyful moments.

Biblical stories provide examples of both successful and unsuccessful praying. David believed when he faced Goliath; and the Benjamite-Judean coalition, aroused to action by his belief, won a victory. Abigail believed when she took supplies to David. Ahab, however, believed the yea-saying prophets instead of Micaiah's insight that God was saying "No" for that battle. Since YHWH God had sent both messages, two armies met at Gilead Heights, and Ahab did not survive the battle against Ben Hadad. Hananiah and Jeremiah both believed their words were from YHWH, but Hananiah

---

13. This complex intermediacy explains the way the ancients identified and named gods and goddesses for sun, storms, sex, war, etc. and makes sense of Ken Wilber's grid which can include the myths and fables of childhood.

PART 5: In the Perspective of Hero Tales

was mistaken. Evidently some external observation is needed to confirm the meme that rises in the human mind. A glimpse of God between the pickets or as a "still small voice" in a cave needs to be followed by a more tangible confirmation.

To whom can we pray after Nietzsche announced the death of God; and why accept Richard Dawkins' declaration that the God presented by prelates and preachers is a delusion for the naïve and superstitious, a means of verbal control over mass behavior? In his experience that may seem to be true, except that Dawkins claims not to be naïve and superstitious. He is like the five-year-old explaining to a three-year-old sister that Santa Claus is only a story. Remnants of superstition remain for all of us, but we need to think and pray beyond the obscurities and our childish imaginings of God. We can step forward believing God as Abraham did, when his step was "reckoned to him as righteousness" (Gen 15:6).

As we noted in chapter 1, Holmes Rolston III, has sketched a way from biological beginnings to emerging human personalities. This evolutionary idea allows the possibility of a personal Omega Point[14] where all forces converge in full personal glory, already embodied in Jesus Christ, "the firstborn of a large family" ("many brothers" in the Greek of Rom 8:29). We, devout Christians, Jews, Muslims, and probably others, can think of ourselves as a continuing, if imperfect manifestation of God's presence among the world-weary in spite of our contribution to the conflicts that divide us. So we instinctively utter fearful thoughts as prayers for support and healing.

God has Spoken

The Hebrew Bible is structured in a way that suggests that God has spoken to the human race in at least three voices, not necessarily in succession, but through a marvelous interweaving of thoughts and ideas.[15] Through the five books of the Torah God spoke as stern but loving lawgiver. In the "Prophets" we hear the "still small voice" of God's presence in Elijah's mind and God's challenging summons to a court where sins are judged. Or we may hear God in the declaration of Amos 1:9 that the world has not remembered the "covenant of brothers." Finally, in the "Writings," Job, the preacher of Ecclesiastes, and the Psalmists found the freedom to talk back to God and to ask God to talk with them in dialogue, as they sought the removal of obstacles to a long and happy life.

Reporting a second anointing of Solomon as king and the establishing of Zadok as priest, the Chronicler reminded post-exilic Jews that God had provided the Temple for continuing conversation with God and the Davidic dynasty for stable governance.[16] All three sections of the Hebrew Bible [TaNaK] can thus be heard as God's voice, which addresses us human beings and gives worshippers a language for confessing sins and finding forgiveness and vindication for faithfulness.

---

14. The term is from Teilhard de Chardin, *The Phenomenon of Man*.

15. Hebrews 1:1–2 declares "in any and various ways."

16. First Chronicles 29:22–24 reports that "they made David's son king a second time; they anointed him as the Lord's prince, and Zadok as priest."

That these three voices correspond loosely to the voices of the three Persons of the Christian Trinity—Father, Son/Brother and Comforting Spirit—is probably neither accidental nor a figment of a speculative mind, though it may simply be a Christian's effort to justify what Jews have seen as a departure from Israelite traditions. Jewish traditional faith has preserved and insisted on the worship of only one God, and lives in the hope of a peaceful restoration to a land promised to Abram/Abraham. In a similar but different faith, followers of Islam have heard a single voice through the words of Allah dictated to the prophet Muhammad, now written and commented on by his Islamic followers. Islam's faithful, like Jews and Christians, look forward to a world united in the service of God and to an afterlife with God. Three essentially monotheistic faiths proclaim similar ethical principles and call people to worship a unifying Spirit out of the midst of the chaotic materialism of the modern world.

The three faiths nevertheless identify an opposing spirit that attempts to pervert those obedient to the leading of God's good Spirit. Muslims have resisted forcefully the material and political inroads of the complex culture of the western world, bringing on the current political impasse between Judeo-Christian and Muslim believers. Exercising violent strategies, both east and west consider it moral to attempt to destroy the followers of "Satan," the supposed alternate deity of their enemies.

The columnist Charles Krauthammer writes regarding the politicizing of faith utterances preparatory to the 2008 presidential campaign that: "The God of the Founders, the God on the coinage, the God for whom Lincoln proclaimed Thanksgiving Day is the ineffable, ecumenical, nonsectarian Providence of the American civil religion whose relation to his blessed land is without appeal to any particular testament or ritual. Every mention of God in every inaugural address in American history refers to the deity in this kind of all-embracing, universal, nondenominational way."[17]

Thus, without waiting for theological "proof" of the existence of God, ordinary, relatively untutored people respond to the voices of religious and political leaders with an affirmation of faith in God, an unseen but strong deliverer. A thousand media channels may bring confused and confusing specific messages about God, but many people agree that the God of the shadows continues to talk both to and with humans, helping us tune our thinking and planning for ever greater good.

A God who Engages in the Human Dialogue

The metaphor of speaking suggests that God not only gives orders, but also hears and responds to what his creatures are saying, both to each other and to God. God interacts, entering into many of our dialogues as a third party with strong inner encouragement or discouragement. Remember that when Jacob and Laban made a formal covenant to replace the informal bargains of their household, they registered their covenant with the supreme God of their differing family traditions. Thus what appeared to be an exchange between two men and their clans was integrated into a larger covenantal picture which became a new aspect of God's work in the world.

17. Krauthammer, "Huck's Unholy Dance," n.p.

Part 5: In the Perspective of Hero Tales

History was made: an immaterial concept, covenant, "cut" by two men, became woven into the created world when animals were sacrificed and their flesh eaten (Gen 31:44–54). The memorial cairn did more than symbolize a new reality which a speaking and hearing God could recall. Laban and Jacob, not one or the other but both working together with their servants, piled stone upon stone to build the cairn. The text does not say "both working together," but a modern church where black and white members do cleaning and repairs together experiences a surprising sense of companionship between the races and the feeling that God is pleased with their work.

Covenant and cairn, a formal agreement to live separately, became a sacramental part of the created world, blessed and sustained by God. In accepting the material/spiritual cairn was God also changed, perhaps ever so slightly, but nevertheless like a thought written on a piece of paper?

In some such way *our* memories of working together become part of the ongoing creation. That is to say, a history preserved in people's minds as well as in history books has a reality that has entered into the natural world. Every manifestation of God has, and will have, a physical duration, like a person, for a time. At the personal level, believers offer God thanks for the lives of departed loved ones and trust that the God of the shadows accepts our thanks and *remember* their lives with and through our friends and children.

The sharing of memories and ideas is not limited to recording in the "Book of Life," but may be seen in a process of wider publication. Current brain/mind research tells us that neurons which replace dying ones during a human life, in addition to preserving memories, are capable of "broadcasting" to other regions of the brain, just as people can share ideas with the communities in which they live. When the king of Jericho heard that Israelites had come to investigate his city, Rahab is reported to have told the Hebrew spies, "I know that the Lord has given you the land, and that dread of you has fallen on us . . . for we have heard how the Lord dried up the water of the Red Sea" (Josh 2:9).

And when YHWH "tuned in" to what was being said and done in Sodom, God sent messengers to warn and rescue Lot (Gen 19:1–11). God has so ordered the creation that its spiritual aches and pains as well as its physical ones call out for restoration to health. At every level including the cellular the healing processes respond. When our spirits cry out, God hears and responds.

Science says essentially the same thing as religion, but changes the word "God" to "nature" or "the body's immune system." There is also, possibly an analogous societal immune system. In the covenantal paradigm almost personal figures, "infection" and "the immune system," bargain for dominance while needing to cooperate for life. At one point for Israel, the figures of the paradigm were a sinning people and "Assyria, the rod of my anger" (Isa 10:5).

People see, hear, feel, think, and act; so God sees, hears, feels, thinks, and acts. We do not usually say this about the natural world, but if we choose not to use the word "god," an alternative may be the plurality of hostile and friendly observing agents. The

Creatio ex Nihilo, Imago Dei, and Talk with God

complete picture requires us to include many surrounding animate and inanimate, even microscopic, "creatures," that both threaten and support our lives.

In this perspective our eyes and ears are the organs of God's perception, our hearts and minds are the seat of God's emotions and thought, and our tongues are the agents of God's blessing and cursing. God's will may be thought of as a composite of everything people do in the human part of the experiment. However, since we customarily think of God as good, our minds balk and prefer to think only of everything good as God's doing, while we ascribe evil to a Satanic being and our guilty selves.

The author of the Book of Job imagined the discussion about the character of Job, which the hero did not hear, so readers could get one more glimpse of God. This ambiguous glimpse also appears in the two reports of the census David ordered late in his reign. Second Samuel 24:1 says that "the anger of the Lord was kindled against Israel and he incited David against them saying 'Go, count the people of Israel and Judah.'" Except for identifying the voice as Satan's, 1 Chronicles 21:1 reports the event in identical words but begins, "Satan stood up against Israel and incited David . . ." Both accounts tell how Joab objected but then proceeded to count the people. The historians do not try to assess David's motivation—or Joab's objections—but it is fairly clear that since the census was associated with the siege of Rabbah, David was beginning to have imperial ambitions instead of being the human partner of YHWH in the building of a united Israel.

After the census was taken, God's displeasure with David continued, and the seer Gad announced three possible forms of punitive correction to David: "three years of famine, or three months of devastation by your foes, while the sword of your enemies overtakes you; or three days of the sword of the Lord, pestilence on the land, and the angel of the Lord destroying throughout all the territory of Israel" (2 Chr 21:12).

All three would prune the counted population, and weaken the nation's war capability, but three months of devastation by enemies would be a human form of correction, which David would believe was instigated by YHWH. Having confessed to the "sin," David followed God's instructions relayed through the seer and bought the threshing floor of Ornan "for its full price." David set that spot aside for sacrifices and it was there that Solomon built the Temple. God directed the illness, but David and his people followed the instructions for the cure.

Viewing this partnership between God and human beings, I conclude that we are something like the software of a fantastic organism, with God directing our bodies by way of our minds—with the participation of our willing selves—to make history. The metaphor of scientific experiment clarifies the NOW moment of Deuteronomy and points to the way in which history is made by the partnership of God and humans. People—Israelites in Egypt, exiles in Babylon, negro slaves in nineteenth-century America—faced what appeared to be insuperable opposition to their free survival, but a thought was expressed when the voice of YHWH God inspired experiments which they attempted in the real world. Moses initiated the experiment for his time: the performance of a cleansing ritual led to the actual movement out of homes in Egypt, and the Exodus was under way. More experiential projects became human history, and at

PART 5: In the Perspective of Hero Tales

the same time God's achievement. The stories can be seen as superstition, not genuine history, but to the eye of faith they are evidences of God, and the words reach ears of believers as God's. In the minds of believers they do not need proof.

Jewish exiles in Babylon participated in a God inspired experiment which Cyrus decreed, "the Lord, the God of heaven . . . has charged me to build him a house at Jerusalem . . . whoever is among you of all his people, Let him go up" (2 Chr 36:23). Believe it or not, some Jews got the message, returned to their homeland and built a new temple in Jerusalem. The language through which God participated in this bit of dialogue was probably Aramaic for the Jews, but a dialect of Babylonian was on the cuneiform cylinder which records the entrance of Cyrus "as a friend" to the city of Babylon.[18] Knowing and trusting Marduk as God, Cyrus acted for God in his day as a bit player in the human drama.

The emancipation of slaves in the United States and the Exodus from Egypt may appear to differ until we remember that some powers to which the slaves were subject participated in their release—"the Egyptians urged the people to hasten their departure from the land, for they said, 'We shall all be dead'" (Exod 12:33). Abraham Lincoln, a somewhat unorthodox believer in God, issued a Proclamation announcing freedom for the slaves of his southern enemies. The announcement and the freedom "became flesh . . . among us."

Only fractured bits of the dialogues between people and God have been preserved, since actions of fleshly beings often took the place of words. God's words were heard, however, possibly only as ideas germinating in minds. The biblical record states that the ideas came from God, in the Hebrew/Israelite period as YHWH's voice, and to them the Israelites replied with words and actions.

An Embodied Deity

The God who lurks in the shadows is more believed in than proved to exist, yet human beings have persisted in declaring that God has appeared in audible, almost tangible forms. Abraham, Moses, Gideon, the mother of Samson, the boy Samuel, Elijah, and many others through history have been certain that Someone more than man or woman visited them and delivered a message for people. Most embodiments and their results were brief episodes, but were intense enough to require reporting to the rest of the community, which could do no less than embody the message in the directed action.

How can I write definitively about a God who has made such fleeting appearances in an ancient time? Providentially, my experience of being called to a ministry in a modern Christian denomination is similar enough to that of biblical prophets to recognize an essential likeness of both the Voice and the directed action in my life.

---

18. Pritchard, *Ancient Near Eastern Texts*, 315–16: "My numerous troops walked around in Babylon in peace, I did not allow anybody to terrorize (any place) of the [country if Sumer] and Akkad . . . I brought relief to their dilapidated housing, putting (thus) an end to their (main) complaints."

Creatio ex Nihilo, Imago Dei, and Talk with God

From the perspective of Christians a major turning point in world history took place with the birth of the teacher from Nazareth who responded to the Voice at his baptism and was recognized as the "Anointed" [Christ] and "only begotten" Son of God.[19] With the experience of disciples on the day of Pentecost, the gospel of John and the writings of the apostle Paul and his successors, a comforting Holy Spirit shares honor and power with Jesus and the patriarchal "Lord" of the earlier witness. I continue to affirm the essential declarations of the Nicene and Apostles' Creeds, but with two reservations: (1) I understand the "persons" of the Trinity as a chronological but overlapping succession of three modes of God's manifestations in history. The God of the shadows was manifest to eyes of faith in the first century CE as a second person essentially one with the "Lord," (YHWH) who had given thoughts for prophets to voice. God continues to save those who repent in the name of Jesus and to build "churches" through the continuing work of the Holy Spirit. (2) Instead of the first-century worldview that visualizes an essentially material heaven and hell as final destinations for humans after death, my worldview comprises a cosmos in which forces interweave to create inanimate "things" and animate creatures including human beings. I see God as one creative and loving Mind in a total working with human minds. Thus I find support in the activities of the Persons of the Trinitarian Deity.

What Kind of God?

What kind of a God *can* I believe in in today's world? Not a god who can be sculpted or painted, but for whom a mental image of dynamic spirit is appropriate. That Spirit both creates and sustains manifestations that are observable in vastly diverse forms, forms that have the capacity to reproduce themselves and to create previously unknown new forms, some biological and others mechanical, economic, and social.

What kind of God *must* I believe in in today's world? My spirit turns to a creative Spirit who works in ways like the human mind, which is both opportunistic and thoughtful, responding impulsively in direct physical action, to seize or reject, like or dislike, entities in the dual environment of Patricia Williams' "matter-and-law" after the big Bang. Appearing as pawns in a vast chess game, people nevertheless express likes and dislikes, make choices as the God of the scriptures does. My God is such an Entity, sometimes seemingly ambivalent in the presence of stubborn obstacles to intended action, but intent on good that does not appear until it is realized.

What kind of God *may* I believe in in today's world? I *may* create aspects of a mental image of God and put them in words in the language I use to communicate with fellow humans. The God I believe in allows this, just as YHWH guided prophets and poets to write the scriptures. But efforts to tie down and contain God have never worked. Instead, what scripture writers wrote originated in quiet moments of

---

19. Jesus, being known as the fully human son of Mary, was thus distinguished from angels, "eons," and other supernatural powers of first and second century philosophies. That distinction may not be needed in a day when science no longer refers to the supernatural, but distinguishes common material and political experience from the hidden fields of force that operate in biological as well as the underlying nuclear relationships.

reflection, which made possible thoughts that transcended ordinary activities. This transcendence of thought over experience permits us to assert a unity beyond diversity, like the full spectrum of distinct radiant frequencies in white light.

While believing as a scientist might believe without full understanding, I fall back on the evolved beliefs from childhood which feature a personal being like father or mother, brother, sister, wife, or friend. These manifestations of God's being are not the full God of the shadows, but their presence in my prayer world comforts me, provides guidance and the companionship of God that can also be felt in fellowship with like-minded friends and family.

In a brief essay entitled *Belief in God in an Age of Science* John Polkinghorne proposes a continuing dialogue between scientists and theologians, which he believes could occupy the human race for centuries. On one hand scientifically inclined minds will continue to ask "how" questions and find many detailed answers; on the other hand theologically inclined humans ask and attempt to answer "why" questions. At present neither interlocutor can give an entirely satisfactory answer to the other's questions.

Perhaps the most discouraging answer to the baffling question of sin in human life is the Westminster Shorter Catechism's statement: "Sin is any want of conformity unto or transgression of the law of God." While the happiest answer comes from the Catechism's third question which defines the chief end of man: "Man's chief end is to glorify God and enjoy him forever." Deuteronomy's rule that the ancient worshipper should diligently observe the annual festivals anticipated the practice of churches, synagogues, ashrams, and other gatherings of worshipful people. Obedience to the statutes and ordinances of the Pentateuch is leading to new festivals in which Jews, Muslims, Christians, humanists, Buddhists, and others may worship in a joyful fellowship with every manifestation of God, Father, Son/Brother, and Spirit.

Bibliography

Ackerman, Diane. *A Natural History of Love*. New York: Random House, 1994.
Ackerman, Susan. *Under Every Green Tree: Popular Religion in Sixth-Century Judah*, Harvard Semitic Monographs 46. Atlanta, GA: Scholars Press, 1992.
———. *Warrior, Dancer, Seductress, Queen: Women in Judges and Biblical Israel*. New York: Doubleday, 1998.
Albright, Madeleine. *Madam Secretary: a Memoir*. New York: Miramax, 2003.
Alexander, Bobby Chris. *Victor Turner Revisited: Ritual as Social Change*. Atlanta, GA: Scholar's Press, 1991.
Alter, Robert. *The David Story: A Translation with Commentary of 1 and 2 Samuel*. New York: Norton, 1999.
Anderson, L. K. "Incidents and Recollections of Missionary Service 1926–1965." David Allan Hubbard Library archives, Fuller Theological Seminary, Pasadena CA.
Ashbrook, James B. *The Human Mind and the Mind of God: Theological Promise in Brain Research*. Lanham, MD: University Press of America, 1984.
Barrow, John D. *The Book of Nothing: Vacuums, Voids, and the Latest Ideas about the Origins of the Universe*. New York: Vintage, 2000.
Brooks, David. "Social Animal." *The New Yorker*, January 17, 2011, 26–32.
Brown, et al. *A Hebrew and English Lexicon of the Old Testament*. Boston: Houghton Mifflin, 1907.
Brueggemann, Walter. *Theology of the Old Testament*. Augsburg: Fortress, 1997.
Buchanan, George Wesley. *The Consequences of the Covenant*. Leiden: Brill, 1970.
Burland, C. A. *The Aztecs: Gods and Fate in Ancient Mexico*. Echoes of the Ancient World. London: Orbis, 1975.
Calvin, Jean. *Institutes of the Christian Religion: 1541 French Edition*. Translated by Elsie Anne McKee. Grand Rapids: Eerdmans, 2009.
Campbell, Joseph. *The Hero with a Thousand Faces: Commemorative Edition* Princeton: Princeton University Press, 2004.
Chalcraft, David J. *Social-Scientific Old Testament Criticism*. Sheffield: Sheffield, 1997
Childs, Brevard S. *The Book of Exodus: A Critical, Theological Commentary*. Philadelphia: Westminster, 1974
Claessen, H. J. M., and Peter Skalnik. *The Early State*. The Hague: Mouton, 1978.
Cloud, John. "Americans Love Marriage, But Why?" Time (Feb 19, 2007) 56. Online: http://www.time.com/time/magazine/article/0,9171,1587273,00.html
———. "Are Gay Relationships Different?" Time (Jan 17, 2008) 78. Online: http://www.time.com/time/magazine/article/0,9171,1704660,00.html
Dawkins, Richard. *The Selfish Gene*. Oxford: Oxford University Press, 1976.
De Chardin, Teilhard. *The Phenomenon of Man*. New York: Harper, 1959.
DeWaal, Frans B. M. "How Animals Do Business." *Scientific American* 292:4 (2005) 72–79.
Dewey, John. *A Common Faith*. New Haven: Yale University Press, 1934.
Dewey, John and Arthur Fisher Bentley. *Knowing and the Known*. Beacon, 1949.
Diamant, Anita. *The Red Tent*. New York: Picador, 1957.
Diamond, Jared. *Guns, Germs and Steel: The Fates of Human Societies*. New York: Norton, 1997.

Bibliography

Douglas, Mary. *In the Wilderness: The Doctrine of Defilement in the Book of Numbers.* Oxford: Oxford University Press, 2001.

Eagleton, Terry. *Reason, Faith, and Revolution: Reflections on the God Debate.* New Haven: Yale University Press, 2009.

Eisler, Riane. *The Chalice and the Blade: Our History, Our Future.* New York: HarperCollins, 1987.

Ellis, George F. R. "Does the Multiverse Really Exist?" *Scientific American* 305:2 (2011) 38–43.

Erikson, Erik, et al. *Vital Involvement in Old Age: the Experience of Old Age in our Time.* New York: Norton, 1986.

Feynman, Richard. *Six Easy Pieces: Essentials of Physics Explained by Its Most Brilliant Teacher.* New York: Basic, 1995.

Fletcher, Joseph F. *Situation Ethics: The New Morality.* Louisville: Westminster, 1966.

Freud, Sigmund. *Major Works.* Vol. 54, *Great Books of the Western World.* Translated by Robert M. Hutchins. Chicago: Encyclopedia Brittanica, 1930.

Gomez, Peter J. *Covenant Connection.* 4:4 (December 2001) 4.

Gopnik, Adam. "The Back of the World." *The New Yorker* (July 7, 2008) 52–54.

Gottwald, Norman K. *The Tribes of Yahweh: A Sociology of the Religion of Liberated Israel 1250 – 1050 BCE.* Maryknoll, NY: Orbis, 1979.

Green, James Benjamin. *A Harmony of the Westminster Presbyterian Standards.* Richmond, VA: John Knox, 1951.

Guerber, H. A. *Myths of Greece and Rome.* New York: American Book Co., 1893.

Herman, Judith L. *Trauma and Recovery: the Aftermath of Violence—from Domestic Abuse to Political Terror.* New York: Basic, 1971.

Heyward, Carter. *The Redemption of God: A Theology of Mutual Relation.* University Press of America, 1982.

Ibata, Rodrigo, and Brad Gibson. "The Ghosts of Galaxies Past." *Scientific American* 296:4 (May, 2007) 40–45.

James, William. *The Varieties of Religious Experience: A Study in Human Nature.* Edited by Martin E. Marty. New York: Penguin, 1982.

Jaynes, Julian. *The Origin of Consciousness in the Breakdown of the Bicameral Mind.* Boston: Houghton Mifflin, 1976.

Jenks, Alan W. *The Elohist and North Israelite Traditions.* Atlanta, GA: Scholars Press, 1975.

Johnstone, William. "The Use of Leviticus in Chronicles." In *Reading Leviticus: A Conversation with Mary Douglas*, edited by John F. A. Sawyer. Sheffield: Sheffield Academic Press, 1996.

———. "The 'Ten Commandments': Some Recent Interpretations." *Expository Times* 100:12 (1989) 453–61.

Krauthammer, Charles. "Huck's Unholy Dance." Times-News (Dec 7, 2007) n.p.

Kurtz, Paul. *Forbidden Fruit: the Ethics of Humanism.* Buffalo, NY: Prometheus, 1988.

Laato, Antti. *The servant of YHWH and Cyrus: A Reinterpretation of the Exilic Messianic Programme in Isaiah 40–,55.* Stockholm: Almqvist & Wiksell International, 1992.

Laffey, Alice L. *An Introduction to the Old Testament: A Feminist Perspective.* Minneapolis, MN: Fortress, 1988.

Lapsley, Jacqueline E. "Unintentional Sins." *The Princeton Seminary Bulletin*, 26:1 (2005) 160–65.

Lipton, Bruce H. *The Biology of Belief: Unleashing the Power of Consciousness, Matter & Miracles.* Santa Rosa, CA: Mountain of Love/Elite Books, 2005.

Lovelace, M. H. "Abomination." In *The Interpreter's Dictionary of the Bible.* (New York: Abingdon, 1962) 1:12–13.

Marshall, Jay W. *Israel and the Book of the Covenant: An Anthropological Approach to Biblical Law.* Vol. 140, *SBL Dissertation Series.* Atlanta, GA: Scholars Press, 1993.

McBride, Jenny. "'Prison Madness': Seen from the Inside." *Hospitality* (Aug–Sept, 2009) 4. Online: http://opendoorcommunity.org/wp-content/uploads/2008/02/August-September-2009-small.indd.pdf

McFague, Sallie. *Body of God: An Ecological Theology.* Minneapolis, MN: Fortress, 1993.

McKenzie, John L. "The Internal Word in History." In *No Famine in the Land: Studies in Honor of John L. McKenzie*, edited by James N. Flanigan and Anita Weisbrod Robinson. Missoula, MT: Scholars Press, 1975.

Bibliography

Mendenhall, George E. *The Tenth Generation: the Origins of the Biblical Tradition*. Baltimore, MD: Johns Hopkins University Press, 1973.
Miller, Maxwell, and Hayes, John H. *A History of Ancient Israel and Judah*. Louisville: Westminster, 1986.
Miller, Patrick. *Israelite Religion and Biblical Theology: Collected Essays*. Sheffield: Sheffield Academic, 2000.
Nelson, James B. *The Intimate Connection: Male Sexuality, Masculine Spirituality*. Philadelphia: Westminster, 1988.
Neuwirth, Robert. "Global Bazaar," *Scientific American* 305:3 (2011) 56–63.
Newman, Katherine S. *Law and Economic Organization*. Cambridge: Cambridge University Press, 1983.
Nicholi Jr, Armand M. *The Question of God: C.S. Lewis and Sigmund Freud Debate God, Love, Sex, and the Meaning of Life*. New York: Free Press, 2002.
Niebuhr, H. Richard. "The Triad of Faith," *Andover Newton Bulletin* 47 (1954) 3–12.
———. *An Interpretation of Christian Ethics*. New York: Harper, 1935.
Norman, Donald A. *The Design of Everyday Things*. New York: Basic, 1988.
Orr, H. Allen. "Testing Natural Selection," *Scientific American* 300:1 (2009) 44–50.
Palmer, John D. *The Living Clock: The Orchestrator of Biological Rhythms*. Oxford: Oxford University Press, 2002.
Park, Alice. "David Ho: The Person Who Could Beat AIDS." Time (Jan 25, 2010) 46: Online: http://www.time.com/time/magazine/article/0,9171,1953703,00.html
Pinker, Steven. *How the Mind Works*. New York: Norton, 1997.
Plato. *The Repuiblic*. Vol. 7 of *Great Books of the Western World*, Translated by Benjamin Jowett. Chicago: Encyclopedia Brittanica, 1930.
Polkinghorne, John. *Belief in God in an Age of Science*. New Haven: Yale University Press, 1998.
Pritchard, James B. *Ancient Near Eastern Texts Relating to the Old Testament*. Princeton: Princeton University Press, 1955.
Rissolatti, Fogassi, et al. "Mirrors in the Mind." *Scientific American* 295:5 (2006) 54–61.
Robinson, James M. "The Enternal Word in History." In *No Famine in the Land: Studies in Honor of John L. McKenzie*, edited by James W. Flanagan and Anita Weisbrod Robinson, (Missoula, Montana, 1975)
Rolston III, Holmes. *Genes, Genesis, and God: Values and their Origins in Natural and Human History*. Cambridge: Cambridge University Press, 1999.
Safire, William. *The First Dissident: the book of Job in Today's Politics*. New York: Random House, 1992.
Sagan, Carl. *The Varieties of Scientific Experience: a Personal View of the Search for God*. Edited by Ann Druyan. New York: Penguin, 2006.
Scham, Sandra. "The Lost Goddess of Israel." *Archaeology* 58:2 (2005) 26–40.
Sheres, Ita. *Dinah's Rebellion: A Biblical Parable for our Time*. New York: Crossroad, 1990.
Shermer, Michael. "Free to Chose." *Scientific American* 296:4 (2007) 32.
———. *The Science Of Good And Evil: Why People Cheat, Gossip, Care, Share, and Follow the Golden Rule*. New York: Times, 2004.
Sidman, Murray. *Coercion and its Fallout*. Boston: Authors Cooperative, 1989.
Smart, James B. *History and Theology in Second Isaiah: A Commentary on Isaiah 34, 40–66*. Philadelphia: Westminster, 1965.
Smith, H. Shelton. *Changing Conceptions of Original Sin: A Study in American Theology Since 1750*. New York: Scribners, 1955.
Taylor, Barbara Brown. *Speaking of Sin: The Lost Language of Salvation*. Cambridge: Cowley, 2000.
Taylor, Charles. *Varieties of Religion Today: William James Revisited*. Cambridge: Harvard University Press, 2002.
Van Seters, John. *The Life of Moses: the Yahwist as Historian in Exodus–Numbers*. Louisville: Westminster, 1994.
Via, Dan O. *Self-Deception and Wholeness in Paul and Matthew*. Minneapolis, MN: Fortress, 1990.
Wall, Steve, and Harvey Arden. *Wisdomkeepers: Meetings with Native American Spiritual Elders*. Hillsboro, OR: Beyond Walls, 1994.
Wilbur, Ken. *The Integral Vision*. Boston: Shambala, 2007.
———. *A Theory of Everything: an Integral Vision for Business, Politics, Science and Spirituality*. Boston: Shambala, 2000.

Bibliography

Williams, Patricia A. *Doing Without Adam and Eve: Sociobiology and Original Sin.* Minneapolis: Fortress, 2001.

Wilson, Edward O. *Consilience: The Unity of Knowledge.* New York: Knopf/Random House, 1998.

Wilson, Victor M. *Divine Symmetries: The Art of Biblical Rhetoric.* Lanham, MD: University of America Press, 1997.

Wink, Walter. *Engaging the Powers: Discernment and Resistance in a World of Domination.* Minneapolis, MN: Augsburg Fortress, 1992

Whitelam, Keith W. *The Just King: Monarchical Judicial Authority in Ancient Isreal.* Sheffield: JSOT, 1979

Wright, G. Ernest. *God Who Acts: Biblical Theology as Recital.* London: SMC Press, 1952

Wright, Robert. *The Evolution of God.* New York: Little Brown & Company, 2009

Bible Citations from:
New Revised Standard Version
c 1989, Thomas Nelson Inc
Nashville, TN